Firms, Networks and Business Values

The British and American Cotton Industries since 1750

This book explores the long-term forces shaping business attitudes in the British and American cotton industries from the eighteenth to the twentieth century. Mary Rose traces social, political and developmental differences from the early stages of industrialisation. She demonstrates how firms become embedded in networks, and evolve according to business values and strategies. The book examines local and regional networks, the changing competitive environment, community characteristics and national differences. Rose's findings challenge traditional views with new evidence that the character and achievements of each industry uniquely reflect local circumstances and historical experience. This is a critical synthesis of the multidisciplinary literature on the cotton textile industries of two major industrial nations and a study of the changing forces influencing decision-making. An important contribution to comparative business history, this book will be of interest to graduates and scholars in all areas of business and economic history.

MARY B. ROSE is Senior Lecturer in Business History in the Management School at the University of Lancaster. She is the author of *The Gregs of Quarry Bank Mill* (1986) and received the 1996 Alan Ball prize for her edited volume *The Lancashire Cotton Industry: A History since 1700.* She is past president of the Association of Business Historians and currently Director of the Pasold Research Fund.

Cambridge Studies in Modern Economic History

Cambridge Studies in Modern Economic History is a major new initiative in economic history publishing, and a flagship series for Cambridge University Press in an area of scholarly activity in which it has long been active. Books in this series will primarily be concerned with the history of economic performance, output and productivity, assessing the characteristics, causes and consequences of economic growth (and stagnation) in the western world. This range of enquiry, rather than any one methodological or analytic approach, will be the defining characteristic of volumes in the series.

For a complete list of titles in the series, please see end of book

Firms, Networks and Business Values

The British and American Cotton Industries since 1750

Mary B. Rose

University of Lancaster

PUBLISHED BY THE PRESS SYNDICATE OF THE UNIVERSITY OF CAMBRIDGE
The Pitt Building, Trumpington Street, Cambridge, United Kingdom

CAMBRIDGE UNIVERSITY PRESS
The Edinburgh Building, Cambridge CB2 2RU, UK www.cup.cam.ac.uk
40 West 20th Street, New York NY 10011-4211, USA www.cup.org
10 Stamford Road, Oakleigh, Melbourne 3166, Australia
Ruiz de Alarcón 13, 28014 Madrid, Spain

First published 2000

Printed in the United Kingdom at the University Press, Cambridge

Typeface Plantin 10/12 *System* QuarkXPress™ [SE]

A catalogue record for this book is available from the British Library

Library of Congress Cataloguing in Publication data

Rose, Mary B.
Firms, networks and business values: the British and American cotton industries since 1750 / Mary Rose.
p. cm. – (Cambridge studies in modern economic history 8)
Includes bibliographical references.
ISBN 0 521 78255 4 (hardbound)
1. Cotton trade–Great Britain–History. 2. Cotton trade–United States–History. I. Title. II. Series.
HD9881.5.R67 2000
338.4′767721′0941–dc21 00-024472

ISBN 0 521 78255 4 hardback

Contents

To Tony

Figures

Tables

Acknowledgements

My interest in both comparative and business history began in the early 1970s, when I was an undergraduate at Liverpool University. Fascination with the cotton industry and family business also started at Liverpool, but grew and developed when, as a Ph.D student at Manchester University, I analysed the evolution and subsequent collapse of the Greg cotton empire. Cambridge University Press published the resulting book in 1986. After over a decade of teaching comparative economic and business history, at Lancaster University, it was a logical step to try and bring together all these strands of interest and experience and this study of the British and American cotton industries is the result. British business has so often been viewed from an American perspective that I was tempted to try to understand the historical, social and political differences embedded in the two countries and demonstrate the peculiarities which led to divergent ways of conducting business. A faith in the explanatory power of history led to my choice of a long time-scale in what inevitably became a multidisciplinary study. The book changed, evolved and grew involving more than seven years of research, writing and re-writing.

My principal sources have been secondary and embrace the historical, sociological, political, economic, industrial and managerial literatures for both Britain and the United States, as well as business histories and the technical literature of the cotton industry. My especial thanks are due to the patience and helpfulness of the Interlibrary Loan staff at Lancaster University. They must have wondered at times whether there could possibly be any more books on the cotton industry. Thanks are also due to the staff of Lancaster University Library, Manchester Central Library, John Rylands Library, the British Library (both Bloomsbury and St Pancras), the Guildhall Library and the London School of Economics. Where primary sources were used, as supplements to the secondary literature, thanks are due to the staff of the Lancashire Record Office, the Archives Department, Manchester Central Library, John Rylands Library and Greater Manchester Record Office.

I am grateful to the Pasold Research Fund and to Lancaster University Research Committee for grants to fund research travel and to present papers relating to the book at conferences in Britain, the United States and Germany.

During the 1990s academic colleagues read early versions of individual chapters, or responded to conference and seminar papers relating to themes addressed in the book. Thanks are due to V. N. Balasubramanyam (Baloo), Stanley Chapman, Marguerite Dupree, Mike French, Les Hannah, David Jeremy, Maurice Kirby, Ken Lipartito, Andy Marrison, Phil Scranton, Geoff Timmins Steve Toms and Oliver Westall for commenting on individual chapters. Katrina Honeyman and Douglas Farnie read the whole manuscript before I submitted it to the publishers and made invaluable observations. I am especially grateful to Geoff Jones for reading all the chapters at their various stages, as well as the entire finished manuscript. He repeatedly helped me to see what was missing and offered broader perspectives at just the right time, while showing me how to move forward when I felt like giving up.

The participants at seminars and conferences at North Andover (MA), Munster, Victoria University of Manchester, Manchester Metropolitan University, University of Hull, University of Leeds, University of Central Lancashire and the International Business Research Group, Lancaster University all made helpful and constructive suggestions. In 1992 and again in 1996 members of the joint business history conferences between the Universities of Reading and Lancaster – later to include Leeds University and the Norwegian School of Management – were also supportive.

I am indebted to two anonymous referees who went to endless trouble to help me improve the manuscript. Their comments provided a good balance of encouragement and entreaties for clarity. I am very grateful too, to Richard Fisher of Cambridge University Press, who has been enthusiastic and encouraging and endlessly patient through a long writing period.

Most thanks are, however, to my husband Tony Breakell, to whom this book is dedicated. He has provided great intellectual, practical and psychological support and tremendous friendship. Despite a demanding career and long-distance commuting he has done far more than his fair share of household chores and much more and, with a dry sense of humour, has helped me to keep things in perspective. I could not have written this book without him.

MBR
Lancaster

1 Introduction: the evolution of two industries

Themes

This book is an analysis of the long-term forces shaping the British and American cotton industries over two hundred years, from the eighteenth to the twentieth century. The choice of a very long-term perspective deliberately highlights both the continuities and changes in the forces shaping business behaviour and the evolution of business culture, which may be obscured when shorter historical periods are studied. Inevitably this means that this is a work of critical synthesis, which tries to make sense of general trends, rather than being based on an extensive use of primary sources, which are used instead to fill inevitable gaps in the secondary literature. This multidisciplinary study derives insight from management, political economy and industrial sociology as well as from the methodologies and empirical studies of business, economic and textile history.

Contemporaries began commenting on the differences between cotton manufacturing in Britain and the United States during the second quarter of the nineteenth century. This began with an awareness that New England industrialists were producing cotton cloth in ways that were quite different from those found in Lancashire and with dissimilar social consequences. Attention has been particularly focused on the variations which occurred in organisation, technology and most particularly in labour productivity. Diverging experience, particularly from the late nineteenth century onwards, has been explained in terms of resource allocation, of relative product and factor market conditions, of differences in entrepreneurial energy and in institutional development. Where culture has been discussed it has largely been in the context of the 'anti-industrialism' which supposedly characterised British society in the nineteenth century and contributed to the failure of the economy in general and the staple industries in particular (see, for example: Montgomery 1840; Cotton Spinning Productivity Team 1950; Cotton Weaving Productivity Team 1950; Habakkuk 1962; Sandberg 1969; Sandberg 1974; Jeremy 1981; Lazonick 1981a; Mass 1984; Wiener 1981).

Irrespective of the interpretative stance, there has been a tendency to view the British cotton industry through American spectacles, with an inbuilt assumption of American superiority stemming from an undeniable labour productivity gap. Yet, if the cotton industry lay at the heart of early industrialisation in both Britain and the United States it has also been closely associated with relative economic decline, a phenomenon which, in different ways, afflicted both industries in the twentieth century. In discussions of the growing problems of the British cotton industry, in the twentieth century, the tendency has been to assume that its performance would have been enhanced by American-style technologies, vertically integrated corporate forms, a growing use of semi-skilled and unskilled labour and by more centralised systems of labour relations. Yet the question needs to be asked how far the features of United States strategies in the cotton industry were, to a considerable degree, a product of the peculiarities of its history, rather than being necessarily superior. In addition, it is important to explore just how well United States firms performed from the interwar period onwards, in comparison with those in Britain. If it can be shown that firms in the United States also experienced difficulties, despite their technological and organisational form, it will be hard to sustain the idea that British cotton firms could have avoided their twentieth-century difficulties merely by using American methods. This is not to suggest that modernisation was not needed in Britain, but rather to question the desirability of United States-style methods in a European context. The degree to which the United States model of cotton manufacturing is truly representative has already been addressed in debates relating to the relationship between technological and organisational change in the cotton industry, but has yet to be taken to its logical conclusion in a long-term, comparative and historical study (Saxonhouse and Wright 1984: 507–19; Clark 1987: 141–73).

The evolution of the cotton industry displayed a number of peculiarities on either side of the Atlantic, which helped to shape the expectations of businessmen and hence both the culture of their firms and the strategies they pursued. These included the relationship between the historical experience of industrialisation and late nineteenth- and twentieth-century technological, organisational and product choices. Of equal importance is the relationship between government and industry and the effect which this had upon market expectations and the process of innovation. It is not, however, possible to understand differences in business behaviour unless the consequences of the peculiar political and developmental status of Britain and the United States are remembered. The cotton industry lay at the heart of early industrialisation in both Britain and America. However, whereas Britain was a colonial power and the first industrialiser, the United States was both an ex-British colony and the first country of recent settlement to industrialise. This book will explore the often profound long-term consequences of these factors for the pattern of change and the development of business expectations in the cotton industry.

It is vital, when comparing business decisions in the cotton industries of Britain and the United States to place them in their appropriate economic, social, political and historical context. As a result this book explores the formation of decision-making in relation to historical developments. However, to counterbalance the unrealistic determinism of path dependency, where technological or organisational choices are principally dictated by the internal resources of firms, almost to the exclusion of external circumstances, this approach is set against the background of a changing environment in the nineteenth and twentieth centuries. Forces such as shifting patterns of trade, import substitution, the international spread of industrialisation, the American Civil War and two World Wars altered for ever the external environment faced by all cotton manufacturers. Consequently, whilst analysing the continuities, the book will explore the way in which the development of varying business cultures contributed to the differing impact and responses to these pressures, especially after 1945.

The institutional environment is central to the study of business and the formation of businessmen's expectations for, as a system of formal and informal rules it influences government–industry relations, the operation of political, legal and financial systems, and inter-firm and labour relations. As a result it represents a major force moulding business responses through time (Davis and North 1971). This is because firms and the markets they serve are 'embedded in political and social institutions [and conventions] and are [as much] the creation of government and politics [as of economic forces]' (Zysman 1994: 243). By implication, however, the institutional environment cannot be separated from the social fabric of both business elites and working people, whose values and behaviour both influence and are influenced by it.

National characteristics are inevitably a vital starting point for the comparative study of business. However, in the eighteenth and nineteenth centuries there emerged numerous and quite varied family-controlled cotton firms, which can only be understood in the context of their local and personal networks. International and intranational differences in networking behaviour, the effectiveness of loose groupings, how they changed through time, their long-term consequences and their cultural underpinnings form one of the core themes of this book. Designed to increase confidence and reduce uncertainty, through the development of mutual trust and flows of information, networks have become an increasingly important way of understanding business arrangements in recent years (see for example Biggart and Hamilton 1992; Granovetter 1985, 1996; Gerlach and Lincoln 1992; Hudson 1986). It is vital, therefore, to explore the forces which led to contrasting types of community-based financial, labour, organisational and commercial strategies to be found in the nineteenth-century cotton industry, especially in the United States, but also in Lancashire, and the way in which such networking behaviour evolved. In this context the notion of the Marshallian industrial district, based upon the self-sustaining reservoir of skills and network of interdependent specialist firms, becomes critical. Much attention will be given to identifying the local distinctiveness of industrial districts in the cotton industry in the nineteenth century as well as to the difficulties they encountered in the twentieth (Marshall 1890).

Analysis of networks will not, however, be confined to the organisation of commercial and financial transactions nor only to communication within communities. They operated between communities and more especially between business and other organisations, especially government. This inevitably raises the question of how far differing political and social systems affected the way in which inter-institutional networks operated and the impact this had upon the behaviour and expectations of businessmen in the British and United States cotton industries. Economic, technological, political and demographic changes from the late nineteenth century onwards, meant that the role of community in the behaviour of those involved in the cotton industry did not remain static. It will also, therefore, be important to assess how far external changes made community-based networks, and hence the industrial districts of which they were part, redundant and how far changes in the relationship between communities had implications for the national competitive environment. Equally, the relationship between community-based networks and the ability to create defensive collusive arrangements, designed to stifle competition, needs attention. From the standpoint of the United States, discussion of this issue will pivot upon the impact of the rise of the South as a centre of cotton manufacturing, whereas in Britain it will focus on the relationship between the spatial and business structure of the Lancashire cotton industry in the nineteenth century, the development of price associations and the emergence of horizontal holding companies in the late nineteenth century and the interwar period.

Concepts

This historical study makes use of a number of closely interrelated concepts, including theories of firms and of networks and of business and community culture and the way in which they are underpinned by the institutional environment of rules and customs which govern behaviour. These tools are, for the most part, used implicitly in the book so it is important to clarify them in this introduction.

An awareness of the peculiarities of both British and United States experience and the social, political as well as economic forces which moulded it is essential if the divergent business strategies that occurred in the cotton industry are to be explained. It is the contention of this book, therefore, that the explanation of diverse policies of cotton firms, within and between the United States and Britain, requires theoretical tools which, whilst taking account of the contributions of both transaction cost economics and the institutional school of business history, explain variety rather than predicting convergence. These include evolutionary theories, on the one hand, but also both 'old' institutionalism and those 'new' institutional theories with a cultural dimension, as well as theories of networks.

Evolutionary theory has explored the way in which patterns of innovation may be shaped by a firm's inheritance and as such derives directly from Schumpeter's analysis of entrepreneurship and Edith Penrose's *Theory of the Growth of the Firm*. Schumpeter saw innovation as far more than simply technological change, including: 'The introduction of a new good . . . a new method of production . . . the opening of a new market . . . the conquest of a new source of raw materials [and] the carrying out of new organisation' (Schumpeter 1934: 63). Yet, the precise innovative strategy chosen will be shaped by the past, as Penrose demonstrated when she originated the idea of (if not the term) organisational inheritance and concluded that:

> There is a close relationship between the various kinds of resources with which the firm works and the development of ideas, experience and knowledge of its managers and entrepreneurs . . . and changing experience and knowledge affect not only the productive services available from resources, but also demand as seen by the firm. (Penrose 1959: 85)

By highlighting the development of organisational capabilities, evolutionary theory is potentially extremely fruitful for a book of this sort (Nelson and Winter 1982). This is because the theory demonstrates the impact of firm-specific routines, which have developed through time, on the choice of technology and, by implication, of organisation, and as such is invaluable in the explanation of divergent as opposed to convergent business arrangements. Recently it has been successfully used to develop a 'dynamic theory of business institutions'. In *Firms, Markets and Economic Change: A Dynamic Theory of Business Institutions* Langlois and Robertson demonstrate that, since the late nineteenth century, the large and centralised corporate enterprise is but one route to innovation and economic growth. Whether loose networks of small firms, coalitions or joint ventures are preferred and form the basis of competitive advantage, depends upon 'the nature of the problem . . . the stage in the product life cycle and the availability of information' (Langlois and Robertson 1995: 150). Since this book is concerned with relationships between firms, between firms and their communities and between different types of organisation, the notion that networks represent a competitive alternative to integration is an important conclusion.

This approach, with its emphasis on diversity and change, provides far greater possibilities for the comparative study of business and, especially, business networks in Britain and the United States than Williamson's new institutional, transaction cost theory or the empirical work of either Chandler or Lazonick. This is predominantly because of its greater flexibility and movement away from using the United States as a starting point for best practice in business. Equally the work of the 'old' institutionalists, most notably John Commons and Douglass North, is invaluable for the understanding of the formation and behaviour of all kinds of networks (Commons 1934; Davis and North 1971; North 1990).

The sense that the operation of the market is not costless lies at the heart of transaction cost theory, where it is used to explain the circumstances under which firms, as opposed to markets, represent the most efficient institutional arrangement (Coase 1937; Williamson 1981). Williamson's comparative static analysis starts and finishes with contractual relationships within and between firms, whereas Chandler's 'stages approach' to the growth of firms, although not directly based upon transaction costs, concentrates on the forces leading to the development and growth of the business corporation. Basing his conclusions firmly on empirical evidence, Chandler has focused on the complex, dynamic interaction between the innovative growth strategies of firms pursuing substantial economies of scale and scope and the development of professionally managed hierarchical structures. According to Chandler, the combined impact of technology and market growth led to the rise of the modern business enterprise from the late nineteenth century. These firms came to enjoy spectacular competitive advantage, especially in capital- and technology-intensive sectors in the United States (Chandler 1990: 235–94).

Chandler's 'stages approach' both underpins and is further developed by Lazonick who emphasises the shifting nature of international competitive advantage through time. Lazonick's perspective draws on the idea that, whereas in the nineteenth century Britain's proprietary capitalists enjoyed international competitive advantage, the characteristics of a business system, featuring high levels of specialisation and labour relations based upon collusion between employers and employed, served as barriers to innovation in the changing world of the twentieth century. Accordingly he suggests that competitive advantage shifted in favour of America's managerial capitalism with its professionally managed, vertically integrated corporations using advanced technology to displace skilled labour. Equally this model proposes a further shift in international competitive advantage with the eclipse of managerial capitalism by Japanese collective business systems (Lazonick 1991). While the notion of internationally shifting competitive advantage is compelling, the suggestion that the persistence of proprietary capitalism in Britain was the primary cause of loss of competitive advantage generally or in the cotton industry, in particular, has proved controversial (Jones and Rose 1993: 1–16; Church 1993: 17–43). Moreover, the experience of the 1990s with the collapse of the Japanese economy and the renaissance of the United States economy seriously undermines the predictive power of Lazonick's model.

Chandlerian theory has transformed the way we think about business history, turning the discipline from one which was primarily descriptive to one with a powerful conceptual foundation. Yet there are real difficulties in applying his ideas outside the United States and to sectors where competitive advantage is more reliant on the quality of information flows than simply on technology and capital intensity. (See for example Hamilton and Feenstra 1995; Granovetter 1996; Jones and Rose 1993). In this respect, part of the problem is that although Chandler is extremely sensitive to differences in the economic underpinnings of business internationally and both he and Lazonick built their analysis on the power of historical forces, their perspectives use the United States as a starting point for the study of business behaviour. In addition, neither gives much attention to the forces, whether political or developmental, which may have made the culture of business in the United States unusual, rather than being an appropriate blueprint for business worldwide, in the twentieth century. Yet this is precisely the criticism which Gerschenkron made of Landes' and Sawyer's comparison of the United States and French business over thirty years ago. He warned against a simple causality between social values and business performance if the superiority of American values was assumed (Gerschenkron 1966: 63–4). This debate continues in the 1990s and Thomas McCraw's recent textbook dismisses the idea of the United States as a model of capitalist development as 'not only parochial [but] seriously mistaken' (McCraw 1997: 302).

Institutionalists undertaking comparative studies make the underlying assumption of international convergence in business activity (Fruin 1998:

122–36). By contrast, sociologists perceive that: '[e]conomic action is socially situated [and] cannot be explained by reference to individual motives alone. It is embedded in ongoing networks of personal relationships rather than being carried out by atomised actors' (Granovetter and Swedberg 1992: 9). This focus on personal relations and hence upon social networks leads to an emphasis on the divergence of business systems which proves especially apposite for this study.

If the intention of this book is to move away from using the United States as the starting point in studying the cotton industry, it is also contended that business behaviour and the perceptions of businessmen are critically influenced by the networks of which they are part. It becomes easier to understand both the significance and persistence of networks in business, if discussion is shifted from the purely economic and formally contractual arrangements to be found in Williamson's work, to include social ties. This change of emphasis means that power and authority, and indeed cultural forces, become significant variables in economic organisation. Analysis in this book centres upon the ways in which 'embedded' historical, cultural and political forces meant that the cotton industries of Britain and the United States evolved in often contrasting ways rather than converging.

The so-called 'old' institutionalists, with their emphasis on the formal and informal 'rules of the game' which influence all aspects of business behaviour, provide some useful tools for the study of networks, whether between firms or between firms and other organisations. Institutions may be either the formal laws created by government or the informal codes of practice and behaviour found within families or within particular communities or groups of individuals. Either way, they are important because they help to create order and the basis for co-operation in an otherwise uncertain world. For example, formal laws and regulations are the basis of property rights, whilst informal codes underpin trust and shape expectations of the likely behaviour of associates. As a consequence, the institutional environment is the critical reference point and foundation stone which affects the evolution of organisations, whether economic or political, and influences expectations and human responses (Davis and North 1971; North: 1990: 1–5). Such theory is invaluable for making sense of international differences in business behaviour whilst throwing light on networks at the community level, where specific sets of social values and norms of behaviour may prevail.

The idea that 'institutions matter' and that an understanding of the 'rules of the game' is crucial to an appreciation of economic behaviour has been applied by some 'new' institutionalists (Hodgson 1988; Casson 1991) and some have evolved transaction cost theories, based upon family and family-like firms, which provide a partial theoretical underpinning to the study of networks both within and between firms. Theorists such as Ben-Porath and Pollak have, for example, applied transaction cost theory to family behaviour whilst complementary analysis has highlighted those circumstances which make informal 'clan-like' control arrangements, within firms, more successful than formal bureaucracies (Ben-Porath 1980: 1–30; Pollak 1985: 581–608; Ouchi 1980; Alvesson and Lindkvist 1993). Implicit in the transaction cost approach is the idea that where regular transactions are conducted in a hazardous environment bureaucratic arrangements, by reducing uncertainty, will increase efficiency. It has been suggested, however, that some circumstances are so hazardous that they cannot be regulated either by the market or the firm. As a result transaction costs will be reduced within firms when control is on the basis of shared attitudes, goals and aspirations, either through a shared background or the creation of a business culture, rather than rules and regulations. Therefore:

> In the clan form, with its lower demands on formalised, sophisticated information – common ideas, beliefs and values instead function as information carriers – yielding sufficient guidance for action, providing sufficiently good measures of the values to be exchanged. (Alvesson and Lindkvist 1993: 430)

Understanding the development and success of networks, therefore, clearly requires an appreciation of the way in which power and trust relationships develop and the impact which they have upon business behaviour. Inevitably sociology provides invaluable insights on such issues whilst comparative management theorists such as Hofstede, Hampden-Turner and Trompenaars allow for culturally based comparisons of business behaviour (Weber 1978; Hofstede 1984; Hofstede 1991; Hampden-Turner and Trompenaars 1993).

New institutionalism is not, however, always acultural and Casson's work, by linking the notion of transaction costs to that of trust, provides insights into entrepreneurial behaviour and the formation of networks within and between firms. Building upon the idea of social norms underpinning trust, it is especially helpful in the study of the boundaries of the family firm which can be viewed as including that extended kinship group of cousins, in-laws and connections in the local business community, especially from within religious groupings. It consequently represents more than just a reservoir of skill, labour and finance. It is a network of trust, the use of which reduces the transaction costs and the dangers and uncertainties of business activity. Thus, although the family might represent an internal market for managerial labour, a source of funds for establishment and expansion and of market information, the boundaries of the family business have usually lain within a rather wider group with a shared culture and values (Casson 1982: 302–7; Casson 1991: 69–70; Casson 1993: 30–54).

Undoubtedly network theory, which is based upon the importance of trust and its relationship to flows of information as well as to flows of goods, finance, commerce and labour, is invaluable in the study of business in early industrialisation. Consequently this book calls attention to the emergence, operation, effectiveness and differences in the predominantly family firm networks in both cotton industries in the eighteenth and nineteenth centuries. Yet networks, although often unstable, are by no means only a stage on the route to the integrated corporation. Similarly the significance of social relationships to business may change as economies mature but it does not disappear and may have repercussions for the interaction between and within even fairly large firms or between firms and governments in the twentieth century. This book will, for example, examine how far in the United States interlocking directorships, which have been inseparable from the idea of the corporation since the eighteenth century and form vertical social ties in business, have had implications for the behaviour of firms throughout the economy, including the cotton industry in the nineteenth century (Mizruchi 1982: 28–9).

It is not intended to suggest that either the British or the American cotton industries were organised on an anti-competitive collusive basis during industrialisation, or that when cartels did emerge in the late nineteenth century and interwar period they were especially effective – at the very least, the structure of both industries precluded this. Rather, the explanation of the varying motivations for and configurations in networking behaviour may well depend upon the differing types of individualism identified in the two societies. The history of the United States, it has been argued, has created an 'outgoing, pragmatic and democratic society [where] they are taught from birth that co-operation for mutual benefit is good'. This environment led to a kind of individualism which does not prevent co-operation for the common good and which differed from the position in Britain in the eighteenth and nineteenth centuries (Cochran 1971b: 102). Without the background of a Frontier society, a collective approach to business problems in Britain was far less common or necessary in early industrialisation. This is not to say that business networking did not occur in Britain, but it was far more fragmented and more commonly linked to the well-being of individual families than to that of an entire community.

These differences will be used to explain the causes and consequences of varying types of family firm networking within both Britain and the United States and between the two societies in the nineteenth century and will form the core of the book. In addition, there will be discussion of the forces which undermined and altered these patterns as societies, economic conditions and the legal and political environments surrounding the two industries changed. In this context two issues will be important: the quest for and effectiveness of collusive arrangements and the changing role of networks in determining the form of government–industry relations and lobbying. The evolution and behaviour of political pressure groups is clearly a vital element of network arrangements.

Collective economic arrangements by groups of firms lead to the creation of cartels to control output and prices, while trade associations and pressure groups increase the political power of business and facilitate negotiations with civil servants and politicians (Grant 1993: 33). Indeed, inevitably there exists a correlation between heavily cartelised sectors and the ability of groups of industrialists within them to exercise political power. Equally the attitudes of government, in framing legislation relating to collective arrangements, will influence their prevalence, organisation and prospects of success. Consequently in some societies, such as the United States, although economic collusion has been outlawed since the late nineteenth century, lobbying is seen as an integral and essential part of the democratic process and as a vital way of preventing the development of undue concentrations of power (Grant 1995: 23). In other words it forms part of the culture of government–industry relations in the United States and is also inseparable from a decentralised political system. It will be necessary to consider the implications of these characteristics for government–industry relations especially set against the very different position prevailing in Britain with its centralised political system.

Individual networks have been likened to networks of trust where a coincidence of values and attitudes reduces transaction costs and encourages collective activity (Casson 1991: 169–70). Clearly in looking at groups intent on exercising political power such attributes are vital. However, the effectiveness of pressure groups does not merely depend upon the internal cohesion of a group, but also upon its ability to communicate effectively with other organisations, an ability which is itself partly culturally determined. What is crucial here is both the values and attitudes of the members of a pressure group and the extent to which they are capable of understanding and adapting to the priorities and behaviour of politicians and civil servants. This will, in turn, determine how far they can pursue 'insider' as opposed to 'outsider' strategies with respect to their dealings with the state.

'Insiders' typically operate within the political system in which the state and civil servants set the 'rules of the game' and in which pressure groups adapt their strategies to fit these norms of behaviour and in so doing enhance their bargaining power. 'Outsiders', on the other hand, may often appear politically naïve and undermine the power of their case through a lack of appreciation of appropriate codes of behaviour and a parochialism in appreciating wider considerations (Grant 1995: 22–3). Consequently even the most united grouping may be unable to influence a government if profound cultural differences between industrialists, civil servants and politicians prevent meaningful interaction. Yet education, social background and the like, whilst vital, are not the only factors determining whether any campaign will have an impact. Much also depends upon the extent to which the wider political and economic priorities of the state and of the narrower concerns of an industrial pressure group coincide both historically and in any particular period. In addition, the ability to convince a wider audience of the public welfare gains of a specific course of action may also be critical determinants of success or failure (Grant 1993: 130). The choice of insider as opposed to outsider activity may depend heavily upon historical forces shaping the cultural characteristics of pressure groups and those within the political system. The ability to shift from outsider to insider activity may change through time depending upon the nature of the cause and the ability of those involved to build an understanding of the priorities, procedures and practices of those within. Such choices are also likely to vary internationally, as a result of differences in the cultural background of politicians, industrialists and the norms of behaviour surrounding their interaction.

Inevitably the evolution of government–industry relations also involves a discussion of changes which occurred in the wider institutional environment within which business operated and the implications which these changes had. It is a process which involves drawing on the work of both Gerschenkron and North. Gerschenkron's theory of relative economic backwardness highlighted the tendency in traditional economies, which industrialised late, for the state to be a substitute for spontaneous private enterprise. Developed initially to explain the distinctive pattern of industrialisation in Russia, there are obvious hazards in applying this theory to the United States. Indeed, as the United States was not burdened by tradition, in the way of many late industrialisers, it is possible to see its experience as that of a relatively advanced industrialiser, rather than a backward economy. However, Gerschenkron's emphasis on the relationship between the timing and pattern of industrialisation and the wider institutional environment is of value in considering the reasons for differences in government–industry relations to be found in the two cotton industries in Britain and the United States (Gerschenkron 1966). Equally the link which Davis and North have demonstrated between institutional change and the distinctive pattern of American economic growth and industrial development is of critical importance to understanding why the attitudes and policies of cotton manufacturers differed on either side of the Atlantic. They concluded that the 'wedding of economic theory with an explanation for institutional change is essential for further understanding of the process of economic growth – past, present and future'. In other words they demonstrated that business reactions and the pattern of development are closely intertwined and shaped by both the legal system and shifts in government policy (Davis and North 1971: 270).

If firms are conditioned by the institutional environment, business culture can be defined as the values, attitudes, rituals and myths which give a firm identity. As Eldridge and Crombie have suggested:

> The culture of an organisation refers to the unique configuration of norms, values, beliefs, ways of behaving and so on that characterise the manner in which groups and individuals combine to get things done. The distinctiveness of a particular organisation is intimately bound up with its history and the character building effects of past decisions and past leaders. It is manifested in the folkways, mores and the ideology to which members defer, as well as in the strategic choices made by the organisation as a whole. (Eldridge and Crombie 1974: 89)

Business culture, an idea apparently coined in an influential article in *Business Week*, therefore reflects the history and sociology of businesses and has been most usually applied to the image and capabilities of twentieth-century corporations (*Business Week* 1980). The notion that external, as well as internal forces shape business culture is a vital consideration and one which is developed extensively in the work of Hofstede. In a book using IBM, in the late 1960s and early 1970s, as a case study, he set out to show that business organisations are 'culture bound'. He identified a number of key national cultural characteristics including Power Distance Relationships, Uncertainty Avoidance, Individualism and Masculinity. Underpinned by a complex mix of historical, familial, legal, political, ideological and linguistic characteristics these factors, he argued, represent the main distinguishing features of national cultures, which may themselves change through time. Hofstede believed that these were the principal factors shaping behaviour within organisations and which explain why United States-based theories of management and business behaviour were rarely applicable elsewhere (Hofstede 1980). The shifting importance of national cultural characteristics on business has also been employed to explain international shifts in competitive advantage and the changes which have taken place since the 1970s (Hampden-Turner and Trompenaars 1993).

Business culture is therefore an important concept and one which has already been fruitfully used by business historians (see, for example, essays by Church, Rose and Westall in Godley and Westall 1996). It can also give form and shape to the study of the relationship between business behaviour and national culture which has interested business historians in recent years (Wilson 1995).

In this book the formation and evolution of business culture and its relationship to the external environment are applied, not only to twentieth-century business corporations, but to firms large and small over a 200-year period of history. It will be demonstrated that, affected by past events, the strategy and structure of firms reflect responses to changes in the external environment, real or anticipated. Yet, at the same time, the ability of firms to adapt and the form that any adjustment may take will be shown to be influenced by, among other factors, their internal culture which is inseparable from the society of which it is a part. In other words the behaviour of a business, its responsiveness to change, ability to innovate and the shape of that innovation will have been modified by the organisation's cultural system which, in turn, will have been shaped by external social, political, economic and historical forces which together build nations (Allaire and Firsirotu 1984: 210). From the perspective of this book, one of the most important influences on business culture, however, is the relationship between a firm and its local community, especially during early industrialisation, and the implications which this has for the types of family firms that emerged and the way they changed through time.

Historical trends

Theoretical tools help to make sense of the past and are vital if generalisations are to be made. However, if an over-simplistic determinism is to be avoided analysis must be set against the appropriate historical context, one which conveys a sense of change as well as of continuity. In order to explain the contrasting sets of business attitudes which emerged in the British and American cotton industries, this book is broadly chronological. Part I will identify the way in which cotton businesses developed and will explore the influence of historical forces, of the structure of product and factor markets and of the institutional environment on the values and attitudes of cotton entrepreneurs in Britain and America. The purpose of Part II is, on the other hand, to explain the responses made to changes in tastes and preferences, in the international economy and in the institutional environment. It will demonstrate that the complex differences in business behaviour, which had evolved prior to 1860, had major consequences for the patterns of response. It will demonstrate, too, that attitudes were not static and in turn evolved to accommodate new expectations. Chapters 2–5, therefore, explore the early development of distinctive technologies and patterns of industry, the emergence and operation of family firm networks, the management of labour and patterns of government–industry relations. Chapters 6–8, by contrast, analyse strategic responses in the two industries between 1860 and 1980. They demonstrate the extent to which fundamental changes such as the Civil War, the growth of foreign competition and the World Wars altered the commercial and political environment, the way in which businessmen reacted and how far their responses, if not trapped by past cultures, continued to be dominated by the past. These chapters will also trace the extent to which responses represented departures from customary practice.

This introduction has intentionally said little about the cotton industry itself since its importance as a field of study and its international role in early industrialisation is dealt with at length in Chapter 2. However, this is first and foremost a comparative analysis of the evolution of an important industry in two countries which, whilst sharing a language and initially, since America was a British colony, a common institutional heritage, soon became economically, socially and politically very different. Given that one of the central themes of the study is the idea that these differences were critical to the emergence of diverging business behaviour it is necessary to look more closely at the most obvious variations and briefly to explore the changes which took place through time.

The most frequently identified economic difference between Britain and the United States and one which undoubtedly influenced technological choice are the differences in the relative price and supply of factors of production. First Habakkuk and later Sandberg used the tools of neo-classical economic analysis to explain business behaviour in the British and American cotton industries. They argued that choices of technology, especially between the flexible labour-intensive mules and skill-saving ring frames, reflected rational responses to factor and product market signals (Habakkuk 1962; Sandberg 1969).

Of equal importance to the attitudes and behaviour of businessmen in general, as well as cotton manufacturers, and closely linked to the factor and product market conditions, is the idea of abundance. This book, however, makes only passing mention of the neo-classical debate surrounding resource allocation since this has been extensively rehearsed in the literature. Instead the emphasis here is on how far this force permeated notions of product markets, as well as sources of raw materials and motive power, in the United States (Licht 1995: 41; Atack 1979; Temin 1966a). In a comparative context an understanding of the way these circumstances contrasted with 'island Britain' where, if pre-industrial skill was readily available, supplies of many raw materials were not and, along with markets, were often to be found overseas, is also vital. The very scale and newness of the United States, for example, is likely to have influenced locational decisions and attitudes towards technology providing options unavailable or unattractive in Britain. Similarly, a key question must be the relationship between characteristics of markets, the organisation of firms and the objectives of their owners. How far, in other words, did a vast domestic market and relatively high labour costs lead American cotton manufacturers to pursue production-driven strategies, with scale and technology becoming icons, the central constructs of their cultural values? Conversely, in Britain, there is the question of whether the exceptional export orientation of the cotton industry influenced the culture of business and also had social and political implications. (Collins 1990: 150; Rubinstein 1993: 9; Cochran 1985: 49).

In a nation-state of recent settlement, which was also a continent, abundance became 'a basic condition of American life', with implications for social attitudes, for mobility and for the role of community. It held out, for example, the prospect of equality through the commercial and industrial exploitation of resources (Potter 1954: 84–96). Most significantly the opportunities for individual advancement which this offered involved migration, which became a way of life from the colonial period onwards (Cochran 1985: 6). High levels of mobility, which American society featured from the eighteenth century, contrasted sharply with England's experience in the same period. It would, however, be wrong to exaggerate the contrasts between Britain and the United States since levels of intraregional migration were rising in England throughout the eighteenth century and industrialisation brought with it rapid urbanisation. The difference lay in the distances travelled, for long-distance migration remained rare even after the Industrial Revolution. Indeed in 1851 83 per cent of the residents of Preston, the Lancashire cotton town, had been born within it or within a radius of thirty miles (Winstanley 1996: 148–9). In addition, regular and frequent geographic movement was far less of a feature of British life than it was in America. In the context of the cotton industry, this book will explore the implications which these differences had for attitudes to consumption, to business communities, to labour management and training, for the effectiveness of trade unions and for political activity by workers.

If transiency became a feature of American society at an early stage, societies did not become atomistic since migration was in the company of friends. In addition, political forces meant that the collective importance of local communities was reinforced rather than undermined in the nineteenth century at least until the Civil War (Bender 1975: 72, 92, 96). As in Britain it was indeed from local communities that the principal stimuli for industrialisation came in nineteenth-century America, but, whereas in Britain this was spontaneous and unplanned, the underdevelopment of the United States was an important, though not the only reason, for a more planned and indeed collective approach to business development.

As a developing country it is to be anticipated in America that the role of the state might be greater in this process than in a more advanced economy such as Britain. However, historical forces, not least their colonial experience, brought a deep-seated suspicion of concentrations of influence among Americans and a consequent fear of strong government. America's founding fathers sought to divide power within the government and within society, an objective entrenched in the Constitution. Within the federal government, executive power was to rest with the president whilst legislative power was to lie with Congress, as the guardians of state interests. As a consequence individual states' identity, legislative power and ability to raise domestic taxes were preserved, with control divided between federal and state governments. This preserved and reinforced the social and political differences and idiosyncrasies of individual states. Hence individual states, rather than the federal government, aided local or regional development chiefly through the corporation, which became so embedded in American life as to become part of its culture (Bender 1975: 83; Cochran 1985: 21; Temin 1997: 279). This meant that whilst it would be going too far to argue that the American Constitution promoted industrialisation, it most certainly created an environment which favoured it (Licht 1995: 93).

The granting of charters to public corporations, by state legislatures, for the collective benefit of communities in eighteenth-century America, laid the institutional foundations for business development as the economy modernised. As a financial device which facilitated raising the large resources necessary to develop services, infrastructure and business in often virgin territory, it was a necessity. The corporation was, therefore, a community instrument which came to underpin often collective endeavours at development, including hospitals, educational establishments, canals, railways, banks and eventually manufacturing. Its operation, therefore, reflected both the requirements and the values of new societies (Horwitz 1977: 109; Hall 1984: 72–3).

The relationship between community and business was every bit as potent in Britain as in the United States during industrialisation. However, a differing institutional environment and a more advanced economy meant that whilst collective action was by no means absent, especially for the provision of services and infrastructure, community-based networks tended to be informal rather than necessarily contractual. It is fair to say that in British business communities in the eighteenth and much of the nineteenth centuries, the partnership form of business was both a reflection of the business and legal environment and became a vital feature of both social and economic relations (Rose 1994). This book will explore the extent to which these differences led to distinctive family firm cultures between Britain and the United States, whilst highlighting the ways in which community values moulded the behaviour of firms within the different societies.

Differences in the internal organisation of communities, between the United States and Britain, were likely to have implications for relationships between communities and for the ability of interest groups to lobby governments on their behalf. It is to be anticipated that this will be shaped by the institutional environment, especially those laws relating to political representation and to the construction of the system of government more generally thus affecting the capabilities of lobbying groups to manipulate government policy in their favour. A full appreciation of the contrasting forces shaping business attitudes in the British and American cotton industries involves an analysis of the evolution of political as well as economic power. It requires an appreciation of such factors as the extent of political representation of industrialists, the impact of constitutional issues and the social and economic underpinnings of government–industry relations.

Summary

The tendency to view the United States model of business as a blueprint for international competitive advantage has often masked the exceptional nature of American economic change. This comparative study of the development of business attitudes in the British and American cotton industries, by placing business behaviour in its historical social, political as well as economic context, will explore the reasons for different business strategies through time. The next chapter will explore the beginnings of this process by looking at the forces which led industries with common technological origins to pursue divergent market, product and organisational strategies.

Part I

The culture of business networks 1750–1860

2 Industrialisation and the cotton industry in Britain and the United States

Textiles and industrialisation are synonymous and almost everywhere the first factories have been in the cotton industry. The position of clothing as a basic necessity, early success in mechanising textile production, and the comparative simplicity of technology, have meant that textiles in general, and the cotton industry in particular, are often the earliest industries to be modernised. Labour- rather than capital-intensive and requiring limited skill of operatives, the cotton and related textile industries suited both the resource profiles and the domestic markets of many early industrialisers and continue to do so. Similarly, textile production was developed extensively prior to modernisation in many countries. As a result basic skills became available to industrialists, even though prejudice against changing working habits might lead to significant labour market imperfections when factories and mechanisation were introduced. Moreover modest financial and technological requirements meant that relatively few barriers to entry existed until after 1960 when the industry became increasingly capital-intensive (Chandler and Tedlow 1985: 140; GATT 1984: 4; Kriedte, Medick and Schlumbohm 1982: 8; Pollard 1991: 33). These factors have meant that, whilst the cotton industry could form the basis of early spontaneous development in many countries, it has also been a prime candidate for government support as part of import substituting strategies aimed at speeding up the industrialisation process (Hoffman 1958: 2–4).

The cotton industry emerged as a dominant sector in the 'take-off' of both Britain and the United States although the macroeconomic consequences may be unclear. The two industries shared common technological origins as new ideas on manufacturing diffused comparatively rapidly from the first industrial nation to her one-time colony. However, although the two industries shared many similar features, this did not mean that a replica of the early British factory system was transferred to the United States in the late eighteenth and early nineteenth centuries. The identification of the distinguishing characteristics of the two industries will help to explain why and how the development of a modern cotton industry varied on either side of the Atlantic. Yet, since nationally differing factor endowments are only part of the story, consideration of the range of historical and socio-political factors which interacted with economic forces is necessary if the foundations of two such distinctive patterns of business attitudes and business culture are to be fully understood.

Cotton and the British Industrial Revolution

Variously described as 'the original leading sector in the first take off' and as the pacemaker of industrial change, the cotton industry came to symbolise the British Industrial Revolution and to be a reflection of industrial greatness (Rostow 1968: 25; Hobsbawm 1968; Landes 1969: 42). Between 1780 and 1800 British raw cotton consumption virtually doubled whilst in the same period fixed investment in the cotton industry grew by 165 per cent to reach £4.9m (Mitchell 1988: 330). It was a growth which continued into the nineteenth century. By the 1830s cotton manufactures were Britain's largest export industry and accounted for nearly half of total exports (Davis 1979: 15).

Although during the Industrial Revolution the cotton industry's rate of growth dwarfed all other British industries its overall impact on the macroeconomy was relatively limited (Farnie 1979: 7). Certainly cotton's productivity growth in the cotton industry vastly outstripped that achieved in other manufacturing industries between 1780 and 1830. However, the traditional sector of British industry at this time was so large that advances in cotton manufacturing did little to lift national productivity levels. Set in this context cotton represented a 'small island of modern industry' amidst a 'veritable sea' of pre-industrial sectors (Pollard 1981: 25). In such a world, still broadly agricultural, any idea of the cotton industry dominating the British economy in this period is impressionistic and is not borne out by the evidence. By 1811, therefore, 'the cotton industry's contribution to British national income was only between 4 per cent and 5 per cent; [and] it offered employment opportunities on a smaller scale than the armed forces' (Deane and Cole 1962: 191–2).

The dramatic expansion of cotton manufacturing did, however, transform the economies and societies of those parts of Britain which were reliant upon it, most especially Lancashire where, by the end of the Industrial Revolution the cotton industry was increasingly concentrated. Therefore, if 'cotton was the motor . . . in the first instance it was Lancashire rather than England that was the vehicle driven by it' (Pollard 1981: 17). It was cotton which stimulated this classic industrial region and reinforced many trends which predated the Industrial Revolution. In a comparatively small corner of Lancashire, south of the Ribble, the cotton industry did indeed act as a leading sector. The stimulus, which came initially from a growing taste for cotton cloths at home, reinforced by the rapid growth of diverse export markets, created a highly specialised and sophisticated local economy encompassing manufacturing, commerce, finance, transport, mining and ancillary industries by 1830. The problem of why cotton, an exotic, entirely imported fibre, should become so important in a small corner of England is a complex one. It owes as much to changes in tastes and preferences, to advances in design, as to the nature of resource allocation in Lancashire. To understand how and why this industry developed in Britain and why it became localised increasingly in Lancashire, it is necessary to explore the forces which shaped it. These led to the evolution of interrelated technologies, products, methods of organising work and business structures which influenced market arrangements and hence the development of the industry. However, if the peculiar features of the rise of the cotton industry in Britain are to be understood and used for the purposes of international comparisons, localised business development must be placed in the wider context of political and social as well as economic relationships (Zysman 1994: 243).

An area's traditions include that patchwork of customs, experience of work, technology, attitudes, contacts and organisations which have evolved through time and are inseparable from its socio-political development. These shape a region's capabilities, help to mould business strategy, the behaviour of labour, capital and product markets whilst at the same time influencing responses to external stimuli and underpinning any emerging culture of business.

Britain's textile tradition predated the Industrial Revolution and was dominated by woollens which were largely produced in East Anglia, Wiltshire and Yorkshire. Cotton mills were built in the late eighteenth and early nineteenth centuries in the traditional woollen areas of Yorkshire. However, the development of a modern cotton industry was not the result of a general textile tradition or one based upon wool. Rather, cotton mills were built in areas producing linen-based cloths or concentrating on framework knitting, not least because demand for these goods proved far more buoyant than for woollens in this period. The early cotton industry developed, therefore, around Manchester and Glasgow where fustians, checks and smallwares had been produced from the seventeenth century onwards (Wadsworth and Mann 1931: 25). At the same time early factories were also built in those areas of the East Midlands which had been associated with light hosiery and lacemaking since before the Civil War as well as in North Wales (Chapman 1967). In all of these areas, by the early eighteenth century, skills, technologies and work practices had evolved, based on extensive putting out and artisan systems of production supported by often complex networks of commerce, finance and market intelligence. These proto-industrial communities were thought to have emerged as a result of the infertility of small landholdings in upland regions, which made family income supplements from industry vital to survival. It has been suggested that the wealth and skills created by the process, combined with the acceleration of population growth, which proto-industrialisation encouraged, formed the basis of the future growth in individual regions (Mendells 1972: 241–61).

Superficially the development of the cotton industry in Lancashire, south of the Ribble, followed this pattern. There was an almost perfect geographic coincidence of eighteenth-century fustian manufacture with the location of the modern cotton industry. Fustians were often produced in upland areas where poor agricultural land made supplementary employment in outwork inevitable. Equally there had developed, in seventeenth- and early eighteenth-century Lancashire, a complex network of middlemen and commercial credit which connected rural producers to their markets. In addition, the evolution of pockets of skill was of critical importance to the subsequent development of the cotton region in Lancashire.

However, the wide variety of experience in Lancashire suggests that the process was more complicated (Walton 1989; Timmins 1998). One of the county's most important specialisms in the seventeenth and early eighteenth centuries was, for example, smallwares produced, not in rural areas, but in Manchester (Wadsworth and Mann 1931: 113). Equally, the existence of proto-industry was by no means an automatic passport to modernisation. This is not, of course, to deny that the shape and pace of the development of Lancashire's factory-based cotton industry *was* critically influenced by past traditions. Rather, it is to emphasise that, even within a single county, regional differences in economic, social and cultural characteristics may lead to alternative paths towards industrialisation (Sabel and Zeitlin 1985: 133–76).

Pre-industrial technologies, in all stages of the production of fustians and hosiery, were relatively simple and labour-intensive and, until the middle of the eighteenth century, innovation proved comparatively slow. However, two important inventions were developed in the textile districts of Lancashire and the East Midlands which were to form crucial parts of their evolving textile tradition. Lee's stocking frame had been invented in the late sixteenth century (perfected by Nottingham workmen by 1732) whilst the fly shuttle, which transformed handweaving, was patented by John Kay of Bury in 1733. Both these hand-operated machines increased labour productivity whilst subsequent improvements, especially of the stocking frame, allowed product innovation. As these technologies diffused they carried major implications for the direction of subsequent complementary technological development and for the emergence of craft-based machine-making capabilities in the textile areas. More importantly, by making available new fabrics and products, they increased the attractiveness of cotton goods even before the coming of the factory system transformed production processes (Timmins 1996: 37–8; Chapman 1987: 13–14).

Since most textile activities were not skill-intensive it is quite hard to identify the nature of pre-industrial skills and to determine with whom they resided. Yet at the very least the concentration of workers, some of whom had craft skills, in relatively narrow geographical areas brought a familiarity and dexterity with textiles and an ability to adapt existing machinery to allow the development of new fabrics. In close-knit communities new ideas diffused rapidly, reinforcing competitive strategies based upon regular product innovation.

Moreover, in both Lancashire and the East Midlands a sexual division of labour had emerged even before the Industrial Revolution. In the eighteenth century, therefore, spinning and preparation, the commonest of industrial processes, were normally carried out by women and children whilst weaving and warping were more generally, though not exclusively, undertaken by men (Timmins 1996: 31). Commenting on the Warrington sail cloth and sacking trade in 1771 Young, for example, highlighted a significant division of tasks and observed that:

> the manufactures of sail cloth and sacking are very considerable. The first is spun by women and girls who earn about 2d per day. It is then bleached, which is done by men, who earn 10s 0d per week; after bleaching it is wound by women, whose earnings are 2s 6d a week; next it is warped by men, who earn 7s 0d a week; and then starched. . . . The last operation is weaving, in which men earn 9s, the women 5s and boys 3s 6d a week. The spinners in the sacking branch earn 6s 0d a week and are women. (Young 1771: 163)

In framework knitting putting out and artisan systems coexisted. Framework knitters were typically male and were normally artisans rather than outworkers. However, hosiery and net made on stocking frames tended to be finished by women and children in villages in Nottinghamshire, Leicestershire, Yorkshire and Staffordshire (Chapman 1967: 19).

A growing number of merchants and middlemen residing in the emerging commercial centres co-ordinated the various stages of production. In Lancashire at the very centre of the industrial and commercial process were the linen drapers. These merchant-manufacturers were involved in 'buying and selling [and] putting out linen yarn [and] cotton wool to . . . spinning, winding, warping and weaving', whilst in Nottingham and

Leicester the merchant-hosiers fulfilled a similar role (Wadsworth and Mann 1931: 73; Chapman 1967: 20). Their personal and financial networks linked Lancashire and the East Midlands to London, Britain's prime centre of commerce, design, and calico printing. Extensive contacts with London were crucial to access to trade credit and to domestic and overseas commercial intelligence.

A significant proportion of the raw materials for both hosiery and fustian manufacture were imported and this considerably increased the complexity of both the linen drapers' and the merchant-hosiers' activities. Some directly imported the raw materials they dealt in or put out for manufacture. However, it was often safer and more convenient to use the services of specialist middlemen such as yarn jobbers and raw cotton dealers in the ports. Linen yarn from Ireland and the Continent was, for example, imported via the ports of London, Hull and Liverpool. On the other hand, raw cotton came from the Levant, the West Indies and Brazil and, until 1795, London remained the most important port of entry. However, Lancashire's west coast ports of Lancaster and, more especially, Liverpool were increasingly the recipients of raw cotton from the West Indies and Brazil (Edwards 1969: 107; Wadsworth and Mann 1931: 233–6). Therefore, while many of the raw cotton dealers operated in London, by the mid-eighteenth century an increasing number could be found in Liverpool with some also in Manchester. There, until the 1770s, cotton dealing was commonly combined with both yarn dealing and manufacturing. London's seventeenth- and early eighteenth-century commercial importance was not confined to the import trade, for the metropolis was the most important fashion centre in Britain, as well as being the hub of both the domestic market and the export trade for textiles. The capital's specialist middlemen were therefore vital to both Lancashire's linen drapers and Nottingham's merchant-hosiers, reducing the uncertainties of dealing with distant and often rapidly changing markets. Some provincial merchant-manufacturers brought this expertise within their firms by taking a London partner. Yet, for many the services of the London warehousemen, who sometimes combined selling goods with purchase of raw materials, were invaluable (Chapman 1987: 12).

The importance of middlemen was not, however, confined to the purchase of raw materials or the sale of finished products for they played a part at every stage of the production and distribution process. Some linen drapers, it is true, operated a putting out system directly from their warehouse. More generally as the scale of activity grew and the geographic spread of their outworkers increased, the services of middlemen, especially of the fustian masters, were crucial. Some of these were manufacturers in their own right and purchased raw materials from the linen drapers on credit, while selling the finished goods for profit. Many were, however, true middlemen, who acted as the agents of the manufacturers co-ordinating the putting-out system in return for commission on the delivery of finished goods. These relatively complex systems of production involved 'the purchase in bulk of imported raw materials, and the lapse of an interval of several months between the time when it was distributed to the workpeople and the final sale of the finished cloth' interacted with an equally elaborate, if largely informal financial system (Wadsworth and Mann 1931: 71–91).

In Nottingham a single bank was active in the hosiery industry as early as the 1740s (with others appearing from the 1760s), although in Lancashire there were none until the 1770s. As a result credit, prior to that date, was non-institutional and largely based upon the bill of exchange and on personalised financial arrangements. A complex interlocking web developed which reinforced the importance of both provincial merchant manufacturers and the London middlemen who sometimes went into partnership. This network was essential to the expansion of both the fustian and hosiery trades (Hoppit 1986: 91–2; Chapman 1967: 22).

In Lancashire every stage of the putting-out system operated on the short-term credit extended by the linen draper. The purchase of raw materials and the sale of goods were similarly underpinned by the London warehousemen. Relying for security on the standing of the London house, a linen draper received payment for goods sold in the form of a bill drawn on London. Since these bills could then be used to meet local debts, the fortunes of Lancashire and those of London became inextricably linked by a network as extensive as it would have been with a banking system. Similarly the growing commercial importance of Liverpool increased the significance of her merchants and brokers in the financial health of the fustian trade, though in the eighteenth century they too remained reliant on the London houses. The sophistication and elegance of Lancashire's eighteenth-century commercial and financial network facilitated business expansion and spawned the first generation of Lancashire's bankers in the 1770s. Not surprisingly, as one-time merchants their principal role lay in discounting bills of exchange rather than in note issuing (Wadsworth and Mann 1931: 248–9; Anderson 1972: 252–5).

The dominance of the putting-out system in Lancashire's eighteenth-century textile industry, made short-term credit of fundamental importance. However, demand also materialised for long-term loans for mining, iron founding and for building textile workshops, especially for sail cloth manufacture. Lancashire was, in the seventeenth and eighteenth centuries, predominantly rural, so that far more wealth was held in land than in trade and industry. In the absence of banks, ignorance and mutual suspicion could have restricted the long-term flow of funds between landed groups and those in trade and industry. Yet, in both Lancashire and the West Riding of Yorkshire such difficulties were circumvented because local attorneys acted as financial intermediaries. Attorneys were involved in real estate dealings and had intimate knowledge of most aspects of their local communities. This placed them in an ideal position to co-ordinate the mortgage market and in turn facilitated the long-term flow of funds between land and industry (Anderson 1966; Hudson 1986: 211–34).

If the evolution of local historical traditions is to be fully appreciated it should be set against the political, legal and institutional environment which surrounded it, because the national political climate can have far-reaching and often unforeseen effects for local interests and the development of business. In seventeenth- and eighteenth-century Britain a combination of restrictive and mercantilist government policies had significant consequences for the localisation of the textile industry, for the types of products made and markets served, and ultimately for the pattern of expansion after 1750.

A decisive factor explaining the concentration of fustian making in Lancashire in the sixteenth and seventeenth centuries was that it was exempt from the Weavers' Acts of 1555 and 1558 restricting the numbers of apprentices who could be employed by a master weaver. Similarly in Nottinghamshire local magistrates successfully thwarted attempts by the London Company of Framework Knitters to constrain entry into their craft in 1728 and encouraged the migration of the trade from the capital to the East Midlands (Daniels 1920: xxviii–xxix, 3–6; Chapman 1967: 18).

For Lancashire an even greater stimulus to the development of fustian manufacture was the county's exemption from the Calico Acts. Originally introduced in 1721 to prohibit the importation of printed fabrics from the East, the Calico Acts were soon extended to apply to the use or wearing of all printed fabrics irrespective of where they had been dyed. However, fustians, Lancashire's specialism, could be sold on the home market. Moreover, whilst these Acts meant that the cloths of the Blackburn–Oldham–Manchester triangle found a growing market at home they also help explain the origins of the overseas orientation of Lancashire cottons. Although the sale of printed calicoes was banned in England it was permitted to print cotton cloth for export. This strategy was further encouraged by the relative success of British mercantilist naval policies internationally from the sixteenth century onwards. Especially important was the acquisition of the American colonies which, by the eighteenth century, were described as the centre of the British Empire both as a source of raw materials and a market for British manufactures (Brogan 1985: 88; Montgomery 1970: 36). That the American market was pursued by Lancashire manufacturers is confirmed by numerous orders from Boston, New York and Philadelphia merchants for English calico and chintz between 1721 and 1740 and by the growing eighteenth-century reputation of such Lancashire firms as Peels and Hydes. However, European markets were not neglected and large quantities of Manchester goods (often finished in London) went to France in the middle of the eighteenth century (Daniels 1920: 20–3; Wadsworth and Mann 1931: 150; O'Brien, Griffiths and Hunt 1991: 395–423; Montgomery 1970: 17, 22 and 40).

The often-interconnected features of local economies do not explain the dramatic rise of the cotton industry in Britain. This resulted from the complex and seemingly self-reinforcing interaction of first domestic, and then overseas demand, with technology. However, the characteristics of traditional economies do help to determine both the location of early cotton factories and the technological, financial, labour or market strategies which millowners subsequently pursued in response to a changing eighteenth-century environment and the initiatives they undertook to alter that environment.

Traditionally, technological change has lain at the heart of studies of the Industrial Revolution, nowhere more so than in the cotton industry, where the cumulative nature of innovation, first in spinning and preparation and later in weaving, was associated with the evolution of the factory system and the consequent dramatic rise in output (Landes 1969). Certainly the emergence of supply bottlenecks in spinning, as a result of both the fly shuttle and the stocking frame, encouraged a quest for a machine which could produce multiple threads of reliable quality. That quest, which was concentrated within Lancashire's textile community, built upon existing technical knowledge and was initially encouraged by a prize from the Royal Society of Arts. The first advance came with Hargreave's spinning jenny in the mid-1760s which, whilst difficult to operate and having a tendency to spin unevenly, did produce multiple threads suitable for relatively coarse wefts. This was followed in 1769 by Richard Arkwright's water frame which spun more regular multiple threads, suitable for use as warps, on rollers. However, fine spinning remained a greater challenge and it was not until 1779 and the introduction of Crompton's mule that fine yarn could be spun mechanically although it required great skill, strength and dexterity on the part of spinners. Complementary inventions were also

Table 2.1. *The scale of the British cotton industry, 1801–61*

Date	Raw cotton (m lbs)	Numbers employed	Spindleage (m)	Loomage (000s)	Fixed investment (£m)
1801	54	242,000	n/a	n/a	3.3
1811	89	306,000	n/a	n/a	6
1821	129	369,000	n/a	n/a	8.44
1831	263	427,000	9.0[a]	110[b]	15.21
1841	438	374,000	17.0[c]	n/a	28.84
1851	659	379,000	20.9	250	44.92
1861	1,007	446,000	30.4	400	n/a

Notes:
[a] This is the spindleage figure for 1832.
[b] This is the loomage figure for 1835.
[c] This is the spindleage figure for 1845.
Sources: Mitchell 1988: 370; Farnie 1979: 180; Chapman and Butt 1988: 124–5.

made in both preparation and weaving with Arkwright's carding engine dating for 1775 and Cartwright's power loom for 1787, a device which was significantly improved by William Horrocks in 1802 (Timmins 1996: 39–46).

If most cotton spinning processes had been mechanised by the end of the eighteenth century, the idea that technological change caused the rise of the factory system and the initial rise in output from the late eighteenth century has been controversial. This is not least because all the new spinning technologies could be operated outside factories which makes for a somewhat blurred causality. More important, however, is that in the very period when overall cotton textile output was growing most rapidly (see Table 2.1) the diffusion of the power loom was relatively slow and most of the expansion came in the hand section. Therefore, technological and organisational change certainly continued apace in spinning and by the end of the late eighteenth century spinning and preparation were fully mechanised though not all spindles were in powered factories. However, cotton cloth was still predominantly traditionally produced and finished, until the second quarter of the nineteenth century or beyond, in some regions of Lancashire. Indeed until the 1830s the rise of factory spinning and preparation led to an expansion in handloom weaving.

By 1813 there were still only 2,400 power looms in Britain whilst the number of handloom weavers did not peak until 1825 when they reached 250,000 (Walton 1987: 109–10; Timmins 1993). The persistence of handloom weaving can partly be explained by technological considerations. Certainly productivity was greater on the power loom but it was unsuitable for the production of all but the coarser cloths until the 1840s and was not successfully adapted for finer or fancy cloths before 1850 (Bythell 1968: 254). Hand-woven cloths, especially in the finer branches, were quite simply superior to the machine-made varieties. Moreover, the flexibility of outwork, in the face of volatile fashion markets for finer cloths, combined with the long-standing artisan handweaving traditions of north-east Lancashire, meant that until at least the 1820s it was possible to expand the scale and the scope of cotton cloth production without a marked investment in new technologies (Timmins 1996: 56).

The idea that the centralisation of production was predominantly technologically driven has also been challenged by those who believe that either the desire for greater control of labour or the reduction of transaction costs was a more important cause of the centralisation of production (Marglin 1974: 60–112; Williamson 1980b: 5–38; Jones 1994: 31–60). Yet, whilst the rise of the factory resulted in some loss of labour freedom and more satisfactory information flows, the extent should not be exaggerated, especially in the early stages of the Industrial Revolution. Moreover, even where factories did bring such consequences this cannot be taken as proof that they were the principal motivating forces. Such predominantly supply-side interpretations deny the importance of changing consumption patterns.

The interaction of technology and consumption combined to make the factory important to virtually all branches of the British cotton industry by 1850. Despite the subsequent export orientation of Lancashire's cotton industry it originally developed to serve the home market. Indeed in the 1770s two-thirds of the output of cotton cloth was consumed domestically. The appeal of cotton cloth in England originated with the Oriental imports of the East India Company, in the late seventeenth and early eighteenth centuries. Despite efforts by vested interests in the woollen sector, between 1721 and 1774, to stifle this trade cotton goods achieved a remarkable level of popularity very quickly. Initially a luxury good, cotton rapidly became accessible to a wider market through the development of the London second-hand clothing trade, while the Repeal of the Calico Acts in 1774 widened the potential market still further (Lemire 1979: 3–42; Wallwork 1968: 144). This in turn encouraged the diffusion of, first, new hand technologies and later mechanisation with the application of power. Labour productivity expanded dramatically with mechanisation and the number of operative hours to spin 100lb of cotton falling from 50,000 in the eighteenth century to just 135 by 1825 – a development which, combined with relatively low wages for all but the mule spinners, ensured that there was a steady supply of cheap cotton goods (Chapman 1987: 20; Catling 1970: 54).

New technology did not, however, only increase productivity. In addition it allowed new products to be manufactured which in turn increased the popularity of cotton goods, reinforcing the need for further technological improvement. In 1758, for example, Jedediah Strutt introduced the highly successful 'Derby rib' hose whilst numerous adjustments and experiments extended the use of the stocking frame to include 'underwear, breeches, gloves, handkerchiefs, waistcoats, elasticated knitwear and various imitations of cushion lace'. In Lancashire, on the other hand, a growing range of mixed fabrics was available by 1750 (Chapman 1967: 19; Shoeser 1996: 189). The dramatic expansion of the production and consumption of cheap cotton goods is, however, best explained by the rise of the factory system and the mechanisation of spinning and especially mule spinning. In the 1770s no calicoes or muslins were made in Britain simply because British hand spinners could not produce threads which were as fine as those produced in India. The introduction and perfection of the mule improved the quality of British cloth while reducing costs to a fraction of their previous level. Thus, whereas in 1779 in early trials of the mule, yarn was sold at 43s 9d per lb, by 1812 this had fallen to 4s 9d per lb. It was this combination of cost and quality advantages which helps to explain the growing popularity of British goods at home and in world markets where, for a while, they enjoyed an absolute advantage (Davis 1979: 15).

The centralisation of production in cotton spinning from the 1770s became inevitable with the application of power, first horse, then water and finally, especially after 1790, steam leading to indivisibilities. This speeded up machinery and increased productivity and simply rendered outwork in spinning impractical. As a result, during the 1770s powered cotton mills began to appear in the old fustian area and in Derbyshire and Nottinghamshire and the rise of the factory system was underway (Walton 1987: 105; Chapman 1967).

Evidence of the early growth of the cotton industry is extremely patchy, and high bankruptcy levels, stemming from the shortcomings of the credit system and a large number of young new entrants, make it hard to track development patterns. In the 1770s, although mills were built in Lancashire, the quest for water power meant that other areas, especially the East Midlands, Yorkshire, Scotland and North Wales, saw quite considerable mill building (Chapman 1981: 5–27). However, it does seem as though by the late 1780s the industry was becoming more concentrated in Lancashire, with its high proportion of new mills especially within the Oldham–Bolton–Manchester triangle. By 1787, of 145 Arkwright type-mills, 43 have been identified as in operation in Lancashire (Honeyman 1982: 61). By 1791 there were 18 mills in Oldham alone, though competition for water power meant that many were horse-powered. Thereafter mill building expanded dramatically. By 1811 Crompton's census of spindleage pointed to upwards of 650 cotton mills operating within 60 miles of Bolton (Daniels 1933: 107–11). However, Crompton was trying to gain recognition and financial compensation for the impact of the mule on the cotton industry. As a result, he underestimated the numbers of water frames and jennies and hence the overall scale of the cotton industry. In addition, he may have exaggerated the concentration within Lancashire at this time.

In the eighteenth century some geographic diversity remained. In the nineteenth century a growing localisation of the cotton industry in Lancashire surfaced; there, by 1841, 70 per cent of Britain's cotton textile production resided in 1,105 firms (Fong 1932: 25; Gatrell 1977: 98). Within the county, activity centred particularly on south-east and central Lancashire with small adjacent concentrations around Glossop and in north-east Cheshire (Walton 1987: 103). In addition, by 1840, 127 calico printing works, the majority either within north-east Lancashire or close to Manchester, were also active (Wallwork 1968: 144). This all had profound implications for Lancashire's employment profile. The marked labour intensity of the cotton industry, at the beginning of the nineteenth century, combined with a relatively narrow industrial base, meant that in 1811 over one-third of the county's population was employed in cotton. As the century progressed, even though cotton's proportionate impact on employment declined once new industrial sectors emerged, total Lancashire employment continued to grow, reaching 446,000 by 1861 (Farnie 1979: 2, 24).

This growing concentration of cotton activity in what had been a traditional textile area stemmed from a combination of existing proto-industrial skill, finance and commercial networks which had developed in these areas by the middle of the eighteenth century. However, concentration of the cotton industry in this narrow geographical area also required the transition from water to steam power, which began in the 1780s and gathered momentum in the 1820s with improvements to the steam engine. Moreover, the significance of the increasingly sophisticated commercial facilities in Manchester cannot be underestimated.

During the late eighteenth century, although their exact numbers or location is not known, cotton mills proliferated in established textile regions with good water power. In Lancashire, for example, in the 1770s and 1780s cotton mills were built on good water sites in the fustian regions, especially around Oldham although some mills were built in other towns including Rochdale, Blackburn and Burnley in the early 1780s.

Still, relatively limited water supplies in Oldham itself encouraged the persistence of horse power, alongside water, quite late in the eighteenth century. Large numbers of early mills were also sited on the banks of the Irwell, Irk, Tame, Roch, Calder and Darwen and their tributaries. These sites, although isolated below the Pennine and Rossendale Moors, were within easy reach of established textile areas (Hills 1970: 91; Ashmore 1969: 44).

During the 1780s overcrowding on water sites sent industrialists to the outer peripheries of both Derbyshire and Lancashire and indeed up to the borders with Westmorland, often well away from concentrations of skilled labour and from established networks of connections. However, if water power led to the dispersal of the cotton industry within and outside Lancashire the spread of steam power would eventually help reverse this trend, though it was initially a slow process beginning in the late 1780s and only gathering momentum in the 1820s and 1830s. Yet as late as 1838 water accounted for 22 per cent of motive power in the cotton industry (Musson 1976: 415–39). The technical limitations and unreliability of early steam engines, combined with the sustained improvement of water technology, meant that steam power brought few cost advantages before the 1830s. However, continued improvements meant that the sojourn of the cotton industry north of the Ribble and in some of the more remote parts of Derbyshire was relatively short-lived and largely vanished after the Cotton Famine. From the 1860s, therefore, increasingly the cotton industry was concentrated in Lancashire, in established cotton areas within easy reach of the coalfield in the south of the county (Rodgers 1960: 138). Certainly cotton spinning, hosiery and lacemaking remained in the East Midlands but the scale of Lancashire's production and employment dwarfed this region.

It is true that the pursuit of water power widened the boundaries of the cotton industry beyond the confines of the traditional textile areas. However, it is misleading to assume that the relative cost of power was the only, or even the most important, reason why cotton manufacturing became so concentrated in south-east Lancashire. Despite the relatively brief extension of cotton manufacturing to the county's periphery, industrial and commercial growth of the 'core' areas served to reinforce pre-industrial advantages. The Industrial Revolution encouraged further development of industrial skills and wealth in such towns as Oldham, Bolton, Manchester, Preston and Rochdale. In addition, the growing specialisation of commercial and financial institutions in Liverpool and Manchester, combined with infrastructure development, increased the locational advantages of the south-eastern corner of Lancashire. These brought significant cost advantages and improved information flows, both vital in the intensely competitive world of the nineteenth-century cotton industry (Farnie 1979: 45–77). In addition, from the 1820s and especially the 1830s, industrial concentration also spawned important ancillary industries such as textile machine making which grew up in individual towns to serve the needs of specialised textile manufacturers there. Machine makers served Lancashire's requirements whilst some, such as the engineering giant, Platt Brothers of Oldham, were instrumental in the international diffusion of textile technology in the late nineteenth century (Farnie 1990: 150–65). All this was to form the basis of Lancashire as an industrial district.

The concentration of the Lancashire cotton industry was, therefore, a cumulative process where pre-industrial influences were reinforced by the Industrial Revolution. Yet despite the remarkable geographical concentration of the cotton industry, experience varied considerably in Lancashire. It was not simply the case that large tracts of the county were untouched, or only fleetingly touched, by the cotton industry. Even where cotton predominated sharp contrasts emerged in the sources of enterprise, in the organisation of firms, in the division of labour, in labour relations, in technological traditions and in products and markets served. These differences highlight the extent to which business development in eighteenth-century Lancashire was inseparable from the evolution of distinctive local communities. In the early eighteenth century it is not surprising that businessmen preferred, where possible, to conduct their business dealings on a largely local basis or through a trusted friend or relation, largely because bankruptcy rates were relatively high, communications poor and markets relatively limited. Yet the economic, social and demographic changes of the Industrial Revolution and the domination of mainly small-scale, family businesses employing mainly local labour reinforced the role of the local business community in British business and most especially within the cotton industry.

Some of the most profound contrasts can be detected if the two spinning towns of Oldham and Bolton are compared in 1811. Although both towns shared a technology, the mule, both their product strategies and the size of their firms diverged. In Oldham the majority of firms were generally small, and spun mainly coarse counts. In Bolton, by contrast, mills were generally larger and produced fine yarns, a reflection of a pre-industrial concentration on muslin manufacture and the local invention of the mule by Samuel Crompton (Honeyman 1982: 87–114). If differences in experience were especially striking between Bolton and Oldham they were to be found throughout the cotton area during and after the Industrial Revolution. In Rochdale, therefore, with its earlier tradition of woollen manufacture, small masters engaged in water frame and later throstle spinning in relatively small firms. Nor were such trends only a feature of spinning, for the persistence of handloom weaving, in the finer branches and in the rural parts of north-east Lancashire, has been linked to the long-standing tradition of craft-organised hand work. In these areas, therefore, it was not until the 1880s that handloom weaving was finally extinct (Timmins 1993; Swain 1986: 147). Similarly, the persistence of tiny small-scale jenny workshops in Wigan, until at least the 1820s, is inexplicable without reference to the characteristics of the local economy and to the technological traditions which had developed there. The jenny has been portrayed as the least enduring of the key cotton spinning inventions. Never a powered machine, it was overhauled in terms of both quality and efficiency, first by the water frame and then the mule by the early nineteenth century. By 1811 Crompton's evidence suggests that only 3.1 per cent of the 5,066,396 spindles in use in the cotton industry were jennies, in small hand workshops operated by marginal producers (Daniels 1933: 107; Chapman 1967: 51; Edwards 1969: 5; Aspin 1964: 46).

What is striking, however, is that nearly 80 per cent of the surviving jennies in 1811 were in just two centres – Stockport in Cheshire and Wigan – with a further 8 per cent in Manchester (Daniels 1933: 108). In Wigan there were 40,386 jenny spindles in use, often in small workshops. Of the 28 mills recorded by Crompton in Wigan, 16 used jennies exclusively. These were tiny hand workshops, employing on average 13 spinners typically on 126 spindle jennies (Crompton Census).

The concentration of jenny workshops has not gone without comment, but more research is needed to explain the phenomenon fully (Aspin 1964: 52–7). It is unlikely, however, that the Wigan jenny cluster could be explained without reference to the local economy, its traditions and resources. Local labour market conditions meant that there were better employment opportunities for men in mining. In addition, an early technological and machine making tradition centred on the jenny, whilst poor water power and demand from the local sail cloth and sacking industries were all likely to have contributed to the persistence of jennies and inhibited the spread of, first, water frames and then mules.

Although there was some convergence within the cotton areas of Lancashire before 1830 the experience of the Industrial Revolution in the Lancashire cotton industry reinforced many pre-industrial differences. Despite quite considerable organisational integration by firms in the 1820s, technical integration was slow and by 1841 the majority in Lancashire remained small and single process, using limited amounts of power and employing a small number of workers. Even in Manchester, where there were a number of large-scale enterprises like McConnel and

Kennedy, the typical business was at best medium-sized and employed between 150 and 500 operatives. Yet what is even more striking than the relatively modest size of firms generally is the considerable variation in scale between the main cotton parishes. Those with the largest factories employing on average more than 200 operatives included Blackburn, Manchester and Preston, while in Oldham, Rochdale and Whalley, on the other hand, the average per factory was fewer than 90 (Lloyd-Jones and le Roux 1980: 72–82).

This overview of the development of the cotton industry in Lancashire during the late eighteenth century demonstrates the significance of pre-industrial economic and social experience in determining its location and development patterns. In the eighteenth century, the Lancashire economy had a relatively advanced craft economy based on fustians which made it an ideal home for the cotton industry. The growing localisation of the industry in a small corner of the county (with Manchester at its core) made the process of development cumulative. The Industrial Revolution saw the development of technical, financial, entrepreneurial and commercial capabilities and the reinforcement of the reservoir of skills. This meant that in this close-knit industrial district, Lancashire firms were capable of producing a substantial range of cloths suitable for a wide array of markets both at home and abroad. Conditions in the United States could not have been more different and therefore it is not surprising that although sharing a common technology the American cotton industry displayed very different characteristics and capabilities.

Technological diffusion and the United States

On the face of it, the United States did not offer a promising prospect for successful technology transfer in the eighteenth century. From a purely economic standpoint market and supply deficiencies, in a country of recent settlement, meant that even as late as 1790 America's chances of industrialisation looked fairly remote. Moreover, the constraining influence of colonial rule seriously inhibited any stirrings of pre-industrial development, in textiles, of the kind which underpinned the industrialisation of Lancashire. It has long been argued that differences in resource allocation led to diverging technological trajectories in Britain and the United States (Habakkuk 1962). Some doubt has been cast on the extent to which differences in resource allocation were real or illusory (Temin 1966b: 277–95). However, to understand both the process of technology transfer and the diverging characteristics of cotton manufacturing in Britain and the United States it is not enough to concentrate only on economic variables. It is also vital to trace the political, social and cultural forces shaping industrial development in a newly independent nation.

Ironically, given the subsequent importance of the home market to American development, a scattered population, inadequate transport and few cities meant that the initial potential of the domestic market was limited. In contrast with Britain, for example, where urbanisation was beginning to gather pace in the second half of the eighteenth century, in America only 5 per cent of the population lived in towns of more than 25,000 inhabitants. Equally, superficially at least, eighteenth-century America's resource allocation seemed likely to counteract any stirrings of industrialisation. This was because, whilst labour was scarce, the abundance of land could divert it away from industry and inflate wage levels. Wage rates were, as a result, significantly higher than those in Britain with the gap being particularly pronounced between 1790 and 1800 when even unskilled wages were, on average, 79 per cent higher than in Britain (Adams 1970: 502). In addition, despite commercial development on the eastern seaboard, financial resources were also relatively scarce in capital markets which were personalised and fragmented. By 1840, the capital costs per yard of production in the United States were twice as high as those in Britain, while ten years later real costs stood 57 per cent higher in the Massachusetts cotton industry than in Lancashire (Jeremy 1990: 38; Broadberry 1997: 187).

Yet if there was a relative scarcity of some factors of production, there was an absolute shortage of skill. Hence wage rates in the United States were virtually double those in Britain between 1790 and 1800. The General Court of Massachusetts 'encouraged' textile production as witnessed by a proclamation of 1656:

> that all hands not necessarily employed on other occasions, as women, girles and boyes shal and thereby are enjoyned to spin according to their skill and ability; and every towne do consider the condition and capacity of every family and accordingly to assess them as one or more spinners . . . that every one thus assessed for a whole spinner doe, after this year 1656 spin for 30 weekes every year 3 pound per week of lining, cotton or wooling . . . under penalty of 12 for every pound short. (Tryon 1917: 32)

But despite these efforts to remedy material shortages, America's pre-industrial economy was far less advanced than Europe generally and Britain in particular (Cohen 1990: 19; Ware 1931: 11; Chandler 1977: 62). In addition, in colonial America, as in Britain, textiles were seen as appropriate employment for the poor. Drawing no doubt on British social policy, in a number of colonies including Massachusetts, New York, Pennsylvania and Virginia, parishes built houses 'in which poor children were to be educated and instructed in the arts of spinning, weaving and other useful occupations and trades' (Tryon 1917: 39). However, although such enterprises must have encouraged the development of some indigenous skills, the overall impact was surely limited, especially if the experience of British workhouses was replicated across the Atlantic (Rose 1989: 5–32).

What America lacked, therefore, was a well-developed pool of skill underpinned and supported by a network of commercial and financial institutions. Outwork and artisan systems of textile production, which had developed so extensively in Britain and specifically in Lancashire, were unusual in America before the coming of the factory. There were some pre-colonial handicraft industries, such as shoemaking and coopering, it is true. However, at the time of the Revolution Philadelphia was the only American city where a long-standing tradition of craft-based weaving, traceable to the seventeenth century, had developed (Lindstrom 1978: 27; Clark 1929: 187; Hood 1999: 135–51). Mainly English and Ulster artisans had settled there by the 1770s, concentrating on the production of print goods, including linens and muslins for all kinds of 'gowns, curtains, carpets, bed furniture, chair bottoms, covers for dressing tables, handkerchiefs and shapes for men's waistcoats' (Montgomery 1970: 88). Inevitably, such development was supported by a growing number of related craftsmen who understood and built admittedly rudimentary machinery.

More generally, however, instead of a capitalist-based outwork and artisanal system, most pre-industrial American manufacturing, including textiles and clothing, operated on a subsistence basis in individual households. Although inevitably more prevalent in the eighteenth than the nineteenth century, this form of work persisted at the Frontier until railways brought factory-produced goods within reach of the mass of the population. Lacking any specialisation of task, household manufacturing was a typical organisational response to underdevelopment. It helped provide the necessities of life, at a time when inadequate transport and scattered communities meant there were few market incentives for greater division of labour or formal outwork systems (Clark 1929: 87–8). It is clear, therefore, that the United States' status, as a country of recent settlement, provides a partial explanation of the prevalence of household manufacturing. That other distinguishing characteristic of American history, the country's position as a British colony, also explains the relative backwardness of its manufacturing industry and the slow development of craft skills.

The Navigation Acts, first introduced in 1651 and renewed in 1660, intended to stimulate English shipping, generate both invisible and visible exports and protect English raw material supplies. One Bristol merchant summed up the role of the North American colonies as:

to tak[ing] off our product and manufactures, supply[ing] us with commodities which may either be wrought up here or exported again or prevent fetching things of the same nature from other places for or home consumption, employ our poor and encourage our navigation. They were in other words seen as a market for British goods and a source of raw materials. (quoted in Montgomery 1970: 36)

On their own, the restrictions which these laws placed on America removed the incentive to develop manufacturing. However, between 1699 and 1750, further legislation explicitly restricted the development of colonial manufacturing. In America, this legislation and the decision, in 1765, to tax the colonies undoubtedly strengthened colonial governments' resolve to promote economic independence and led to consistent policies, regarding the encouragement of household manufacture, which became a matter of political defiance (Tryon 1917: 11–27, 43). Moreover, there were numerous gestures to encourage the consumption of domestic manufactures whilst in 1776 Congress proposed the formation of societies in all colonies for the promotion of such manufactures. Household manufacturing extended to the Southern colonies where, in South Carolina, efforts were also made to promote workshops with larger plantations running weaving shops using both free and slave labour to make goods both for their own use and for sale within local communities (Rezneck 1932: 786; Lemert 1933: 17).

However, the scale of this response was limited, and inevitably during the Revolution actual levels of production were low. In addition, the cloths produced have been described as the most primitive in the civilised world and were quite unlike those of pre-industrial Lancashire. They may have met Frontier needs but around the eastern seaboard, the availability of Philadelphia textiles notwithstanding, tastes favoured more sophisticated imported cloths. Indeed from the 1740s, when there was a sharp increase in advertising of imported English consumer goods, wealthy east coast Americans developed an increasing preference for fabrics which could only be made in England (Breen 1986: 486). Only in sail cloth production, which was encouraged rather than restricted by the Navigation Laws, was there any significant workshop type development (Tucker 1984: 193). As with other non-household production this was in Philadelphia, where there is evidence of a manufactory in 1767 'set up about 3 years ago . . . for making sail cloth, ticking and linens' (quoted in Scranton 1983: 77). As a consequence of the limited pre-industrial development, an estimated 9–10 per cent of colonists' per capita income continued to be spent on British textiles and the products of the East India Company and, at the time of the Revolution, America had a very limited reservoir of indigenous textile skill (Shammas 1990: 64–5). In addition, the thriving commercial community along the eastern seaboard specialised in the import of manufactures and

Table 2.2. *The transatlantic transfer of British cotton technology to the United States, 1774–1812*

Name of technology	Date of invention	Date transferred to United States
Arkwright's Carding Engine	1775	1783
	invented 1764	
Hargreave's Jenny	patented 1770	
patented 1770	1774–5	
Arkwright's water frame	1769	1791
Crompton's mule	1779	1790–3
Cartwright's power loom	1787	–
Horrocks' power loom	1802	1812
Cylinder printing	1785	1809

Sources: Jeremy 1981: 76–117; Timmins 1996: 29–62; Jeremy 1996: 210–37.

the export of primary produce, rather than in the co-ordination and finance of industrial activity as in Britain.

Inevitably such a backward economy should depend on borrowed technology. Geographic proximity meant that most eighteenth-century technology transfer was between Britain and Continental Europe. However, trading links, a shared if diverging history and technological tradition and, most importantly, a common language, meant that the Atlantic was a relatively small barrier to the diffusion of technology (Jeremy and Stapleton 1991: 31; Tryon 1917: 64; Dickson 1966). As Table 2.2 shows, between 1774 and 1812 the major textile technologies were transferred from Britain to the United States.

The transfer of technologies was actively discouraged by British governments which, between 1718 and 1782, introduced a succession of pieces of restrictive legislation. These threatened fines and imprisonment for skilled workers who tried to emigrate, for those enticing artisans abroad or for the export of machinery. At the same time industrial secrets were jealously guarded by British manufacturers. However, neither legal restrictions nor the secrecy of industrialists prevented the flow of technological information between Britain and the United States.

In the post-revolutionary period, industrial espionage was sanctioned and indeed promoted by American state governments especially after the depression of 1783–7 rekindled an enthusiasm for manufacturing (Lipset 1967: 53). At the same time the gift of Americans for forming voluntary associations was fully exploited in this period. For example, the Pennsylvania Company for the Encouragement of Manufactures and Useful Arts, established in 1787, engaged in what was essentially state-financed industrial espionage. It openly proclaimed its aims as being: 'borrowing European inventions, utilising European immigrant skills and emulating European methods of encouraging manufactures' (quoted in Jeremy 1973a: 24). Although common, this type of activity was, however, a hazardous and uncertain process and the success of Francis Cabot Lowell in acquiring plans for the power loom, during a visit to England between 1810 and 1812, was far from typical. Most similar visits failed to produce the hoped for rewards and, even where plans and designs were procured, they were no guarantee of a successful transfer of new technology, especially if it was relatively sophisticated (Jeremy 1973a: 16–31).

Clearly the limitations of indigenous skill, the position of Philadelphia notwithstanding, had implications for the speed of assimilation of new technologies. It meant that the diffusion of more complex machines could be a protracted process even if plans and diagrams were acquired. Consequently, whilst the jenny was introduced into America in 1774, the mule proved a very different proposition requiring a combination of skilled managers, machine makers and operatives who were rare other than in Philadelphia. Not surprisingly, therefore, that city became the only substantial centre of mule spinning before the 1820s (Jeremy 1981: 20; Jeremy 1973a: 39–40, 47–8). In such circumstances it was inevitable that the diffusion of new technology depended heavily upon the transfer not of drawings or even machinery but of knowledge and expertise. The migrant artisan was, therefore, the single most important force in the successful transfer of textile technology from Britain to the United States.

So great were the potential prizes offered, by American states, for those supplying information, expertise, machinery or drawings and for those successfully utilising them, that British legal restrictions had little deterrent effect. Between 1774 and 1812, therefore, British methods for the preparation, spinning, weaving and finishing of cotton yarn and cloth were introduced into the United States, even though legal restrictions on the migration of artisans and the export of machinery were not repealed until 1825 and 1843 respectively (Tryon 1917: 27; Jeremy 1977: 1–34).

Skilled migrants, who contributed to the development the United States cotton industry, fell into two categories. There were those who had been involved in establishing pioneering British mills and who could secure generous premia in return for their knowledge. In addition there was a much larger group of mainly handicraft workers whose skill became vital to the competitive advantage of firms in some regions. In the first group were men who had been employed in key technological or managerial roles, by Britain's industrial leaders and especially by Richard Arkwright. They included men like Samuel Slater who successfully introduced the water frame to America. This one time apprentice to Arkwright's partner, Jedediah Strutt, went to America in 1789, lured by newspaper advertisements offering rewards for the technically proficient. For a while Slater worked in a jenny workshop belonging to the New York Manufacturing Company. However, his knowledge and expertise, derived from experience at the technological apex of the British cotton industry, placed his skills at a premium. In 1790, in return for building water frames and preparatory machinery at Pawtucket, Rhode Island he was able to secure admission to the family partnership of Almy and Jones (White 1836: 37; Tucker 1984: 24, 56). Similarly, Thomas Marshall, who had been the manager of Arkwright's Masson Mill, left for America in 1791, attracted by the offer of a salary of £100 a year to manage a mill built by the Society for Establishing Useful Manufactures, at Great Falls, Paterson New Jersey (Fitton 1989: 81).

Men of this sort, whose practical experience of new technology had been gained in the world's fastest growing cotton industry, had a disproportionate impact on early American textile development. Moreover, immigrant machine makers contributed both to the initial application of new techniques, and were also instrumental in founding American machine-making traditions which were increasingly reflected in subsequent adaptations of technology (Jeremy 1981: 142–78; Jeremy 1977: 3–4; Jeremy and Stapleton 1991: 35). Such men, in the vanguard of technological change, were, however, in the minority. The majority of British immigrant textile craftsmen, between 1770 and the 1820s, were handloom weavers or mule spinners many of whom were in retreat from modern machinery and work organisation. Given the limitations of preindustrial manufacturing in the United States, they provided a vital supplement to indigenous skill.

That the new nation could begin to overcome the potential obstacles to industrialisation owes something to its colonial past which fostered a fervour for economic independence from Britain, once political separation had been secured (Rezneck 1932: 785). This, in turn, encouraged the formation of voluntary associations to promote manufacturing, some of which received state support which, taken together, were vital to the industrialisation of what was, after all, a largely agricultural economy. Indeed the potential obstacles to the development of factory industry were such that government support was essential if further progress was to be made. It became so considerable during the forty years following the Revolution, that it has been concluded that 'the North Eastern United States had a culture, including instruments of government, [which was] . . . uniquely stimulating to new economic activity' (Cochran 1981: 15). Resolutions favouring a focus on domestic as opposed to imported goods were made in a number of towns whilst, in 1786, Massachusetts' political office holders were requested to wear only clothes made in America for the performance of their duties. These moves were further reinforced in 1788 by the Grand Federal Procession, held in Philadelphia to ratify the constitution demonstrating a national awareness of the need to foster and protect new manufactories (Montgomery 1970: 85; Rezneck 1932: 790). In addition, to counteract their technological deficiencies, the new states set up numerous societies to foster development and to 'borrow' British technology (Cochran 1981: 76; Jeremy 1973a: 28–31; Jeremy 1981: 17; Rezneck 1932: 784–811).

Much pressure for government support of industrial development came from commercial communities in individual states and especially in Massachusetts. Believing, rightly, that political independence from Britain did not mark the end of their economic disadvantages, they demanded that new manufactories should be erected and fostered by the government. Effective political pressure from this powerful group meant that experimental spinning factories were established and were able to turn to state legislatures, not only for tacit support, but also for financial assistance. In 1790, therefore, a group of Massachusetts merchants received a state grant of £1,000 to set up the Beverly Company to help create a flow of exports as well as serve the domestic market (Jeremy 1990: 153; Handlin and Handlin 1947: 104–5, 121–2). Such industrial encouragement was underpinned, from 1789, by a federal government whose sympathy for the needs of the business community materialised in the introduction of a series of tariffs. Still, these were predominantly for revenue purposes and cannot, therefore, be described as truly protective in intent. However, from 1790, although imported cotton and linen goods were subject to a tariff of 7.5 per cent, the duty on Indian goods, especially calicoes which were most likely to be in competition with America's coarse textiles, stood at 12.5 per cent (Clark 1929: 271).

Without government support, however, it is doubtful whether even the faintest stirrings of industrialisation would have occurred. Between 1774 and 1806 the halting development of factory spinning appeared in only a small corner of New England, in the Philadelphia area and in New York State with some very limited experimentation in the Southern states. This was based upon the largely complementary technologies of the jenny and the water frame. Introduced into Philadelphia in 1774, the jenny was rarely used, in anything but tiny workshops, at the Beverly Manufactory in Massachusetts from 1790 and subsequently in scattered workshops in Baltimore, New York and South Carolina (Jeremy 1981: 15; Clark 1929: 191–2; Lander 1969: 3–4). As in Britain, however, the jenny remained hand operated whilst power was first applied to Arkwright's water frame

Table 2.3. *British exports of selected cotton goods to America, 1780–1806 (£000)*

	1780	1786	1790	1796	1800	1806
Cottons and linens (printed)	80	49	94	317	802	1,427
6d–18d before printed	–	134	440	1,152	931	2,331
Stuffs (white)	–	–	2	6	148	1,249
Muslins	–	–	38	292	222	145
Manufactures	–	–	–	–	406	950
Stuffs (plain)	–	–	15	20	n/a	31
Manchester and fustians	35	26	83	196	119	76
Totals	115	209	672	1,983	2,628	6,209

Source: Edwards 1969: 246.

when Samuel Slater introduced it at Pawtucket, Rhode Island late in 1790. There is evidence that Hugh Templeton's factory in Statesburg, South Carolina began mechanised production several months earlier than Slater and employed slaves; however, it struggled and eventually failed five years later. In any event the backwardness of the entire American economy meant that by 1806 there were still only 15 cotton mills known to be in operation, with over half being run by Samuel Slater, his partners or his ex-employees (Chandler and Tedlow 1985: 152; Tucker 1984: 21, 89; Coleman 1963: 130–1; Ware 1931: 30, 128, 301–2; Wright 1979: 661). Certainly these mills did not meet the United States' growing demand for cottons, while American handloom weavers continued to produce fairly rudimentary cloths. As a consequence imports of British cotton goods (especially the fine or fancy varieties which Americans could not produce) continued to grow throughout the late eighteenth century, as Table 2.3 demonstrates.

There was, therefore, remarkably little sign of the spontaneous development of factory-based cotton manufacturing using imported technologies in this period. As in Britain early factories were confined to the spinning and preparation of yarns. This was partly because the transfer of calico printing using cylinders and power loom weaving was delayed until 1809 and 1812 respectively (Jeremy 1981: 92–107). Yet despite government enthusiasm for the development of manufacturing industry and the advantage of cheap supplies of domestically grown raw cotton, it took until the 1820s for there to be any really significant progress. This clearly is a measure of the obstacles to industrialisation faced by an ex-colonial country of recent settlement. Moreover, in the absence of further government intervention it is not at all clear how long it would have taken for the emergence of a factory-based cotton industry to gather momentum.

The United States cotton industry, especially in Massachusetts, received a vital fillip from the deterioration of relations with Britain which began with Jefferson's Embargo in 1807 and culminated in war from 1812 until 1814 (Clark 1929: 272). This was because these developments brought isolation from British cotton textiles and a strengthening of the resolve to achieve economic independence from the former mother country. The resultant shortage of cotton goods encouraged state legislatures to renew their efforts to promote manufacturing. In New York State, for example, an Act Relative to Incorporations for Manufacturing Purposes was passed in 1811 to encourage investment in yarn manufacturing for household weaving (Seavoy 1982: 65). It was, however, in Massachusetts that the response was most profound. In part to reduce the impact of the Embargo on Boston's powerful mercantile community the governor encouraged manufacturing. Increasingly, however, the development of industry was seen as a critical weapon in the war against England, becoming a symbol of patriotic zeal just as it had during the Revolution. The formation of corporations was encouraged and bounties and tax exemptions granted to a wide range of activities including cotton factories. Indeed, the Commonwealth granted exemptions to a wide range of business activities including cotton manufacturing (Handlin and Handlin 1947: 127–62).

It was against this background that cotton manufacturing began to expand in the United States in the early part of the nineteenth century. By 1809, therefore, there were 62 cotton mills in operation with a further 25 under construction while, in the next five years, 244 cotton and woollen mills were incorporated in the United States (Jeremy 1981: 160; Atack and Passell 1994: 122). By 1814 Tench Coxe estimated that as many as 243 cotton mills operated within 15 states, with Pennsylvania, Massachusetts, Rhode Island and New York seeing the largest concentrations (Ware 1931: 57), though numerous small mills were established in the Carolinas, in Virginia and in Kentucky. This southern expansion was, in part, a response to the quest for markets for raw cotton which, during the Embargo period could not be exported to England and which supplied the numerous local household manufacturers (Wright 1979: 661; Griffin and Standard 1957: 16–20). The gap left in the American market by British imports encouraged an expansion of handloom weaving and in 1810 alone cloth output grew by 153 per cent, with the average annual rate of growth for the period 1807–14 standing at 59.8 per cent (Chandler and Tedlow 1985: 152; Jeremy 1981: 160; Tucker 1984: 113; Zevin 1971: 123).

Table 2.4. *The scale of the United States cotton industry, 1800–60*

Date	Numbers employed	Number of mills	Spindleage (m)	Loomage (000s)	Fixed investment ($m)
1800	1,000	n/a	n/a	n/a	n/a
1806	n/a	15	0.004	n/a	n/a
1809	10,000[a]	62	0.03	n/a	n/a
1814	n/a	243	0.1	n/a	n/a
1820	12,247	439	0.2	1.665	n/a
1832	62,157	795	1.2	33.4	40.6
1840	72,119	1,240	2.3	48.0	n/a
1850	92,000	1,074	4.0	95.5	n/a
1860	122,028	1,091	5.2	126.3	98.6

Note:
[a] This figure refers to 1810.
Sources: Farnie 1979: 180; Cotton Yarn Association 1929: 7; Atack and Passell 1994: 191 and 523; Copeland 1912: 5–6; Lander 1969: 79.

Clearly the wartime expansion was artificial and the peace of December 1814 brought a deluge of cheap British imports which forced many established producers, as well as recent new entrants, out of business. It was, however, a collapse which inspired further government intervention through the extension of tariffs in 1816.

Whilst protection was by no means the only force stimulating the growth of cotton manufacturing it undoubtedly promoted 'learning by doing' which increased productivity (David 1970: 521–601) and the industry enjoyed rapid and sustained growth, as Table 2.4 shows. Consequently numbers employed reached over 62,000, a growth of more than 400 per cent in just 12 years between 1820 and 1832. The number of cotton mills also rose from 439 to 795 and spindleage reached 1.2m with loomage rising to 33,433 (Jeremy 1981: 162–3). The most rapid changes appeared in New England and especially Massachusetts where a regional take-off, based on cotton goods manufactured on American built machinery, began in the 1820s. By 1831–2 Massachusetts' spindleage and output dwarfed other states surveyed by Montgomery and by 1840 28 per cent of the nation's spindles and 29 per cent of those employed in cotton manufacturing were in the state (Montgomery 1840: 160–1; Lander 1969: 79). Indeed Massachusetts emerged as the most thoroughly industrialised portion of the globe, outside Great Britain, and the United States generally was second only to Britain in the production of manufactured goods, with textiles in pole position. By 1860 the value of cotton goods manufactured had reached $115,682,000 and the industry employed 122,000 people whilst capacity stood at 5.2m spindles and 126,300 looms (Table 2.4) (Cotton Yarn Association 1929: 7, 9; Rostow 1975: 203; Dalzell 1987: 3).

The rapid growth of cotton manufacturing in Massachusetts needs to be set against the paradoxically slow development of a factory-based cotton industry in the Southern, cotton growing states in the ante-bellum period. In the early part of the nineteenth century, although there was experimentation with manufacturing, the South remained dominated by cotton growing. Even during the 1840s, when William Gregg became a vocal and active enthusiast for cotton manufacturing, its emergence was limited (Wright 1979: 656). Therefore, of the 1,074 cotton mills identified in the 1850 census over half were in New England, while only 178 operated in the Southern states, which accounted for less than 7 per cent of all cotton spindles in the United States. Indeed by 1860 there were more spindles at the town of Lowell than in the entire American South (Lemert 1933: 38; Atack and Passell 1994: 191). Explanations of the brakes on cotton manufacturing in the South include the high profitability of cotton growing at a time when both international and domestic demand for raw cotton was rising, the lack of a local market in the self-sufficient slave economy and labour scarcity among conservative, plantation owners who feared the destabilising influence of both industrial concentrations of slaves and waves of immigrants. In addition, whereas in the North wealthy commercial elites favoured factory production as a means of protecting their social standing, in the South the only wealthy groups were the plantation owners who believed the only way to preserve their status, which came from land, was to bolster the traditional values of plantation society (Licht 1995: 37–41).

American adaptation

The initial development of the United States cotton industry clearly relied upon textile technology transferred, mainly illegally, from Britain. The early machine makers were attached to textile factories and were predominantly British migrants. However, the flow of migrant machine makers between 1820 and 1832 was insufficient to meet the needs of the rapidly expanding cotton industry and increasingly these new technicians were Americans. In this period, therefore, employment in machine making rose from 757 in 1820 to 3,206 in 1832 with less than half of the increase consisting of immigrants (Jeremy 1981: 164). The emergence of an indigenous textile machine-making capability had profound implications for the future industrialisation of the United States when during the nineteenth century firms diversified first into steam engines and turbines and later into specialist machine tools, which were to provide one of the Second Industrial Revolution foundations. For the cotton industry this capability was of fundamental importance to the successful absorption of textile technology and its subsequent adaptation to American conditions. Consequently it was of vital importance to the development of a cotton textile tradition or, more particularly, to a number of regionally distinctive traditions, which were peculiarly American.

The American cotton industry clearly shared technological roots with Britain. However, with differing factor and product market conditions, stemming partly from variations in resource allocation and reinforced by contrasting historical forces, it was inevitable that their trajectories would diverge. The abundance of natural resources, the high price of labour, and the position as an imitator rather than an initiator, are among the factors which differentiated the nascent American cotton industry from that in Britain. Despite difficulties at a micro level, the British cotton industry developed against a background of labour surplus but relative shortage of water power (Rose 1989). By contrast, in America, relatively scarce labour, especially skilled labour, was counter-balanced by plentiful supplies of water, in northern Massachusetts at least, and by cheap, high quality, domestically grown, raw cotton (Habakkuk 1962: 32–3; Jeremy 1981: 65; Cohen 1990: 28–54). This encouraged American machine makers to adapt technology to take account of their own resource conditions and increasingly from the 1820s to develop technologies which were wholly their own. From an early date, in comparison with Britain, the aim in America was to achieve high labour productivity, using relatively capital-intensive technologies where the demands on skill were comparatively low and where it was possible to economise on labour by using better grades of cotton than their English counterparts (Habakkuk 1962: 33; Jeremy 1990: 35–9).

If, from the 1820s, a distinctive resource allocation affected United States technology, a number of factors led manufacturers to pursue increasingly distinctive product market strategies. Firstly, Britain enjoyed the market power of the early starter and had a sufficient depth of skill to produce an increasingly diverse range of high quality goods for export. In these circumstances it is clear that if they were to gain a foothold in their own domestic markets American producers had to concentrate on coarse and medium cotton goods, where Britain's competitive advantage was least (Jeremy 1973a: 41). However, the limited skill base made the idea that there was any choice academic. Secondly, the tastes and preferences of the majority of the population, in a country of recent settlement, were profoundly different from those in Britain and it would have been surprising if had it been otherwise.

The tastes of the wealthy merchants on the eastern seaboard certainly favoured sophisticated English cloths. However, the sustained flow of migrants, with the westward movement of the Frontier, meant that early nineteenth-century American consumers were primarily rural (Cochran 1981: 12). They were admittedly 'relatively prosperous by European standards . . . [but had] a strong preference for moderately priced household furnishings, durable goods and equipment [including coarse textile fabrics]' (Rosenberg 1972: 48). Their tastes were comparatively simple and, indeed, one English migrant to Illinios, in 1833, observed:

> you would smile at the extreme simplicity of dress in these parts; we look rather singular by being dressed in broad cloth. Stockings seem quite out of fashion as a common article of dress, and shoes also . . . in the wilderness people must not expect what we call comforts, for it is quite necessary to abolish all artificial wants as much as possible. (quoted in Jeremy 1981: 182–3)

Population growth in the western states averaged 6.2 per cent per annum between 1810 and 1840 so that there emerged a buoyant market for simple standardised products (Zevin 1971: 137). However, if the Frontier represented the largest segment of the American domestic market for cotton textiles, the emerging and prosperous cities on the eastern seaboard represented a significant and more demanding niche which was partly met by United States producers.

As American machine-making capabilities developed there emerged a complex interaction between product markets and technology on the one hand and technology and factor market conditions on the other. Clearly it is possible to identify distinctive national resource and market characteristics which have been linked to the emergence of textile traditions quite separate from those in Britain. However, analysis of that evolution reveals a far more complicated picture. It has, for example, been demonstrated that cotton textile manufacturing grew more dramatically in Massachusetts than elsewhere in the United States. Yet, it is not just the case that there were regional variations in the rate of growth of production. The strategies used to accommodate the peculiar conditions faced, in the American economy, were not universal within the United States.

Between 1820 and 1840, as Table 2.5 demonstrates, the growth of the American cotton industry was associated with the emergence of three distinctive technological and organisational traditions in northern Massachusetts, Rhode Island, southern Massachusetts and Connecticut and in Philadelphia. On the other hand, although organisation was distinctive and shaped by local conditions, the South never developed its own technological tradition, remaining entirely dependent upon Northern machine makers and often on migrant mechanics (Lander

Table 2.5. *Regional differences in organisation, technology and products of the American cotton industry by 1840*

Features	Rhode Island	Philadelphia	N. Massachusetts	Southern states
Business form	Proprietors/partnerships (giving way to corporation)	Partnership	Corporation	Some proprietors, mainly corporations
Organisation	Technical but not organisational integration before 1820s, thereafter vertical integration	Vertical specialisation	Vertical integration of production	Little integration, though beginning by 1840, mainly spinning only
Technology	Throstle warps, mule weft, handlooms (power looms late 1820s)	Mules Handlooms	Throstles Power looms	Throstles Handlooms Some power looms by 1840, but rare
Power	Water/some steam, late 1820s	Water/steam/Hand	Water	Water, steam rare before 1840
Labour	Family	Male skilled	Female unskilled	White female unskilled
Product	Plaids and checks	Fancy goods and specialties	Coarse sheeting and shirting	Coarse yarns, where power weaving: sheetings and shirtings

Sources: Jeremy 1981: 163–4, 204–15; Jeremy 1973b: 44–5; Gibb 1950: l, 32; Dalzell1987: 28; Ware 1931: 63; Tucker 1984: 115; Scranton 1984: 243; Scranton 1983: 51–6; Clark 1929: 553–6; Griffin and Standard 1957: 15–35 and 131–64; Lander 1969: 25, 95–7.

1969: 12; Griffin and Standard 1957: 23–5, 132, 139). In northern Massachusetts the emphasis was on the bulk production of standardised cloths on skill saving technology in vertically integrated corporations. This contrasted with both Rhode Island and Philadelphia where there was a higher level of product differentiation, greater specialisation and a greater use of skilled labour.

That regional variations occurred in the development of the cotton industry in the United States in the second quarter of the nineteenth century is unsurprising. In a country where intraregional transport was poor until the coming of the railways, regional differences in technology and business organisation, even within a comparatively small geographic area, are to be expected. Imperfect communications gave rise to localised markets, and meant that differences in business practice, technology and product were commonplace. As Gibb has observed with respect to textile machinery:

> The fact that two different manufacturing systems and divergent viewpoints evolved in two neighbouring areas [northern Massachusetts and Rhode Island] is an indication of localised trade and essential independence. Trade in heavy equipment actually grew more rapidly between seaports hundreds of miles apart than between inland towns separated by a few dozen miles of abominable roads. (Gibb 1950: 45)

It was not, however, merely imperfect communications which contributed to regional variations in both technology and organisation. Inevitably the industrial growth which began in 1807 intensified competition, whilst the influx of cheap British cloth following the end of the war, in 1814, produced a wave of bankruptcies (Tucker 1984: 90; Dalzell 1987: 36). These forces meant that in order to survive firms had to develop competitive strategies which reflected regional differences in resource allocation, technological and business traditions. As a result the distinct textile regions of the Northern states became increasingly non-competing. Instead they met different, initially domestic needs, in different ways.

The incorporation of the Boston Manufacturing Company in 1813 with an initial capitalisation of $400,000 and the establishment of a vertically integrated cotton mill at Waltham, represented a departure from what had been the norm in the American cotton industry. In terms of scale of investment alone the enterprise dwarfed previous Rhode Island developments, whilst the use of corporate rather than partnership form reflected an apparent departure from convention by the financiers, the Boston Associates (Dalzell 1987: 27; Jeremy 1981: 204). It was, however, the establishment and development of Lowell in the 1820s, by the same group of investors, and of other towns subsequently, which saw this distinctive system of manufacture come to maturity in northern Massachusetts.

Lowell was a comprehensive, purpose built, factory town which owed its existence to the abundant water power of the Merrimack River (Gibb 1950: 64). Not surprisingly, given common financial, technological and entrepreneurial origins, Lowell followed a similar pattern to Waltham. Production of coarse cloth was on a vertically integrated basis, using a predominantly female workforce, drawn from surrounding rural areas. It was, however, on a far more extensive scale. Beginning with the foundation of the Merrimack Company in 1822 and the Locks and Canals Company in 1824, Lowell expanded apace during the 1820s and 1830s. A growing number of jointly owned corporations produced goods which were, initially at least, complementary. The machinery, building and housing needs of these quasi-independent firms were met by the Locks and Canals Company. This company also co-ordinated the use of water power and the allocation of land. Thus, unlike Waltham, machine building was not formally integrated with manufacturing, the extensiveness of the development stimulating specialisation (Gibb 1950: 66–76). Nor was investment restricted only to manufacturing. Increasingly, the Boston Associates invested in a range of ancillary services, including banking insurance and transport. On the other hand, although marketing remained external, it was handled by a firm owned by Nathan Appleton, a prominent Associate (Dalzell 1987: 88–98). Lowell therefore represented 'complete industrial planning co-ordinated to an extraordinary degree', where mills were standardised in size, power use and spindleage and part of a comprehensive industrialisation programme (Dalzell 1987: 67–8).

The sharpest contrast in industrial organisation, product and technology is to be found when Philadelphia, with its large concentration of handloom weavers, is compared with New England, especially northern Massachusetts, in the 1820s and 1830s. Where northern Massachusetts producers manufactured a limited range of cloths for the growing Frontier market, in Philadelphia which was, until the 1850s, America's largest textile city, the array was endless (Lindstrom 1978: 42). Where Waltham–Lowell producers were integrated, in Philadelphia specialisation was the norm. Rather than trying to compete with Lowell's bulk producers of coarse sheeting, Philadelphia manufacturers, building upon the city's craft traditions, pursued a niche market strategy based on increasingly diversified production. There was a factory system where, by 1824, relatively fine cotton yarn was produced on mule spindles in steam- and water-powered mills. Some vertical integration followed, but cotton mills combining spinning and weaving usually retained networks of handweavers to provide flexibility during upswings, at least until the 1840s. At the same time many large mills were sublet on a room and power system and, where the power loom was used, it was of a different type from that at Lowell. Philadelphia cloth manufacturers were serving 'temporary demands' rather than mass markets; thus as the power loom diffused it was sufficiently sophisticated to allow for rapid pattern changes (Scranton 1983: 52). In woollens and mixed cloths, however, the industry was characterised by a proliferation of proprietorships and partnerships, where mainly male handloom weavers produced fancy goods and specialities. These trends were reflected in the growth of handloom weaving in Philadelphia in the 1820s and 1830s where even in 1859 there were 6,000 handloom weavers engaged in the production of cotton goods, carpeting and hosiery (Jeremy 1981: 163). These textile sectors were served by a number of bleacheries and dyehouses and goods were sold, at least in the 1830s, in Philadelphia's comparatively wealthy western hinterland (Lindstrom 1978: 93–119).

Even within New England contrasts in business structure and technological strategy are to be found in the 1820s, between northern Massachusetts and adjacent areas. In Rhode Island, southern Massachusetts and Connecticut, for example, partnerships using family labour at rural, water-powered mills, concentrated on producing ginghams and checks rather than the coarse sheetings of the Lowell mills. Most mills were in small villages and towns and whilst increasingly spinning and weaving were integrated, scale tended to be smaller than in northern Massachusetts. Technologically the Rhode Island system can be differentiated from Lowell, since mule rather than throstle spinning predominated. As the century progressed, incorporation replaced the partnership, especially in rapidly growing Fall River. It will emerge, however, that as in Lowell and a number of other Massachusetts mill towns, this incorporation reflected a community-based family firm strategy, rather than a divorce of ownership from control (Cohen 1990: 121–4).

Regional differences in resource allocation undoubtedly played a significant role in explaining these variations in technology, product and organisation. Thus in Philadelphia the comparative labour intensity and decentralised structure were partly explained by resource and market considerations. In the first place, in this urban centre, labour was far more plentiful than in northern Massachusetts, reducing the need to introduce labour-saving technology. In addition, bulk production of the Lowell type would have been quite inappropriate to the needs of Philadelphia producers, with their increasingly diversified outputs. The rapid fluctuations of the fancy good and speciality markets, and the need for novelty, encouraged batch production, using a system of flexible manufacturing and employing skilled workers (Scranton 1983: 10). The characteristics of manufacturing in Philadelphia thus represented an alternative to the large-scale vertical integration which characterised Lowell. In Rhode

Island, on the other hand, resource and market factors created a regionally distinctive cotton industry. A shortage of capital relative to the commercially wealthy area of northern New England, helped create technological and organisational strategies which were different from Lowell. Given the greater variability of the market served, a prime consideration was versatility. As a result shorter rather than longer production runs were favoured. At the same time the use of a different type of power loom on which could be woven a wider array of threads enhanced flexibility, in the face of rapid market change (Jeremy 1981: 50).

The Southern states were distinctive for the limited scope and patchy development of antebellum cotton manufacturing. Moreover, unlike the Northern textile areas they did not develop a distinctive technological tradition but remained reliant on the North. Northern influence of the South in this period began when, during the depression which followed the war with England, some Yankee entrepreneurs moved south. However, much of the expansion of the 1830s and 1840s can be linked to Northern machine makers who played a central role in the transfer of technology, skill and credit to Southern mill owners (Lander 1969: 13; Griffin and Standard 1957: 132). Initially Southern water-powered mills were only involved in coarse spinning to serve the needs of local household weavers. However, several of the 20 mills built in North Carolina during the 1830s were integrated, whilst by 1840 there were two steam-powered mills (Griffin and Standard 1957: 131–64).

As the American cotton industry developed, therefore, there emerged a symbiosis between markets, products and technology at the regional level which was inevitably reflected in the process of innovation and invention and became embedded in business strategy. British technologies were consequently adapted to accommodate the specific conditions of different regions which, in turn, became associated with particular products and technological traditions. This led to the emergence of families of interconnected technologies with changes to one stage in the production process having implications for others. It was no accident, therefore, that in northern Massachusetts, where cotton manufacturing was dependent upon predominantly throstle spinning, power weaving and cylinder printing, there emerged from 1813 a series of interconnected adaptations to these and related technologies to improve overall levels of productivity and cost competitiveness. In Rhode Island, on the other hand, there was an emphasis on the saving of both capital and labour. However, since the general aim was less to achieve productivity gains than to allow a movement up market, the region's technological traditions reflected this. Consequently in the 1820s and 1830s plaids, checks and ginghams continued to be produced on handlooms, whilst power looms were adapted to make a range of cloths rather than the standardised goods of northern Massachusetts. At the same time, since versatility rather than uniformity was of prime importance, adaptation of the mule and the development of a self-acting mechanism rather than the adoption of improved throstles occurred in 1827. In Philadelphia, technological change was slower but occurred incrementally with versatility stemming from the adjustments made by skilled handworkers in an intimate industrial region (Jeremy 1981: 180–217).

Summary

The above analysis has demonstrated that whilst the cotton industries of Britain and the United States shared common technological origins their development contrasted sharply. This cannot simply be explained in terms of identifying factor and product market variations, but has required an analysis of the very real historical differences which reinforced them.

In Britain, the expansion of mechanised cotton manufacturing owed much to a combination of localised pockets of pre-industrial skill, finance and commercial activity with the increasing popularity of cotton cloth in clothing and home furnishings. At the same time the mercantilist policies of seventeenth- and eighteenth-century British governments ensured that markets were available in the Colonies to supplement those in Europe. By contrast, as a colonial country of recent settlement America had few economic advantages, while restrictive British legislation acted as a positive deterrent to the development of pre-industrial manufacturing. Certainly in Britain the expansion of factory industry was slow and patchy, with changes to both technology and organisation being evolutionary rather than revolutionary, in the period before 1830 at least. However, until 1807, despite government efforts to stimulate manufacturing, the obstacles to industrial development in the United States meant that progress was meagre, even though there had been a steady rate of transatlantic technological transfer. In the introduction to this book it has been suggested that America's colonial history led to a suspicion of strong centralised government making it impossible to paint a simple Gerschenkronian picture of state intervention, in a relatively backward economy. However, it is highly questionable whether without positive government support, at both federal and state levels, a modern cotton industry could have developed. The gaps in terms of skill, finance and communications were simply too great, while continued reliance on British manufactures and those of the British East India Company made the problems even greater.

Moulded by contrasting influences the cotton industries of the United

States and Britain diverged at an early date. However, in each there evolved distinctive regional technological and industrial traditions. In Lancashire, these subsequently became the basis of an emerging spatial specialisation. In the United States, on the other hand, geographic concentration of the cotton industry was delayed until the twentieth century and occurred outside the north-eastern United States. Until the late nineteenth century, firms in northern Massachusetts, Rhode Island, Philadelphia and indeed the few in the Southern states pursued largely complementary industrial strategies. The intimate relationships between technology, organisation and product, which developed on both sides of the Atlantic during industrialisation were shaped by economic, historical, cultural and political factors. At the same time they were inseparable from the development of business culture which also displayed sharp regional differences. At both the national and intranational level it is possible to identify differences in the culture of family firms in the cotton industry which both shaped and were shaped by variations in industrial profile. The analysis of these interrelationships and the implications which they had for both the structure of business and the organisation of work will be the subject of the next two chapters.

3 Family firms, networks and institutions to 1860

Historically family firms have been vital during industrialisation throughout the world and were synonymous with the early development of cotton textiles in both Britain and the United States. Whether as the result of institutional failure stemming from underdevelopment, or as a reflection of pre-industrial wealth patterns, or a combination of the two, family businesses lay at the heart of the First Industrial Revolution on either side of the Atlantic. In eighteenth-century Britain family firms proliferated in most branches of manufacturing, commerce and finance. With the spectre of bankruptcy ever present in the hazardous world of the eighteenth and nineteenth centuries, a combination of the common law partnership and unlimited liability meant that many businessmen preferred to be associated with their family connections than with outsiders. This was less a reflection of conservatism than a strategy to ameliorate the worst effects of uncertainty. In the United States too, the regional take-off of New England and Pennsylvania was based upon personal capitalism which proved crucial in the cotton industry. Similarly in the Southern states the, admittedly limited, development was founded on family-based, community-oriented firms.

The popularity of family business in the early British and American cotton industries in both manufacturing and commercial arrangements was, therefore, a predictable response to instability. However, national differences in the sources of uncertainty, in economic circumstances, in the institutional environment and in that complex array of historical forces which shape both business and national culture mean that, whilst ownership and control were united in both countries, the form which this took and the strategies pursued were at times strikingly different (Gerschenkron 1953: 1–19; Kindleberger 1964: 113–14). As a result, in the British cotton industry before 1840, most family firms were small-scale partnerships. In the United States, on the other hand, although partnerships did proliferate, the corporation was a far more common vehicle for family business.

That British and American family firms differed is not surprising given the diverging experience of industrialisation, while the structure of enterprise and the nature of technology were partly dictated by the extent and constraints of both product and factor markets. Such differences led to the international differentiation of technological and product strategies. Variations in both the timing of industrialisation and the sophistication of the pre-industrial economy also meant that family businesses had to develop distinctive capabilities in Britain and the United States, not least because the origins of uncertainty diverged. Yet it will become clear that differences in family firm strategy were not only national.

In both Britain and America the early cotton industry grew on local as opposed to national lines and the distinctive characteristics of business communities were related to both technology and product. Not surprisingly, the resulting regional variations were a reflection of, and inseparable from, the strategies of family firms. It will emerge, therefore, that it is not possible to appreciate the boundaries, structure or capabilities of family firms, other than in the context of the local business communities of which they were part. Just as at the national level, so locally, differences in resource and product markets, as well as cultural and political characteristics, were to be found at the community level in both Britain and the United States.

Established businesses normally choose to reinforce their positions and reduce uncertainty further by diversification. For the family enterprise, in the early stages of industrialisation and operating within a localised business community, insurance strategies often involved externalisation rather than internalisation. Not only was this facilitated by a common culture, but such strategies reinforced the founding family's security within a community. In labour markets too, family business owners have sometimes tried, through paternalist strategies, to create or change community culture in an effort to reduce conflict and uncertainty. This is not to say that competition is not intense in developing communities. Rather it is to suggest that where the external environment is potentially volatile, the desire to reduce the danger of failure will inform the policies of family businesses. Since family and family firm strategy are inseparable, decisions will, in turn, be the consequence of cultural norms, values and legal systems. Inevitably, therefore, the characteristics of family businesses may vary intranationally as well as internationally. In addition, in the case of the early cotton industry, some contrasts in the sources of uncertainty in Britain and America contributed to variations in the form which such networks took. Moreover, such variations had repercussions for family firm strategy, especially in terms of the organisation and structure of business, during industrialisation.

National characteristics of family firms in the British and United States cotton industries

Entrepreneurship is inseparable from risk-taking and innovation. However, since risk is also associated with failure, it is to be expected that an important aspect of entrepreneurship, in an uncertain world, is the construction of an environment which facilitates change while reducing the likelihood of bankruptcy. The creation of a relatively high trust environment in which to conduct business will diminish uncertainty and transaction costs by improving information flow, on the one hand, while reducing the dangers of cheating by business associates on the other. In addition, greater market security can itself be a stimulus to innovation.

During early industrialisation family business represented a predictable response to instability and became the central pivot of a network of trust (Casson 1982: 302–7; Casson 1991: 169–70; Casson 1993: 30–54). In Britain, uncertainty stemmed from the hazards of small-scale firms operating in the capricious world of the eighteenth-century economy in a nonetheless relatively advanced business system. An intricate network of middlemen facilitated flows of commercial information and finance within Lancashire and between Lancashire and other commercial centres, especially London and abroad.

Imperfect and often slow communications over poor roads, or by sea, vastly increased the hazards of business in Britain, in this period, by impeding information flows and increasing the danger of loss or damage to goods. Equally, the much applauded bill of exchange, which oiled the wheels of commerce in the eighteenth century and which was inseparable from the networks of middlemen (Crouzet 1972: 44; Mathias 1979: 88–115) was open to abuse and was thus itself a source of business anxiety (Hoppit 1986: 64–78). In addition, when country banks finally appeared in Lancashire in the 1770s, they were private partnerships usually made up of ex-merchants. The principal function of these early banks was the discounting of bills of exchange, an activity which was innocent of any regulation. As a result they were themselves a source of instability (Pressnell 1956: 507; Ashton 1953; Crick and Wadsworth 1936: 142). Moreover reliance upon agents for both commercial and financial information could be hazardous in itself. This was because the transaction costs of conducting business were comparatively high and trust low. In an effort to counteract potentially poor information flows and financial malpractice, wherever possible, middlemen came from within the extended circle of family and friends (Wadsworth and Mann 1931: 71–96). As a result, the usually small family partnership, which characterised the early British cotton industry, was part of a complex, usually vertical network, even though competition could be intense within any sector.

However, if the position of Britain's early cotton manufacturers was at times precarious, the risks were, if not greater, then certainly different in America. In the early decades of the nineteenth century, away from the cities of the north-eastern seaboard, America was untouched by the trappings of development. Much of New England was virgin territory lacking industrial traditions, infrastructure and financial and commercial institutions and, in comparison with Britain, distances were vast, making personal contact between regions extremely difficult. If family businesses represented a response to uncertainty, it was inevitable that enterprises operating in such a hostile environment would develop different capabilities from those in Britain.

Contrasts in the level of development between Britain and America help to explain variations in business structure which emerged by the middle of the nineteenth century. The vertically specialised structure of the Lancashire cotton industry in the second half of the nineteenth century may have been less a symptom of the conservatism of family businesses than of advancement of the local economy. Conversely, the growing trend towards vertical integration in the American cotton industry, from 1820, was conceivably a product of comparative backwardness. Given the newness of the American economy at this time it is conceivable, therefore, that industrialists chose to fill the gaps in the economic system by provision within their firms (Stigler 1951: 150).

Economic and geographic factors were not the only determinant of family business strategy, however. Family firms were inseparable from value systems, attitudes and the legal framework which were also critical determinants of ownership patterns and the way business was conducted. In the first place there is evidence that the business corporation was viewed differently in Britain and the United States by the end of the eighteenth century and that these differences had repercussions for its use.

In England the Bubble Act of 1720 restricted incorporation to those firms gaining a Royal Charter. Whilst this costly process excluded all but the largest undertakings, lawyers and businessmen were adept at evading it. The unincorporated joint stock company represented an increasingly popular alternative, for capital hungry ventures, in the years before repeal in 1825 and beyond (Cottrell 1980: 40). There is, however, little evidence to suggest that such legislation as the Bubble Act, by confirming the partnership as the most popular financial and organisational device amongst British industrialists, inhibited early textile factory development. The modesty of financial requirements in cotton, for example, rendered joint stock status unnecessary. What memory of the South Sea Bubble left instead was a legacy of suspicion of the joint stock company and all that went with it (Cottrell 1980: 41) which Americans generally did not share. In this context, far from being seen as an impediment, the unlimited liability which was inseparable from the notion of partnerships, became vital to prudent managerial practice well into the nineteenth century, whilst the limited liability of the corporation was seen as a dangerous tendency likely to increase speculative behaviour and, ironically, the hazards of business. Indeed even in the late 1850s, Henry Ashworth, the Bolton cotton master, was especially vehement in his condemnation of the introduction of any limitations to liability, claiming they would mean that:

> failure and success would be shielded from reproach; the law would become the refuge of the trading skulk, and as a mask over the degradation and moral guilt of having recklessly gambled with the interests of trades, and then the stain which now attaches to bankruptcy would cease to exist. . . . The position of our mercantile character is a treasured object, and demands the best security we can obtain for the upholding of it. On that account we cannot hesitate to prefer the security of a man who without reservation offers to stake his whole property and the treasured estimate of his own respectability upon the result. . . as against the pretentions of another who requires to be fenced in by conditions. (quoted in Hunt 1936: 11)

Similarly one critic described the Limited Liability Bill of 1856 as 'An Act for the better enabling Adventurers to interfere with and ruin established traders, without risk to themselves' (quoted in Jeffreys 1977: 28). With attitudes such as these it is no surprise that corporate enterprise was so slow to touch the cotton industry in nineteenth-century Britain.

The Bubble Act was extended to the colonies in 1741, but its impact was generally short-lived. After the American Revolution, state legislators pursued more liberal policies granting corporate powers, first to public and then to private undertakings, so that increasingly state governments became the facilitators of business (Clark 1929: 265). The granting of corporate status to religious, charitable and educational foundations in late eighteenth- and early nineteenth-century America ensured early social acceptance for the business corporation. The respectability and public utility which these developments accorded to the corporate form undoubtedly made it easier for businessmen to set up joint stock companies in manufacturing (Seavoy 1982: 78).

It is misleading to suggest there was no hostility to the separation of ownership and control in America or residual suspicion of the corporation, especially within the eighteenth-century mercantile community. Tucker, for example, has pointed to the commitment of merchants and traders in northern American ports to the family partnership in the early nineteenth century and to their distrust of outsiders, which was very similar to that displayed in Britain (Tucker 1984: 24). There is, however, a world of difference between the natural caution of businessmen operating in a deeply uncertain pre-industrial world and an ingrained suspicion of an organisational form, which generations of business practice served to confirm. It is significant, however, that in Pennsylvania, where the partnership form did predominate in much nineteenth-century business, that corporations were characterised as 'monopolies, aristocracies which violated the social contract [and as a] monarchical imposition against popular sovereignty' (Roy 1997: 52). Even though Pennsylvania became extensively involved in chartering public and private corporations in the nineteenth century, there remained an anti-corporate legacy which was embodied in the close monitoring of their activities. More generally the family partnership, whilst the norm for commerce and manufacturing in the eighteenth century, did not become institutionalised during American industrialisation, in the same way that it did in Britain.

As well as entrenched attitudes, an important reason for the greater popularity of the corporation in the United States than in Britain was simply the greater financial requirements of business development on greenfield sites in a young economy where distances were great and institutions were limited. Moreover, the early American corporation was deemed to serve the collective needs of the community and to perform tasks which could not be funded by taxation. It was a view which undoubtedly affected their private use in business, especially in Massachusetts where it became a critical dimension of collective business strategies. The combination of these forces had important consequences for the position of the corporation in the two cotton industries in the nineteenth century. In Britain, until the early 1870s the majority of firms in the cotton industry were not joint stock companies, with only comparatively modest changes in the next 20 years, despite waves of incorporation. In the United States, on the other hand, by 1899 70 per cent of all establishments were under corporate ownership, a state of affairs which had significant consequences for family firm strategy (Cohen 1990: 206).

If the corporation became a common business form before the end of the eighteenth century it should not be assumed that ownership and control were divorced. Early American business corporations were as much family businesses as were partnerships. In a developing country, where there were numerous institutional gaps, the corporation provided an ideal vehicle for development through the collective action of usually interrelated families. At the same time the interlocking directorship, which had originally emerged in social institutions such as medical societies as a check on specific interest groups, became a device for reducing uncertainty and maintaining family control in early manufacturing corporations

(Hall 1984: 100). These vehicles for collective action in some states, especially in Massachusetts, stimulated economic activity but, by increasing the cohesion of participating families, contributed to their political bargaining power in the early part of the nineteenth century. As the nineteenth century progressed and as networks of interlocking corporations emerged in the major textile towns of New England, this also significantly increased the power of employers in labour disputes (Cohen 1990: 116–24). It should not, of course, be inferred that these corporations were immune to intense competitive pressure. However, those controlling them were able to exert quite considerable impact on their local environment.

Contrasting cultural forces created very different family firms in the United States from those in Britain. The United States' position as a country of recent settlement undoubtedly shaped attitudes to the family and, since the objectives of families and family firms were inseparable, business policies also. For example, the British desire to found a family dynasty meant that 'British entrepreneurs . . . viewed their businesses in personal rather than organisational terms, as family estates to be nurtured and passed on to heirs' (Chandler 1990: 286). It has been argued that this tendency was far less strong in the United States. There, in theory at least,

> High mobility, both geographic and social, also weakened family ties; men expected to leave home early, and in many cases the farm of their early childhood memories was soon sold. The same was true of family business firms. Few sons felt the obligation, common in continental Europe, to perpetuate the farm or firm as a family enterprise. Money, or 'economic rationality' rather than land and family ties, was the common measuring rod of the society. (Cochran 1985: 12)

Partible inheritance rather than primogeniture was the norm and there was also seemingly less of a tendency to 'found a family' by landholding than in Britain. In addition, the United States Constitution aimed to dilute any tendency towards the power and privilege which came from birth (Farber 1972: 77–8). By implication, American businesses became more dynamic and responsive to change than their British counterparts. Such a broad cultural interpretation of family firm differences between Britain and America can, however, be misleading. In the first place there is ample evidence that only the very wealthy British manufacturers founded substantial landed estates. For them, as an alternative source of income and security for loans, the ownership of property could be a positive advantage (Rose 1979: 79–96; Rubinstein 1981: 125–47; Howe 1984: 310). Within the Boston mercantile community, on the other hand, there was clearly little incentive to found a landed family in the British sense. Nevertheless, it will emerge that it was their capacity, as an elite, to act collectively which gave them the option to move into new areas and adopt new modes of organising business. This networking also helped them to reduce the uncertainty of their business environment in ways which determined the technological, organisational and product strategies of their firms.

What is even clearer, however, is that nothing so simple as differences in national culture can be used as an explanation of varying family firm strategies in Britain and the United States. During the early stages of industrialisation in both countries family businesses, though the consequence of differing national characteristics, were firmly embedded in and indeed inseparable from their local communities, which were themselves highly distinctive.

The early stages of industrialisation in both Britain and the United States presented the owners of family firms with a range of challenges. These included whether to enter a new and potentially profitable but risky sector, what to produce, the sources of finance to use and how to respond to the competitive environment. In addition, businessmen, in relatively underdeveloped economies, struggled to compensate for any market or institutional failures through the pursuit of 'entrepreneurial gap-filling'. This usually took the form of the building of kinship- and community-based networks to improve flows of either information or finance. In these circumstances informal socialisation strategies could either supplement or be a substitute for more formal institutional arrangements. However, the form they took and the extent to which they could lead to any systematic planning and co-ordination of activity, to reduce risk further, very much depended upon the social and economic characteristics of communities.

Business communities derived their distinctiveness both from their economic base and from the complex array of traditions, attitudes, skills and values which together made up their culture. Historical differences in the development of communities, even within the same region or in similar sectors, could lead to contrasts in values and attitudes and in the measures adopted to ensure familial security in both Britain and the United States. Clearly family firms did not act independently to counteract uncertainty. The existence of locally based networks of trust, which reflected far more than flows of finance, ensured that the strategy and structure of family firms were closely bound up with the culture and institutions of the surrounding community. Equally, since business communities were composed of the owners of family firms, depending upon the relative importance of a business group, the culture of the firms impacted on the surrounding society. This meant that there existed in the early British and United States cotton industries a diversity of locally sculptured family firm strategies which complicates any idea of national tendencies. An appreciation of these differences and the competitive environment which they reflect is critical to the understanding of subsequent strategy in the two industries. There were intranational variations in technological and product strategies of firms in both countries and these were inseparable from and partly the result of local differences in family firm strategy. These also had significant implications for the kind of networks built to facilitate communication within communities and between communities and their markets.

Understanding of the evolution of family firm strategy in Britain and the United States requires an analysis of the origins of enterprise and the position which early entrepreneurs occupied within their communities. It will then be possible to explore the extent to which their responses to uncertainty or market failure involved informal rather than institutional arrangements and the degree to which they impacted on the societies and economic systems of which they were part.

Networks and family firm strategy in Lancashire

Lancashire has been described as 'the America of England'. The analogy has been drawn between the spread of the cotton industry in a relatively inhospitable corner of the British Isles, between 1780 and 1840, and the upsurge of economic activity in the United States in the nineteenth century (Farnie 1979: 324). Yet, in terms of the evolution of family firm strategy, in many respects, the contrasts were far greater than the similarities. While the cotton industry, with its complete reliance on imported raw materials, was an artificial transplant to Britain, it emerged most strongly and lastingly in regions of Lancashire with some previous textile tradition. Clearly this had a bearing upon the development of distinctive technological and product strategies in different regions of Lancashire during the Industrial Revolution. This is not to suggest that the economic and social system fossilised at some point in the eighteenth century. Rather, it is to argue that the process of change was conditioned by the past which, in turn, affected the direction of innovation, responses to internal and external shocks and policies adopted by family firms to reduce uncertainty. To understand this process it is necessary to look first at the experience of industrialisation and the origins of enterprise to evaluate the variations in the types of family firms which emerged in different communities. Secondly, discussion of mercantile arrangements will demonstrate how a combination of regular personal contact and loose networks of firms ensured that information flowed between communities within Britain and meant that commercial intelligence flowed between Lancashire and numerous overseas suppliers and customers.

The Industrial Revolution in Lancashire was an organic process based upon the past capabilities of the textile areas. Technology was rudimentary so the start up capital was modest. Between £3,000 and £5,000 was enough to build and equip a purpose built Arkwright style mill of 1,000 spindles in the 1780s and considerably less was needed where adapted buildings and second-hand machinery were used (Chapman 1987: 27). However, this does not mean that the majority or even a significant minority of the pioneer factory masters were self-made men. Rather they tended to be men of moderate wealth, which they had normally accumulated within the local economy, whether in commerce, industry or small-scale landholding or a combination of all three. As the Industrial Revolution progressed and fixed capital requirements rose, with steam powered mills costing in the region of £10,000 from early 1800s, mill-owners continued to come mainly from the middle ranks of society (Honeyman 1982: 57). For the majority movement into factory industry was a logical progression and in many cases a diversification strategy designed to protect the future of the families concerned by widening the basis of wealth creation. Initial finance was therefore personal or from within the immediate family circle.

The early factory masters, however, did not spring from common origins although in the vanguard of the industry, by the 1790s, 60 per cent of the leading cotton firms had been founded by those who already had commercial wealth. Of those almost half, as might be anticipated, were Manchester fustian merchants (Chapman 1970: 249). There were, however, significant local variations in the sources of enterprise and hence finance even in towns which shared technological traditions. Such variations inevitably had repercussions for the scale of firms which emerged and the subsequent shape of business strategies. In Oldham, for example, there were a large number of small mule mills with an average spindleage of 6,000 by 1811. There, the more substantial early millowners had originally been involved in landowning and coal mining while the majority of small masters had been hatters or fustian weavers, Oldham's previous textile specialisms. Bolton's larger mule mills, with an average of 9,500 spindles, on the other hand, had usually been established by those who had made more substantial wealth in textiles (Honeyman 1982: 87–114; Cohen 1990: 12).

The precise relationship between the interrelated sources of entrepreneurship and capital and the product strategies and scale of firms in these two towns is difficult to determine. Oldham was home to Lancashire's earliest cotton mills. There, at the dawn of the Industrial Revolution only relatively coarse counts could be spun first on jennies and then on mules. In addition the shortage of water power around Oldham meant that mills remained small and often horse powered quite late in the eighteenth century. This meant that the levels of fixed investment were relatively modest, at around £2,000 for a water powered mill. This made cotton an ideal investment for relatively wealthy landowners and mineowners looking to diversify their family interests. However, the far smaller investments required for horse powered mills offered opportunities for less wealthy textile journeymen (Honeyman 1982: 87–98).

In Bolton, by contrast, earlier concentration on fine muslin spinning meant that, whilst coarse mills did appear, the shift to the factory system was delayed until the 1790s. Only then was it technically possible to produce fine yarns on powered as opposed to hand operated mules. This brought prosperity to muslin spinners, many of whom amassed quite substantial industrial fortunes. Such wealth in turn flowed into factory industry at the point when motive power shifted from water to steam, increasing the required start up capital. This inevitably created a barrier to entry to men of modest means and served to differentiate the structure of industry in Bolton from that in Oldham (Honeyman 1982: 99–100).

Such complex interaction between the social and economic characteristics of communities was replicated throughout Lancashire during the Industrial Revolution, leading to considerable diversity in ownership patterns and the scale and internal characterisitics of firms. Power weaving was far slower to develop than machine spinning. Handloom weaving continued to be on a master-manufacturer basis during the late eighteenth and early nineteenth centuries and proved most tenacious around the north-eastern fringes of Lancashire. When the spread of power weaving finally accelerated with the relatively rapid diffusion of the plain loom, after 1840, industrial structure was also very different from that which had emerged in spinning. The persistence of 'handloom traditions' of both finance and organisation offered far more opportunities for 'small capitalists' than did spinning. Weavers frequently rented space and power and were able to operate on the combination of credit from yarn merchants and advances from Manchester cloth agents. Inevitably the socioeconomic relationships within such towns as Nelson and Colne were very different from those areas of Lancashire more reliant on spinning (Farnie 1979: 284–5).

It is clear, therefore, that there were sharp contrasts in the evolution of characteristics and capabilities of Lancashire's family firms during the Industrial Revolution. The combination of diversity of business types and competitive pressures meant that by 1840 Lancashire's businessmen could be divided into two principal categories. At the one extreme was that elite group of cotton magnates including the Gregs, the Brights, the Horrockses and the Fieldens employing sometimes over 1,000

Table 3.1. *Size of firms in the cotton industry, 1841 (nos. employed)*

Sector	1–50	51–100	101–150	151–200	201–250	251–500	500+
Fine spinning	1.9	11.1	11.3	13.7	4.4	27.7	29.9
Coarse spinning	8.9	14.8	18.7	13.6	10.2	25.6	8.2
Combined	0.7	2.6	4.0	6.6	6.2	29.3	50.6
Weaving	10.4	29.4	29.1	11.2	9.4	10.5	–
Subsid.	36.2	13.5	5.5	11.1	5.1	17.5	11.1
Calico printing	0.2	4.1	3.3	6.7	9.3	31.1	45.3
Bleach works	0.8	9.3	17.1	23.1	14.2	14.2	20.5

Source: Howe 1984: 5.

workers, and at the other was the massive tail of tiny employers engaged in intensive competition in often shared accommodation (Howe 1996: 95). In the early years of the Industrial Revolution Arkwright has been identified as a price leader. By 1840, however, although there was a distinct dynastic tendency among Lancashire's elite, there had also been a continued proliferation of small- and medium-sized firms. This meant that there could be no question of any single firm exerting overwhelming dominance by this period. In 1833, for example, the Gregs controlled less than 1 per cent of the cotton yarn market and only slightly over 1 per cent of the cotton cloth market even though they were, at that time, the largest coarse spinning and weaving firms in the country (Rose 1986: 40).

Table 3.1 demonstrates that there were considerable sectoral variations in the size of firms. This confirms that firms remained tiny in weaving, with nearly 70 per cent employing fewer than 150 workers in 1841. At the other end of the spectrum nearly 30 per cent of fine spinners employed over 500 operatives, as did over half of those firms combining spinning and weaving, whilst scale was also a feature of both calico printing and bleaching. Given the differing capabilities of businesses in the various Lancashire towns sharp variations in the economic structure of communities were inevitable, as Table 3.2 illustrates.

Reliance on imported raw materials, the persistence of handloom weaving and the tendency for the finishing trades to be separated from spinning and manufacturing reinforced pre-industrial commercial and financial arrangements which tied Lancashire's communities to one another and to London, then the commercial heart of Britain. However, although the growth of manufacturing may have been closely linked to the availability of commercial facilities, by placing additional demands on those arrangements, the Industrial Revolution spawned new ones. The expansion of overseas trading activity, for example, made it increasingly

Table 3.2. *Average number of employees per factory in the principal cotton parishes in Lancashire, 1841. Employees per mill (including subsidiary trades of waste spinning and weaving and yarn doubling)*

Parish	No. of firms	No. of workers	Workers per firm
Blackburn	49	13,829	282.2
Manchester	115	30,316	263.6
Ashton	93	22,476	241.7
Bolton	55	11,965	217.5
Preston[a]	35	7,161	204.6
Bury	87	14,113	162.2
Whalley	127	14,683	115.6
Rochdale	77	8,084	105.0
Oldham	201	15,947	79.3

Note:
[a] Figures for Preston are for 1838 and are derived from H. D. Fong, *Triumph of the Factory System* (Tientsin, China: Chihli Press), p. 29.
Sources: Gadian 1978: 168; Sykes 1980: 168.

important that firms had access to accurate information on the trading conditions and tastes and preferences of distant markets. This required institutional changes and increasing specialisation in both commerce and finance. It also involved the evolution of formal and informal arrangements by family firms to reduce the hazards of such activity and the agency costs which they incurred.

Intense competition characterised every stage of the production and distribution process of the Lancashire cotton industry. Yet this was very far from impersonal atomistic competition. Risk and uncertainty were significantly reduced by loose ties of personal contact which markedly reduced transaction costs within and between communities. Arrangements varied between day-to-day contact in business and social institutions, intermarriage and associated kinship-based networks of partnerships, through community-based involvement in institutional and infrastructure development to the more formal internalisation of activity. The development of networks and the behaviour of individuals within them depended heavily upon the social composition of their membership and the structure of the surrounding community. This affected their bargaining power and level of cohesion. In Lancashire, the evolution of distinctive communities tied together by complex economic, social, religious and political ties further complicated the picture. This meant that despite the high level of geographic concentration of the county, which facilitated the emergence of intracommunity ties pivoted on Manchester, there were sharp differences in community culture and hence in family firm behaviour.

Networks were vital to flows of commercial information within and between communities. Consequently there was a range of institutions which were underpinned by more informal community-based contacts. In eighteenth- and nineteenth-century business in Lancashire, in the days before the telegraph, regular day-to-day contact was vital for the negotiation of contracts, the distribution of goods and the arrangement of credit terms. The interaction between manufacturer and middleman, therefore, formed a vital element of every stage in the production process.

The shift in the nucleus of the raw cotton trade from London to Liverpool, with the emergence of the United States as an increasingly important source, reduced some of the problems of communication within the British cotton trade. However, separated by space and time, the producers of raw cotton and its consumers were increasingly reliant on specialist middlemen whose function it was to transmit market information between American planters and shippers and Lancashire spinners (Edwards 1969: 111; Buck 1925: 55). The British importer was an agent of the planter. Usually commission agents, these middlemen made all arrangements, including insurance and warehousing of the raw cotton, though the risk remained with the American commercial house or the planter. It was rare for the importer to sell direct to the spinner who instead dealt with other specialist agents, and predictably, given the risks involved, even rarer for the importer to have connection with manufacturing, a notable exception being Fielden Brothers & Co (Law 1996: 75–82). In general, after the end of the Napoleonic Wars all of the principal cotton towns, particularly Manchester, had cotton dealers who sold to the spinners either by public auction or by a private sale organised from a warehouse and normally on credit. This commercial specialisation meant that importers concentrated on the complex transactions with their overseas contacts, while spinners gained both a specialist service and finance based upon personal and regular contact (Buck 1925: 37–8; Lloyd-Jones and Lewis 1987: 80).

As the complexity and scale of the cotton trade grew, so commercial arrangements became even more specialised and selling and buying brokers began to replace the dealers. This process began as early as the 1790s but really only gathered pace after 1820. Based in Liverpool, the selling broker acted on behalf of the importer whilst the buying broker represented spinners and even dealers. They usually offered spinners far less generous credit terms than the dealers had done (Edwards 1969: 117–19).

London was the traditional centre of the textile trade in the seventeenth and eighteenth centuries. Long association with the muslins and calicoes of the East India Company meant that extensive warehousing emerged, whilst as a fashion centre it was also a nucleus of textile design and calico printing (Lemire 1992; Schoeser 1996: 187–95). The metropolis retained its significance as an importer of raw cotton during the 1780s and early 1790s and much the same can be said about the sale of goods. In the eighteenth century London wholesalers, who were the focal point of the home trade especially in fashion goods, were also active in overseas trade, either dealing with foreign representatives through their London-based auctions or travelling abroad obtaining orders through personal contacts overseas. Between 1780 and 1815 London remained the major market for cotton cloth, with its home trade houses maintaining significant competitive advantage throughout the nineteenth century (Edwards 1969: 162; Chapman 1987: 39–40; Chapman 1996: 82–3; Chapman 1992: 69–74).

In tracing the evolution of the home trade houses from the eighteenth to the twentieth centuries Chapman has shown that, by the middle of the nineteenth century, the London wholesalers came to dominate the home trade despite the efforts of Mancunian merchants. Their prominence can be explained by a range of forces including the wealth which had been accumulated in the woollen trade and their realisation of opportunities offered by the Napoleonic War period.

If London's importance, especially in the home trade, remained, the nineteenth century saw the evolution of institutional arrangements for the cotton trade centred on Manchester. There, proximity to the manufacturing areas meant that merchants were in closer touch with manufacturers and were hence able to exert more precise control over their suppliers. Such control was doubtless reinforced by the financial ties which existed between commerce and industry, and meant that Manchester warehousemen were in an exceptionally powerful position by the end of the Napoleonic Wars.

Manchester's position as Lancashire's commercial centre began to develop well before the end of the war with France and by 1815 its warehouses were the vital link in the manufacturing process which facilitated the flow of goods between the factory spinning sector and the growing numbers of handloom weavers. Since the finishing trades were typically separated from production, Manchester warehouses again played a vital role (Lloyd-Jones and Lewis 1987: 81–3).

As Table 3.3 demonstrates, by the middle of the 1820s Manchester had emerged as the commercial heart of Lancashire, being the home of the intermediate yarn market, the grey cloth market and of the finishing trade. In addition it was increasingly the centre of Lancashire's growing interna-

Table 3.3. *The development of Manchester as a commercial centre, 1825–50*

Type of firm	1825	1836	1850
Agents and commission dealers	103	169	312
Cotton dealers	88	72	38
Cotton twist and weft dealers	81	51	18
Manufacturers and dealers in cotton goods	309	366	467
Merchants	184	242	416
Country manufacturers attending Manchester market	635	989	918
Bleachers	n/a	32	61
Calico printers	159	167	139

Source: Jones 1978a: 168 and 173.

tional trade. Its origins as a commercial, as opposed to an industrial town, lay in the need of country spinners within and without Lancashire for warehousing in order to distribute their goods (Chapman 1987: 40).

It was a system which depended heavily upon face-to-face contact, on market days, between country manufacturers and warehousemen in the numerous inns in Manchester's developing commercial area. The focal point and barometer of Manchester's commercial activity was, however, the Exchange. It became, in the nineteenth century, the very nucleus of Lancashire's international trade in cotton goods. By 1860 the city had become 'a city of a hundred mills and a market for the products of another two thousand mills' (Farnie 1993: 4).

Originally set up as a raw cotton market in the 1720s, the Exchange was re-opened in 1804 as the principal Lancashire yarn and cloth market. With the ending of the monopolies of the various chartered trading companies, between 1813 and 1834, the international business of the Exchange expanded and its membership grew from 1,500 on its establishment to 4,000 in 1860, reaching 10,000 by 1913. The growth in activity occasioned an extension to the original building in 1841 and complete rebuilding between 1867 and 1874 (Chapman 1992: 74–5; Howe 1996: 105). By the 1830s, the Exchange was not just a centre of trade but has been described as the 'power house' of Manchester and the 'nerve centre' of the increasingly spatially specialised Lancashire cotton industry. It was, in effect, a private if increasingly large, club where members met regularly. 'It centralised the supply of information both private and public, as the indisputable basis of all transactions. Members conducted their business beneath a congenial cloak of secrecy' (Farnie 1979: 97–8). It was the Exchange, more than any other single institution, which facilitated communication between

Lancashire's numerous specialised manufactures and the myriad of foreign shipping houses which emerged in Manchester during the nineteenth century.

Business institutions such as the Exchange clearly facilitated the day-to-day contact essential if business uncertainty was to be reduced. Other organisations such as the Manchester Chamber of Commerce, which was the mouthpiece of Manchester's commercial community, reinforced such ties of contact and, as with the Exchange, facilitated contact across the county. In addition, social institutions, such as the Manchester Literary and Philosophical Society, strengthened such ties. In the cotton towns local links were cemented by similar local institutions.

Ties of personal contact proved vital to the establishment of the trust necessary for smooth business arrangements and to facilitate the flows of credit, which underpinned commercial transactions. Yet entirely informal arrangements were not enough, especially when the discount of bills of exchange and the finance of international trade increasingly became the province respectively of local banks and the London acceptance houses. As far as Lancashire's banking was concerned, its relatively late development and the close ties of ownership between the county's merchants and country bankers, before 1825, did reduce the transaction costs of bill discounting, though by tying industry, commerce and banking together increased the danger of local collapses. The coming of joint stock banking served to reinforce these ties with industrialists and merchants being prominent promoters, directors and shareholders in banks in their localities. Although this trend undoubtedly improved information flows, the desire for secrecy, which was so much a feature of Lancashire business, led to conflicts of interest and practice. That said, as the nineteenth century progressed both London acceptance houses and Lancashire joint stock banks devised methods of credit assessment and credit rating which required local business intelligence.

Credit links flowed between rather than simply within communities and continued to involve commercial as well as financial institutions. Flows of financial intelligence were clearly reinforced by the existence of local business, social and institutional ties. Networks of kinship, community and ethnic-based partnerships were also commonly used to reduce uncertainty and improve information flows. These, usually vertical, ties were especially noticeable among the family dynasties and in international trading arrangements.

Dynastic tendencies have been identified in the Lancashire cotton industry between 1800 and 1850, with a growing proportion of entrepreneurs, among the leading firms, being from the second or third generations of textile families. Growing capital intensity in spinning, combined with the high financial costs of trading arrangements and intense competitive pressures in the 1820s and 1830s reinforced the position of the hereditary owners (Howe 1984: 6–15). Accumulated wealth and the array of contacts, which came with long establishment, made expansion easier during upswings and survival more likely in depressions.

Within these families intermarriage with other commercial and industrial families, a distinctive feature of Lancashire textiles, meant that they became part of an extended network of contacts, which further reinforced their position (Howe 1984: 77). This provided the basis for regular social interaction which increased levels of trust in commercial and business dealings. It could also form the platform for the creation of, usually, vertical networks of interlocking family partnerships, which improved information flows further without any need for formal integration. Amongst the Liberal Congregationalists, the Lees of Salford, the Armitages of Salford and Bolton and the Kershaws of Stockport and Manchester were all linked by marriage in the second half of the nineteenth century, ties which united commercial and manufacturing interests. Similarly a range of vertical ties can be traced in Blackburn and Darwen uniting cotton, engineering and ironmaking families whilst the social, political and economic cohesion of Bolton was also reinforced by intermarriage (Joyce 1980: 12–19). Clearly the pursuit of such kinship-based networking, over two or three generations, significantly reinforced the economic position of the participating families and their ability to survive during downturns and crises.

Of the Nonconformist sects the Unitarians and Quakers were of overwhelming importance, especially within the often overlapping dynasties which had been built on established wealth. A 'charmed circle' of Unitarian commercial–industrial families were, for example, dominant in Manchester until at least 1850. Intermarriage between such families as the Philips, Potters and Gregs created 'a web of family connection [which] was the source of Manchester Unitarians' great strength' (Gatrell 1982: 25). Manchester's Unitarian chapels were more than just religious meeting houses; they were social institutions which brought together the town's wealthiest families (Seed 1986: 25–46). The same group also dominated the Manchester Literary and Philosophical Society, whose meetings, by providing further opportunities for contact, cemented the coherence of the elite (Seed 1982: 4).

Networks of partnerships were even more important in international commerce than they were within the domestic economy in this period. In general, throughout the nineteenth century, the risks and uncertainties of overseas trade deterred the majority of manufacturing firms from becoming involved in foreign marketing and success in manufacturing and commerce was unusual. For the majority of small family manufacturing firms the integration of marketing was not an option nor, given the high bankruptcy rates in commercial activity, was it necessarily desirable.

Most goods exported from Britain to the United States were purchased in the United Kingdom either by a British or an American merchant who bore the risk of all transactions (Buck 1925: 99). The growing trade with Europe, the Middle East and the Far East, on the other hand, was increasingly handled by numerous German and Greek emigrant merchants who congregated in Manchester from the late eighteenth century onwards, becoming one of the keys to Lancashire's overseas success. From a handful, prior to the 1820s, numbers grew so that by the 1870s there were more than 400 foreign merchants in Manchester (Chapman 1992: 139). Initially most foreigners were agents of Continental firms but, from the 1830s and 1840s, they were increasingly employed in branches of foreign firms or operated on their own account. These shipping houses were experts in particular geographic segments of overseas trade although they were dependent on the financial services of the City of London acceptance houses (Chapman 1992: 68–74).

Given the complexity of foreign markets this kind of specialisation was essential, for:

> the particular knowledge of each market, the management of credit and other details of administration are so different, in several countries and the close attention required to follow and adapt one's arrangements to all the changes constantly going on in them is so great, that it is found most advantageous to limit the field of operations to, at most, a few well marked spheres. (Helm 1900–1: 58–9)

Commercial intelligence flowed through networks of partnerships overseas, based often on religious and ethnic minorities in foreign commercial centres such as Hamburg and Frankfurt. By having detailed personal knowledge of the customs, tastes and preferences of specific Continental markets the foreign shipping houses significantly reduced the risks of overseas trade and helped to ensure that goods were appropriate to specific markets. As time passed some also became involved in British trade with Latin America (Chapman 1992: 165–6). American mercantile houses were less common and permanent residence was rare, though there is evidence of American merchants settling in Liverpool as early as 1808 (Buck 1925: 107).

The risks of trade with the Orient were far greater than those with Britain's traditional markets and it was there that the agency houses, the most distinctive commercial institutions, were set up. Originating as commission houses acting on behalf of British manufacturers or merchants, they evolved into extensive interlocking partnerships tied together by often Scottish family ties. They engaged in an unusual level of investment in the host economy to improve both the local infrastructure, later diversifying into plantation and factory owning whilst playing a significant role in the provision of credit to customers in India. Unlike the international houses, these firms were connected with the City of London, Liverpool and Glasgow rather than Manchester, though of course they acted on behalf of Manchester firms (Chapman 1992: 117–28). If interlocking partnerships facilitated information flows in foreign markets there is also evidence of networks stretching backwards into manufacturing.

The tendency of firms to prefer looser networks of partnerships to more formal arrangements for business does not mean that integration of the various stages of production and between manufacturing and commerce did not occur in Lancashire. Rather, such activity was the preserve of the dynastic families and particularly of the giant firms which made up the elite. In the eighteenth and early nineteenth centuries a few of the wealthier pioneer factory masters whose origins lay in commerce, such as the Gregs, combined factory-based manufacturing and handloom weaving with overseas selling. Rather than use the services of either a British or American merchant based in Manchester, Samuel Greg made direct sales into the American market, although using a Philadelphia agent. The Peels on the other hand employed agents in both Continental and North American markets (Chapman 1996: 68).

The integration of marketing with manufacturing was therefore a comparative rarity. This partly stemmed from the position of the firms' owners at the very vanguard of Lancashire's elite dynastic families. These families had the accumulated wealth, reputation and contacts to pursue this type of policy. Even where marketing was not added, the economic strength which the hereditary owners enjoyed enabled them to pursue wide-ranging diversification strategies from the 1820s. These strengthened the position of their families and protected their firms during periods of crisis and financial stringency. It was these families who were able, after 1825, to combat the falling profit margins, which came with the collapse of yarn prices, by integrating forward from spinning into weaving. This tendency appeared first and most vigorously in the south-east of the county and after 1830 in the north-east and was confined to the coarse end of the trade, with 94 per cent of all integrated firms producing sub-50s counts of yarn in 1833 (Temin 1988: 902). The greater capital intensity of this method of organising business meant they were particularly the preserve of the more long established families such as the Horrockses, Fieldens and Ashtons, but less wealthy dynasties were also involved. The integration of spinning and weaving was at its peak in 1850, when these firms employed over 60 per cent of the Lancashire workforce. However, changing competitive pressures and export growth prevented their continued expansion during the nineteenth century (Farnie 1979).

Diversification within industry was one way of increasing the security of families; landowning was another. However, just as vertical integration was generally undertaken by dynasties, so the small scale and short life of the majority of firms meant that landownership was a luxury denied the majority of Lancashire's businessmen. A modest villa in the leafy suburbs of the cotton towns was likely to be the full extent of the property expenditure of the majority of cotton men and their families. Consequently less than 20 per cent of cotton masters captured in the 1872 *Return on Owners of Land* had what could be described as 'great estates' of more than 1,000 acres (Howe 1984: 30). Yet by further widening their economic base, landowning increased the dynastic tendencies of the elite families and their ability to survive economic shocks.

The forces reinforcing the strength of dynastic families in the nineteenth century should not be mistaken for the emergence of a unified group capable of the collective formation of networks in Lancashire as a whole. Certainly within individual communities activity could be co-ordinated by elite groups who often dominated both local industry and politics. Their interlocking marriages and regular meetings at social gatherings increased their ability to act as a group. In Manchester in the 1820s, for example, a powerful group of mainly Tory merchants pursued a vigorous and successful policy of collective diversification. These merchants created a network of public utilities, infrastructure and financial institutions 'to serve the needs of the local economy' and prevent their commercial fortunes from being eroded by external pressures (Pearson 1991: 413). Elsewhere in Lancashire the promotion of banks and utilities by leading industrialists helped to improve the economic environment. The endowment of social institutions in the cotton towns, from the 1840s onwards, has been seen as a form of 'new paternalism' by factory masters who intended to adapt communities and reduce social and labour unrest (Joyce 1980). Yet any notion that Lancashire's elite families enjoyed a coherence which allowed for any wider collective action in the nineteenth century was precluded by both the survival and indeed growth of a large number of tiny firms. In addition, the social, economic, political and cultural diversity of Lancashire's communities prevented the emergence of a countywide elite. Certainly intermarriage between elite families meant that some had contacts in more than one community. However, the continued distinctiveness of Lancashire's cotton towns is a testimony to the limited degree to which this proved significant.

By the end of the nineteenth century Lancashire had emerged as the world's most concentrated industrial district. Within it was to be found an unparalleled degree of vertical and spatial specialisation, reflecting the distinctiveness of communities within the county. Within any locality competition was extremely intense as witnessed by the high bankruptcy rates. However, from the 1830s and 1840s, as the cotton industry matured, there emerged a sophisticated web of community-based services, ancillary industries and financial institutions to support the cotton towns. In towns such as Bolton and Oldham the ties between machine makers and the firms that they served were close and it was the specialisation of these firms, on the perfection of machinery for specific types of cotton manufacturing, which helped to give towns their distinctive qualities. Consequently in Oldham Platts and Asa Lees specialised in machinery for the coarse trade while in Bolton Dobson and Barlows and Threlfalls made mules for the fine end of the trade (Clay 1931: 12). Manchester's commercial sector, on the other hand, acted as a conduit for intermediate goods and services while the numerous international houses formed the bridge between the county's manufacturers and their ever more diffuse international markets. Informal arrangements, based upon ties of regular contact, were reinforced by relatively loose vertical networks of ownership within and between communities.

Networks and family firm strategy in the United States

One of the crucial differences in the early development of the cotton industries of Britain and the United States was the level of geographic concentration. Whereas in Britain both manufacturing and commerce were increasingly centred in Lancashire, in the United States the idea of a regional take-off in the north-eastern states should not be confused with a high level of concentration. The growing importance of New York as the centre of both commerce and the clothing trade certainly had some parallels with the position of Manchester. Yet differences in the market orientation of manufacturing firms, the goods they produced and the competitive environment led to often contrasting institutional arrangements. In addition, within Lancashire manufacturing, regional differences in family firm strategy were reflected mainly in a growing level of spatial and vertical specialisation. In the United States, on the other hand, there emerged, before 1840, these regionally distinctive cotton industries in northern Massachusetts, Rhode Island, southern Massachusetts and Connecticut and Philadelphia with limited development occurring in the Southern states. In addition, while there were similarities in the competitive environment faced in Philadelphia with that in Lancashire, there emerged within New England at the community level a degree of co-operation quite unmatched in Lancashire.

Variations in product and factor market conditions provide a partial explanation of the variety of family firm strategy but they are not enough to explain the various paths pursued by cotton manufacturers in America after 1820. Responses to external pressures were also the product of attitudes, expectations and past experience of those in control of firms. In family business diversification and innovation were financed by those who controlled the firm and who thus designed business culture. They in turn derived their values from the community of which they were part. Just as was detected in Lancashire, local differences can be found in the patterns of development, experience and composition of different business communities.

In the case of the United States, such variety came partly as a response to and a reflection of institutional and legal variations between different states. Not surprisingly, therefore, the cultural characteristics of communities were not uniform, and displayed instead considerable diversity. Given the intimacy of the relationship between family firm and community, such regional variations helped to shape business culture and hence strategy in important ways. In other words the differences in the organisation of firms exhibited in four regions of the United States, stemmed, in part at least, from varying family firm cultures between communities.

The sharpest contrast in the nineteenth-century American cotton industry lay between Philadelphia and northern Massachusetts. Equally, differences in the composition, attitudes and aspirations of the business communities of Philadelphia and Boston can be detected. In both, family firm and community culture were linked to business strategy in the textile industries, but in sharply divergent ways. Both were substantial ports in the eighteenth century, with considerable mercantile communities. Yet, whereas Philadelphia's handicraft manufacturing tradition was long established, in Boston artisan production was, by comparison, more limited, though not absent (Lindstrom 1978: 23). In the early nineteenth century the commercial communities in both ports faced similar pressures. Increasing competition from New York and the uncertainties of the Embargo period threatened to erode the economic and social position of these powerful elites. Differing attitudes, value systems and past traditions within the two communities, meant that the responses to this external threat diverged, a bifurcation which had significant consequences for the future shape of manufacturing in the two areas. Boston's mercantile elite protected their established wealth and standing by moving into large-scale, factory-based manufacturing in northern Massachusetts. Philadelphia's merchants, on the other hand, saw finance, internal improvements and the extractive industries as the most attractive directions in which to move (Dalzell 1987; Lindstrom 1978: 39–40). Indeed, it has been observed that:

Had Philadelphia's industries relied upon consistent commercial prodding, they would have performed far less successfully than they did. Instead, 'self sustenance' had been achieved by the late 1830s and manufacturing rivalled commerce as the major source of urban income. (Lindstrom 1978: 41)

Just why the mercantile elites were drawn in opposing directions in the two ports is not clear and could only be established by more detailed research. Contrasts in rates of return, real or anticipated, between manufacturing and the primary and tertiary sectors, must have been a factor. Yet an important cultural distinction should not be forgotten. Although the state of Pennsylvania had a long history of promoting cotton manufacturing, its attitude to the business corporation in manufacturing was at best ambivalent and at worst downright hostile. In Massachusetts, by contrast, company law was far more liberal (Merrick Dodd 1954: 436). There the business corporation was crucial to the manufacturing strategy of the Boston mercantile community and was embedded in the evolution of the Commonwealth of Massachusetts from its earliest days (Handlin and Handlin 1947: 106). On the other hand, Philadelphia merchants may have been drawn towards those areas where the use of the corporation was acceptable, though there is no conclusive evidence one way or another.

Thus although around Boston, before 1840 at least, the strategy and structure of cotton manufacturing firms reflected the collective culture of the mercantile elite, this was not replicated in Philadelphia. There, by mid-century, family firm strategies were increasingly a reflection of the culture of a very different group – that of immigrant craftsmen attracted to the city by its handicraft traditions (Scranton 1983: 138). Family firms remained important in both, at least until 1840. Yet, as has been shown, they pursued contrasting policies and adopted sharply varying organisational forms, which are best understood in the context of their particular communities.

The all-embracing approach to regional industrialisation, which the Boston Associates adopted at Lowell, was doubtless partially designed to compensate for the deficiencies of an underdeveloped region. In addition, the wide-ranging integration and use of the business corporation was clearly affected by eighteenth-century attitudes to development in the Commonwealth of Massachusetts. In the eighteenth century, therefore, 'the Commonwealth's concern with the entire productive system, its solicitude for the welfare of many diverse activities, all interdependent and all adding to the strength of Massachusetts, all quickly put the corporate form to use of many ventures' (Handlin and Handlin 1947: 106). Yet, as applied by the Boston Associates this approach was, at heart, a family firm strategy built upon the perceptions, attitudes, past experience and values of the Boston mercantile community. Dalzell may have overstated his case, when he suggested that the development of the Waltham–Lowell system could only be understood in the context of the political and social priorities and cohesion of the Boston mercantile community. Nevertheless, without an appropriate cultural context, the subtleties of the behaviour of the Boston Associates would remain obscure (Dalzell 1987: 11).

The interlocking corporations, which together controlled the early development of cotton manufacturing in northern Massachusetts, were collectively owned by the Boston Associates. Their early success was as much a product of the ability of these investors to behave as a group, as with the nature of the business and technological innovation. Conversely, in the absence of such a cohesive network of investors it is probable that both the risk and the scale of the undertaking would have rendered it still-born.

A select group of 11 representatives of Boston's leading mercantile families joined Francis Cabot Lowell in 1814 to form the Boston Manufacturing Company and construct the Waltham factory. As well as the Lowells this group of families included at its heart the Appletons, the Amories, the Perkinses, the Lymans, the Brookes, the Bootts, the Cabots, the Lawrences and the Jacksons and it is no accident that within this elite were some of the very same families who had been associated with Cabot's Beverly Company in the 1790s (Handlin and Handlin 1947: 104; Tucker 1984: 113). Waltham was, however, just a start; it was the development of Lowell in the 1820s which saw the emergence of both a distinctive system of manufacturing and more particularly of collective business behaviour which became a model for much of New England's industrial development.

Lowell was a comprehensive, purpose built, factory town, which owed its existence to the abundant water power of the Merrimack River (Gibb 1950: 64). It followed a very similar pattern of development to Waltham, producing coarse cloth on a vertically integrated basis, using a predominantly female workforce, drawn from surrounding rural areas. It was, however, as Table 3.4 indicates, on a vast scale. Beginning with the foundation of the Merrimack Company in 1822 and the Locks and Canals Company in 1824, Lowell expanded apace during the 1820s and 1830s. A growing number of jointly owned corporations produced goods which were, initially at least, complementary. The Locks and Canals Company met the machinery, building and housing needs of these quasi-independent firms. This company also co-ordinated the use of water power and the allocation of land. Thus unlike Waltham, machine-building was not integrated with manufacturing, the extensiveness of the development stimulating specialisation (Rosenberg 1963: 414–63). Lowell therefore represented 'complete industrial planning co-ordinated to an extraordinary degree', where mills were standardised in size, power use and spindleage (Dalzell 1987: 67–8).

Table 3.4. *The development of the Lowell cotton manufacturing companies to 1835 (1853 scale in brackets)*

Company	Founded	Capital ($)	Employed (M)	Employed (F)	No. of mills	Activity
Locks and canals (reorganised 1845)	1824	600,000	200	–	n/a	Machine shop, sale of pre-packaged mills
Merrimack	1822	1,500,000	437 (650)	1,321 (1,650)	5 (6)	Prints sheeting (21–40)
Hamilton	1825	900,000	200 (750)	800 (406)	3 (4)	Prints, flannels, ticks, sheeting (14–30)
Appleton	1828	500,000	70 (120)	475 (400)	2 (3)	Shirting sheeting (14)
Lowell	1828	500,000	150 (500)	330 (800)	1 (1)	Cotton carpets
Suffolk	1830	450,000	70 (100)	460 (400)	2 (3)	Drillings
Tremont	1830	500,000	80 (100)	450 (400)	2 (2)	Sheetings shirtings (14)
Lawrence	1830	1,200,000	(not available) (500)	 (1,200)	4 (5)	Print cloths shirtings sheetings (14–30)
Boott[a]	1835	1,200,000	120 (260)	950 (870)	4 (5)	Print cloth weaving, sheeting shirting, jeans
Massachusetts[a]	1839	1,200,000	150 (300)	665 (1,250)	4 (5)	Sheetings (13s) drillings (14s)

Note:
[a] These mills were founded after 1835, capital and employment data relate to 1843.
Sources: Dalzell 1987: 48; White 1836: 255–6; Gibb 1950: 68 and 103; Rosenberg 1969: 308–9; Jeremy 1990: 172.

Critical to the co-ordination of activity was the network of finance based upon the Boston Associates (Dalzell 1987: 45–73). Conservative in management, the investors themselves often filled the key position of treasurer in the early years at least. Thus, whilst in theory ownership and control were divorced, strategic decisions were controlled from Boston (Dalzell 1987: 50; McGouldrick 1968: 21; Tucker 1984: 115–16). At the same time the Locks and Canals Company and its machine shop, also owned by the Associates, represented the linchpin of activity. This was because: 'no enterprise could locate advantageously in Lowell except on Locks and Canals land, and no wheels could turn except by means of Locks and Canals water' (Gibb 1950: 70). By 1853 there were at Lowell 35 cotton mills employing 7,720 women and 2,638 men. These workers operated 320,732 spindles and 9,954 looms and produced 2,137,000 yards of coarse cloth a week (Rosenberg 1969: 308–9).

The financial interests of Boston's elite mercantile families did not, however, end with Lowell or with the cotton industry. Textile developments at Manchester, New Hampshire, Lawrence, Massachusetts, and on the Connecticut River at Chicopee and Holyoke, Massachusetts, also received their financial backing. Similarly the Associates initially dominated stock holding in such regional ancillary services as railways, banks and insurance companies, after 1830 (Dalzell 1987: 79–112, 233–8).

The establishment of infrastructure and an institutional framework were essential if the industrialisation of previously virgin territory was to progress. Yet, as a business strategy it did not represent a radical departure from previous practice, since the eighteenth-century origins of commercial banking lay with the mercantile elites. The first New England bank, the Massachusetts Bank, was founded in 1784 by the very same cabal of families who co-operated in the Beverly Company seven years later. Other less well-known networks followed them, so that by 1810 there were 52 New England banks – a complement which reached 172 by 1830 and 320 in 1837 (Lamoreaux 1994: 113).

The formation of banks by the Boston Associates after 1820 was, therefore, part of a deep-rooted collective kinship strategy which had become inseparable from business policy well before their move into manufacturing. By promoting banking corporations they were able to widen the resource base of their group which, in turn, became crucial to subsequent commercial and industrial expansion as 'insider lending' became the norm (Lamoreaux 1994: 1–89). By 1845 the group had come to contain:

> about eighty men with interests in 31 textile companies. Together those companies controlled 733,981 cotton spindles or 1/5 of total capacity of the American industry in 1850. Meanwhile, in 1848, 17 of the same individuals served as directors of 7

Boston banks commanding over 40 per cent of the city's authorised banking capital. (Dalzell 1987: 77)

Yet even as shareholding widened and the scope of the Associates' activity grew, the dominance of the 11 families continued, with nearly 40 per cent of shareholders being drawn from their number. The group was initially able to act collectively from a shared set of values, regular social contact and an outlook born of their experience in the mercantile community. Cohesion became self-reinforcing, however. Interlocking directorships in the array of textile and ancillary companies increased common interests that were repeatedly bolstered by intermarriage within the elite. A network of trust was thus the basis of economic activity in northern Massachusetts before the 1840s. It was a network where the transaction costs of financing activity were low and where risk was reduced to manageable proportions.

In the ante-bellum period New England industrial and financial institutions evolved in a symbiotic way. Any tendency towards the divorce of ownership and control was counteracted in both sectors, which were in fact drawn closer together. In the case of the banks the limitations of deposits in new areas of operation meant that lending tended to be financed by the sale of equity. However, the largest shareholders were the insurance companies which had also been promoted by the Associates. In addition, the use of interlocking directorships between the manufacturing corporations and the banks ensured the banks remained the servants of their manufacturing promoters until the Civil War. This interrelatedness, in turn, had consequences for the financial gearing and corporate governance of the Lowell Corporations. Between 1827 and 1860, whilst equity continued to predominate as a source of finance, the debt–equity ratio of these corporations rose as they expanded. This meant that any dilution of control by the Associates was comparatively limited (Davis 1957: 189–203).

Close analysis of the activities of the Boston Associates reveals a family firm strategy built upon the culture of the mercantile world. It was a community in which status derived from commercial success and social standing came from public service facilitated by wealth. It has been inferred that external threats to the prosperity of the elite galvanised them into action. Gibb has therefore argued:

Few could see it clearly, but an economic system was crumbling, and [in] its accelerating decay was threatening a whole social order. Saco-Lowell's parent companies were part and parcel of this upheaval – experiments in an experimental age, launched by merchant capital, managed by merchants who hoped to find in an untried field of manufactures a medium for creating new wealth and perpetuating old dynasties. These companies were clearly an answer to an economic challenge. (Gibb 1950: 3)

Yet, whilst moving into seemingly uncharted waters, the form which their action took bore all the hallmarks of New England mercantile business and community culture. Collective behaviour by the mercantile community was not new; rather it built on prevailing New England business practice. From the seventeenth century New England's overseas trade and shipping had been organised within loose family networks. Within these, 'relatives operated in a constantly shifting series of combinations, as partners, as agents, as customers to each other' (Bailyn 1950: 63). Not just in Boston, but in neighbouring Salem, there existed an increasingly cohesive web of family and business relationships (Hall 1977: 44). An important consequence of such a business and social configuration was a capacity and an inclination for collective action. The implication has been that: 'The intense competition within the merchant class required the pooling of family resources and the creation of family alliances to embark on commercial ventures with some sense of security' (Farber 1972: 201).

There existed then in early New England, a business culture born of uncertainty which embraced the family and a network of family connections as a source of safety. The early post-revolutionary years brought a high degree of co-operation to Boston's networks which was underpinned by intermarriage, the formation of political alliances and the joint promotion of corporate enterprises (Hall 1977: 180). Such eighteenth- and early nineteenth-century cohesion meant it was a comparatively small step to the investment by the Boston Associates in interlocking corporations in cotton manufacturing. It was, in essence, a conventional family firm strategy grounded in mercantile practice, whilst the use of interlocks derived directly from practice in the early social institutions of the Commonwealth of Massachusetts.

For all the prudence and care of this extended family network, the policy was an innovative one. Such scope in activity and scale of investment can, however, be interpreted as a legacy of the mercantile origins and perceptions of the investors. The 'culture of expansiveness' may have been born of experience in overseas trade and shipping and applied to manufacturing. In Gibb's view therefore:

> The concept of great size, large capital and wide markets was a direct legacy from the merchant world. Applied to the manufacturing world it dwarfed contemporary undertakings and laid open a new and timely vista to American capitalists, to whom big business had previously been associated with sailing vessels, counting houses, lumber, rum, molasses, trade and barter. (Gibb 1950: 60)

Whilst it is an exaggeration to explain the nature of industrial development in northern Massachusetts purely in these terms, the impact of mercantile attitudes should not be discounted.

That the business corporation, rather than the partnership, was favoured, was a reflection of the scale of the investment. Yet as a departure from mercantile convention it is worthy of comment. Wariness of an unfamiliar company form might be expected. Indeed McGouldrick interpreted the exceptionally high liquidity ratios of the Lowell Corporations as a reflection of 'suspicion . . . if not hostility to the corporate form' from a group more attuned to the partnership (McGouldrick 1968: 23). Yet, if the Associates were strangers to the business corporation in their personal commercial activities, it had become increasingly familiar in the Boston community, widely used by the Massachusetts State Legislature to secure finance for road-building and for the relief of poverty. As such, joint stock companies had become identified with stability. At the same time investment in them was increasingly viewed as a public service, from which social cachet could be drawn (Dalzell 1987: 27). Thus when, in the early 1800s, the law of incorporation was liberalised with respect to manufactures in Massachusetts, the business community had already accepted the corporate form. What industrialists lacked before 1830 was, however, limited liability. This omission, far more than any aversion to the joint stock company *per se*, would have encouraged high liquidity ratios, in what were effectively family owned firms, as a form of protection (Merrick Dodd 1954: 430).

Given their pedigree it comes as no surprise to find the divorce of ownership from control was distinctly limited in the interlocking corporations. To Chandler, although the integrated textile mills of northern Massachusetts were pioneers in modern technology, they had little impact on the development of management. This he argued, was because 'traditional businessmen had not been pressed to alter traditional ways' (Chandler 1977: 72). The Lowell development represented, in essence, a network of family firms. The corporations were owned and controlled by the same mercantile group who, whilst appointing mill managers from outside their group, frequently occupied the key strategic position of treasurer (Wortzel 1982: 199–220).

What is especially interesting is that such an approach to inter-family security was not unique to the Boston mercantile community. In the cotton town of Fall River, in southern Massachusetts, although merchants pursued differing technological strategies from their Lowell counterparts, from the 1820s their collective action was very similar. Thus:

> The key group in the establishment and development of Fall River was the . . . extended kinship family joining together its early entrepreneurs. For 50 years after the founding of the first mills or until the panic struck the city, this family structure founded in the seventeenth century and eighteenth century was still close knit. Its individual members usually exerted personal control over the major institutions formed there during that half century. (Hall 1977: 97)

There, as at Lowell, interlocking corporations which, by mid century, encompassed far more than cotton, reinforced both the security and local power of a small group of families whose interlinkages stretched back to the seventeenth and eighteenth centuries along with their involvement in local trade. Thus by the 1870s, seven families controlled roughly 40 per cent of directorships in 32 Fall River cotton corporations. These same families also dominated the boards of the Fall River banks and transportation houses (Cohen 1990: 122). Similarly mercantile families in New Bedford created a dense and complex interlocking web within cotton manufacturing and between manufacturing and local financial institutions which endured until the twentieth century (Wolfbein 1944: 92).

In New England, therefore, economic, institutional and cultural forces led to the development of collective family firm strategies by commercial groups. These in turn became inseparable from the local communities which they created. However, an examination of the development of 'personal capitalism' in Philadelphia brings into relief the way in which community-based value systems can shape family firm strategy. As in Boston so in Philadelphia, the family and the family firm lay at the heart of business and community culture in the nineteenth century. Yet the policies of the manufacturing proprietorships and partnerships evolved in very different ways from those of the Boston merchants. In the first place, it has already been shown that Pennsylvania's corporate law was far less liberal than that in Massachusetts. It seems likely that this helped to entrench the partnership within the community. At the same time, the attitudes, values and composition of Philadelphia's manufacturing community could not have been more different from Boston's mercantile elite. Although forming a cohesive and deeply interdependent group, Philadelphia's manufacturers cannot be described as an elite in the sense of the Boston Brahmins. Instead they comprised a group of immigrant proprietary capitalists who, according to Scranton, perpetuated and perfected a craft culture.

Thus by 1860: 'There existed in Philadelphia a complex of specialised and flexible manufacturing enterprises of all sizes, employing labour of recognised skill in the production of wools, cottons, blends, hosiery, carpets, silks and trimmings' (Scranton 1983: 10). The symbiotic relationship between the immigrant owners of factories and workshops and the skilled, largely foreign-born craft workers helped to give the Philadelphia textile industry its distinctive character. Equally, the complex network of small, specialised firms were mutually dependent upon each other for both services and credit. The result was 'fragility combined with flexibility involving the necessary linkage of textile capitalists in related sectors of the industry' (Scranton 1983: 227).

Philadelphia's craft traditions stretched back to the pre-revolutionary period. Nevertheless, the city was not a preferred destination for redundant British handloom weavers before the 1820s (Jeremy 1981: 168). A combination of the spread of the power loom in New England and the strategic decision by Philadelphia's cotton manufacturers to move up market, in the 1820s and 1830s, made the city a magnet for foreign handworkers. During the decade when power weaving diffused rapidly in New England, handloom weaving grew apace in Philadelphia. A staggering 70 per cent of the city's textile workforce were handloom weavers in 1830 (Jeremy 1981: 165). Nor was their position transient, since by the 1850s there were no fewer than 7,180 handloom weavers working in Philadelphia (Scranton 1983: 86).

The immigrant handloom weavers were the linchpin of Philadelphia's flexible manufacturing system. It was their skill which facilitated rapid pattern changes in response to demand fluctuations. It is, however, the relationship between community and business which is of interest here. The values and attitudes of foreign handloom weavers, often living in close-knit, ethnically distinctive neighbourhoods, reinforced existing Philadelphia traditions. These both contributed to the product strategies of the city's manufacturers and had profound effects on business culture.

It was the ability of skilled workers to become proprietors which meant that the values of this group became embedded in the culture of Philadelphia's family firms. The growing number of hand workshops which appeared, especially in woollens and in carpet-making, in the middle of the nineteenth century, were essentially 'schools of entrepreneurship' for craft workers. At the same time, the persistence of the room and power system, in the cotton factory sector, made upward mobility by artisans a real possibility. As a result the craft-oriented values of the immigrant worker became inseparable from that of the employer. Conversely, a significant proportion of the immigrant entrepreneurs, who comprised the Philadelphia manufacturing community, began their careers as craftsmen (Scranton 1983: 56; Scranton 1986: 40–62).

The relatively small number of family firms emerging in the Southern states in the ante-bellum period were different again. The behaviour of these coarse yarn and later cloth producers is impossible to understand without reference to the plantation society of which they became a part. Local storekeepers, who supplied the numerous household manufacturers with yarn, often initially founded these family-controlled corporations. In a plantation society where, it was believed, prosperity depended upon the preservation of the social and economic institution of slavery, there was deep suspicion and hostility towards manufacturing. In such a society where the returns on raw cotton growing were high, industrial capital was scarce as were managerial skills, whilst infrastructure was often minimal. In this environment cotton mills were inseparable from their local communities which were the principal markets and sources of labour and finance and within which workers were housed. They were risky affairs which were generally built, as in the 1830s and 1840s, when raw cotton prices were low and when they often received support from newspapers arguing that diversity would contribute to the economic independence of the South rather than destroying the basis of prosperity (Griffin and Standard 1957: 135; Lander 1969: 21–3; Wood 1986). What is striking, if the family firms of North Carolina are considered for the nineteenth century as a whole, is that, despite high failure rates, there was a considerable level of continuity in the families involved in the industry. Even during and immediately after the Civil War, when the position of cotton firms was especially precarious, there was no complete breakdown in the industry. As a result mills in the textile expansion of the 1880s:

> were operating under the same family management and had the same families of workers since the 1830s and 1840s. It was this asset – a number of communities with manufacturing traditions and training and enough mills to form a nucleus of further growth – that attracted capital and made North Carolina Piedmont the textile centre of the New South. (Griffin and Standard 1957: 160)

Evidence of nationally and locally distinctive family firm strategies was not confined merely to manufacturing but extended to commercial arrangements. Clearly the complexity and high level of specialisation of commercial arrangements in Britain were a reflection of the export orientation of the industry which was reinforced by the development of foreign commercial policy in the nineteenth century. Conversely, the type of institutional networks which evolved, especially in Far Eastern markets, was a product of both domestic family firm strategy and British empire policy.

In the United States, on the other hand, whilst arrangements for marketing cotton goods became increasingly sophisticated during the nineteenth century, concentration on a protected domestic market also determined the kind of institutions in evidence and their relationship to manufacturing firms. In Britain, such was the diversity of markets served that only comparatively few giant manufacturing firms undertook their own marketing at any stage in the nineteenth century. Instead British exports were handled by a myriad of family firms, which demonstrates the versatility of such networks, especially when financial and ethnic links stretched overseas. In the United States, on the other hand, the domestic orientation of trade in manufactures made for a simpler commercial structure, though until the Second World War forward integration into marketing was every bit as rare as in Britain. In addition, by the Civil War, there was a comparatively sophisticated network of import houses and a number of mainly New York-based selling agencies for the domestic market, but hardly any export houses. In Britain, by contrast, although international financial arrangements were based on London, Manchester had emerged as Lancashire's international commercial heart and spawned increasingly specialised export houses. This was quite apart from the home trade houses which were mainly based in London and the raw cotton trade centred on Liverpool. However, differences in the institutional arrangements did not stop at the national level since the contrasting family firm strategies, detected in cotton manufacturing in the United States, were inevitably extended to commerce.

Prior to 1815 British merchants often using American agents had largely undertaken trade in British cotton manufactures in the United States. These firms were usually based in Boston or Philadelphia but had representatives in London or Liverpool. The trade they were engaged in was financed either by British commercial houses or by bills drawn on such Anglo-American banking houses as Brown Shipley & Co of Liverpool. There were, of course, exceptions such as Nathan Appleton who, during the Embargo period, emerged as a large-scale importer in the Anglo-American trade. As a partner, first in Nathan Appleton and Co and then in Eben Appleton and Co in Liverpool, from 1810, he was engaged on trade at his own risk. However, the majority of firms were acting as agents for British firms rather than trading in their own right (Buck 1925: 117; Chapman 1996: 81; Gregory 1975: 114). International banking, which played such a part in the spread of British commercial activity overseas was severely restricted in the United States until 1914, certainly one of the factors which reduced the direct activities of American import houses overseas (Carosso and Sylla 1991). However, by 1830 increased availability of financial services from the merchant banks of both the City of London and Liverpool encouraged American importers to make purchases in England rather than simply acting as consignees for British firms. In addition, British international bankers also set up branches in the United States which encouraged further development of United States importing houses and meant that Anglo-American trade was, to a growing extent, based on bills drawn on London (Buck 1925: 154).

Since the expansion of cotton manufacturing in the United States, after 1820, was mainly spurred by the increase in domestic demand, this inevitably placed pressure on the distribution network. The combination of increased volume of cotton goods coming on to the market and the movement of the Frontier westward led to significant changes in the relative importance of different commercial centres and in the types of institutions within them.

In the late eighteenth and early nineteenth centuries, commerce focused on the New England wealthy coastal commercial centres, such as Boston, Salem, Gloucester, Marblehead, Newburyport, Portsmouth and Portland and also on Philadelphia. However, the New England towns became impoverished after 1809 as a result of the Embargo and later the war with England, making them a far less attractive market. Moreover the end of the war with Britain in 1814 undermined the New England commercial community still further, leading to innumerable mercantile bankruptcies. Indeed, the move into manufacturing by the Boston Associates was a direct response to this threat to their economic and social standing. The movement of the Frontier westward and improving communications saw an increasing shift of commercial activity from New England to Baltimore, Philadelphia and most especially New York, all of which could better serve the new markets. However, it was the opening of the Erie Canal in 1817 which, by vastly improving New York's communications with the west, transformed it from regional distribution centre to a major commercial city. As the nineteenth century progressed it proved a magnet to both the domestic selling agents and, in the late nineteenth century, to the growing clothing trade (Gregory 1975: 226; Ware 1931: 166–71).

As the nineteenth century progressed, in the export-oriented British cotton trade commercial activity became increasingly specialised, with differing types of institutions evolving to handle trade with specific parts of the world. In addition, the commercial opportunities offered by such a buoyant trade encouraged a steady entry of new, often networked family businesses. Although the domestic orientation of the American cotton industry did not spawn the same range or diversity of firms, the geographic variations in production, strategy and the physical distances involved meant that in most sectors middlemen were every bit as important to commercial activity as they were in Britain. Moreover as industrialisation progressed innovations in commercial institutions had a significant impact on ensuring that products reached the markets they were intended to serve. Direct selling was, on the other hand, comparatively rare and the integration of marketing and indeed finishing with production was also unusual.

Commission agencies lay at the heart of the United States home trade from the eighteenth to the twentieth centuries. In the very earliest days of the cotton trade these were nothing more than retail storekeepers in the large commercial centres of the eastern seaboard and, because of the monetary fluctuations which occurred between states, exchanges were often in goods rather than money. Reliance on numerous storekeepers to distribute goods was a hazardous and often unsatisfactory arrangement, which placed significant limits on the markets which could be reached. Increasingly during the early nineteenth century, however, retailing and mercantile activity became separated as commercial agencies became more specialised (Chandler 1977: 19). Intimately related to the early nineteenth-century growth of cotton manufacturing were the emerging wholesale houses in Philadelphia, Baltimore and New York, which enabled factory owners to serve wider markets more effectively. Some, such as Almy and Brown's Philadelphia agent dealt exclusively in American goods, whilst the Philadelphia Society for the Encouragement of Domestic Manufactures also ran a successful home trade warehouse from 1807–13 (Ware 1931: 167–8).

Commission houses were true intermediaries, which charged fees of between 2.5 and 4 per cent, but passed all bad debts back to the manufacturer who consequently continued to bear the risk (Ware 1931: 163–7; Tucker 1984: 208). In addition, they could do little to combat surpluses, especially after the influx of British goods after the Napoleonic Wars, so that auctions became an increasingly common, if not an always popular, feature in the distribution of cotton goods during the 1820s (Ware 1931; Buck 1925: 140). However, just as the development of manufacturing in Massachusetts was collective so there were also co-operative efforts to break the power of the old commission houses, undermine the auction system and generally reduce the degree of risk involved in trade. The first came in the 1820s and was initiated by the Boston Associates.

One of the objectives of the Boston Associates, in establishing their planned, vertically integrated corporations, was the creation of a manufacturing system where risks were significantly reduced and which could serve a wide and growing western Frontier market by using rapid throughput technologies. It is clear that, in view of these objectives, existing commercial systems were unsuitable and they were among the forces which stimulated further commercial change in the United States. From the 1820s onwards selling houses were established which would take a manufacturer's entire stock and, for an additional commission, would also take responsibility for all financial risks and, in effect, act as bankers (Ware 1931).

Initially these selling agencies were inseparable from the co-operative capitalism of the Boston Associates and from the mercantile flair of Nathan Appleton. In 1815, at the head of Benjamin Ward & Co in which he had a financial stake, Appleton undertook to handle the entire output of the Waltham Company for a commission of 1 per cent. However, it was not until 1828 and the establishment of J. W. Paige and Co, again with Appleton at the head and financed by the Associates, that the first modern selling agency was founded. Established with the express purpose of acting as the exclusive sales agent for the Waltham, Merrimack, Hamilton and Appleton Corporations, Paige and Co was also heavily involved in their financial affairs. Accordingly Paige and Co took responsibility for commercial credit and bad debts, while regularly making advances to the firm for the payment of wages, for cotton purchases and for dividends when sales were slow. The selling agency, which was a reflection of the Associates' mercantile past and acumen, was thus vital to their success and significantly reduced the level of risk involved. Moreover, their financial function was especially important given the shortcomings of the banking system in rural Massachusetts (Ware 1931: 179; Gregory 1975: 214–51). As these early selling agencies dealt exclusively in American goods and were a direct response, by Appleton in particular, to the damaging effects of British dumping via the auctions in the 1820s, they can be seen as an institutional reaction to efforts to promote industrialisation in the United States, whilst at the same time being an integral part of the Boston Associates' co-operative capitalism.

Although the Associates originated the first selling agency, independent firms began to emerge in the 1820s and 1830s as the numbers of corporations grew and cotton manufacturing expanded. Consequently, by 1836 there were 21 selling agencies dealing in domestic goods in Boston alone. Accordingly A. & A. Lawrence became sales agent for the Lowell, Boott and Tremont companies and James K. Mills & Co became agent for Chicopee Mills whereas the Boston firm Francis Skinner and Co acted for a number of small cotton and woollen mills before becoming agent for Pepperells, the James Steam Mill and the Naumkeag Steam Mill by 1850. As time passed selling agencies acted for a growing number of firms so that by 1860 Frank Skinner and Co had added the Bates, Porter, Kennebec, Portland, Uncasville and Portsmouth Mills – all shirting and sheeting manufacturers – as well as selling the doeskins and cassimeres of the Burlington, Otter River, North Vassalboro and Wamsetta Mills to a range of firms. By the twentieth century independent selling houses typically dealt in the goods of 5–75 firms. These agents, initially based mainly in Boston, were in turn part of an emerging commercial network centred upon New York, which gave access to growing western markets as the century progressed. By way of illustration, 77 per cent of the 136 firms with which Mason and Lawrence had dealings, in the 1830s, were in New York. To facilitate arrangements and ensure personal contact with the growing numbers of cutters-out, jobbers and clothiers serving the retail trade, many of them, including Skinners, set up branches in New York as the nineteenth century progressed. In some cases manufacturers, keen to make the widest possible use of facilities, changed to a New York selling house. Bootts, for example, abandoned A. & A. Lawrence in 1865 in favour of another Boston firm George C. Richardson only to shift to the New York firm of Smith, Hogg and Gardner in 1871, attempting to widen sales. By the interwar period, as a result of these trends, most of the major selling houses had their headquarters in New York (Gregory 1975: 228; Chandler 1977: 71; Michl 1938: 88; Knowlton 1948: 73–7; Gross 1993: 42; US Department of Commerce 1939: 308).

Having the exclusive agency of a mill's output and being financially involved gave the selling houses considerable leverage over the companies whose business they handled. They set prices and increasingly controlled production and styles (Siegenthaler 1967). Mason and Lawrence, for example, handled the goods of the Cocheco Company of Dover, New Hampshire, a print cloth manufacturer, and became increasingly involved in the firm's product strategy (Afleck 1987: 25). Similarly the Naumkeag Steam Cotton Company established close financial relations with a succession of selling agents during the course of the nineteenth century and into the twentieth. It was not unusual by the early twentieth century for their agents to be involved in detailed production decisions, to become embroiled in disputes with their bleachery, and in product and financial strategies: indeed, in anything that might have bearing on the profitability of sales (French 1994: 227–42).

Selling houses emerged as one of the crucial go-betweens in the chain of communication between the mill and the retailer. Since grey cloth was a substantial proportion of the total cloth passed to the selling houses the other most important intermediary was the converter. Mainly based in New York, the converters assumed 'the responsibility and risk for the selection of styles and finish for cotton fabrics' (Burgy 1932: 206–7). They bought grey cloth either from brokers or more often from selling houses and had it 'bleached, dyed, printed or finished for resale to cutters up, wholesalers and retailers' (Burgy 1932: 206–7; see also Michl 1938: 90–1).

Selling agencies were set up to accommodate the peculiar needs of the bulk producers of northern Massachusetts and were ideal for handling standardised products such as sheetings, shirtings and print cloth for mass markets. However, they were neither universally popular nor necessarily well suited to the more diverse and specialist needs of both the Rhode Island check manufacturers and Philadelphia's proprietary capitalists. In 1836, the Rhode Island Cloth Hall Company was established by 28 Rhode Island, Connecticut and southern Massachusetts manufacturers to facilitate the display and sale of their wares and to provide additional financial services. It was a dismal failure, perhaps because, unlike the Boston Associates, these manufacturers lacked the necessary commercial background and they turned increasingly, if often reluctantly, to selling agents (Ware 1931: 176–7). Selling agents were not widely used by Southern coarse manufacturers who, perhaps because of their origins as storekeepers and the coarseness of their products, initially preferred the services of local commission merchants. Only market leaders like William Gregg of Graniteville, South Carolina, made use of New York houses (Lander 1969: 49–52).

The essence of competitive advantage for Philadelphia's proprietary capitalists was their product rather than their price strategies. These involved seasonal flexibility in the face of rapid changes in demand in the New York fashion market (Scranton 1983). This meant that sales agents, with their emphasis on price, were less appropriate for Philadelphia firms than direct selling. Until the 1890s the majority (though not all) relied for their market information, not on selling agents, but largely on personal contact through twice-yearly trips to New York and on the services of jobbers who purchased goods outright while giving advice on likely trends and styles (Scranton 1989: 69).

Summary

The analysis of the evolution of family firm strategy in Britain and the United States has revealed that in both countries family firms tended not to stand alone. Networks, as opposed to more formal integration, were preferred on either side of the Atlantic before 1860. However, the form that they took varied considerably as a result of economic, social and institutional differences.

In Britain, for the most part, loose networks of interlocking partnerships improved information flows and reduced transaction costs in both industrial and commercial arrangements at home and overseas. In the United States, on the other hand, the most prominent networks were the result of the collective activity of groups of merchants throughout New England. There the corporation rather than the partnership was used as the institutional device through which businessmen were able to affect their environment. What is particularly striking, if family firm networks are compared on either side of the Atlantic, is the degree to which activity in American communities was collective and planned. Clearly this was partly explained because American cotton towns began as greenfield sites. The development of these required planning, whereas in Lancashire apart from the factory colonies such as New Eagley, development was on a more ad hoc basis. However, the far simpler social composition of the elite American groups, compared with the Lancashire cotton masters, brought greater coherence of action. In Lancashire, even at the level of individual communities and still more in the industry as a whole, there was considerable social and economic diversity among cotton manufacturers and merchants. In New England, on the other hand, until the 1840s, manufacturing was dominated by a single interlocking group of powerful families. Even when other groups followed their lead, in the 1850s and 1860s, they were a far less socially diverse group than their Lancashire contemporaries were. In addition, the greater openness of American society, as compared with Lancashire with its tendency towards secrecy, encouraged co-operative arrangements. Only in Philadelphia, with an economic profile more akin to Lancashire than New England and where manufacturers displayed considerable ethnic diversity, were loose networks of partnerships preferred to planned corporate networks.

It was not only in manufacturing that differences between the policies of British and American family firms were found. The contrasting market bias of the British and American cotton industries had a profound impact on the type of commercial arrangements which emerged. In Britain such was the diversity of markets served, only comparatively few giant manufacturing firms undertook their own marketing at any stage in the nineteenth century. Instead British exports were handled by a myriad of family firms which demonstrates the versatility of such networks, especially when financial and ethnic links stretched overseas. In the United States, on the other hand, the domestic orientation of trade in manufactures made for a simpler commercial structure. In addition, by the Civil War there was a comparatively sophisticated network of import houses and a number of mainly New York-based selling agencies for the domestic market, but hardly any export houses. These selling agencies were sometimes tied to the manufacturing firms, over which they exerted considerable financial control, by interlocking directorships.

By 1860 the extreme spatial division of Lancashire into spinning in the south-east and weaving in the north had yet to be achieved. Indeed in the second quarter of the nineteenth century there was a trend towards vertical integration which changing market conditions subsequently reversed. Spatial specialisation was, however, already apparent in calico printing which occurred within the Blackburn–Stockport–Manchester triangle and overlapped with bleaching which was even more closely concentrated in Bolton. Similarly whereas Manchester was renowned for fine spinning and Bolton for the production of medium fine counts, Oldham was already the county's principal coarse spinning centre (Howe 1984: 1–3). In the United States, on the other hand, differing family firm strategies in New England, Pennsylvania and in the Southern states meant there was little direct competition between the three regions. Yet on both sides of the

Atlantic the last four decades of the nineteenth century brought political, social and economic changes which disturbed the mid-nineteenth-century balance and had significant implications for business strategy. Consequently the impact of the rise of the Indian market for Lancashire firms on the one hand, and of the American Civil War for firms on both sides of the Atlantic can only be understood in the context of the earlier evolution of family firm strategy outlined here.

4 The management of labour to 1860

Differences in the relative supply of labour, land, power and raw cotton differentiated the American from the British cotton industry and contributed to contrasting patterns of costs, technological development, productivity performance and business organisation. Before 1840 American cotton masters, in general, were faced with less plentiful and less elastic supplies of labour than their counterparts in Britain. Yet there were, nevertheless, sharp contrasts in the labour markets faced by the water-powered Lowell corporations in the 1820s and 1830s and those in urban centres such as Philadelphia, quite apart from the peculiarities of labour markets in the Southern states. Equally in Britain, although the factory system evolved against a background of relative labour surplus, there were imperfections in regional labour markets, especially where water power was used. Inevitably, therefore, in early industrialisation there emerged an array of labour and related technological strategies tailored to meet local, as opposed to purely national, conditions.

Disparities in the evolution of business institutions, of technology and of product strategies cannot be understood exclusively in terms of differing price relativities. Similarly, national and regional dissimilarities in the development of labour management also need to be set in a wider context. The cultures and capabilities of family firms in the cotton industries of Britain and the United States were inseparable from their community cultures during the eighteenth and nineteenth centuries and this symbiosis extended to the management of labour. Thus networks that underpinned financial and commercial arrangements, on either side of the Atlantic, were also a feature of labour relations, the arrangement of work and of training. Moreover, the formation of regionally and locally distinctive product and technological strategies by family firms cannot be understood unless set against the background of local labour markets and evolving community cultures. Product markets, by helping to shape technology and hence the skill requirements of labour, also influenced labour strategies. Yet, as at the national level, so at the local, variations in the composition and attitudes of both the workforce and the business community, helped to create distinctive approaches to labour management. In Philadelphia, for example, there was a concentration of predominantly British immigrants working in a world of proprietary capitalism. It has been suggested that this gave rise to a form of community-based paternalist labour relations, which bore closer resemblance to practice in Lancashire than to that at Lowell (Scranton 1983: 25). There, by contrast, before 1840, the labour force was predominantly composed of native-born American girls (McGouldrick 1968: 13; Ware 1931: 64–5; Dublin 1975: 99–116).

A complex array of influences, of which the reduction of risk in an uncertain world was perhaps the most important, meant that early British and American factory masters often preferred arm's length to direct management. The use of external and internal contracting represented attractive alternatives to direct management of labour, in both nations. Distinctiveness in technology, and the attitudes, composition and unionisation of labour on the one hand, and the power of employers on the other, meant, however, that the long-term influence of such strategies varied. Contracting, whether external or internal, rarely represented an entrepreneur's only management strategy, nor was its use universal, even amongst early factory masters. The extent of its adoption depended upon such considerations as the nature of product markets and the composition and skill of the labour force.

Whether direct or indirect managerial control of labour was favoured, there is also evidence of the use of varying types of paternalist labour strategies by British and American cotton manufacturers in an effort to create quiescent labour relations through reinforcing or forging links between the factory and the community, with the intention of promoting industrial harmony. However, differences in both the organisation of labour and employers and the type of community in which they operated had profound implications for the bargaining power of each group in case of conflict.

The labour force in Britain and America to 1850

The relative scarcity of labour in the United States, as compared with Britain, has long been at the heart of discussion of contrasting productivity and industrial performance in the two countries. Influencing technological and organisational strategies in varying ways, labour, and more particularly skill shortage, is thought to have helped to shape the American cotton industry by the middle of the nineteenth century. In partial confirmation of this thesis it will be demonstrated that where labour, and especially skilled labour, was more plentiful, as in Philadelphia, this contributed to the development of multifarious strategies.

Labour in America was dearer relative to capital than was the case in Britain. In addition, it was also less elastic in supply and thus harder to recruit. The attractions of independent farming in a land-abundant country, poor transport and the geographic remoteness of early water powered factories, all served to increase the difficulties of labour recruitment faced by the early American factory masters. As a result, the incentives to save labour by enhancing productivity were considerable (Habakkuk 1962: 11–16). This explanation of the development of American technology, in terms of the interaction of relative factor prices, has been found to be wanting on both empirical and theoretical grounds (Temin 1966). Doubt has especially been cast on the significance of the labour cost divergence in the two countries. It has, for example, been suggested that variations in education, hours and intensity of work, make British and American wage rates non-comparable (Saul 1970: 4). Equally, early nineteenth-century observations of wage differentials became exaggerated in the telling while the productivity gains under the Waltham cotton textile system were less than assumed (Rosenberg 1967: 27, 221–9; Jeremy 1990). Nevertheless, whilst the general validity of the so-called Habakkuk thesis as an explanation of the shape of American technology may be in doubt, and some of the detail questionable, it would be wrong to ignore the impact of labour scarcity. It was one of several factors which included the nature of demand and the availability of cheap raw cotton, which helped to shape strategy in the American cotton industry during the early stages of industrialisation (Jeremy and Stapleton 1991: 38).

The availability of an abundant supply of cheap labour was of fundamental importance during British industrialisation (Pollard 1978: 102). Population growth, steady before 1780, accelerated afterwards to reach a rate of 0.91 per cent per annum over the next 20 years. By 1800 Britain's population had reached 10.5m and over the next 50 years doubled to stand at 20.9m in 1851 (Lee and Schofield 1981: 17–35). The level of urbanisation also rose so that by 1801 34 per cent of the population lived in towns, a figure which reached 54 per cent by 1851. At the same time there is evidence of rising poverty levels in some urban centres and underemployment in agriculture, pointing to a labour surplus (Crouzet 1982: 20, 90). The contrast with America was pronounced. In a vast, new country, America's population was tiny and scattered in the eighteenth and early nineteenth centuries. Thus, despite a growth which averaged 3 per cent per annum throughout the eighteenth century, the population of the United States had reached a mere 3.2m by 1790. In terms of density, the contrast with Britain was even more striking. In 1790 only 5 per cent of the American population was urban with virtually the entire population being east of the Appalachian mountains. Even in 1840, only 11 per cent of Americans lived in towns (Atack and Passell 1994: 239). Thus the American population was both smaller than Britain's as the cotton industry developed and more scattered, even allowing for a concentration in New England. In addition, in a large and underdeveloped country, both intra- and inter-regional communications were poor, reducing the potential pool of labour for the early millowner.

Despite these demographic patterns, there were marked similarities in labour requirements, problems of recruitment and the sources of labour in the eighteenth-century British and American cotton industries. Given their common technological roots and sources of power this is not altogether surprising. The American cotton spinning industry initially utilised British methods, and both industries were at first reliant on water power. Hence in both countries mills were built: 'Where streams were found capable of affording the requisite power to work the machinery. . . . In the neighbourhood of many, indeed most of these new erections the population was extremely limited'.[1] Thus in late eighteenth-century Britain, mills were scattered throughout the Pennine regions, as well as upland areas of Scotland and Wales. Similarly America's pioneering mills were to be found on water sites in Rhode Island, Massachusetts and Delaware. As a result, the recruitment and retention of a labour force has been described as being one of the most intractable problems faced by pioneer cotton manufacturers in each country (Chapman 1967: 156; Pollard 1965: 191, 196; Ware 1931: 198). Nevertheless whilst geographic isolation, prejudice and suspicion of factories and, in the case of the United States, a general sparsity of population, undoubtedly created some difficulties for early millowners, the scale of the problem should not be exaggerated. The labour requirements of early rural millowners were, in Britain and particularly in America, relatively modest, whilst pockets of poverty in both countries facilitated recruitment. The primitive wooden construction of early water wheels, for example, placed a ceiling on the potential size of mills (Hills 1970: 25). In Britain, therefore, even 'state of the art' mills such as those of Arkwright or Strutt in the 1770s initially employed a modest number of workers on each site, whilst the workforce of Samuel Greg's mill at Styal in 1796 was around 200 (Rose 1986: 25). The majority of British mills were, however, much smaller and as late as 1841 23.8 per cent of firms employed fewer than 50 workers (Gatrell 1977: 98). There is little systematic evidence on the overall size of America's small number of early cotton mills. Yet it is clear that the number of mills grew much more slowly than in Britain in the eighteenth century, and if anything they were even smaller in scale. Thus Samuel

[1] Parliamentary Papers, *Poor Law Commissioners*, 1836, p. 414.

Slater employed a mere 68 operatives at one of his Rhode Island mills as late as 1816 (Ware 1931: 199).

Britain

In Britain's eighteenth-century rural cotton factories, water frames, spinning coarse yarns, were operated primarily by women and children. Before power was applied to the mule in the 1790s, the only men to be found in cotton factories were overseers and mechanics. This employment pattern in part reflected the desire of millowners to minimise labour costs. At the same time it replicated the division of labour common under the domestic system, from which much labour was drawn.

Poor communications and the operation of the Settlement Laws created local rather than national labour markets in eighteenth-century Britain. The development of factory-based cotton spinning in areas where there was already a textile tradition meant that early factory masters were able to draw at least part of their workforce from the part-time textile workers in the environs of their mills (Pollard 1978: 130; Lazonick 1990: 82). In the case of larger and expanding mills, however, by no means all operatives came from local textile communities, even though wages superior to those in agriculture were offered (Rose 1986: 27). Dispersed population and the well-known prejudice against factory work led the more substantial employers to look beyond the immediate surroundings of their mills. Recruitment strategies ranged from the offer of non-pecuniary benefits to persuade families to uproot themselves, to a widespread recourse to parish authorities who had responsibility for finding employment for the poor. Numerous advertisements in the provincial press point to efforts to attract labour from further afield. Knowing that enhanced wages alone were unlikely to attract sufficient families, some offered housing, allotments, livestock, agricultural employment for men and guarantees of regularity of employment (Chapman 1967: 157–68). In a world where the Settlement Laws and consequent fears of unemployment in a distant parish constrained inter-regional migration, such undertakings proved invaluable.

Enforced paternalism was, however, costly. Where, as was so often the case in eighteenth-century England, there existed pockets of poverty, millowners frequently turned to parochial authorities for assistance in amassing their workforce. Indeed there was an intimate relationship between eighteenth-century social policy and the recruitment of labour by millowners (Rose 1989: 5–32). Factories became vehicles for the employment of the poor, on the model of the 'houses of industry', and were thus initially welcomed by parish authorities, if not by local inhabitants (Pollard 1965: 193; Lane 1977: 187). Manufacturers consequently could trawl the poor in the immediate locality of their mills with ease, and with the support of the Overseers of the Poor, who were keen to reduce poor-rate burdens. Arkwright and his Midland contemporaries, for example, found declining Derbyshire mill villages useful sources of labour (Chapman 1967: 167). Occasionally poor families were recruited but, more often millowners were interested only in the children. These were employed either under contract, while continuing to live with their families, or as parish apprentices. Although the children of the local poor frequently met the needs of the majority of smaller cotton factories, larger employers and those wishing to expand often turned to distant urban parishes, such as London. In so doing, they were acquiring labour in what had become a time-honoured way. Overburdened metropolitan parishes and charities had been sending batches of poor children to the provinces for at least 20 years before the first cotton factory. As a result lines of communication already existed and parishes with children to apprentice placed almost as many newspaper advertisements as did millowners in search of labour (Rose 1989: 5–12).

From the 1770s until at least the 1790s, the parish apprenticeship system proved mutually beneficial to millowners and parishes. Parochial authorities favoured apprenticeship of their poor children less for the training they received (which was minimal in any event) than because it reduced the burden of support. On payment of a premium maintenance passed from the parish to the millowner for the duration of the indenture. If the employer happened to reside in another parish this was even better, since the recipient parish then became responsible for any future support (Rose 1989: 7–8). For factory owners, especially the larger ones, the benefits, at least before Peel's Act of 1802, would seem to have outweighed the costs. In other words the well-known inconveniences of using large numbers of parish children – high weekly costs not counterbalanced by premia, inflexibility, truancy and general discipline – were outweighed by the advantages. For these firms, the system not only provided a supply of unskilled labour far in excess of that available locally, but also facilitated economy of both fixed and working capital. Thus although millowners incurred weekly maintenance costs, these were more than counterbalanced by savings on cottage building. At the same time, since they could force parish children to work at night, they increased speed of trade turnover and hence reduced their credit requirements (Rose 1989: 19–20).

The significance of parish apprenticeship in the British Industrial Revolution generally should not, however, be exaggerated. In the early nineteenth century only about a third of the cotton labour force was apprenticed (Redford 1926: 28). Unfettered use of pauper children was only really an option in the eighteenth century. From the 1790s onwards a combination of public pressure, belated parochial concern for the fate of their children and, ultimately, legislation, meant that apprentices became less readily available. It is true that several large rural mills and even some urban ones continued to expand their factories, by using batches of poor children until the 1820s or even later. Nevertheless, overall demand declined, as technological change altered the locational patterns and the industry's product base (Rose 1989: 20–4). The spread of steam power, which gathered momentum after the Napoleonic Wars, meant that mills became increasingly urban. Similarly the application of power to the mule in 1790 heralded a decline in water-frame spinning and increased production of finer yarns. Building on the outwork traditions of hand mule production, urban millowners delegated the recruitment and disciplining of child labour to the male mule spinners (Lazonick 1990: 80–5).

The transition to the factory system was far more protracted in weaving than in spinning. The persistent use of outwork systems, dictated partly by technology, partly by abundant rural and some urban handloom labour, and partly by a desire for flexibility in the face of market uncertainty, freed most manufacturers from the need to recruit factory weavers until at least the 1820s. Integration, where it occurred, was organisational rather than technological. Thus, where millowners combined spinning and weaving they relied on external contracts with handloom weavers. From 1825 until 1850, however, during a brief flirtation with technological vertical integration, millowners were able to draw their power weavers from the ranks of by now mainly female handweavers (Lyons 1985: 419–26). This set a precedent which was followed for the rest of the nineteenth century. Thus as firms became increasingly vertically specialised as the industry matured, there were more female than male weavers (Pollard 1978: 132).

The division of labour which had emerged in Lancashire by 1840 persisted at least until the First World War. As factory legislation progressively discouraged the use of child labour during the 1830s and 1840s, so the proportion of female cotton operatives rose. In 1833, therefore, whilst 41 per cent of the workforce in the British cotton industry was female, by 1911 the proportion averaged 65 per cent throughout Lancashire, though there were significant variations between towns depending upon differing characteristics of local labour markets and the economic profile of towns (Winstanley 1996: 130). One activity, however, apart from overseeing remained overwhelmingly male – mule spinning. Bolstered by a combination of tradition, increasingly powerful unions keen to exclude women, and the need for physical strength, mule spinning remained a male preserve long after the coming of the self acting mule in the 1840s (Freifeld 1986: 319–43; Lazonick 1990: 82–93).

America

In terms of available population, the problem of creating an industrial labour force, especially where skill was required, was more acute in America than in Britain in the late eighteenth and early nineteenth centuries. Nevertheless smaller mills and slow development before 1807 did ease the problem. At the same time, parochial authorities, an inheritance from the British colonial period, welcomed factories as a means of relieving poverty. As a result, although the American cotton industry was far behind the British in the early phases of development, their sources of workers and methods of recruitment were similar, as was the division of labour. However, during the expansion of the industry after 1807 and more especially in the rapid growth of the 1820s contrasts emerged, at least in those factories based upon the Waltham model. There, instead of comparatively poor family labour, young married women drawn from the respectable farming community dominated the workforce. Throughout the period from 1790 to 1840, however, what is striking is that with the exception of Philadelphia, immigrant workers played a very marginal role in the creation of America's first industrial labour force. Before the mid-nineteenth-century waves of immigration, employers were forced back on to, and indeed often preferred, indigenous labour.

As in Britain so in America, a large proportion of the early, unskilled factory workforce was made up of children (Goldin and Sokoloff 1982: 741–74). Several factors favoured the employment of juveniles in the cotton factories of the 1790s. In the first instance, comparatively high earnings for adult males, in this land-abundant country, made them unattractive to early millowners like Samuel Slater (Jeremy 1981: 10). Secondly, high birth rates and immigration made America's population very youthful. In addition, even though it has been suggested that some Americans, including Franklin and Jefferson, believed that manufacturing had a corrupting influence on the morals of children (Jeremy 1981: 10), there is ample evidence that general attitudes favoured it, especially for the children of the poor. Thus in 1791 Alexander Hamilton, who promoted the development of manufacturing, observed that factories would provide employment for:

> persons who would otherwise be idle (and in many cases a burden on the community) either from the bias of temper, habit, infirmity of body or some other cause, indisposing or disqualifying them from the toils of the country. It is worthy of particular remark, that in general women and children are rendered more useful, and the latter more early useful, by manufacturing establishments, than they would otherwise be. Of the number of persons employed in the cotton manufactories of Great Britain, it is computed that 4/7, nearly are women and children; of whom the

greatest proportion are children, and many of them of tender age. (quoted in Bremner 1970: 172)

In the same year, expressing sentiments regarding childhood which were reminiscent of those found in seventeenth- and eighteenth-century Europe, another writer warned of the dangers of idleness amongst children. Enos Hitchcock, an eighteenth-century author of books on child guidance, suggested that children who had not learnt a trade could fall into bad habits and end up as candidates for the gallows. He argued that:

> In order to prepare children to live in the world, it is necessary to train them up in the knowledge of business and the habits of industry. . . . Childhood and youth may be considered as a term of apprenticeship in which they are exercised in those employments whereby they are to live. (quoted in Tucker 1984: 73–4)

In the circumstances, therefore, Samuel Slater's early use of child labour at Pawtucket was entirely predictable.

The reservoir of children available to Slater and his contemporaries, whilst by no means as large as in Britain, was nonetheless fairly substantial. In the 1790s, for example, 10 per cent of New England's population were classified as poor (Tucker 1984: 69). It was from this pool of labour that Slater's early child workforce was drawn. Based on the British model, parish apprenticeship in America was intended to provide support for 'indigent, illegitimate and orphaned children'. Given America's rural bias, the majority of apprenticeships tended to be into agriculture, yet there is evidence that Slater made some use of the system in the 1790s. However, the hostility of many apprentices, combined with the system's inflexibility, expense and general inefficiency, led him to abandon it. Slater switched instead first to children who, whilst residing with their families, worked for him under contract and thence at Webster and Slatersville to a distinctive form of family labour (Tucker 1984: 74–7). It would seem, therefore, that whereas in Britain the pattern of poverty drove pauper children into factories, in the United States it drove whole families into a new lifestyle in Slater's mill communities. Moreover, the emphasis on family labour, with its similarities to pre-industrial household manufacture, helped to overcome some of the not inconsiderable prejudice against factory work amongst the Yankee poor (Brody 1989: 46; Tucker 1984: 79).

Just as Slater's sources of labour resembled those in Britain, so his methods of recruitment were not dissimilar, perhaps because of his own British roots, or more likely because he had little choice. Once he had moved towards a family system of labour he also increasingly provided houses. He pursued this system of factory colonisation especially vigorously at Slatersville after 1806 and at Webster after 1811 (Tucker 1984:

126–9). Whilst building on New England value systems Slater's rural mill communities resembled the factory villages to be found in Britain during the early years of industrial expansion. A paternalism born of necessity, such community development reflected the desire of early factory owners to procure a workforce. It is striking, however, that whilst in Britain an important objective was to build a stable community, which certainly by the 1830s helped to achieve low labour turnover, American factory masters had no such expectations or intentions. Between 1813 and the mid-1830s Slater records for Dudley and Oxford demonstrate a remarkably high level of transiency. Labour turnover fell below 100 per cent per annum only twice between 1813 and the mid-1830s with annual turnover averaging 162.7 per cent over this period (Prude 1983: 144). However, whereas in Britain, where levels of labour turnover were far lower, mill-owners complained of the 'restless and migratory spirit' of the workforce, in the United States there was no expectation of long attachments by workers or effort to retain them. Rather, social norms and attitudes in a new country of recent settlement meant that it was anticipated that factory work would be a stepping stone to some other activity which would almost certainly involve movement (Prude 1983: 144; Kirk 1994 vol. I: 67–8; Chapman 1987: 46).

The expansion of factory spinning from 1807 until 1814 in New England, Philadelphia and the Southern states must have placed a strain on America's traditional sources of labour, though high bankruptcy rates following the end of war with Britain and more especially the Napoleonic Wars, doubtless provided a temporary respite. It was, however, after 1812 and more especially after 1820 that fundamental changes began to occur in both the division of labour in much of the American cotton industry and in the sources tapped. At the same time it was in this period that American labour strategies partly diverged from those in Britain.

Innovation, both technological and organisational, occurred under the Waltham system, which introduced the power loom, and integrated it with spinning, dyeing and finishing. Still water powered, the corporations established by the Boston Associates involved both more substantial levels of investment than earlier mills and larger numbers of operatives in each. Child or family labour was never employed under the Waltham system. Instead Lowell and founders of the town which bore his name employed predominantly single girls. Coming from respectable families, these girls were recruited chiefly for short terms from New England farms (McGouldrick 1968).

Explanations vary of female labour's predominance under the Waltham system. It has, for example, been suggested that child labour was inadequate to make the family system viable in northern Massachusetts, whilst there was only a small, highly inelastic supply of unskilled male labour (McGouldrick 1968: 35). Undoubtedly male mule spinners could attract far higher wages in this area than in Delaware or Rhode Island (Jeremy 1981: 261). Yet the availability of an alternative supply of underemployed female workers, who could easily be trained to operate throstles rather than mules, was also significant. The growth of female employment can thus be explained by the decline of household manufacturing, which created a supply of underemployed young women, prepared to work temporarily in the mills. Indeed Nathan Appleton, a leading Boston Associate, said as much when he observed: 'There was [in New England] little demand for female labour, as household manufacture was superseded by improvements in machinery. Here in New England was a fund of labour, well educated and virtuous' (quoted in Chandler and Tedlow 1985: 162).

Tapping this source of respectable middle-class young women helped to shape the entire Waltham system as the availability of such labour dictated product and technology. At the same time, creating a well-ordered community, where the worst excesses of industrialisation were avoided, became imperative if rural families were to allow their daughters to join the workforce. Lowell corporations constructed dormitories in the purpose built towns, whilst extensive use of water power and the speeding up of machinery compensated for the limited physical strength of the women. Instead of forming a permanent, experienced workforce, these young women worked only temporarily in the factories to supplement their families' income. Rapid turnover of labour and its consequent limited experience increased the need for mechanical control and for automation (Jeremy 1973b: 47). This meant that throstle spinning and power weaving were ideal technologies, given the available workforce.

It would be wrong to exaggerate the impact of the Waltham system on employment and recruitment patterns in the 1820s and 1830s. Less than 30 per cent of workers in Massachusetts were employed in the Lowell sector in 1832 (Cohen 1990: 170). Nevertheless as power weaving spread, the practice of employing female weavers was replicated in Slater-style mills. Only in Philadelphia, where handloom weaving remained important, were there significant numbers of male weavers. As female employment rose child labour declined accordingly. Thus, although in 1820 over half of Rhode Island's cotton operatives were children, by 1831 this proportion had fallen to 41 per cent, whilst in Massachusetts the level had dropped to 21 per cent. In the same period female employment in Rhode Island had risen from a quarter to 39 per cent and in Massachusetts had reached 80 per cent (Jeremy 1981: 210; Siracusa 1979: 188). Child labour in America's cotton mills did not disappear completely, however, and indeed grew in the middle years of the nineteenth century as immigrant

Irish families supplemented their incomes by allowing their children to work. It was only with increased concern over hours, conditions and education, which began in the 1830s and gathered momentum in the 1840s and beyond, that controls over the employment of children were introduced and the practice declined. By 1860 child labour in Rhode Island had fallen to 7 per cent and family labour had been eclipsed. Family labour continued in southern Massachusetts into the 1860s, only declining when state laws to regulate child labour were introduced in 1865 and 1866 (Gitelman 1967: 245; Siracusa 1979: 182–230; Tucker 1984: 220–1). Although individual New England states introduced controls on child labour, it was not until 1916 that the Child Labor Act was passed, although uniformly opposed by Southern congressmen. This delay in the evolution of a national policy meant that child labour remained a feature of mills in the Southern states in the ante-bellum period and, indeed, became increasingly important (and controversial) in the late nineteenth and early twentieth centuries (Lea 1975: 492).

In Britain the employment of men was limited in early factories and so it was in the American cotton industry before 1840, where male employment was also restricted to mule spinning, to supervision and to skilled activities (Cohen 1990: 67). The more limited use of the mule as compared with the throstle and the employment of women on self actors after 1840, however, meant that there were proportionately even fewer men in the New England cotton industry than in Lancashire. In the early 1830s, less than a third of the American cotton textile workforce was male, whilst in Lancashire the proportion was not far short of 40 per cent (Jeremy 1981: 211).

Prior to 1840 there were only a handful of mills in the South. Even after the expansion of the 1840s, when there was a 6 per cent decennial growth of employment in cotton manufacturing in the cotton growing states, the labour force was only 16.37 per cent of that in New England. At the best-known example of ante-bellum Southern development, William Gregg's Graniteville, both the methods of recruitment and the sources of labour used were similar to those in the North. There was, therefore, reliance on white rural female labour and families lived in heavily subsidised housing. However, more generally in the South, although labour recruitment was very localised and remained so throughout the ante-bellum period, the concentration on white rural women, so much a feature of the New England states, has been questioned. Instead black and white, free and slave labour was used to counteract labour shortages in regions where the demand for labour to produce raw cotton for the expanding industrial North and Europe was growing (Wright 1979: 667; Ward 1987: 328–48).

Any analysis of the emergence of an industrial labour force in America would be incomplete without an assessment of immigrants. What is especially striking is the limited role played by this group before 1840. Prior to 1820 it is true that a relatively few skilled British migrants did have an important impact on the shape of the American cotton industry. Yet it appears that the expansion of the industry in both Rhode Island and Massachusetts during the 1820s and in the South in the 1840s owed little to British migrants, whether skilled or unskilled. Between 1820 and 1832, for example, employment in the American cotton industry grew more than five-fold to reach 62,157, only a small portion of which was met by British immigrant textile workers (Jeremy 1981: 161–2). In the first place, there was a shortfall between the level of immigration and the growth of the American cotton industry, whilst in the second, in much of the industry, immigrant labour in general and British in particular was not especially sought after. Mills organised under both the Waltham and Slater systems employed predominantly indigenous labour, and indeed appeared to prefer it, fearing drunkenness and militancy would be the consequences of immigrant concentrations (Cohen 1990: 89; Prude 1983: 87). In the Hamilton Company at Lowell, for example only 3.4 per cent of the workforce were immigrants in the 1830s, whilst at Fall River in 1826 only 6 per cent of 612 mill operatives were foreign-born. The one exception to this general pattern in the 1820s was Philadelphia where, in the cotton mills of Manayunk, British immigrants formed a significant part of the workforce (Dublin 1975: 107; Cohen 1990: 91; Scranton 1983: 249; Shelton 1986: 56).

It was only after 1840, in New England, that a combination of growing difficulties of factory recruitment and a surge of European and French Canadian migrants, meant that a rising proportion of the cotton textile workforce were born overseas. At Lowell, for example, even though a significant percentage of operatives were still Yankees in the 1860s, over half were Irish, making them the largest ethnic group. In the southern part of New England on the other hand, the Slater towns saw an upsurge of Irish and Canadian immigrants whilst Fall River, where weaving was combined with mule spinning, attracted mainly redundant British spinners in the 1850s and 1860s (Gitelman 1967: 242; Prude 1983: 187, 224; McGouldrick 1968: 13; Ware 1931: 117; Early 1980: 37; Silvia 1975: 232; Cohen 1990: 94). Philadelphia was also an increasingly popular destination for another group suffering from technological unemployment. Long a centre of handloom weaving, Philadelphia attracted a significant proportion of Lancashire's redundant handworkers during the 1830s and 1840s (Scranton 1983: 213).

British factory operatives were not the only group of workers to be passed over by early New England factories. Differences in training, industrial organisation and attitudes rendered British managers and mechanics far less popular after 1820 than they had been in the eighteenth century. Thus, whilst it is not immediately clear from whence the native-born mechanics in the Waltham machine shop were drawn, only one English mechanic may be found in its records (Gibb 1950: 52). British mechanics were accused of being unimaginative and suspicious of change, in comparison to their New England contemporaries who:

> From the habits of early life and the diffusion of knowledge by means of free schools there exists generally among the mechanics of New England a vivacity in inquiring into the first principles of the Science to which they are practically devoted. They thus frequently acquire a theoretical knowledge of the processes of the useful arts, which the English labourers may commonly be found to possess after a long apprenticeship and life of patient toil. For this reason the American mechanic appears generally more prone to invent new plans and machines than to operate upon old ones in the most perfect manner. The English mechanic, on the contrary, confining his attention simply to the immediate performance of the process of art to which he is habituated from early youth, acquires wonderful dexterity and skill. (Gibb 1950: 178)

By contrast the Irish became increasingly important in New England as the nineteenth century progressed.

This brief analysis of the emergence of an industrial labour force in America, whilst highlighting some contrasts with Britain's experience, has also shown that at times patterns converged. Labour was more scarce in America than in Britain, but the tiny scale of the industry in the late eighteenth century meant that the demand for labour was limited. In the early phases of development, therefore, the poor – whether women, children or whole families – were important in each country. During the rapid expansion of the American cotton industry of the 1820s, patterns of recruitment and technology did diverge and American firms came to employ a higher proportion of female labour and ran their machines faster than was the case in Britain. Yet the distinction was less acute than might be assumed and stemmed more from the importance of the mule in British cotton spinning, than from the markedly different division of labour in power weaving.

It is also clear that until the second third of the nineteenth century, America's first industrial labour force arose from predominantly, though not exclusively, indigenous sources. In this it was similar to Britain. That this should have been possible, despite America's relatively small population, is not altogether surprising. The output of the American cotton industry did grow eightfold during the 1820s (Zevin 1971: 123–4). Yet the advance built on very small beginnings and was achieved in part by productivity improvements. Even in 1831, the total workforce was a mere

14.5 per cent of Britain's cotton textile labour force (Jeremy 1981: 161; Farnie 1979: 82). As the nineteenth century progressed immigrant labour increasingly replaced indigenous labour in the Northern states but this did not entirely undermine management policies developed in an earlier era. However, since labour management was so closely tied to community culture the alteration of the ethnic mix had implications for social cohesion, even if the turnover of personnel meant that the evolution of traditions was far less embedded than in Britain.

The management of labour: conflict and co-operation

The transition to the factory system was a protracted and patchy process. Labour strategies contributed to this evolutionary change, but were also a response to the peculiar difficulties of centralising production. Through the use of first outwork and later subcontracting within mills, early factory masters could delegate responsibility for such activities as recruitment, training and discipline to the workers themselves. Conversely, the coming of the factory system and the application of power to machinery did not always mean that workers relinquished control over their work. If experience in the British and American cotton industries is compared, it seems that in both countries millowners used external and internal contracts before 1840 (Kirk 1994 vol. I: 39). Nevertheless characteristics in product, technological bias, tradition and the bargaining power of both unions and masters meant that, with the exception of Philadelphia, subcontracting persisted far longer in Britain than in America.

Historically the rise of centralised production and, more particularly, the business corporation has been associated with the replacement of external and internal contracts with workers, by managerial direction. Efficiency in the production of standardised goods for mass markets has thus been associated with the ability of management to regulate all aspects of its increasingly unskilled workforce's environment. Between the two extremes of the independence of the artisan and direct control of all aspects of work within the large corporation, there exists, however, a wide array of alternatives.

Examination of the labour strategies of British and American cotton manufacturers, during the eighteenth and nineteenth centuries, reveals that the process of change in the organisation of work was by no means linear. Even in America, where the decline of craft control was more rapid, regional divergences occurred. In their search for suitable and, by implication, profitable methods of managing labour, businessmen took account of a range of factors. Technology, labour and product market considerations are all relevant to shopfloor arrangements and to the resultant relations between employer and employed. At the same time cultural considerations, such as levels of education or attitudes, which may be specific to a community, are also significant. Equally, decisions concerning the introduction of changes to work practices may be influenced by a combination of past practice, trade unions and the collective power of employers.

In the early stages of industrialisation of both Britain and America, the factory system more often led to an expansion of outwork than to replacing it. The technological deficiencies of crude machines, the availability of labour, the desire to spread risk or increase flexibility, all contributed to the persistence or in some cases the emergence of outworking systems. External contracts, which confirmed rather than reduced the control of labour over its working environment, thus remained a feature of the early factory system. In Britain, for example, spinning millowners wishing to reduce risk and compensate for the early failings of the power loom, surrounded their factories with networks of handloom weavers, well into the second quarter of the nineteenth century. In addition, early technological deficiencies of the mule meant that before 1790 it was used in cottages rather than factories (Lazonick 1990: 82). In America, on the other hand, the factory system fostered outwork rather than evolving from putting-out networks; there is also ample evidence of the use of external weaving contracts by factory spinners who, before the second decade of the nineteenth century, lacked the power loom. Yet once under way, the disappearance of outwork systems in much of the New England cotton industry was fairly rapid and was complete by the early 1830s. In Philadelphia, by contrast, the town's factories and skilled handloom weavers enjoyed a symbiotic relationship until quite late in the nineteenth century. For the factory owners, even those who also used power looms, skilled outworkers allowed them flexibility in both product and levels of output. Handloom weavers, on the other hand, enjoyed continued craft status, whilst the proliferation of small-scale firms producing woollens, mixes and fancy goods held out the possibility of craft workers becoming proprietors (Scranton 1983: 55–6).

External contracts therefore gave way to factory production, more quickly in America than in Britain. Similarly, subcontracting of responsibility within factories was less widespread in the American cotton industry, though its final demise was more rapid. A system of internal contracting prevails when:

> the management of a firm provided floor space and machinery, supplied raw material and working capital, and arranged for the sale of the finished product. The gap between raw material and finished product, however, was filled not by paid employees arranged in the descending hierarchy . . . but by contractors, to whom the production job was delegated. They hired their own employees, super-

vised the work process, and received a piece rate from the company for completed goods. The income of the contractor consisted of the difference between his wage bill and his sales to the company, plus the day pay he earned as an employee himself. The company's largest single expense was the amount paid to contractors for finished goods. (quoted in Littler 1982: 165)

In an uncertain world, when most factories were owned by family partnerships whose members were inexperienced in many aspects of management, the attractions of internal contracting were considerable and thus prevalent in early factories in Britain and America. The system allowed manufacturers to avoid management rather than embrace its complexities. By passing responsibility for labour recruitment and management to certain key workers, the subcontract spread risk and responsibility. Sometimes, though not exclusively associated with the use of family labour, the subcontract could ensure that familial authority or at least community relationships were transferred into the mill. Subcontracting systems thus generated their own hierarchy, which through financial incentives ensured stabilisation of effort and the allocation of tasks within a mill. It also confirmed the independence and status of the skilled worker. By behaving as a small entrepreneur, the subcontractor could make a profit from the gap between the price he was paid and the wages he provided for his workers (Littler 1982: 66–7; Garside and Gospel 1986: 101; Cohen 1990: 57).

The use of the subcontract, which perpetuated pre-industrial work relationships, was commonest in male-dominated, craft-oriented, highly paid activities such as mule spinning. Conversely in throstle spinning and power weaving, where there was a predominantly female workforce of machine minders, it was virtually unknown in both Britain and America. Instead foremen carried out supervision and a range of ancillary activities (Cohen 1990: 56). In Britain subcontracting persisted in mule spinning well into the twentieth century. In America, on the other hand, the arrival of the self acting mule in the 1830s and 1840s, heralded the demise of internal contracts. To establish why this was so it is necessary to compare attitudes, business structure, labour supply and long-term historical experience in the two countries.

British hand mule spinners, who exhibited a combination of skill and physical strength, had gained craft status under the domestic system. By strict adherence to apprenticeship rules, they restricted entry to their trade and thus commanded high piece rate wages which reflected a predetermined 'customary price'. In general, centralisation of production led to a substitution of child and female labour for expensive male labour. Mule spinning proved to be an exception, however, since application of power only partially automated the process. Common mules continued to require considerable strength and whilst women and children were employed on smaller frames, the majority of mule spinners were male. Their market power, reinforced by early unionisation and the desire of millowners to avoid active management, enabled them to transfer their influence over recruitment and training to factories (Lazonick 1990: 80–5; Chapman 1899: 592; Chapman 1900: 467–8; Turner 1962: 62–3). Factory mule spinners controlled virtually all aspects of their work from maintenance of their machinery to the choice of helpers. Out of piece rate wages they recruited, trained and remunerated their piecers who in turn could look forward to the prospect of rising to become spinners. It was a hierarchical system, therefore, which almost exactly replicated the craft-based apprentice system (Chapman 1900: 468–9). It also represented a fairly effective method of factory management for:

> The spinners had an economic interest in seeking out the most dependable assistants, while at the same time their location in the families or communities . . . gave them advantage in assessing the likely qualities of recruits. (Lazonick 1990: 95)

Past restrictive practices were thus perpetuated and reinforced with the acquiescence of millowners, keen to reduce the burdens of management. Of British cotton mills in the 1830s Montgomery could observe:

> in the mule spinning department, there are men who have the charge of their own work, and are only paid for what they do, and [are] responsible both for the quality and quantity of their work; they can also be made sensible of the consequences that would result from any degree of carelessness on their part; and hence it is not necessary that the master should always be present. (Montgomery 1836: 272 quoted in Cohen 1990: 61)

The automation of mule spinning, with the introduction of the self actor in the 1830s and 1840s, by removing the need for physical strength, should have transformed the division of labour in the sector. Instead, male dominance continued and, far from being undermined by technical change, the craft orientation of mule spinning was reinforced by both employers and unions. As spinners became machine minders, increasingly well organised unions protected the internal contract system. For their part the employers accepted the minder–piecer system as an effective method of shopfloor management. By progressively incorporating minders into the hierarchy of management, their hidden agenda was doubtless the hope of union moderation. The supervisory and maintenance function of minders thus became implicit in the piece rates they received. These were perpetuated, especially after 1850, within local Wages Lists, any changes to which were dependent on the unlikely acquiescence of increasingly powerful, albeit fairly conservative unions (Lazonick 1990: 95; Singleton 1991: 4). As a result, this relic of pre-industrial practice came to characterise British cotton spinning until after the Second World War (Singleton 1991: 53). In the interwar period it was observed:

> The textile workers of the country are so thoroughly organised in trade unions that the organisation of labour is practically entirely in their hands, and the management must organise almost exactly on the lines laid down in a series of rules recognised by master and man as a basis upon which they must work. These rules have almost the force of laws, and they apply chiefly to the number of people to be employed, their duties and their remuneration. . . . Here is the place to emphasise the vast importance of good management, a recognition of a set of fixed conditions established after a long and dreary warfare between master and man, and the clear exhibition to his workmen of his intention to abide by these conditions. (Taggart 1923, quoted in Lazonick 1990: 111–12)

Contrary to Lazonick's view that subcontracting was unknown in New England (Lazonick 1990: 99), the work patterns in American mule spinning before the 1830s and 1840s were remarkably similar to Britain (Cohen 1990: 55). Only in the integrated corporations of northern Massachusetts was centralised management rather than internal contracting the norm. Thus at the Greene Manufacturing Company of Warwick, Rhode Island, in 1815 a mule spinner made an agreement for both for his own labour and for his son who was to 'tend two sides of a spinning frame and keep his ends up as well' (Zonderman 1992: 128). Similarly in Philadelphia and in such Pennsylvanian mill villages as Rockdale, mule spinners recruited and trained their own helpers (Wallace 1978: 143, 177–80, 366). Such discrepancies in no sense detract from Lazonick's general thesis that differences in past practice explain diverging labour strategies in the British and American cotton industries. Rather, as a reflection of regional diversity in the United States cotton industry they provide confirmation of the influence of historical factors. The distinguishing characteristics in shopfloor hierarchies that can be detected in American cotton mule spinning are thus a reflection of the organisational, technological and product peculiarities which had emerged in cotton textiles by the 1830s. They also stemmed from contrasts in the composition of the labour force and in socio-economic environment in the various textile centres. In southern New England, for example, the proliferation of family firms, using family labour systems between 1807 and 1815, helped to foster subcontracting (Cohen 1990: 58). In Philadelphia, on the other hand, not only were there numerous family firms and proprietorships, but also a long-established textile tradition, combined with a growing concentration of British immigrants influencing the organisation of work. Further research is needed to establish the precise explanation of the incidence of subcontracting in Philadelphia's mule spinning industry. Nevertheless it would be surprising if the bias of the town's mule spinners towards finer counts during the 1820s did not affect work patterns and the division of labour. At the same time the role of the British immigrant should not be neglected. Alone of the textile centres in the 1820s and 1830s, Philadelphia's mills employed a significant proportion of immigrant workers. Transatlantic transfer of pre-industrial practices could, therefore, have created a continuity with Britain, which was absent in parts of New England, at least until the 1840s and 1850s.

Quite why, alone of American textile areas, northern Massachusetts largely avoided subcontracting in mule spinning is intriguing. Still the most likely explanation of the relative absence of internal contracting in this region is a simple one. The relative scarcity of mule spinners in this virgin textile area vastly inflated the wages they could enjoy. As a result mule spinning was exceptionally rare in the Boston Associates' mills. In 1817, for example, of the 125 workers employed by the Boston Manufacturing Company only two were mule spinners (Gibb 1950: 54). By the late 1820s improvements in throstle spinning meant that the Merrimack Company was producing cloth made entirely from throstle spun yarns (Jeremy 1981: 115).

The introduction of the self acting mule heralded the decline of subcontracting in most of the American cotton industry. In much of New England, automation meant that the power of the overseer replaced that of the mule spinner. Why it was that the impact of automation on work practices should have been so different in America than in Britain requires some comment. Lazonick has suggested this discrepancy can be explained by distinctions in past practice, attitudes and institutions as compared with Lancashire. For him, just as the persistence of the minder–piecer system in the British cotton industry was a legacy of eighteenth-century organisation, so foremanship in New England mule spinning from the 1830s and 1840s was merely a continuation of past practice. He suggested, therefore, that the mode of supervision on self acting mules: 'conformed to common mule practice in the New England cotton mills, in which top down hierarchical authority prevailed and internal subcontract systems were virtually unknown' (Lazonick 1990: 99). Yet whilst this might apply to the Lowell Corporations, it cannot be applied to all the textile areas. There is, however, evidence that attitudes to management elsewhere were beginning to change. Increasingly in the 1820s and 1830s American employers took the view that: 'control over production, recruitment and piece rates was the sole prerogative of management' Cohen 1990: 103). Thus even before 1840, in Slater's mills at Dudley and Oxford, Massachusetts there is evidence of a decline in the use of family labour in mule spinning, with operatives allowing management to select their helpers (Prude 1983: 118).

Elsewhere several organisational and financial changes may have helped to stimulate change. In the first instance the spread of vertical integration to Rhode Island, southern Massachusetts and Connecticut in the 1820s, increased the incentives to centralise labour management if rapid throughput was to be achieved. Secondly, as the business corporation replaced the family partnership in, for example, Fall River, so firms' ability to centralise management increased (Cohen 1990: 121). The rise of the integrated business corporation contrasted sharply with experience in Britain where, apart from a brief flirtation with the integrated factory, many of Lancashire's cotton firms became vertically specialised. That New England textile manufacturers succeeded in undermining the craft status of mule spinners was also a reflection of the limitations of trade unions which were in any event illegal until the 1840s. Resistance did occur, but it was sporadic, localised and uncoordinated. Even the wave of strikes in Fall River, masterminded by disgruntled British immigrants in the 1870s, achieved only limited success. This was the result of inadequate union organisation, combined with co-ordinated action by the owners of an array of interlocking Fall River corporations. Any gains in the form of uniform Wages Lists were counteracted by the limitations of these agreements. At the same time the spinners' militancy merely served to hasten the introduction of ring frames as an alternative technology in Fall River (Cohen 1990: 104–34; Sandberg 1969: 129; Lazonick 1990: 115–18).

While the characteristics of the shopfloor are critical to competitive advantage, they are but one facet of labour relations and need to be placed against a wider spectrum of policy options. In an effort to counteract or avoid the upheavals of industrialisation, a number of industrialists in both Britain and America introduced paternalist labour strategies in which internal contracts formed an integral part of certain types of management. It has been shown that one of the aims of subcontracting was to cement a unity of interest between skilled workers and their employers. As an economic relationship between employer and employed, paternalist labour management was similarly linked to a desire to promote industrial harmony and efficiency (Abercrombie and Hill 1976: 413). British and American cotton manufacturers believed that the wage bargain was the beginning rather than the end of relations with their workforce, while efforts by employers to mould the outlook of their operatives abound.

Yet when paternalist strategies are compared, some striking dissimilarities emerge, variations which help to explain the extraordinary difficulty, not to say futility, of defining paternalism. This is because: 'Paternalism does not exist indiscriminately across time and place. Specific paternalisms represent specific social and cultural bridges across the gap [of ultimately] irreconcilable interests' (Fox-Genovese and Fox-Genovese 1983:

130). Given the cultural, historical and organisational features of British and American cotton industries it would have been surprising had their nineteenth-century paternalist strategies been identical. That said, certain common elements, such as the use of water power, clearly influenced the physical manifestations of paternalism, if not its ethos. Diverging experience was, however, not solely international. For paternalism to have any real meaning and, by implication any noticeable effect as a labour strategy, its form and content had to vary depending on the context. By relating production to community culture, its various forms reflected differing social relationships, forms of business and product strategies. This has meant that it has been possible to identify an array of regionally distinctive paternalist strategies coexisting in the American cotton industry before the 1840s (Scranton 1984: 235–57). Shaped by a range of economic and social influences, paternalist labour policies varied within and between countries. Equally, with the passage of time changes in attitudes, expectations and competitive pressures could render previously successful policies ineffective.

In the British context, though interestingly less in the American, paternalism has sometimes been used as little more than a synonym for benevolence and philanthropy, practised primarily by a few religious minorities. It was, in essence, an economic relationship between employer and employed and whilst many early British paternalists were either Quakers or Unitarians this was not inevitable (Child 1964: 393–415; Fitzgerald 1987). Although America was a haven for Britain's dissenting sects, it would nevertheless be misleading to suggest that religious ideology held an overriding significance in shaping the labour policy of her industrialists. It has also been shown that benevolence was not always the core of paternalism, but only a part, with authority, guidance and ultimately duty, deference, dependency, exploitation and control making up the whole (Engels 1958: 210–13; Roberts 1979: 5–15; Joyce 1980: 92–4).

Whatever the manifestations of paternalism, the term implies 'fatherly control'. From this starting point it is possible to encompass the full gamut of paternalist relationships – whether between the state and the mass of the population or the employer and the employed. Paternalism implies 'the relationship not only between employer and employee, but also between parent and child, elder and younger siblings'. In such circumstances, the subordinate participants, unable to perceive their own best interests, become reliant upon the senior for protection, whilst the senior in their turn may exert control (Fox 1985: 3–5). Nevertheless, historical patterns in the development of society and of business in Britain and America affected the ways in which paternalism developed.

In Britain, from 1450 until 1800 or beyond, the relationship between rich and poor stood broadly paternalistic, as did work arrangements. Thus, in the eighteenth century: 'the prevailing view of the English aristocracy was to assert that the higher classes were obliged to think for and protect the poor, while the latter had to be submissive, depending entirely upon their betters' (Bendix 1956: 16). The implication then, is of an unequal, authoritarian, hierarchical society in which birth and wealth brought status and power. It was, nevertheless, a stable society in which traditional paternalist bonds meant that duty on the one side was rewarded by loyalty on the other (Roberts 1979: 2–3). Between the fifteenth and the eighteenth centuries British work relationships, as embodied in the apprenticeship system, were also broadly paternalistic. The link between the master craftsman and his apprentices represented a 'quasi-familial paternalism', based upon 'tutelage and deference' (Bendix 1956: 6). The powered factories which began to appear in the eighteenth century undeniably had a dramatic effect on working patterns, the working lives of operatives and the relationship between employer and employed (Thompson 1967: 56–97). As shown above, one of the objectives of the mechanisation of production was to reduce its skill requirements, so that expensive, craft-oriented male labour could be replaced by much cheaper child and female labour. Nevertheless, the factory system's impact on labour relations should not be exaggerated. Formal apprenticeship began to show signs of decay before the late eighteenth century, while in cotton spinning, some early mills exhibited a continuity in the relationship between employer and employed. There is evidence, therefore, that labour discipline was bolstered by a dependence and even a deference born of the work environment, the family and the community. Where skilled labour was employed this could be strengthened by a sub-contract system based upon family labour (Pollard 1963: 513–29; Chapman 1967: 156–62; Collier 1964: 29–31).

The reliance of early British factory masters on water power rendered some of them paternalists almost by default. They were implanting an alien way of life into rural areas, which had cultures suspicious of factory work. Thus the provision of housing could help to reconcile workers to altering their lifestyle. The emergent factory colonies were not, however, merely recruitment devices. By binding workers to their place of work by more than just a wage bargain, employers had the opportunity to mould their workforce to the ways of the factory, create stable labour relations and reduce labour turnover. The very isolation of many early factories, combined with the opportunity for community building, could create a kind of benevolent despotism, where the dividing line between the life of the factory and that of the surrounding community became blurred. Building housing, schools, shops, chapels and providing recreational facilities at such places as Cromford, Styal, Belper, New Lanark and many other early centres of cotton spinning, where often there was only a single substantial employer, created an environment ideal for the practice of an authoritarian, albeit usually benevolent industrial paternalism (Fitton 1989: 187–9; Pollard 1963: 513–19; Rose 1986: 102–22). These were family firms and the millowner and his family normally lived close to the factory and community they had built. The result was an almost squirearchical and certainly hierarchical relationship between employer and employed. Such links were further strengthened by the tendency of key workers to hold positions of authority within chapels and other institutions, whilst Sunday Schools were used to mould workers from an early age (Boyson 1970: 95). The evolution of community-based relations, as a method of labour discipline in many of the best-known British factory colonies in the eighteenth century, can also be seen as a substitute for subcontracting. It has been suggested that whilst such arm's length management was a feature of mule spinning, it did not occur where the throstle and, by implication, the water frame were used. Since the earliest British factory colonies used Arkwright's technology, millowners could exert their own personal power in the community to foster stable labour relations. That is not to deny that whole families ultimately became reliant upon the mill for employment, rather that authority came from above rather than being subcontracted.

The extent of paternalism should not be exaggerated for, even in the best-known factory colonies, this strategy was combined with other types of discipline, such as fines, corporal punishment and even dismissal. It would be equally misleading to assume that all factory masters became community builders or that in reducing labour turnover, equal effort was devoted to all categories of worker. In the first place community development was costly and beyond the reach of most small employers. The so-called 'model' factory colonies such as Cromford, Coalbrookdale, New Lanark and Styal were thus attached to large profitable firms (Pollard 1965: 231–42; Butt 1971: 84; Rose 1986: 13–35). Moreover, even where colonies were built, where efforts were devoted to the retention of labour, it was especially directed towards skilled workers (Rose 1986: 102–22). Such selectivity in paternalist policies was predictable and anticipated attitudes observed later in the century (Lazonick 1979: 231–49).

It is interesting to note that on matters such as hours of work, the employment of children or trade unions, few of even the most benevolent early factory masters were, by twentieth-century standards, enlightened. Parish apprentices were employed, the Factory Acts opposed and sometimes contravened and a number, initially at least, were profoundly anti-union and anti-democratic (Peacock 1984: 197–210; Rose 1989: 5–32; Boyson 1970: 148–9). This is not surprising, for whilst a few early factory masters were influenced by religion or by forward-thinking wives, the majority were paternalists of necessity. It is true that Robert Owen held a far wider social vision and later Samuel Greg Junior conducted a social experiment at Bollington (Rose 1986: 120–2). However, most were paternalists of necessity rather than as a result of social consequence. They wished to attract and retain labour, improve efficiency and reduce labour unrest and their colonies gave them the opportunity to do this. Moreover, in the context of eighteenth- and early nineteenth-century England, there was no contradiction between behaving as a paternalist and being unenlightened. As benevolent despots millowners believed they understood their employees' interests better than workers did, whilst opposing any external interference. Enlightenment came only with time and changing social conditions.

Water power only remained the predominant source of energy in the British cotton industry until the 1820s. As the industry grew, all but those on the best water sites began to turn to steam. As a result, from the 1820s the cotton industry became increasingly localised within the Lancashire coalfield and more and more urban. With the exception of those industrial villages which merged with existing towns, and those communities on exceptional water sites, paternalism of the type just described declined (Marshall 1968: 216–20). The comparatively stable labour relations of the factory colony gave way to a short-termism where economic fluctuations led to growing uncertainty of employment and a willingness of employers to compete via wage cutting. The combination of rapid urban and demographic growth with uncoordinated industrial expansion, during the 1830s and 1840s, thus created social problems of mammoth proportions. Moreover, at the very time when the social costs of industrialisation became magnified, social policy makers denied their duty of support and became increasingly *laissez faire*. The response of a few industrialists to the horrors and upheavals of the industrial city was, by the 1860s, to create their own purpose built towns (Meakin 1905).

Combined with the emergence of unions in the cotton industry and a willingness of employers to act collectively to counteract their demands, these conditions contributed to an upsurge in industrial unrest, in the 1830s and 1840s, culminating in the Plug Riots of 1842. Although this action has been described as the first General Strike and as verging on revolution, its origins in Lancashire were more economic than political and revolved around cuts in piece rate payments as a result of an economic downturn (Mather 1974: 116–17). It was Joyce who suggested that the social unrest and wave of strikes led employers in parts of Lancashire to adopt a 'new paternalism' based upon greater co-operation. This, whilst unlike that in the rural colonies, was nonetheless based upon the relationship between the factory, the family and community relations and resulted in an era of greater co-operation in the middle of the nineteenth century. A logical outcome of *laissez faire* by both government and industry, this new paternalism, 'cut more deeply into operative life than the paternalism of the early founders of industry' (Joyce 1980: xx). Joyce's central thesis is that the marked decline in social unrest, which occurred in England and especially in the textile heartlands of the north of England, could be traced to the organisation of the factory and to ties fostered by textile employers with their local communities where the culture of the town became inseparable from the culture of the industrial community (Joyce 1980: 50).

The 'new' paternalists still relied upon a paternalism based upon the family firm, familial relations and the community, but they constructed such ties in different ways. Gone were the colonies developed for a single mill. Instead they built cotton mills in existing towns, thus saving manufacturers the cost of housing and community development. Lancashire employers by the 1850s, Joyce has argued, tried to foster good relations with their workforce by arranging excursions and celebratory dinners, whilst at the same time promoting education, building churches and supporting self-help institutions for the whole community. Such superficially philanthropic acts helped to mould society and counteract some of the worst evils of industrialisation. At the same time, along with the holding of public office, they enhanced employers' standing within the community and, in theory, their authority within the factory. Joyce went further, however, to suggest that the authority of the factory extended into the community in other ways. The crucial links between factory and the community were overlookers and subcontractors. Of the overlooker Joyce observed: 'His position . . . as the master's agent and yet part of the workforce, gave him a crucial and mediating role in the life of the factory' (Joyce 1980: 101). Similarly the survival of the subcontract in mule spinning created further links between factory authority and community authority. Based on the family unit of employment it ensured that domestic paternal influences were extended to the world of work (Joyce 1980: 112). It has, however, been demonstrated that even though mule spinners undoubtedly recruited from within their own communities, family recruitment was distinctly limited. It would seem therefore that like the overseer, it was the respected position of the mule spinner in the community that was significant here.

The result, Joyce argued, was a stability in urban and community relations, especially where there were larger, established firms, which helped to counteract the social disruption caused by population growth and economic change. In communities such as those in Lancashire by mid-century, where levels of long-distance migration were low, even if there was considerable mobility within an individual town the potential for influence was high (Anderson 1971: 35–7). Deference on the part of workers, illustrated by stable labour relations and also in voting patterns, emerged as a result of a far-reaching dependence of workers on their employers in relatively stable communities. Harmony was ensured because workers and employers increasingly shared the same aspirations, even if these inevitably varied between communities.

There can be no doubt that industrial relations in Lancashire became more quiescent in the middle of the nineteenth century and that the local business community was of vital importance in achieving this. However, it is not at all clear that this stemmed from the emergence of deference on the part of working people. Doubts have ranged from whether industrial and social accord can be reasonably attributable to paternalism, to whether there was any industrial accord at all (Dutton and King 1982: 59–74; Huberman 1987: 187–92). It is, for example, extremely difficult to establish motivation whether of employers or employed. Since only a handful of mid-nineteenth-century paternalist employers left records of their intentions, the motivation of the silent majority must remain open to various interpretations. Certainly some employers may have been paternalist in intent, but it seems likely that most became philanthropists for social gain (Howe 1984: 307). It is, however, infinitely more difficult to form a view of what the majority of working men and women, rather than merely their leaders, actually thought, so that dependence in the labour market and apparent deference in politics and religion may have been nothing more than an illusion (Savage 1987: 5).

Dependency, as Joyce subsequently admitted, was too strong a term for the relationship between working people and their employers. This is because the real change that occurred by the 1860s was that labour relations became a two-way process, and whilst rarely admitting the virtue of unions employers were increasingly prepared to accept them as part of collective bargaining (Joyce 1984: 67–76; Howe 1984: 176). Even prior to this, the persistence of internal contracts in mule spinning, with its arm's length management, can be shown to have been desired by and been mutually beneficial to employers and employees. Since most disputes between employers and the spinning unions in the 1830s and 1840s had been about cuts in wage rates, the establishment of Wage Lists was a critical turning point which in turn served to institutionalise the position of internal contracting in Lancashire communities. These lists fixed rates of pay per pound spun on mules of a given size, regularised the relationship between pay and effort, reduced the incentive for competitive strategy to be based on wages' cuts and hence cut the number of disputes and so brought advantages for both employers and employed. They contributed considerably to industrial harmony and owed little if anything to deferential relations and a great deal to a realisation of an emerging economic interdependence (Huberman 1996: 132–48). Nevertheless it should be remembered that the variations in the social, political and economic characteristics of Lancashire communities meant that any generalisation over levels of labour unrest in the 1830s and 1840s and the achievement of less tumultuous labour relations in the middle of the nineteenth century is extremely difficult. On the one hand the cotton unions were fragmented and sectional, whilst on the other employers' associations were usually sporadic and were linked to particular causes, such as the Factory Acts, and to specific disputes (Howe 1984: 164–6).

The level of industrial conflict, therefore, varied across Lancashire and was especially intense in Preston from the mid-1830s until the mid-1850s. Dominated by a few large firms, the Preston Masters' Association was able to impose piece rate cuts, twice defeating trade unions in the strikes of 1836–7 and 1853–4 (Howe 1984: 164–6; Dutton and King 1982: 59–73; Dutton and King 1981; Russell 1987: 153–73). Thereafter, perhaps shocked by the damaging consequences of the second strike, when their triumph over the Amalgamated Association of Cotton Operative Spinners closed down the Preston cotton industry for seven months, Preston employers became more conciliatory and introduced a Wages List within a decade (Dutton and King 1982; Huberman 1996: 133). In Oldham, on the other hand, where there were far lower levels of economic concentration and where the room and turning system might have been expected to have created a community of interest between employers and employed, there were several bitter and violent strikes during the 1830s and, like Preston, a Wages List was not introduced until the 1850s. The persistence of conflict has been interpreted in part as stemming from traditions of a militant radicalism which was both economic and political in origin and which helped to make the community of Oldham distinctive. At the same time the high mortality rate of firms prevented employers from forming an effective collective response to unrest (Gadian 1978; Sykes 1980: 171; Huberman 1996: 136–7; Farnie 1979: 246). In Bolton, a standard list had already been introduced by 1829 and although there were violent strikes against individual employers relations between the Associated Masters and the Spinners' Union remained relatively cordial in the 1840s. A major strike and lockout was consequently delayed until 1861 which brought a proposed wage cut. Yet the apparent calm has been explained not by a desire for co-operation and still less by working-class deference. Instead it appears that there was social and political conflict within the town's middle-class employers which prevented them from organising effectively, as employers did in Preston (Howe 1984: 172; Taylor 1991: 79–89). The impact of any type of paternalism in Lancashire is, therefore, by no means clear cut whilst its prevalence and form varied regionally and through time.

Similarly in the United States, paternalism was not a universal strategy. Indeed, the sentiments of a mill agent at Holyoke, Massachusetts who declared: 'I regard my work people just as I regard my machinery. So long as they can do my work for what I choose to pay them, I keep them, getting out of them all I can' (Dulles 1993: 75) were doubtless views shared by as many there as in England. However, where paternalist strategies were used the influence of differing social values, demographic trends, labour markets and industrial structures meant that their form often differed from those in Britain. Yet since divergent labour policies have been detected within America, the picture is clearly more complex than would be revealed by simple national comparisons. For example, where paternalist policies were used, whether in Britain or America, their shape was certainly in part the result of national economic and social characteristics. Equally important, however, was whether factories were being implanted in otherwise virgin areas or being spliced on to an existing industrial centre.

In eighteenth-century American textiles the predominance of household manufacturing, rather than craft-based apprenticeship in textiles, undoubtedly influenced labour strategies. It meant that whilst a form of paternalism did exist, it was based directly upon the values and authority of the family, rather than on the master–servant relationship, as in Britain. In addition, in America, paternalist social policy was not designed to bolster the status quo in an aristocratic social order. Institutions such as pauper apprenticeship were surely derived from the British model. Wider philanthropic activity, such as the educational endowments of the Boston Associates, may have been motivated by a desire for social standing within the mercantile elite. Nevertheless, far from reinforcing a society based on birth they helped to foster one based on merit.

The absence of generations of convention and tradition in American work relations did not prevent prejudice against factory work. Centralisation of production, therefore, may not have undermined status in the way that it did in Britain. It was, nonetheless, fairly unappealing to those accustomed to household work and was duly treated with suspicion. Thus one of the origins of paternalism in both Slater's industrial villages and later at Lowell, whilst building on prevailing value systems, was the desire to convey the acceptable face of capitalism (McGouldrick 1968:

34; Tucker 1984: 21). Policies were implemented less from a commitment to social justice than because they proved an effective recruitment device. At the same time paternalism was thought to contribute to the smooth and profitable operation of factories.

Superficially Slater's factory villages closely resembled those surrounding Arkwright-type factories in eighteenth-century Britain. Rural implants, his family owned factories at Webster and Slaterville linked intimately to the community he developed. Agricultural land surrounded family dwellings, with strong religious institutions providing a moral basis for the community (Tucker 1984: 126–34). Yet just as Slater and later Lowell adapted technology imported from Britain to America, so Slater sculpted his Derbyshire experience to New England conditions. Through a combination of distinctive community development and patriarchal authority within the family labour system, Slater created links with past Yankee values which overcame factory prejudice and promoted industrial harmony (Tucker 1979: 116–17). This meant that:

> The patriarchal family structure; the customary division of labour on the basis of age, gender and marital status; the church; and New England factory design were integral to many of the early factory colonies. Such respect for regional culture served to ease the transition, for all elements of the community, from an agricultural, rural economy to one based on the factory system and wage labour. (Tucker 1984: 21)

At Lowell too, Yankee value systems influenced labour policy. There, efforts to procure underemployed rural young women, meant that high priority was given to overcoming their conservative parents' suspicion (Dublin 1979: 2–10). The avoidance of urban squalor of the British type became a top priority (Scranton 1984: 243). The interlocking corporations at Lowell pursued common labour strategies, which involved the building of a sanitary town and the construction of closely supervised dormitories intended to provide the appropriate moral environment for short-term female labour. In planning such 'orderly industrialisation' the Boston Associates also hoped to avoid the social tensions which beleaguered British industrial towns, doubtless acting as much out of a desire to protect their investment as from social conscience. Their labour strategy was thus inseparable from their overall intention of reducing the uncertainty of potentially highly risky and large investments (Dalzell 1987: 13).

The familial paternalism of the Slater system was intimately related to both the family firm and the position of family labour within it. Traditional family authority was thus replicated by mill hierarchy. At Lowell, however, the more formal paternalism of the business corporation helped to embed an order and a discipline into the working environment (Scranton 1984: 240–8). In Philadelphia, by contrast, a form of 'fraternal paternalism' has been identified from mid-century and resembled that found elsewhere in America. The familiar pattern of housing and religious provision was replicated. But variations in the structure and output of industry meant that the relationship between employer and employed was different. It was closer to that of master and apprentice than to millowner and factory operative. Mills, which were often sublet, were similar to schools of entrepreneurship, with skilled, mainly immigrant, workers aspiring to become owners in their own right. Moreover in producing more specialist products than elsewhere in America, Philadelphia's factory masters relied for their flexibility on the skill of their workers (Scranton 1984: 242). It was the potential for social mobility, absent in New England, which made Philadelphia paternalism more akin to that in Lancashire than elsewhere in the United States (Scranton 1983: 248). The identification of a range of paternalist strategies, shaped by business organisation, the nature of products and cultural values is critical to an appreciation of labour policies in ante-bellum America. Business structure in Philadelphia, especially in the room and power system, did resemble that in early Victorian Lancashire. Yet parallels with Lancashire should be treated with caution. It has already been shown that the use of predominantly family labour in Lancashire mule spinning had declined by the 1830s. Equally there is little evidence in Joyce that his paternalism was that of the room and power system, which had in any event declined in the spinning towns by the second half of the nineteenth century. Instead it reflected the behaviour of the elite rather than of the tiny firms which clustered in the weaving sheds of north-east Lancashire and the shared mills around Oldham.

Nowhere is the link between the cultural characteristics of local communities and the nature of paternalism more pronounced than in William Gregg's 'experimental' in the Southern states during the 1840s. There paternalist ideas were developed to suit a plantation society where value systems and attitudes were radically different from New England and where there was a deep-seated suspicion of industry. Rather than antagonise the planters, with their commitment to slavery, Gregg (himself a slaveowner) created a 'familiar' paternalist system which posed no threat to plantation society since mills were intended to employ poor whites in rural areas. He created a self-contained world at Granitesville with strict regulation of the way his female workers lived. This meant that in effect the paternalism of the plantation was transferred to the factory. However, in order to overcome fears of 'white slavery' he emphasised the racial and social superiority of white workers and employed slaves to undertake unpleasant tasks. In the North transiency was seen as a consequence of development so that millowners pursued labour and technological strategies to accommodate this. However, differing social conditions in the

South meant that 'familiar paternalists' as such as Gregg looked to create a stable local labour force where labour turnover was low (Ward 1987, 228–35; Scranton 1984: 246–8).

American employers faced lower levels of labour unrest than was common in Britain, though they were not entirely immune from strikes. The first textile strike occurred at Pawtucket in 1824, while the family labour system entirely lost its grip by the 1840s – a development followed by a growing number of strikes. Equally, the fraternal arrangements which were strengthened in Philadelphia did not prevent a rise in labour militancy in the 1830s and 1840s. Similarly there were turnouts at Lowell in the 1830s whilst the 1840s saw campaigns for shorter working hours. At Fall River, on the other hand, the rapid expansion of the 1860s and the influx of British mule spinners heralded a rise in unrest. Only in the South was labour conflict virtually absent (Scranton 1983; Prude 1983: 141–3; Dublin 1975: 106–13; Silvia 1975). The relationship between paternalism and both industrial harmony and conflict was a complex one in the United States, just as it was in Britain. Therefore by the 1830s and 1840s it would appear, for example, that the very characteristics of the community created at Lowell, where close mutual bonds developed among women in a close-knit community, fostered an ideal environment for unified unrest (Dublin 1975: 99). Nevertheless, there is no escaping the fact that conflict was less frequent, less violent and less effective than equivalent upheavals in Britain in the 1830s and 1840s. The regional variations in labour strategy which have been detected indicate that there was no simple explanation for this. However, a number of factors limited the frequency and effectiveness of labour disputes in the United States cotton industry in this period.

In the first place labour unions were, until the 1840s, patchy and sporadic and regularly declared illegal by employers who had the backing of individual states (Spence 1965: 136–9). In addition, in comparison with Lancashire, where levels of migration were falling and where the factory workforce was local and relatively stable, in New England communities' transiency was an important characteristic. This undoubtedly reduced the ability of workers to organise, whilst the influx of immigrant labour to the Northern states from the 1840s onwards created social tensions and divisions which acted as a brake on effective action (Zonderman 1992: 97–118; Kirk 1994 vol. I: 181). Moreover, in Massachusetts at least, the structure of communities, where employers were tied together through interlocking directorships, meant that they could act collectively in a way that was not echoed in Lancashire. This significantly increased operators' bargaining power in the event of a strike. In the South, on the other hand, community stability should be set against the tight control of an almost feudal society combined with anti-union laws which remained restrictive throughout the nineteenth century.

Summary

Central to the discussion of the comparative performance of the British and American cotton industries in the late nineteenth century, has been contrasts in the management of labour (Lazonick 1979: 231–2). There can be little doubt that by the late nineteenth century mule spinning was far less common in America than in England, while in New England management was by overseers rather than via the subcontract (Cohen 1990: 108–9; Lazonick 1990: 95). Similarly it would be hard to demur from the view that by the 1870s American perceptions on labour management had diverged from those in Britain. Whilst Lancashire millowners helped to perpetuate the subcontract on self actors, American manufacturers, with the exception of the Philadelphia fancy goods producers, sought to centralise management. That they were able to do so despite some striking similarities in early practice was the product of several factors. Of these, differences in unionisation and the superior organisation of employers are among the more important. It should, however, be remembered that even though internal subcontracting had been widely used in the earliest of American factories it never became as entrenched as in Britain. In other words it was easier to break with past practice when it did not stretch back over generations. Conversely, in Philadelphia mule spinning had a longer pedigree and was consistently being reinforced by the attitudes of British immigrants.

The implications of such central control for productivity change in America were considerable. It facilitated the intensification of work through increased operating speeds and longer hours. In Lancashire, by contrast, the millowners relied upon the self-interest of the mule spinner to achieve productivity growth through a system deemed to be mutually beneficial to spinners and owners alike. It should be borne in mind, however, that the dissimilarities in the organisation of work in Britain and New England, so noticeable in mule spinning, were not replicated in other areas of work. Where throstles were used, whether in Lancashire or Lowell, work effort was the responsibility of the overseer. What is significant, however, is that the product orientation of the Lancashire industry meant that mule spinning, with its persistent internal contracting, predominated.

In both countries there is evidence that, whilst relations with labour were influenced if not at times dominated by the trade cycle, employers looked beyond the wage bargain. Paternalist strategies, motivated not by benevolence but as a way of meeting management objectives, prevailed. The form which they took, however, changed through time and with circumstances. Nevertheless, just as the precise motivation behind apparent paternalism is often difficult to identify so the effectiveness of such policies has been the subject of debate. What is clear, however, is that in both countries the conduct of labour relations was firmly embedded in local business communities, further strengthening the links between community and business culture.

5 Networks and the evolution of government–industry relations to 1860

Business behaviour is conditioned by a combination of external institutional forces and by the social and cultural environment of which they are part, which are, in turn, conditioned by historical factors. These influences, by affecting the expectations and attitudes of businessmen, themselves fashion the culture of individual firms leading to significant international variations in business behaviour. The firm embedding of family-owned cotton businesses in the social networks of local communities helped to give these businesses their distinctive characteristics and is reflected in the striking national and intranational differences in the ante-bellum period and also in the political behaviour and relative political power of interest groups.

Business decisions are not, therefore, the result just of the price mechanism but are also affected by both laws and that complex array of rules, formal and informal, which determine human behaviour. Moreover, if the expectations and responses of businessmen are shaped by the institutional environment in which they operate, their changing responses and sometimes their efforts to evade laws may also impact upon the development of the legal system and rules associated with the conduct of economic activity (North 1990: 3–8). This is because laws, whether they relate to property rights, inheritance, the status and regulation of firms or commercial policy, are not formed in an historical vacuum. Instead, they are the product of responses to changing conditions and to the interaction between governments on the one hand and business groups and other interested parties on the other. They may also be a response to particular pressures and events. Since the institutional environment is clearly influenced by historical forces, it has especial relevance for the study of the behaviour of all firms. The development of laws is path-dependent so that there can be, for example, significant international contrasts in both the privileges and restrictions faced by firms. The regulation of business or the level of tariff protection enjoyed may, therefore, vary between countries. As a result, institutional and political forces may be every bit as important, for the formation of family firm strategy, as purely economic ones (Rose 1996).

External networking by family firms has not been confined to contacts with other business organisations, but includes relations with governments. Indeed to understand the freedom of manoeuvre and even the direction of innovation in all firms, whether family or corporate, internal and external decisions need to be placed in the context of government–industry relations (Casson and Rose 1997: 4). In addition, in most societies economic elites emerged whose common backgrounds, values and aspirations made them natural successors. The behaviour of these elites at the local level, and their status and bargaining power nationally, could have considerable implications for the expectations and policies of the majority of businessmen in their particular sector and region.

In the context of the distinctive experience and strategies of British and American cotton firms, it is important to explore the forces which shaped the relative political leverage of local business groups at the national level. This will demonstrate how far differences in the evolution of government–industry relations may have affected expectations and hence business strategy in the period before the Civil War.

The foundations of collective action

Seen in the simplest terms the institutional environment, in both Britain and the United States, from the late eighteenth century onwards, should have meant that in both countries collective action, especially that based upon formal organisations, was a rarity. In Britain, for instance, the withering of the medieval guild system by the seventeenth century and the passing of the Combination Laws in 1799 and 1800, should have generated a growing trend towards competition rather than co-operation (Unwin 1904: 41–6; Redford 1934: 66). Even more in colonial America there was a legal system, inherited from England, which gave little support to collective, stabilising institutions. The post-revolutionary period, on the other hand, saw little legal support for formal anti-competitive arrangements, which were indeed outlawed in a number of states and America's 'dedication to competition' in the nineteenth century became legendary (Galambos 1966: 6).

If there was a legal framework designed to discourage co-operation in business, in reality informal and formal networks, at the community level, hold the key to the understanding of government–industry relations with respect to cotton textiles in Britain and the United States before 1860. Personal, family and community ties, so crucial to the formulation of business strategy, were also vital if groups within industry were to influence policy choices. However, the nature of arrangements was often disparate, with British businessmen exhibiting a preference for formal rather than informal arrangements to a far greater degree than in the United States. At the same time, the ability of local groups to influence national policy and the form such influence took were also shaped by the character of the political system and by a complex array of political forces often only indirectly connected to business.

Collusive arrangements inhibiting changes in price and output were a rarity in early industrial Lancashire (Howe 1984: 162). However, collective commercial organisations designed to influence government policy, albeit often short-lived, appeared especially in Manchester, during the late eighteenth century and reflected a growing range of internal and external threats to the well-being of the cotton interests. Most early bodies were established in response to town meetings to deal with, often local, difficulties while those such as the Committee for the Protection of Calico Manufacture and Print Trade, were set up to protect individual interests. In addition, Pitt's introduction of the Fustian Tax in 1784 triggered the proliferation of outraged, but largely ineffective local associations, the effectiveness of which was greatly impeded by significant sectional differences.

More lasting, though by no means permanent, were the Manchester Committee for the Protection and Encouragement of Trade, established in 1774 and the Manchester Commercial Society of 1794 set up in response to the shock of the outbreak of war with France the previous year. Neither was sufficiently robust to survive the uncertainties and turbulence of the French wars, yet both reflected an awareness of the benefits formal association promised in the face of economic adversity, especially where the goal was to nudge government policy in ways which would bring local benefits. For example, the Manchester Committee for the Protection and Encouragement of Trade became involved in campaigns to reduce industrial espionage and the emigration of skilled artisans, whilst in the 1780s a primary objective was to break Richard Arkwright's monopoly power by attacking the validity of his patent (Redford 1934: 3–6). In addition, the Combination Laws did not prevent operatives making arrangements which, in turn, prompted the formation of sectional groupings of employers which were themselves illegal (Redford 1934: 66).

Given that the majority of early associations were a localised response to a specific set of circumstances, it is not surprising that they were generally short-lived and ineffective. It was not until 1820 that the Manchester Chamber of Commerce emerged as Lancashire's first permanent commercial organisation. A supposedly apolitical body, it had the declared intention of lobbying parliament on issues 'affecting the commercial interests of Manchester and its neighbourhood'. The Chamber recruited relatively widely in Lancashire embracing most regions and sectors. Yet merchants (who made up over 30 per cent of the total by 1860) heavily dominated its membership. Lancashire's enduring family dynasties dominated its council, so that it favoured the interests of large rather than small firms. Indeed there is evidence that the Chamber believed small businesses should be controlled as a major source of over-trading and instability (Redford 1956: 299; Howe 1984: 201). The extent to which the Manchester Chamber of Commerce truly reflected the aspirations and concerns of Lancashire can, therefore, be disputed and some towns, such as Blackburn, believed they lacked representation in the decision-making process and so undertook to establish local Chambers of Commerce and commercial associations (Howe 1984: 197–9). Nevertheless the Manchester Chamber of Commerce was to remain the mouthpiece of Manchester's commercial community, if not the whole of Lancashire, until the twentieth century (Redford 1934: 70).

The development of commercial associations, intent on lobbying parliament, was not the only potential source of political pressure to emerge in Lancashire in this period. The Combination Laws made employers' associations illegal, yet did not prevent clandestine arrangements in the first quarter of the nineteenth century. There remained, for instance, the vestiges of paternalism in domestic sectors with combinations emerging to protect handloom weavers. In addition, from the 1830s onwards true employers' associations began to emerge. These arose in response to a range of forces including waves of labour unrest and trade union activity such as occurred in Preston in 1836 and 1853–4, changes in profit margins due to altered market conditions and the effects of increased government intervention such as came with the extension of the Factory Acts. By the 1860s employers' associations were active in Ashton, Blackburn, Bolton, Burnley, Hyde, Manchester, Oldham, Stockport and Wigan (McIvor 1996: 36–7; Howe 1984: 162–4, 175). In general these remained local organisations in this period though the Manchester Committee and the National Association of Factory Occupiers, formed respectively in 1833 and 1855, represented broader groupings to oppose factory legislation. Accordingly the Manchester Committee represented the interests of eight major textile towns, while Robert Hyde Greg's National Association of Factory Occupiers had an even wider representation (Howe 1984: 179).

If commercial and employers' associations displayed increasing permanence from the 1820s onwards, other organisations sprang up for specific purposes. Of these easily the most important was the Anti-Corn Law League, founded in Manchester in 1839 and disbanded in 1846. However, the less prominent Cotton Supply Association of 1857 was set up: 'not to grow cotton, but to remove existing obstacles to its cultivation.

. . . Supply and demand will be left to shape their own mutual relations; all that will be attempted is to remove impediments . . . [and] stimulate . . . [cotton's] growth by every legitimate means' (quoted in Silver 1966: 85–6).

These single issue associations reflect the importance of certain key causes, such as free trade and raw cotton supply. They also demonstrate the inability of existing organisations to press specific cases with the government, when they themselves were sometimes divided. These single-issue associations represented responses to the limitations of the political system, even after the Reform Act of 1832. Electoral reform certainly meant that, for the first time, the interests of Lancashire's cotton industry were reflected in parliament, with 30 per cent of all Lancashire MPs between 1830 and 1860 having a textile background. However, in a county with significant political divisions, even in those areas linked to textiles and in a House of Commons still dominated by the landed interest, their ability to speak effectively for Lancashire was distinctly limited. This rendered 'pressure from without' vital, at least until the 1867 Reform Act (Howe 1984: 96; Hollis 1974: vii–viii).

The tendency for formal organisations created to exert pressure on governments was less pronounced in cotton regions of the United States than it was in Lancashire before 1860. Instead, especially in Massachusetts the largely informal kinship groupings, which dominated cotton manufacturing in the state, allowed firms to act collectively where necessary to influence decisions at state if not national level. Consequently: 'Joint political action and pre-arrangement for shared expenses ensured maximum effort and minimum risk for all concerned. The corporations were assured a significant voice in the various public fora of the State House' (Gross 1993: 27). Additionally personal contacts within government played a critical role in ensuring that federal as well as state policy decisions, at least until the 1850s, favoured the interests of the Boston Associates. Equally, there was little demand, before the Civil War, for employers' associations of the kind that appeared in Lancashire from the early nineteenth century onwards.

If effective personal networks reduced the need for commercial lobbying groups there were a number of reasons why what can be described as stabilising institutions found little favour among American cotton manufacturers. One possible explanation was the devotion to change which was the product of being a country of recent settlement which may have undermined cartel-type arrangements before they developed. Yet the behaviour of such groups as the Boston Associates must make it doubtful that the average businessman was averse to collusion. More significant, however, was a tendency in the state courts to favour competition rather than co-operation and thus outlaw formal associations (Galambos 1966: 7–8). A major stimulus for Lancashire employers' associations, in the first half of the nineteenth century, had been the spread of trade unions and increased levels of strike activity. Yet in the textile cities of the Boston Associates and at Fall River strike activity before the Civil War was minimal and employer unity easy to achieve. In Philadelphia, where strikes were bitter and violent in the 1830s, the paternalism of the proprietary capitalists reduced the need for employer associations in the ante-bellum period, whilst in the South organised labour unrest was unheard of (Scranton 1983: 33 and 138).

Boards of Trade and Chambers of Commerce developed very slowly and sporadically in America and lacked any significant political influence in the ante-bellum period. In the pre-Revolutionary period, the British government prevented Bostonians from forming any form of trade association and even after Independence development was halting. Not until 1836 was a Chamber of Commerce was established, only to be dissolved six years later on account of its members' apathy. A further somewhat half-hearted effort came in 1855 with the formation of a Board of Trade but it was the 1880s, with the formation of the Boston Chamber of Commerce, before the city had an active and powerful trade organisation. In Philadelphia, too, development was halting and spasmodic, initiated far more by shipping interests than by textile merchants. Certainly a Board of Trade came into existence in the 1830s but, without any permanent meeting place until the 1850s, it is hard to visualise how it made any impact as a trade organisation (Sturges 1915: 23–37).

Reliance on informal as opposed to formal arrangements, to secure political influence, was therefore a characteristic of American cotton manufacturing interests before the Civil War. This state of affairs was further encouraged by a political system designed to prevent the emergence of excessive concentrations of power and in so doing gave real power to the interests of local groups. Unlike the position in Lancashire, even after the First Reform Act, where industrialists exercised local rather than national political power, in the United States the Constitution ensured that local interests were genuinely represented. The identity and legislative power of individual states were preserved, with control divided between federal and state governments. In turn, within the federal government, executive power was to lie with Congress, as the guardians of state interests. Members of Congress, mindful of a desire for re-election, put the likely local consequences of any policy initiative first and voted accordingly, rather than necessarily along party lines (Lees 1969: 36, 189). Since, unlike their British counterparts, American industrialists were enfranchised, this system gave them real leverage.

Government–industry relations

Clearly there were variations in the way the cotton interests in Britain and America sought to exert political influence in the years before 1860. There were also sharp variations in the attitudes and relative influence of cotton industry interest groups in Britain, as compared with the United States in this period. The most obvious of these relates to the policy preferences of the cotton interests on either side of the Atlantic. In the United States a bias for protection, when the industry was in its infancy, was not replaced by any enthusiasm for free trade. On the other hand, initially Lancashire's cotton interests were relatively slow to embrace the benefits of free trade in the eighteenth and early nineteenth centuries. Protectionism in this period took on a number of guises and reflected the relatively divided interests of Lancashire groups. There was, for example, little support for complete freedom of entry of all types of cotton goods into British markets. Meanwhile, many weavers and merchants opposed yarn exports as a potential stimulant to foreign competition, although spinners favoured it as a way of widening markets. Similarly cotton merchants and manufacturers opposed any easing of restrictions on the export of machinery, even though it had strong support from the less vocal and visible machinery makers. Merchants and manufacturers only accepted the removal of restrictions in 1842 in the hope that it might hasten the repeal of the Corn Laws (Musson 1976; Redford 1934: 129). There was, therefore, a certain expediency in Lancashire's support for free trade, even in this period. Yet this measure of support and an enthusiasm based upon self-interest, marked a difference in attitude, as compared with the United States, which stemmed both from variations in the timing of industrialisation and in the market bias of the two industries. Just as the extreme domestic orientation of the United States cotton industry fostered, and was in turn sustained by tariff protection, so in Lancashire the quest for ever wider foreign markets in the nineteenth century became inextricably linked to the doctrine of free trade, especially amongst Manchester's large, wealthy and powerful commercial community.

Several issues relating to foreign commercial policy stimulated nineteenth-century collective action in Lancashire. Of these easily the most famous was the repeal of the Corn Laws in 1846, which attracted industrialists far more on the grounds of self-interest than ideology. However, other matters, including calls for repeal of duties payable on printed cotton goods, on raw cotton and concern over supplies of raw cotton and the future of the East India Company, were all significant issues with direct bearing on the health and well-being of the cotton industry, generating at the very least petitions to the House of Commons.

On the domestic front, factory legislation proved to be an important rallying point which drew a collective, if not always a united, response. The extent to which campaigns were successful depended upon a range of forces of which wider political and revenue considerations of governments were by far the most important. That is not to say that collective action by Lancashire industrialists in the early Victorian period was impotent, rather that in assessing campaigns it is necessary to remember they represented part of a much wider picture.

The Anti-Corn Law League is easily the most prominent and best known of the early Victorian lobbying groups. That it was needed to highlight the economic benefits of free trade stemmed from a reformed political system which still rendered industrialists as 'outsiders' so that the overall impact of local MPs was limited. The Anti-Corn Law League was also a product of the inadequacies of the Manchester Chamber of Commerce's attempts to orchestrate opposition. Certainly the Chamber of Commerce expressed support for the liberalisation of trade during the 1820s, in its dynamic early years, with greater economic freedom and the removal of duties on raw materials, in particular, being among its avowed objectives (Redford 1934: 140–7). However, Chamber of Commerce's stance was at times contradictory, especially when it came to the export of machinery which it opposed. Moreover, during the 1830s an apathy developed which has been likened to a 'seven year sleep', from which it only awoke in December 1838. Even when the formation of the Anti-Corn Law League in 1839 encouraged the Chamber to trumpet its belief in trade liberalisation, it was not unanimous in its enthusiasm nor particularly forthcoming in its public displays. Consequently, although requested by the Board of Trade to call a public meeting expressing wholehearted support for free trade, which could have been used as evidence by the Select Committee on Import Duties, J. B. Smith, the Chamber's Chairman, was not co-operative (Brown 1958: 182).

The Times described the Anti-Corn Law League as 'the most advanced political machine this country has yet seen' (quoted in McCord 1958: 163). It transformed free trade into a national political issue and gained a more prominent position in national life, through its ever-widening propaganda campaigns, than any other radical group (McCord 1958: 15; Howe 1997: 29; Schonhardt-Bailey 1998: 73). Its fundraising activities, which almost became an end in themselves, whereby ever rising sums were pledged in support of repeal, were legendary. Campaigns in 1843, 1844/5 and 1846 raised respectively £50,000, £100,000 and £250,000, much of it from Manchester (Howe 1984: 212). Even electorally, although the League did not secure a Liberal victory in 1841, there were successful Anti-Corn Law candidates in a number of constituencies inside and outside Lancashire. These included: Cobden (Stockport), Bowring (Bolton), Brotherton (Salford), Scott (Walsall), Walker (Bury), Villiers (Wolverhampton), Philips and Gibson (Manchester) (McCord 1958: 95).

Still the balance of the evidence suggests that the League should not be credited with achieving repeal, however. That it did not was a product of both internal and external divisions, the difficulty of achieving meaningful influence in parliament and the complexity of the political map in this period. Many early League initiatives, for example, can at best be described as a shambles and a constant tension endured between the wealthy, influential moderates like Robert Hyde Greg, who were vital to the financial viability of the campaign, and the energetic but often intemperate extremists like Prentice (McCord 1958: 108). Moreover, while the League undoubtedly kept the Corn Laws to the forefront of the nation's minds, it did not succeed in converting those vital to parliamentary success, the landed groups. Nor, for all the rhetoric on the commercial benefits, in terms of widening markets, was Lancashire or even Manchester united on the issue of free trade generally or the Corn Laws in particular. Even though there was wide representation of Lancashire's textile towns on the Council of the League, the economic and social distinctiveness of Lancashire's communities was also reflected in political diversity. Indeed the political map of the county has been likened to three Lancashires with capitals in Liverpool, Manchester and Preston, with only Manchester and its satellite cotton towns staunchly Liberal in the 1830s and 1840s (Hanham 1959: 284; Howe 1984: 210). Taking Lancashire as a whole therefore, of 26 seats contested in the 1841 election, there was an even split between Conservatives and Liberals (Craig 1977). Even returning a Liberal MP and having representation on the League Council was no guarantee that there was total support for repeal. This is illustrated in the case of Preston where the League did not convince the leading cotton masters, who were influenced by the local landed gentry with regard to the repeal of the Corn Laws (Howe 1984: 213). More widely, even when the headquarters of the League was transferred to London, to create a psychological and actual distance between Manchester and the campaign, this did not encourage City merchants to give financial support, even though they supported the principle of free trade (Howe 1997: 34).

Pressure from without was essential to keeping free trade to the forefront of people's minds, at a time when rival causes included Chartism and the Poor Laws. The Anti-Corn Law League had 'turned free trade into a popular moral crusade, converting a "pocket question" for the cotton lords into a symbol of a new community of interest and a new understanding of nation itself' (Howe 1997: 36). Yet the timing and scope of repeal was decided from within parliament and was part of a wider and more complicated political and economic picture than that which concerned the Lancashire cotton interests. In this arena outsiders may have orchestrated pressure, but they did not finally precipitate change, chiefly because the decisive battle was parliamentary and the League, after eight years of struggle, controlled neither the procedure nor the terms utilised (McCord 1958: 203–4). Rather, the timing was partly dictated by the prospect of the Irish potato famine, which gave Peel the opportunity to restructure Irish agriculture and break reliance on the potato, while the long-term support of trade liberalisation from the Board of Trade also proved significant (McCord 1958: 196–7; Brown 1958: 183; Kinnealy 1998: 13; Grampp 1987). Repeal must surely also be placed against wider economic and fiscal issues and especially the rise in government deficits during the severe depression from 1837–42. This made it easier for Peel to restore income tax and reduce duties on semi-manufactured and manufactured goods making the Corn Laws an anomaly. It is inconceivable that it could have been contemplated without these other tariff reforms which Peel secured in his 1842 budget (Lloyd-Jones 1998: 99). As had been the case in 1818, when duties on raw cotton were substituted for those on printed cottons, success in all campaigns for tax reform depended as much upon the revenue requirements of governments and their ability to tap alternative sources, as upon the bargaining power of particular interest groups.

If Lancashire's merchants favoured policy measures that widened the markets for cotton goods there was a creeping awareness, again among the mercantile community, that Lancashire was vulnerable to interruptions in raw cotton supplies from the United States. This affected Lancashire's attitude to India and gave rise to the apparent contradiction of arguing for free trade and *laissez faire* in the mother country, in one breath, whilst favouring government intervention to facilitate infrastructure development in India in the next (Moore 1964: 135–6; Harnetty 1972: 37). The cotton supply issue first raised its head in 1828, but it lacked the public profile accorded to free trade and was supported by only a handful of admittedly prominent merchants in the Manchester Chamber of Commerce. In fairness, by 1850 Manchester's MP Thomas Bazley had become alarmed at continued reliance on the United States, whilst a petition from the Manchester Chamber of Commerce expressed concern over the failure of the East India Company to undertake transport improvements in India (Harnetty 1972: 37). Although the Cotton Supply Association was founded in Manchester in 1857, only the American Civil War gave it any really significant profile in the frustrating process of campaigning for transport improvements in India. Ironically given the complete reliance of the Lancashire cotton industry on imported raw cotton, the Cotton Supply Association lacked the mass appeal of the Anti-Corn Law League even amongst the majority of cotton manufacturers and had very limited leverage as a pressure group. Industrial raw materials, however vital, ultimately ignited less political passion than food had a decade earlier (Silver 1966: 225–91; Howe 1984: 201).

Manchester's opposition to the East India Company's privilege can be traced back to the eighteenth century, when merchants and manufacturers petitioned parliament about the damage caused to their infant industry by the fine textiles the Company imported. With the growing technical superiority of Lancashire this stance shifted, however, to calls and petitions for free trade in the Indies which were, by the 1820s, seen as attractive markets (Redford 1934: 121–3). Progress was slow, however, and even the withdrawal of East India Company privileges did not signal an end to Lancashire's complaints, since the commercial interests believed that the Company's favourable credit arrangements seriously disadvantaged independent merchants. The establishment of the Government of India in 1858 replaced the East India Company. However, the growing importance of the Indian market in Lancashire trade meant that the subcontinent remained the focus of parliamentary petitions. In this period Indian import duties were raised entirely for revenue purposes and their level was very closely related to Indian finances. In 1859 debts incurred during the Indian Mutiny prompted an increase of duties on cotton yarn and goods from 5 per cent on cotton goods and 3.5 per cent on yarns to 10 per cent on goods and 5 per cent on yarn in order to reduce the Government of India's budget deficit. Inevitably Lancashire protested vigorously and eventually a war of attrition led to a restoration of the duties to their original levels in 1862 (Harnetty 1972: 9).

Lancashire's economic, social and political diversity, which at times had confused campaigns on commercial policy, also created divisions regarding domestic government policy, most especially in the sphere of factory reform. In general, hostility towards reductions in the hours children and women could work began with government interference in the 1830s and continued into the 1840s, as opposition to the Ten Hours Movement hardened. Yet there was never a consensus in Lancashire regarding the impact of factory reform, and attitudes were a reflection of the complicated forces influencing individual communities. The idea that those opposed were simply rural owners of water powered mills seeking to protect themselves against more sophisticated urban mills cannot, therefore, be sustained. Instead, those who opposed reductions in hours were mainly concerned about the impact of such restrictions on hours upon international competitive advantage and the consequent unwelcome choice between wage cuts and social unrest (Howe 1984: 182). At the same time, since there was a broad association between particular sectors, processes and technologies and the composition of the workforce, this also affected attitudes to reform. Consequently, in towns where mule spinning was prevalent, with its higher demand for adolescents rather than juveniles and women, support for reform was generally higher. Yet the political as well as the economic profile of individual communities contributed to their attitudes since the issue of factory reform became increasingly party political. Thus Tory employers in Oldham rallied behind radical MPs William Cobbett and John Fielden while there was support for reform in Blackburn, Wigan and Preston. Liberal masters were, on the other hand, more inclined to oppose it (Ward 1965–6: 197; Gray 1996: 107). The existence of such divisions, and their failure to coincide neatly with support or opposition to free trade, make it hard to sustain the argument that the Anti-Corn Law League was a front for the pursuit of the cotton interests' true concerns, namely the repeal of duties on raw cotton and a halting of factory reform. Certainly these were important issues for Lancashire cotton masters, but unity, particularly on factory reform, was even more illusive than on free trade (Anderson and Tollison 1985: 197–212).

The question of the political power of the cotton industry interest groups was every bit as complex in the United States as it was in Britain. There were significant regional variations in both the influence of specific groups and their stances on particular issues. In addition, in comparison with Britain there were inevitably sharp contrasts in attitudes to specific policies and upon those causes likely to stimulate a response. Factory regulation, for instance, so visible on the agenda of the Lancashire cotton masters was virtually a non-issue in the United States before 1860. Indeed the ante-bellum period in Massachusetts has been likened to a 'kind of manufacturer's dreamland' where the regulation of hours and labour conditions was minimal (Galambos 1966: 14). Nevertheless, in Pennsylvania child labour became controversial in the 1830s whilst, in the 1840s, pressure for a ten-hour day mounted in both Pennsylvania and in parts of New England. But legislators were reluctant to interfere in labour market arrangements and even where legislation was passed it was generally ineffective. Not until the 1850s was there any groundswell of support for a ten-hour day in Massachusetts which interestingly stimulated a voluntary reduction to eleven hours in Lowell (Kirk 1994: 153; Scranton 1983: 32 and 38).

If factory regulation was a relatively minor issue, commercial policy in general and protection in particular held centre stage with interest groups throughout this period. The vision of America as a free trade area encircled by external tariffs was embedded in the Constitution of 1787, despite the free trade leanings of some of its architects. Congress gained the right to raise taxes while abolishing inter-state tariffs, thus establishing, from the outset, the significance and sanctity of the domestic market for the new nation. This was followed two years later by the first of a long succession of tariff laws which culminated in that controversial peak of protectionism, the Smoot Hawley Tariff of 1930 (Taussig 1931: 14; Ratner 1972: 10 and 91). The 1789 tariff legislation was: 'necessary for the support of government, for the discard of the debts of the United States and the encouragement and protection of manufactures' (quoted in Ratner 1972: 91).

Set against the range of goods which were to be subject to duty of 5 per cent which included alcohol, food and drink, clothing, paper, a range of household goods and raw materials and a higher rate for luxuries it is clear that, in raising tariffs, Congress's motivation was finely balanced between the revenue requirements of a new hard-pressed government, a desire to protect industry and the need to demonstrate economic as well as political independence. In his *Report on Manufactures* of 1791 Alexander Hamilton observed that:

> a monopoly of the domestic market to its own manufactures [is] the reigning policy of manufacturing nations, a similar policy on the part of the United States, in every proper instance, is dictated, it might also be said, by the principles of distributive justice; certainly, by the duty of endeavouring to secure to their own citizens a reciprocity of advantages. (quoted in Ratner 1972: 100)

This highlighted the need for infant industry protection as essential to the pursuit and achievement of national wealth whilst articulating the central importance of the domestic market for the future prosperity of the United States. Nevertheless, the relative slowness of manufacturing development in the eighteenth century meant that the search for revenue, as opposed to protection, remained the driving force behind tariffs until 1816. However, even in this period, it is worth noting that by 1804 *ad valorem* tariff rates had progressively risen to 17.5 per cent with the increasingly enthusiastic support of industrialists in both Massachusetts and Pennsylvania (Ratner 1972: 95 and 100; Pincus 1977: 8–14; Eiselen 1932).

The war between Britain and France marked a turning point for American cotton textiles, for until this date the industry had received no special protection. The Non-Intercourse Act of 1809 was followed by war with England in 1812–14 when tariff levels were doubled to generate additional revenue to enable the government to finance hostilities. This measure also meant that normal trade was curtailed and the cotton

Table 5.1. *Tariffs and American cotton goods, 1789–1846 (%)*

	Ad valorem	Actual protection
4 July 1789	5	5
13 May 1800	15	15
5 Feb. 1816	35	35
27 Apr. 1816	25	n/a
22 May 1824	25	n/a
1830–2	25	71.12
1833–41	24	82.3
1843–6	30	291.24
1846	25	25

Sources: Taussig 1931: 114; Pincus 1977: 35; Baack and Ray 1974: 107.

industry gained an enormous stimulus (Taussig 1931: 16–17). Peace, however, reversed conditions, generating sharp increases in English imports. These inevitably precipitated a wave of bankruptcies, an upsurge in Anglophobia and immediate demands for increased tariffs (Dalzell 1987: 36; David 1970: 521).

The wartime success of the Boston Manufacturing Company illustrated the collective economic strength of the Boston Associates, whilst their political power and acumen materialised in their role in shaping the 1816 tariff.

Taussig observed that:

> The control of the policy of Congress at that time was in the hands of a knot of young men of the rising generation, who had brought about the war and who felt in a measure responsible for its results. There was a strong feeling among these that the manufacturing establishments which had grown up during the war should be assisted, though not as a permanent policy. (Taussig 1931: 18)

It might, therefore, be anticipated that cotton goods received unusually high *ad valorem* tariff rates under this legislation. As Table 5.1 shows, however, the *ad valorem* tariff was actually lower than during the war period (Baack and Ray 1973–4: 106). Some scholars have implied that both Appleton and Lowell were opposed to anything but a moderate tariff simply because their production methods were so efficient and the cloth they produced sufficiently novel and distinctive to render it unnecessary (Gregory 1975: 299; McGouldrick 1968: 31; Taussig 1931: 34). Such a conclusion would fly in the face of any idea of interest group influence on the shaping of United States government policy in this period. However, a more plausible explanation of the apparent moderation of their request lies in the complex political issues that surrounded it and the unlikely prospect of Congressional agreement to exceptionally high tariffs. At the very least there was likely to be spirited opposition from Southern senators to a prohibitive tariff, which they feared would lead to English retaliation, stifling their principal market for raw cotton. As the producers of the United States' principal export these were an interest group to be reckoned with even at this time. It appears, therefore, that mindful of the likely stance of his opponents, upon whom he and his collaborators relied for supplies of raw cotton, Francis Cabot Lowell successfully lobbied for a proposal which effectively disguised the degree of protection afforded to cotton goods but most especially to those cotton goods produced by the Boston Associates (Temin 1988: 897). As a consequence of his efforts the 25 per cent *ad valorem* tariff was subject to the proviso 'that all cotton cloths, or cloths of which cotton is the material of chief value . . . the original cost at which at the place whence imported shall be less than 25 cents per square yard shall be taken and deemed to have cost 25 cents per square yard and shall be charged with duty accordingly' (quoted in Baack and Ray 1974: 106).

The addition of a minimum specific duty of 6.25c per yard meant, in the first instance, that the cotton industry received significantly more protection than was implied by the quoted tariff rate as Table 5.1 demonstrates. This additional protection continued to be adjusted until the abolition of this disguised protection in 1846. This meant that for 30 years the actual rate of protection was sharply above the *ad valorem* rate. When the *ad valorem* rate rose in 1842 the next four years saw an incredible actual rate of protection of 291.24 per cent (Baack and Ray 1974: 107).

Sustaining the high level and specific form of protection owed much to the political strength of the Boston Associates and their ability to balance political expediency and economic necessity. Tariff protection therefore stemmed as much from the political power of one group of cotton manufacturers, as from the economic case for protection. Appleton's success in the Congressional elections of 1830 reinforced this position and meant the Boston Associates could be confident that their particular brand of protectionism would continue to find support. In addition the financial dependence of leading senators, such as John Davis and Daniel Webster, on the Associates, strengthened this policy further during the 1830s (O'Connor 1968: 35). Between 1816 and 1846 the political tactics of the Boston Associates ensured that they were able to use the duties to fulfil their economic objective – corporate security. The minimum duty aimed to protect the particular type of cloth produced by the corporations and was sustained at the expense of protection for other regions with differing product strategies and less political power. If the Associates' business strategies were a product of the group's cultural characteristics, it is also clear that economic and financial power reinforced their social cohesion and also brought them considerable political strength which simply was not shared by the other regions of the cotton industry. Indeed, despite their city's historic support of protection, the very diversity of Philadelphia's community and the dominance of a free trade mercantile elite meant it was not until the 1880s that its textile men became anything but a negligible political force (Lindstrom 1978: 39–40; Scranton 1989: 28). It is worth remembering, however, that tariff changes between 1825 and 1832 at least benefited both Lowell and Philadelphia (Scranton 1983: 128). Even a short-term coincidence of interests between regions was by no means inevitable, however, and representatives of the Rhode Island cotton industry complained that the 'protectionist' Appleton was indifferent to cries for enhanced protection from outside northern Massachusetts, even though these areas were not in direct competition with them. Moreover, as one of the architects of the 1832 and 1842 tariffs Appleton actually favoured lower rates than Congress was willing to accept (Gregory 1975: 299–300).

Changes in the minimum efficient duty, therefore, can be used to chart the external competitive threats to the corporations' cloths and be taken as a reflection of their product strategies as quality improved. The duties did not, therefore, initially discriminate against English cloth but against low labour-cost, hand-produced Indian cottons. These were the nearest equivalent to early northern Massachusetts cloths and the Associates could not compete with them (Temin 1988: 897–8). By the late 1820s, when the diffusion of power looms brought English sheeting into direct competition with that produced in the United States, the minimum price was raised to 35c with a minimum specific duty of 8.75c per yard. This again afforded considerable additional protection, for at this time the price of English sheeting has been estimated to be well below 35c per yard (Baack and Ray 1974: 106).

The significance of the adjustments to the minimum specific duty stretches beyond protection for particular cloths, however, and embraces wider political issues. These were, nonetheless, of fundamental importance to the overall strategy of reducing uncertainty which underpinned so many of the Associates' decisions. It is clear that one of the origins of the minimum specific duty was the desire to avoid contrariety with the Southern states. Yet, in the 1820s and 1830s *ad valorem* tariffs, at the level needed to provide a satisfactory degree of protection, would have undoubtedly brought the Massachusetts industrialists into direct conflict with the Southern planters. This would, of course, have been disastrous for their interests, at the very time when prominent Associates were trying to steer a middle course over the issue of slavery. Whilst abhorring the notion of slavery, a mixture of political realism and economic self-interest led the so-called Cotton Whigs to pursue a broadly co-operative relationship with an economy which they increasingly saw as complementary to their own. At the same time they favoured a relatively cautious attitude on the tariff as the best way of avoiding rocking the increasingly fragile Union of the United States (O'Connor 1968: 65). From the mid-1840s, however, their political power was undermined, not least by the growing unpopularity of their stand on slavery in Massachusetts. Equally, the dilution of the Associates' financial stake in the corporations reduced their collective impact. This period therefore marked a turning point in both the political and economic power of the Associates. This is not to say that the bulk producers ceased to be a major economic force in the 1840s. However, their ability to initiate tariff changes which met the specific requirements of their corporations shrank significantly. Taken along with free trade tendencies within Congress, whose decision was partly dependent upon Britain's repeal of the Corn Laws (Ratner 1972: 23), this may help to explain the timing of the abandonment of the minimum specific duty in 1846.

With no upward adjustment in the *ad valorem* rate, the 1846 Tariff Act was the nearest thing to free trade to affect the cotton industry in nearly 40 years and remained the pinnacle of liberalism until after the Second World War. If, however, 1846 marked the end of the Boston Associates' power to shape tariff policy to meet their own specific needs, campaigns for protection by the cotton lobby continued. Nor did this period mark the eclipse of the bulk by the batch producers in these quests for support. Moreover whilst tariff rates generally drifted downwards slightly under the 1857 Tariff Act, special consideration was given to cotton duties which remained at very similar levels as in 1846. Nevertheless, after a decade of struggling profits the Massachusetts' cotton manufacturers joined other industrial pressure groups campaigning for higher tariffs (Ratner 1972: 26–8). Clearly, in the United States, in the nineteenth century industry representatives were able to use both their economic influence and cumulative political experience to ensure that, for the most part, the tariff ran in their favour. They were helped by a decentralised political system which provided an ideal basis for interest groups to influence policy.

The balance of power

Given the size and strength of the Lancashire cotton industry by the middle of the nineteenth century, the potential bargaining power of its interest groups plainly exceeded that of equivalent groups in the United

States. It is extremely difficult to quantify the precise impact of interest groups, especially on the basis of international comparisons. This is especially the case because it is far rarer for a pressure group to alter a cornerstone of government policy than to achieve modifications which are broadly in line with government aspirations. Clearly the repeal of the Corn Laws was a major success for the Anti-Corn Law League, but pressure from Lancashire's industrial and commercial community was but one element, if a vital one, in the campaign for free trade. However, if the nineteenth century is taken as a whole the United States cotton industry achieved more consistent government support and favourable responses to pressure than in Britain as a result of the interaction of a range of economic, political and social factors. In many ways the Anti-Corn Law campaign had proved to be a false dawn in terms of the relative power of cotton interest groups. In subsequent years any trend in government policy in favour of cotton came more from a coincidence of wider policy objectives with those of cotton, than from the power of pressure groups.

There were a number of reasons why the power of Lancashire cotton was more limited than that found in the United States. In the first place, direct government involvement in the process of early industrial growth was limited and interactions between 'new' industry and government were more likely to be confrontational than co-operative. This is not to say that government policies had no impact on the nascent cotton industry. However, there was little that was equivalent to the state enthusiasm for industrial development demonstrated by both Massachusetts and Pennsylvania which, through the form of the American Constitution, inevitably fed into federal government policy and to Congressional attitudes to tariffs. In America, for example, the relative power of individual states meant that industrialists were in regular and close contact both with members of state legislatures and with Congressmen, which led to good information flows and enhanced the power of interest groups. The centralised system of British politics left no such opportunities even after the parliamentary and local government reforms of the 1830s. Instead whilst the local power of industrialists was enhanced by these changes, this was not translated into national leverage. Moreover, in Britain some mercantilist policies, such as the Act of 1721 prohibiting the sale, use or wearing of British printed calicoes, initially worked against the development of a cotton industry. It would seem, therefore, that at the very least, there was a greater meeting of minds between northern Massachusetts cotton manufacturers and Congress than ever existed between government and the cotton magnates in Britain.

In the eighteenth and early nineteenth centuries the cotton interests in Britain lacked the cohesion of the Boston Associates. The early British factory masters were a diverse group, scattered across Lancashire, Cheshire, Yorkshire, Derbyshire and Nottinghamshire with a range of backgrounds and religious persuasions, the majority owning tiny, often short-lived firms. This alone prevented the emergence of any coherent political identity during the Industrial Revolution itself. Even in the nineteenth century, as the industry became localised in Lancashire, there was considerable diversity in the religious affiliations, aspirations and political leanings of the county's numerous entrepreneurs. Certainly commercial capital was of fundamental importance to the early factory system and a Unitarian-dominated 'charmed circle' of leading Manchester merchant manufacturers emerged including the Gregs, Kennedys and Philips who were at the core of Manchester's commercial oligarchy. This group did dominate many of Manchester's key institutions and commercial organisations such as the Royal Exchange, the Manchester Chamber of Commerce and for a while the *Manchester Guardian*, while a group of mainly Tory merchants were able to conduct a form of collective diversification in the 1820s (Howe 1996: 102; Pearson 1991). There was, however, no eighteenth- (or even nineteenth-) century equivalent of the Boston Associates which, as an elite cabal, could lobby parliament with a united voice to secure supportive government policies in the cotton industry's formative stage.

Members of Lancashire's leading families may have been able to exert influence within their local business communities but, viewed as a whole, they were an extremely diverse group whose economic, social and political variety reduced any tendency to collective action. It is not, for example, possible to draw a stereotypical view of the Dissenting Lancashire businessman. Indeed by 1851, although Nonconformists did predominate and textile masters were more likely to be Nonconformist than the mass of the population, 49 per cent of Lancashire's cotton masters were Anglicans, who represented the largest single religious group (Howe 1984: 62–72). In addition, although the combination of commercial and industrial wealth meant that the Unitarians enjoyed considerable power and status, within Manchester in the first half of the nineteenth century, this was unusual, however. Outside Manchester, Anglicans more generally dominated mercantile elites and even within the city there existed a prominent group of Anglican merchants including the Birleys, the Cardwells and the Houldsworths (Pearson 1991: 384–5). In Lancashire's cotton towns considerable variation existed in the juxtaposition of different religious groupings within regions of the county and within particular towns and villages. In Lancashire's industrial villages, for example, millowners were predominantly Methodist but significant numbers of Preston's elite families, such as the Horrockses and the Birleys, were Anglican (Howe 1984: 67).

Lancashire's cotton elite was not, therefore, united by ties of religion. The nineteenth-century political map of Lancashire was every bit as complex. Moreover, the gulf between government and industry in Britain during the Industrial Revolution was of course exacerbated by the limited political representation of the cotton interests. In contrast to the political leverage which the Boston Associates could exert, in Britain, the cotton interests had barely any parliamentary representation before the First Reform Act of 1832. Between 1800 and 1831, therefore, only four of the 59 MPs returned for Lancashire had textile connections (Howe 1984: 90). Certainly the First Reform Act brought representation for Lancashire's textile masters and meant that between 1832 and 1859 between 30 and 40 per cent of Lancashire's MPs were from this group, the overwhelming majority of whom were Liberal (Howe 1984: 96). However, the political affiliations of the vast majority of textile employers are marked as much by divisions as by unity, while evidence also confirms significant shifts in affiliation within cotton towns through time. Consequently whereas in Lancashire, as a whole, 58 per cent of cotton masters voted Liberal, only 38 per cent of Rochdale employers voted in this way, as compared with 76 per cent of Oldham employers. Tory employers, on the other hand, although in the minority, were not insignificant in this period (Howe 1984). It was these variations which formed the basis of the social and cultural, as well as the economic distinctiveness of local communities. They also meant that the dynastic tendencies in the Lancashire cotton industry did not result in countywide elite strategies to mould the business environment.

Certainly the electoral reform of the 1830s did bring the first real prospect of political influence, whilst Lancashire's electoral volatility in the 1860s and 1870s meant that the cotton industry had the power to exert pressure on both political parties (Howe 1984: 90; Harnetty 1972: 33; Dewey 1978: 58–9). However, in the late nineteenth century the centralisation of British politics, on the basis of national party organisations as opposed to local political associations, further impaired the bargaining power of the cotton industry which had been organised regionally (Dewey 1978: 58–9).

Although easily the most powerful industrial group in parliament the overall influence of Lancashire's MPs on policy and of cotton pressure groups on government faltered before a profound cultural gap between the provincial commercial groups and factory masters and the majority of the governing classes, whether in London or in India. This was in sharp contrast to the City of London which displayed that considerable cohesion which derived from intermarriage and close personal contact in the square mile. Moreover, intermarriage with the aristocracy meant that

City representatives increasingly shared the cultural attributes of those in government which, combined with the great wealth and power of the merchant banks, placed them in a privileged position with respect to government policy. This meant they exercised infinitely greater bargaining power with government than Lancashire. Thus it has been suggested that cotton industry pressure was only successful if it did not conflict with City interests (Cain and Hopkins 1993: 26–41). Not only was the cultural gap between government and industry not replicated in the United States, there was not a comparable conflict between financial and industrial interests.

Summary

The domestic orientation of the United States cotton industry in the nineteenth century was inseparable from the tariff. In other words the institutional environment had a direct bearing on both the strategy and structure of business. America's political system allowed interest groups to influence tariff policy and this shaped the expectations which moulded business policy. In the nineteenth century that position was, however, complicated by the existence of three regional, initially non-competing cotton industries and a cotton-growing region. For much of the century the interests of northern Massachusetts dominated a reflection of the considerable financial and political power of a cohesive, wealthy and well-connected group of Bostonians. Their comparative security over the domestic market and the expectation that it would remain theirs by right encouraged investment in rapid throughput technologies. On the other hand, in the ante-bellum period, mindful of the consequences of a breach with the South, the Associates' demands for direct protection were fairly modest. In Philadelphia any semblance of political unity among industrialists was vastly complicated by the diversity of the industry and the sectoral divisions which existed.

Tariff protection of cotton manufacturing in the United States has been explained on the grounds of the 'learning by doing' effects on productivity in an infant industry (David 1970; Zevin 1971). There can be no doubt that the distinctive strategies and structures of northern Massachusetts corporations were shaped by protection and that these did involve productivity improvements. At the very least changes to the minimum specific duty brought the relative economic security necessary to encourage investment in the distinctive technologies and organisational forms of the new corporations. Similarly the high rates of profitability (as compared with other cotton textile regions), which lasted until the 1840s, could be linked to the enhanced efficiency which these strategies brought. However, the collapse in profitability on the abolition of the minimum specific duty and the upsurge of English imports, which more than tripled by value between 1844–6 and 1854–6, must make any such conclusion suspect (McGouldrick 1968: 119; Gregory 1975: 301; Davis 1979: 19). It implies instead that the supposed 'learning by doing' effects of tariffs on productivity had been comparatively slow to take effect and that without significant protection the northern Massachusetts cotton industry would simply have been wiped out before reaching maturity (Bils 1984: 1038–45). Indeed it seems that at no time in the ante-bellum period did the productivity gains of the corporations make them proof against foreign imports (Harley 1992: 560). Moreover calculations on the effective rate of protection suggest that after the Civil War the cotton industry received disproportionate if, possibly, unintentional tariff support (Hawke 1975: 87). It is worth remembering that northern Massachusetts received a level of protection not matched in other cotton regions which were, by the nature of their product mix, more susceptible to British competition. The survival and growth of the other regions in different domestic niches, without the benefit of the same degree of protection, implies a competitive advantage that was based upon more than costs and productivity. Indeed it is conceivable that the lower level of protection afforded to Philadelphia, as compared with northern Massachusetts, may have reinforced existing business strategies of flexible specialisation. Although more research is needed, it is plausible that having no chance to compete with British and European producers on price, the incentive for greater American specialisation increased as the nineteenth century progressed. In so doing United States millmen could in part counteract the impact of foreign competitors since they inevitably enjoyed closer contact with the volatile New York fashion markets than did producers overseas.

In the British case early export orientation encouraged increasing commercial specialisation which was reinforced and extended by the coming of free trade. The structure and contours of the British cotton industry were undoubtedly shaped by the characteristics of the markets served and by the coming of free trade and by the tariff reforms surrounding it. The ability to penetrate vast overseas markets and especially access to the India market made Lancashire the home of the world's largest cotton industry with its distinctive vertically specialised structure. Yet reliance on overseas trade brought increased uncertainty, which the Lancashire cotton interests sought to reduce through exerting political influence on government. It has been argued for the twentieth century that the vertical specialisation of the Lancashire cotton industry reduced its ability to respond to change by giving a unified response to external pressures (Lazonick 1986). It is also clear that such a structure made a concerted political response to external threats more difficult. However, it has become evident that even in the nineteenth century, when Lancashire's power was most profound, a number of interrelated socio-political factors reduced its effectiveness as a pressure group, especially in comparison with equivalent groups in the United States.

Part II

Continuity and change

6 Consolidation and change, 1860–1914

The preceding four chapters have explored the forces which shaped the evolution of business attitudes and the emergence of networks in the British and American cotton industries before 1860. Their findings are summarised in Table 6.1 which demonstrates that, whilst sharing the common concerns of production, profitability and market penetration, businessmen on either side of the Atlantic often displayed differences in priorities, perceptions and behaviour. These were born of the varying social, political and economic forces to which they were subject, and in turn were translated into the culture of business. For example, the production-driven strategies, detected in much of the United States cotton industry, clearly only partly resulted from resource allocation. Rather they derived from a combination of collective approaches to community development traceable even to the colonial period, from a faith in the power of technology which was rarely contradicted by the workforce and the habitual transience of the workforce plus a confidence in a protected domestic market. Yet in Britain eighteenth- and early nineteenth-century infant industry protection against cheap colonial imports allowed the successful development of cotton manufacturing. However, the constraints of a small, but strongly differentiated domestic market, combined with overseas opportunities, brought with it greater market complexity than was then the case in America and significantly enhanced the relative power of mercantile groups, as opposed to manufacturers. This factor, combined with a need for cheap imported raw materials, a reliance on overseas markets for business expansion and the social and political forces which brought free trade, led to a shift in government policy in favour of liberalism. This meant that British protection did not become institutionalised in the way that it did in the United States. The pattern of industrial growth, on the other hand, closely matched existing pockets of skill and, where migration occurred, it was over short distances with skilled workers often remaining within a single community, even if not with the same firm. This contributed to the development of distinctive capabilities in particular communities, to the importance of shopfloor

Table 6.1. *Business culture and business strategy in the United States and British cotton industries to 1860*

United States	United Kingdom
1. Forces at work: • recent settlement • colonial past • domestic market • growing homogeneous market • resources and abundance • regional distinctive, largely complementary development • relative strength of manufacturers • regional machine making capabilities • scarcity of skill, labour transience, weak labour organisation • decentralised political system • social sytem based on achievement	**Forces at work:** • proto-industry/advanced economy, skills • protection initially • Empire • small home market • heterogeneous market • geographic concentration in Lancashire • enhanced power of merchants • differentiated labour market, strong skilled labour organisation • community based machine making • reliance on imported raw materials • centralised political system • social system based on land
2. Business attitudes: • willingness to pursue collective community strategies to facilitate development often involving corporations • openness • confidence in domestic market and supplies of raw material • faith in the tariff • belief in power of technology • expectation of short labour attachments • limited training • unwillingness to negotiate with unions	**Business attitudes:** • unplanned but evolutionary community development based on partnerships • secrecy • awareness of market vulnerability (e.g. especially overseas and relating to raw material supplies) • increasing belief in free trade • importance of technological versatility • emphasis on community specific shopfloor training • reluctant acceptance of the position of unions
3. Impact on business strategy: • family business increasingly corporate • production driven • vertical integration • coarse products • high labour productivity • rapid throughput • skill and labour saving technology • co-operative product strategy • interlocking directorates	**Impact on business strategy:** • family partnerships • market driven • trend towards vertical integration reversed by 1850 • spatial specialisation • product specialisation • versatile technology • development of loose vertical networks

training and to the increasing potential (if not always the actual) power of trade unions.

In terms of national industrial structure both industries can best be described as atomistic, displaying low levels of concentration and high rates of business turnover. In both Britain and the United States, however, the local business community was the vital canvas for all aspects of business activity and indeed for social and political influence. Both the internal and external functioning of Lancashire's communities was quite unlike those in New England, however.

National dissimilarities in the historical forces affecting business strategy, which had emerged by 1860, mask local variations which were predicated on the role of community in early industrialisation. The disparate types of family firms, which have been detected in the United States, were a reflection of the distinctive regional cultures of predominantly complementary sectors. Similarly, in Britain, the trend towards spatial specialisation, admittedly then by no means as pronounced as it subsequently became, was in part a reflection of the diverse capabilities and characteristics of individual communities within Lancashire. To understand the development of business attitudes in subsequent periods and the decisions that were made, it is necessary to appreciate the complex changes which occurred within and between communities. Only when regional and local variations in business behaviour are appreciated, will it be possible to make sense of the national picture. Yet, if historical forces moulded responses, forces for change and their interaction at the local and national levels altered expectations and hence business styles and the behaviour of businessmen.

Despite its relatively slow and modest beginnings, by the second half of the nineteenth century the American cotton industry ranked second in the world after Britain, in terms of capacity. Thereafter, as Table 6.2 shows, whereas the giant Lancashire cotton industry experienced sustained if decelerating growth, during the late nineteenth and early twentieth centuries the most rapid expansion of cotton manufacturing in the United States came after 1860 and most particularly after 1880. By 1910 spindleage in the United States had more than doubled and loomage tripled. Although the respective export orientation of British growth and the domestic focus of American growth pointed to considerable continuities with the past and hence to factors which reinforced business attitudes, there were substantial forces for change at work in this period. The American Civil War marked a major watershed in the development of the cotton industries of both Britain and the United States, though in very different ways, whilst world depression in the 1880s and 1890s was also significant for its impact on business behaviour. Equally, growing import

Table 6.2. *The capacity of the British and United States cotton industries, 1860–1914*

	No. of firms		Spindleage (m)		Loomage (000)		Employment (000)	
Date	UK	US	UK	US	UK	US	UK	US
1860	n/a	n/a	30.4[a]	5.2	400[a]	126	452	122
1880	1,874[b]	56	39.8	10.7	485	226	486	175
1890	1,801	905	43.8	14.4	606	325	529	219
1900	1,787	973	43.9[c]	19.5	649	451	523	298
1910	1,977	1,324	53.4	28.3	741	665	577[d]	310

Notes:
[a] This is the figure for 1861.
[b] This is the figure for 1882.
[c] This is the figure for 1903.
[d] This is the figure for 1907.
Sources: Mitchell 1988: 370, 371, 376, 377; Jones 1933: 277; Cotton Yarn Association 1929: 9; Farnie 1979: 180; Robson 1957: 355.

substitution and international protectionism had particularly important implications, especially for the experience of British exporters.

The American Civil War 1861–5

The vulnerability of Lancashire, as a result of an increasing reliance upon American raw cotton, was recognised prior to the Civil War, and is reflected in the formation of the Cotton Supply Association in 1857. On the eve of the Civil War 80 per cent of all cotton consumed in Britain came from the United States (Augur 1979: 36). It is easy to exaggerate the impact of the American Civil War on the supply of raw cotton in Lancashire and the extent to which it precipitated depression. Nevertheless, it had profound and lasting consequences for the profile of the cotton industries in both Britain and the United States. The war affected the competitive environment whilst having ramifications for both technology and for the politics of business on either side of the Atlantic.

The years immediately before the Civil War had witnessed unprecedented industrial expansion in Lancashire and by 1861 there were already signs of over-capacity and the threat of bankruptcies. This meant that the blockade of Southern ports had an enlivening impact on expectations and hence benefited those with growing stock levels. The resultant speculation, mainly by larger manufacturers, on likely future price levels of raw cotton, combined with a willingness among some leading Liverpool merchants to re-export raw cotton for sale to manufacturers in New England, contributed far more to supply difficulties than the generally ineffective Union blockade (Farnie 1975: 157–8). In addition, whilst suspicion that Indian Surat was an imperfect substitute for American cotton remained, it proved more versatile than was anticipated, at least for the coarser types of yarn. By 1864 67 per cent of raw cotton imported into the UK came from India (Logan 1965: 40).

Short-time working became the norm in those Lancashire communities reliant on the cotton industry and, even if there was some exaggeration of the degree to which the workforce was impoverished, the problem of relief was significant. By December 1862 247,230 operatives were out of work and 485,434 people depended on relief (Ellison 1972: 15). However, the impact of the so-called Cotton Famine was felt unevenly in the varied communities. Consequently in towns such as Ashton and Preston, 26 per cent and 21 per cent of the population respectively were in receipt of relief in November 1862, whilst in Bolton, with its reliance on Egyptian cotton, a mere 6.7 per cent of the population were classed as being paupers (Ellison 1972: 222). Experience and responses depended upon a combination of the economic, social and political profile of individual towns. Certainly this was a period of difficulty, but the American Civil War has been described grandly as a 'fundamental turning point in the history of Lancashire' and did prove to be an important precursor of lasting changes in the economic and political balance of the county. Some of these are vital to understanding the national divergence in the capabilities of the British and American cotton industries and to the choices made by businessmen (Farnie 1979: 167).

A town's experience during the Cotton Famine depended upon a range of factors which included the level of economic diversity, the type of product, the type and size of firms, markets served and the cotton used. It was inevitable, therefore, that those towns which had the worst experience were those heavily reliant upon American cotton, which found the substitution of Indian Surat problematic, and where the town was dominated by the cotton industry. In this category lay Ashton-under-Lyne, the worst hit of the cotton towns and where, according to the Factory Inspector's Report of 1864: 'Manufacturers . . . spin and weave numbers finer than 32s [and] find considerable difficulties in their way of producing with a mixture of cotton, yarn and goods equal to what they had been accustomed to make' (quoted in Augur 1979: 52). By contrast, Henry Ashworth could write to Cobden in 1862:

> Bolton, I am happy to say forms a most enviable exception to this deplorable state of misfortune. The mills there are supplied with cotton chiefly from Egypt, the Brazils and to some extent from South Carolina, consequently they are not likely to be deprived of raw material. . . . Their dealings are principally with the stuff manufacturers of Bradford, whose trade is become so largely increased by the French Treaty. (quoted in Augur 1979: 55)

If Bolton weathered the crisis with little damage, it was in Oldham that there emerged creative responses which had lasting implications for the technological profile and ultimately the competitive structure of the industry as a whole. There, the production of coarser yarns, in the first instance, allowed the relatively easy substitution of Indian Surats and increasingly cotton waste – long an Oldham specialism (Augur 1979: 58). Far from being a negative period for Oldham manufacturers, it was during the Civil War that the foundations for their subsequent dominance of coarse spinning were laid. The improvement of the self acting mule, by local machine makers Platt Bros, increased both its speed of operation and versatility so that finer counts could be spun on these machines. Between 1861 and 1863 spinners, who had secured large gains from speculating on rising raw cotton prices, were able to invest profitably in new spindleage on long, fast machines in large, new mills at the very time when many millowners were working short-time. Nor was innovation only the preserve of Oldham, for in Blackburn there was a shift among weavers to the production of bordered Dhooties using technology originally developed in 1858 and reliant upon Oldham yarn. As in Oldham, far from marking a period of contraction, Blackburn loomage rose by a third so that the town accommodated a quarter of Lancashire's looms by the end of the American Civil War. Burnley, on the other hand, developed an increasing reliance upon Oldham for yarn and produced light printing cloths in place of T cloths, while in Rochdale there was a shift towards a greater production of woollens and flannels. In addition, throughout the weaving sector, techniques were developed to accommodate lower quality Surats and to economise on the use of raw cotton; consequently 'steaming' and the use of heavy sizing were introduced.

The years of the Cotton Famine, therefore, saw a reinforcement of patterns of spatial specialisation which, although building on earlier technological, machine making and organisational capabilities, also created new ones. For example, this crisis marked the end of the pre-eminence of the small-scale firm, certainly in spinning, and stifled the early stirrings of co-operation in manufacturing, since cynically both these types of firms lacked the resources necessary to enjoy large, appreciating stocks and to speculate in cotton futures. Conversely, the period provided the foundations of future investment activity for those large firms which prospered in the 1860s. Consequently, of the industrial changes which began with the American Civil War, easily the most important was the shift in the structure of firms, technology and the finance of business which occurred in Oldham, for in due course it was to influence the competitive structure of the entire Lancashire cotton industry. The Civil War also served as the death knell for the peripheral country districts, where cotton manufacturing had originally taken root in the early phases of the Industrial Revolution, which were unable to sustain the impact of rising raw material prices. This in turn reinforced the concentration of the industry in Lancashire's south-eastern corner.

The Civil War marked a political as well as an economic watershed in Lancashire. It can be argued that apart from the riots in Ashton and Preston, the comparative docility of the workforce was a testimony to the success of 'new paternalism' and contributed to the extension of the suffrage to the working man in 1867. Yet the fatal irony for Lancashire's cotton masters lay in the 1868 election, a year after the passage of the Reform Act, when working men exerted a legendary independence from Liberal masters and secured an overwhelming Conservative victory. That they were stirred up in part by an indifference to their plight during the 'famine', which was alleged by the Tory press during and after the Civil War, seems likely (Farnie 1975: 155–76; Farnie 1979: 139–67; Joyce 1980: 150–1). The emergence of working-class conservatism, therefore, provides compelling evidence of the limits of the 'new paternalism'. It also ended the potential for national pre-eminence of the cotton masters, through the Liberal party (Farnie 1975: 176). Despite political divisions in Lancashire this had given them a visible parliamentary presence which could have provided greater leverage on those issues, such as Indian tariffs, which were to become so important in the late nineteenth century as the Indian market grew.

Given the prominence of the Civil War in American political history it comes as a surprise to find that, superficially at least, its immediate impact upon the profile of the cotton industry was relatively limited. Unlike some new industrial sectors, the industry as a whole did not share in the stimulus for change and expansion provided by the war effort. Certainly the huge disturbances to textile markets, caused by the Civil War, led two out of seven bulk corporations to shut down for its duration, while their owners made large profits from the sale of accumulated and appreciating stocks of raw cotton. This meant that for the bulk producers of northern Massachusetts the period was little more than a brief break in the trend of growth, with little lasting impact upon the strategy and structure of firms. No Lowell corporation failed and expansion resumed fairly promptly after 1865, financed in part from wartime gains (McGouldrick 1968: 6;

Gross 1993: 35–6; Scranton 1983: 312). Yet in the relatively rapid resumption of 'business as normal' lay the problem that the inflexibility of the bulk system, for so long a competitive benefit, had neared its limit during the war and would be seriously tested in the changing competitive environment of the late nineteenth century.

By taking what was in effect the line of least resistance during the Civil War, the business strategy of northern Massachusetts contrasted with that pursued in Philadelphia, where batch producers were better able to respond creatively to the challenges of the period. Rather than shut down their firms, Philadelphia's manufacturers, encouraged in part by the 1861 Morrill Tariff, simply switched production to woollens to meet growing government demands for uniforms and in response to shortages of raw cotton. Consequently, many cotton firms shifted with apparent ease into wool and carpet manufacture and their ability to do so was based upon a combination of skill and specialty. In so doing they were pursuing an option that simply was not imaginable for all but a few bulk producers. In Lowell, therefore, only those corporations with a previous history of woollen manufacturing were able to shift. On the other hand, those few firms that did change strategy, in the face of the war, were not especially successful and encountered serious losses and were eventually forced to withdraw from such experiments. In Philadelphia, however, the majority were merely carrying their strategy of flexible production to its logical conclusion. This trend continued into the 1870s and 1880s, and as a result of the Civil War Philadelphia became better known for the production of woollen hosiery, carpets and worsteds than for cottons whilst many firms mixed woollens and cottons with considerable success (Scranton 1983: 212, 280–8).

If the Civil War indirectly demonstrated the economic shortcomings of the Lowell corporations, it ended the political power of the Boston Associates for ever. Their long-standing efforts to keep slavery out of the political arena and their support, after 1846, of lower tariffs were increasingly seen for what they were – an effort to appease the South and so protect their own economic interests. This strategy alienated them from their fellow New Englanders, rendering the so-called Cotton Whigs a spent force and opening the way to the Republicans as the party of industry and not cottons (Dalzell 1987: 221–3; O'Connor 1968: 97–9). This meant that the personal leverage of this once powerful group vanished and, during the confused postwar reconstruction, Boston's merchants and industrialists found themselves compelled to form a somewhat unlikely alliance of convenience with Philadelphia's mercantile community. Both groups were united in a desire that the South should be penalised, especially whilst their representatives were excluded from Congress, and a growing realisation existed that the rise of new industries during the war fundamentally altered the equation with regards to government–industry relations. A whole range of new sectors required infant industry protection, whilst Philadelphia merchants and industrialists were keen for continued protection of their expanding woollen sector. Boston's merchants and industrialists were less than wholehearted about high textile tariffs but, in 1866, allied with Philadelphia to secure the introduction of an excise duty on raw cotton to protect their position in the market for cheap cotton goods in the face of England's increased use of low-value Indian raw cotton (Cohen 1962: 146; Woolfolk 1958).

> Triumphant radicalism, enthroned at Washington, was knee deep in plans to reward the economic faithful. The system of tariffs, drawbacks, tax reductions and bounties and government organised exploitation of the Southern region, sponsored by the Boston-Philadelphia merchant-dominated political alliance, was being pushed to completion with every pressure tactic possible. (Woolfolk 1958: 76)

The failure of this ploy stemmed largely from the economic chaos of the South, which was unable to deliver a large cotton crop. By 1868 Congress abolished the excise duty and Massachusetts' capitalists rapidly abandoned their former allies in their quest for protection, fearing that higher tariffs would stimulate further competition at home (Cohen 1962: 146). High duties on all cotton goods, however, remained until 1872, when a 10 per cent reduction in the *ad valorem* tariff still left rates well above their low point in the 1840s. The 1880s saw a further shift upwards in cotton duties, though this time in ways which favoured the increasingly well organised Philadelphia producers. Significant variations in tariff rates for particular categories of textiles remained, however, and those which could not be produced in the United States such as fine goods, lace and embroideries, continued virtually unprotected in the nineteenth century (Copeland 1912: 232–48; Ratner 1972: 29–30). In the late nineteenth century another force, quite separate from the relative power of interest groups, served to further institutionalise protection of the cotton industry. From the 1880s onwards the tariff became a central foreign policy issue for the federal government. From being essentially a domestic policy issue tied to the interests of industry and the revenue needs of government, the tariff became inextricably linked to nationalism and to a growing isolationism which began to spill over into Anglophobia (Terrill 1973: 3). This shaped Republican legislation in the 1890s which, whilst finding favour in the Republican-dominated Northern states, was unpopular in the South where Democrats remained largely free traders.

Table 6.3. *British cotton piece good exports, 1860–1919*

Date	m yds, av. p.a.
1860–9	2,374
1870–9	3,572
1880–9	4,674
1890–9	5,057
1900–9	5,648
1910–19	5,459

Source: Mitchell 1988: 356–7.

Strategic response in a changing world, 1865–1914

In the years before 1860 British firms enjoyed an absolute advantage in world markets for cotton goods. However, as the nineteenth century progressed, there was an increasing trend towards import substitution and protection, especially in Europe and North America, areas which had been so important to Britain in the first half of the nineteenth century. This altered the trading environment faced by Lancashire and contributed to a shift in orientation towards the diverse markets of Empire. This shift, as Table 6.3 shows, was associated with a sustained, although decelerating growth in exports of cotton piece goods and more especially in yarn exports. Cloth exports peaked in 1913 at 7,100m yds at a time when 80 per cent, by value, of British cotton cloth was exported, a proportion that was far higher than in the early nineteenth century, whereas the growth of cotton yarn exports, on the other hand, peaked by the 1870s (Marrison 1996b: 239).

The opportunity to expand exports to Empire was closely associated with the international financial impact of the City of London, which featured so strongly in the rise in both portfolio and foreign direct investment, especially in resource exploitation and services in the Dominions, the Far East and Latin America (Cain and Hopkins 1993). The combination of infrastructure development with primary production and the expansion of financial and commercial services fostered opportunities for trade throughout the Empire in the late nineteenth century. These forces raised real incomes and hence the capacity to consume in the Dominions which were, in turn, experiencing high levels of immigration. At the same time transport and communications improvements, most especially the development of steam shipping and the telegraph, facilitated long-distance trade and the more rapid flows of both goods and commercial intelligence. These

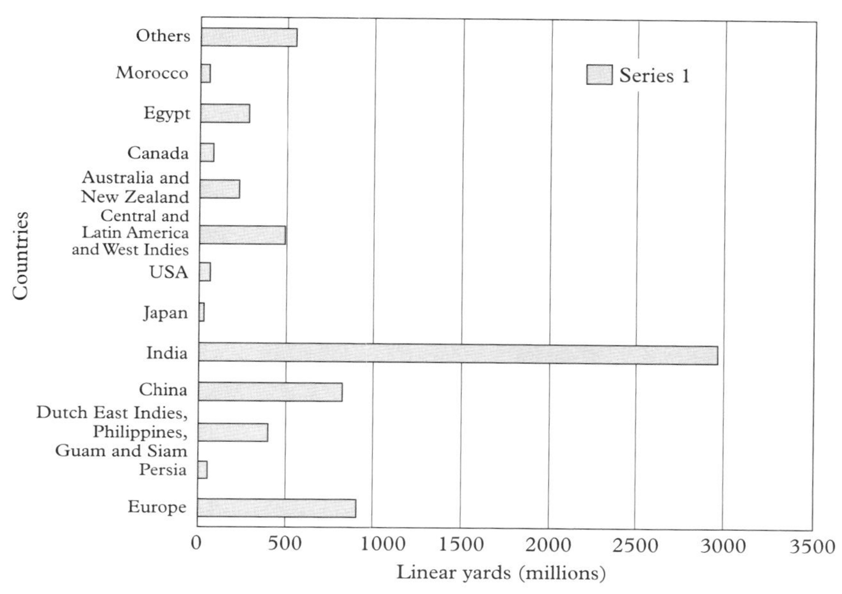

Fig. 6.1 Destinations of British cotton cloth exports
Source: Chapman & Kemp 1915: 169

forces helped to create a diverse array of markets for Lancashire's products, ranging from the high income markets of Canada, Australia and New Zealand to the low income markets of Africa, Asia and the Far East. Of these, by far the largest was India, which consumed almost 31 per cent of the value of Lancashire cotton goods in 1886 and was of overwhelming importance as a destination for exports as Figure 6.1 shows (Farnie 1979: 119).

Inseparable from Britain's external economic policies, the growth of the Indian market critically depended upon India's status within the Empire and upon Britain's maintenance of free trade. The surplus that developed provided, moreover, the key to the smooth operation of multilateral settlements and to the functioning of the international gold standard. A combination of Indian railway development, as British influence grew, and the expansion of British shipping capacity helped to open the Indian market and reduced transport costs, whilst the ability of the British government to restrict Indian tariffs ensured that British exports of cotton goods were relatively unimpeded. On the other hand the opening of the Suez Canal in 1869, which facilitated the export of the subcontinent's primary products, increased India's capacity to import manufactured goods. Of critical importance to the expansion of the trade was the growing network of English- and Scottish-owned agency houses in India and the Far East. They improved information flows and hence reduced commercial transaction costs. In addition, such developments in the organisation of trade, which were the product of group activity by interconnected families, were matched by an increasingly sophisticated network of overseas banks to finance international trade in the region (Chapman 1992: 107–28; Jones 1993: 13–62).

The significance of India for Lancashire, was that it dwarfed all other markets, but Farnie has rightly warned against according it too much significance in Lancashire's overall pattern of development (Farnie 1979: 119). Certainly the vast unprotected Indian market, which continued to grow in absolute if not relative terms until 1913, encouraged the dramatic expansion of the coarse 'American' spinning section of the industry, especially around Oldham, and the expansion of weaving in north-east Lancashire, particularly in Blackburn and Burnley. An 'Indian summer' of capacity-growth therefore occurred before the First World War (Marrison 1996a: 238–64). The impact of the Indian market on the quality of goods exported by Britain was, however, marginal since new evidence suggests that most British yarn exports to India were above 30s (Sandberg 1968: 1–27; Kawakatsu 1998: 297–314). Nor did India give Lancashire its distinctive characteristics as a sophisticated industrial district. What reversed the pre-1850 trend towards vertical integration and led to the unrivalled spatial specialisation was the diversity and changing nature of markets served, especially in the market for cloth, which created opportunities for product and market shifting. This was fostered by, and in turn encouraged, the growing number of specialist and often foreign shipping houses which developed in Manchester (Chapman 1996: 80–1). In addition, although only a small and declining proportion of British cotton cloth was consumed domestically, in absolute terms domestic consumption grew even as this market also displayed considerable diversity.

Cotton cloth had been a fashion good since the early eighteenth century and had featured in working-class dress well before 1800. However, the emergence and expansion of the ready-made clothing trade proved vital in increasing the extent to which cotton cloths were worn across all levels of society. The growing use of the sewing machine and especially the Singer Sewing Machine, once the American company established its factory in Scotland in 1886, brought down costs and widened the market for an ever growing range of goods still further (Godley 1995; Godley 1996; Levitt 1996: 167–76).

Industrial change, at the community level, continued in Lancashire during the late nineteenth and early twentieth centuries in response to these forces. Outstanding, and indeed in many respects atypical, was the sustained growth of Oldham, where between 1866 and 1885 spindleage rose from 3m to 10m, primarily in new Limited Companies. By 1914 the town housed 29 per cent of UK spindles and represented the largest concentration of spinning mills in the world (Marrison 1996a: 244). Limiteds were funded first by Oldham's working-class operatives and skilled ancillary workers. They had developed a taste for co-operatives, whilst changing company legislation gave them the opportunity to apply these principles to industry (Farnie 1979: 252). Working-class capitalism was, however, a relatively short-lived phenomenon in Oldham, yet its aftermath continued to play a role in the town's financial policies and technological strategies in the late nineteenth and early twentieth centuries. Increasingly profits earned in the Oldham Limiteds, especially by those in the ancillary trades, including machine makers, were reinvested (by increasingly wealthy and powerful shareholding groups which initiated new, mainly private ventures via the mill building companies) in the booms of the early twentieth century. Predictably these firms also invested in mules, which in any event, as new evidence suggests, remained profitable at least until the First World War (Leunig 1996; Toms 1996). This outcome had implications for business behaviour generally in the years before 1914. In Lancashire as a whole, but especially in Oldham which was the heart of the county's capital market, although family business retained its importance, a group of entrepreneurs emerged who can be classed as financial capitalists. These individuals owed their wealth to the relatively high dividend payments of the Oldham Limiteds. They created loose coalitions of firms through either share purchases or company flotation and engaged in an extensive mill building campaign in the years immediately before the First World War. Moreover, their activity generated the increasing sophistication of the provincial stock exchanges, of which Oldham was one of the most active. These factors undoubtedly helped to provide a model for Lancashire's distinctive holding company structure while creating wealth which formed the basis of subsequent financial syndicates (Toms 1994: 363–83; Toms 1996: 249–53; Broadberry 1997: 189; Thomas 1973: 145–68).

The rise of the Oldham Limiteds was not replicated in any other cotton town. Yet the emergence of publicly owned companies in cotton spinning broke Lancashire's mould in terms of plant size. Moreover, the new capacity with which this was associated altered the competitive and financial balance of the industry far beyond Oldham. Combined with the external market changes the competitive shock of Oldham's emergence, as Lancashire's major spinning centre, helped to give the county its distinctive late nineteenth-century features. It therefore contributed to the horizontal structure of the industry, to the high level of both spatial and vertical specialisation and to the continued bias for flexible manufacturing technologies and for craft-based work organisation. The expansion of Oldham spindleage also contributed to the intensification of horizontal, mainly local competition, which gave way to a trend, first towards association and then amalgamation, commencing before the First World War and gathering pace in the interwar period. Equally it reinforced the distinctive local cultures of the cotton towns, giving them identities which survived even after the disappearance of the cotton industry in the late twentieth century.

The expansion of south Lancashire's spinning, with its close links to the perfection of steam power and the growth of textile engineering, contributed to the geographical separation of spinning and weaving. Certainly the process of geographic specialisation began well before the 1880s and was underpinned in part by the evolution of loom manufacturing in Blackburn between 1820 and 1880. However, the enlargement of Oldham's yarn production reinforced Blackburn's position and it emerged as the largest single centre of cloth production for the Indian market, relying almost entirely on Oldham's 'American' yarn. As in Oldham, where Platt Brothers and Co played a vital role in the continued trial and error improvements to the mule, so in Blackburn local machine makers and their close and regular contact with manufacturers proved important to the town's response. It was a pattern repeated elsewhere where local machine making industries had developed. Thus Oldham's rise also provided a stimulus to Burnley, whilst Nelson and Colne moved towards finer production using mainly the Egyptian yarns produced by Bolton spinners. Similarly Bolton machine makers Dobsons and Barlow continued to perfect the mule for finer counts (Farnie 1979: 301, 308–11; Farnie 1990: 151; Clay 1931: 25).

Preston's development differed in a number of ways from the other cotton towns. It was dominated by relatively few large firms, lacked a machine making industry and displayed a preference for private rather than public companies. Rather than pursuing price competition with other late nineteenth-century centres, Preston's manufacturers increasingly concentrated on adding value. This was especially the case with Horrockses, one of Preston's oldest and most dominant firms which had expanded exports to the Chinese and Latin American markets in the nineteenth century, while building a strong reputation in the home market (Farnie 1979: 310–11; Chapman 1996: 85).

The thousands of overseas shipping houses which had proliferated in Manchester remained family owned, and whilst many were tiny, some of these firms were vast international houses. Firms such as Ralli Brothers, by means of interlocking partnerships, linked Lancashire manufacturers to numerous international trading centres throughout the world (Chapman

1996: 81). The hazards of the overseas markets, served by the majority of British firms and the diversity of shipping houses for exporting, meant that the majority of the British vertically integrated firms including Horrockses, Fieldens and Rylands were primarily, though by no means exclusively, involved in the home trade. For example, Rylands & Sons, Manchester's leading home trade house employed by its peak in the 1890s 12,500 people in total including 1,200 in the warehouse alone specialising predominantly on the home trade and only one-third of its business went overseas. Its range included heavy textiles, fustians, ginghams, checks, linens and fancy goods whilst in the 1870s it diversified further into clothing (Farnie 1993: 49). Horrockses, on the other hand, although trading with China and the Far East during the nineteenth century, was principally involved in the home trade and developed a strong brand identity when, following the merger with Crewdson Cross and Co it began to build direct links with retailers (Toms 1993: 129–46). Exceptionally, Tootal Broadhurst and Lee & Co pursued this same strategy in both home and overseas markets from the late nineteenth century (Chapman 1996: 85).

Pressure of growing overseas industrial development and over-capacity in periods of depression, in the 1880s and 1890s, led to intensified competition in many sectors of Lancashire's cotton industry and price cutting became common. In response, industrialists in a number of sectors, most especially where there was a high level of spatial specialisation such as in the finishing trades, tried and failed to regulate prices (Cook and Cohen 1958: 135–55; Macrosty 1907: 121). When collusion proved an unsatisfactory and unstable way of reducing uncertainty, the formation of vast horizontal trusts became the preferred option. Between 1896 and 1904 a wave of amalgamations occurred, which significantly altered the competitive structure of especially the finishing and thread sectors of the industry.

Three mergers in thread and sewing cotton (much, though by no means all, of which was produced outside Lancashire, in Scotland and the East Midlands) between 1896 and 1898, created what was, in effect, an oligopolistic, co-operative structure in this sector. J. and P. Coats Ltd of Paisley began the trend towards concentration, by merging with the four strongest thread producers in 1896, to be followed the next year by the formation of English Sewing Cotton Ltd which embraced a further 11 companies and in 1898 by the American Thread Company, which included a further 13 firms. The monopoly power of these three companies was considerable and intentional since they co-operated with one another on the basis of financial ties and interlocking directorships. Of the three thread combines Coats was easily the most successful in terms of management, level of innovation and its degree of vertical integration. A family dominated firm, it was by 1904 Britain's largest industrial company with 16 factories, including mills in the United States, Canada and Russia, as well as 60 branch houses and 150 depots. It began direct dealing with retailers and in so doing by-passed middlemen and increasingly acted as the selling agency for the sector (Macrosty 1907: 127–8; Wardley 1991; Anon. 1897: 612–17). By contrast, prior to its reorganisation in 1902 by O. E. Phillippi of Coats, English Sewing Cotton displayed all the features of moribund, cumbersome management which have led to such criticism of holding companies in British business in this period (Wilson 1995: 107). The strength of this group of firms remained considerable in the years before the First World War since their dominance was international as well as national, a critical determinant of success in a world of growing foreign competition.

The transformation of the finishing trades occurred in this period with the formation of the Calico Printers' Association in 1899 and the Bleachers' Association in 1900; both, as their names suggest, the product of abortive attempts at collusion on prices in the 1890s. The Calico Printers' Association represented a merger of 46 print works and 13 merchant converters and controlled, according to its prospectus, around 85 per cent of the industry with the explicit purpose to raise prices and reduce price cutting (Calico Printers' Association Ltd 1899). The Calico Printers' Association soon ran into managerial difficulties and, as with English Sewing Cotton, reconstruction came in 1902. Interestingly this involved the creation of a board of six managing directors who included Frank Hollins of Horrockses, Crewdson and Co Ltd, Sir William Mather of Mather and Platt, John Stanning of the Bleachers' Association and O. E. Phillippi of J. and P. Coats (Cook and Cohen 1958: 161). While this was clearly an attempt to professionalise the combine's management by employing the talents of successful industrialists, such interlocking directorships were not accidental. They provided an opportunity for those committed to a less decentralised structure for the industry to exert further control on a major sector.

The merging of 53 bleaching companies to form the Bleachers' Association in 1900 covered 60 per cent of the trade and included both successful and ailing companies. Bleaching had long showed a very high degree of geographic concentration in villages where there were close cultural ties between firms, family and community. In common with so many early combines, the Bleachers' Association perpetuated family control and maintained the impact of locality on its branches. By 1911, after some managerial reorganisation, it successfully pursued modernisation strategies which ensured regular dividend payments and profitability in the years before the First World War. The new combine used its market dominance to drive out potential competitors through price cutting campaigns (Jeremy 1993: 163–209; Utton 1974: 56).

Since the Horrockses Crewdson and Co Ltd merger of 1887 created a vertically integrated firm, the only truly horizontal amalgamation in spinning and weaving was the Fine Cotton Spinners' and Doublers' Association (FCSDA) of 1898 which included 31 fine spinning firms (around 40 per cent of the industry) mainly in Manchester and Stockport, which were 'engaged in spinning fine (Sea Island) cotton or doubling yarns used from this or other staples of cotton' (Macrosty 1907: 140–1). As such the Association's promoters sought to differentiate themselves from the other group of fine spinners reliant upon Egyptian cotton, in an attempt to dominate specialist markets. In pursuit of this objective the central core of their strategy was backward integration into raw cotton production and to this end they acquired 38,000 acres of cotton growing lands for around $2.5m and organised two plantations to secure adequate supplies of long stapled cotton at a time when supply difficulties were especially acute. In the event inexperience in cotton growing meant that the cotton was unsuitable for the Association and was sold instead on the open market generating quite considerable profits. Although overall FCSDA was fairly profitable in the years before the First World War, the structure of the spinning sector undermined the trust's plan to exert the kind of monopoly power that the other combines achieved (Macrosty 1907: 140–1; Utton 1974: 56; Wilkins 1989: 351–2).

Variations and changes in product and organisational strategies within late nineteenth-century Lancashire were also mirrored in the technological choices that enterprises made. As Table 6.4 shows there were sharp variations in the distribution of rings and mules, with the largest concentration of sub-40s mules being in Oldham while a third of all ring spindleage was in Rochdale. Ring spinning diffused most readily in those areas where there was already a tradition of throstle spinning. The mule's versatility meant that it very quickly superseded the water frame in popularity whereas the diffusion of the throstle during the nineteenth century was far more limited than in the United States (Cohen 1990: 54). On a small island, inevitably, reserves of water power were far more limited than in the virgin lands of New England. More seriously, expanding industrial activity placed pressure on rivers, leading many good water sites to become overcrowded. In addition, growing concern over the employment of first children and later women in cotton mills stimulated a wave of factory legislation, especially after 1830, which reduced the attractions of such sources of cheap labour. More critically, however, neither the water frame nor the later throstle was sufficiently versatile to meet the needs of increasingly discerning domestic and overseas markets served by British manufacturers. The only major textile town to rely heavily on throstles was Rochdale with its pre-industrial woollen tradition. This legacy, combined

Table 6.4. *Distribution of mule and ring spinners in Lancashire and Cheshire in 1906*

Town	Rings	Mules sub-40s	Mules 40s–80s	Mules 80s+
Ashton-under-Lyne	230	766	352	151
Oldham	511	1,979	1,134	60
Bolton	181	136	1,125	553
Manchester	104	44	–	160
Stockport	340	421	172	54
Blackburn	85	565	69	–
Burnley	147	–	72	–
Bacup	404	197	–	–
Rochdale	1,097	439	248	–
Leigh	–	–	317	143
Preston	–	195	193	140
Accrington	–	28	237	–
Other districts	335	94	44	17
Total Lancashire and Cheshire	3,434	4,864	3,963	1,278

Source: Board of Trade Report of an Enquiry by the Board of Trade into Earnings and Hours of Labour of Workpeople in the UK, vol. I *Textile Trades*, 1906 Cd. 4545 (1909): lxxx.

with an increasing dependence on flannels and flanelettes, which were introduced in the 1880s, explains the concentration of ring spinning in the town in the years before the First World War.

Elsewhere their adoption was extremely patchy and in many instances both throstle spinning and later ring spinning appeared only on the periphery. It was only on exceptional water sites, such as Quarry Bank on the Bollin at Styal, which concentrated on the production of coarse yarns and cloth, where the throstle made any real headway in the nineteenth century. Typically, the employers on these sites were both in a position to evade the Factory Acts and had, by the 1840s, developed substantial factory colonies. Moreover, at Styal, and villages like it, relatively docile labour relations and what amounted to an internal labour market were the natural consequence of a fairly authoritarian form of paternalism. This meant that the introduction of new technology was relatively easy (Farnie 1979: 73; Rose 1986). Much more research into the distribution of throstle frames in nineteenth-century Lancashire is needed, if their influence on the diffusion of rings is to be demonstrated. Yet, at Quarry Bank Mill at least, the impact is clear. There, in the face of increasing competitive pressures, rings were introduced between 1888 and 1892. Instructively, they did not revive the mill's flagging fortunes and Quarry Bank abandoned spinning in 1894 (Rose 1986: 91–2).

If ring spinning concentrated in Rochdale by the early twentieth century, Oldham became Lancashire's biggest spinning centre and also its largest centre for coarse mule spinning. A number of forces explain both Oldham's dramatic expansion and the preference for mule rather than ring spinning. Clearly Oldham's technological heritage lay in mule spinning and in the production of relatively coarse yarns. Although even in the 1830s Oldham had been one of Lancashire's leading spinning towns, the opportunity to expand coarse spinning there came with the growth of the Indian market, which created a demand for relatively coarse fabrics and provided an important stimulus. The improved self actor provided the ideal vehicle for this growth whilst the close financial ties between Oldham's machine makers, the mill building companies and the 'Limiteds' reinforced the trend towards this technology rather than rings. This choice was further encouraged by the highly specialised profile of Oldham's economy and its heavy dependence on spinning. For Oldham spinners, only 7 per cent of yarn could be woven locally so that the much discussed transport cost disadvantages were very real indeed and made mules rather than rings the best choice (Leunig 1996: 110).

Historical and market factors, combined with the late nineteenth-century efficiency of the mule, therefore made it a sensible technological choice whilst Oldham's social distinctiveness was also important. The distribution of shareholdings in the Limiteds which were, in the 1870s, predominantly in the hands of the more highly paid operatives, bolstered the bargaining power of the mule spinners union at the very time when private capitalists in the town were under threat. This may have reinforced Oldham's distinctive pattern of both technology and labour relations. It can surely have been no accident that the successful negotiation of the Oldham piece rate list in 1875 coincided with the first and largest flotation boom of working-class Limiteds (Farnie 1979: 220; Lazonick 1990: 104).

The evolving competitive environment in Lancashire was inseparable from the development of collective bargaining, especially when the forces of depression in the 1880s and 1890s precipitated wage cutting and embittered labour relations. Amalgamations of unions and of employers' associations occurred to form national negotiating bodies, through which local organisations operated. As a result local Wages Lists were subsumed in national lists and any negotiations on pay and working conditions arose on the basis of collective bargaining through the amalgamations. Again the changes which happened in Oldham were significant as in 1891 when, in response to a series of bitter strikes and lockouts, the local and powerful Oldham employers' association succeeded in creating the Federation of Master Cotton Spinners' Association, which covered around 40 per cent of the spinning sector and engaged in collective bargaining with the Amalgamated Association of Operative Cotton Spinners. These bodies were instrumental in negotiating the Brooklands Agreement of 1893, which meant that the influence of the Oldham list extended throughout south-east Lancashire. In north-east Lancashire, on the other hand, the Cotton Spinners and Manufacturers Association surfaced and although in 1890 it represented just 25 per cent of capacity, this had risen to 61 per cent by 1914. However, in weaving, although there was opposition to new technology, to increasing the numbers of looms per worker and to the speeding up of machinery, the smaller scale of firms tended to make for more quiescent labour relations in the late nineteenth century than in spinning (Farnie 1979: 265 and 299; Winstanley 1996: 140; McIvor 1996: 62–3).

The change in labour relations, which served to reinforce the craft-based organisation of work, also confirmed the importance of shopfloor training. This does not mean, however, that both at the level of individual communities and indeed in Lancashire as a whole, more formal education was neglected. Some of the wealth amassed in business communities in the first half of the nineteenth century was channelled into the development of local technical education, which built on the earlier Mechanics Institutes before the 1890s and served to reinforce local technological prowess (Garrard 1983). Similarly it was local wealth which financed Owen's College which was founded in 1851 and later became the Victoria University of Manchester with specialisms both in commerce and in textile chemistry (Guagnini 1993: 22).

The half-century before the First World War, therefore, saw Lancashire emerge as a most advanced and sophisticated industrial district. Yet, for much of this period its industrialists felt themselves under pressure from competition in foreign markets, and accordingly, mainly through the Manchester Chamber of Commerce, campaigned to gain the largest possible share of the Indian market. Yet far from enjoying the power and leverage that might be expected from Britain's premier export sector, cotton industry pressure groups were sometimes treated with derision within government circles and by civil servants, especially those connected with the India Office. These individuals had little understanding and still less patience with the attitudes and concerns of what they saw as a gauche, whinging, parochial interest. For instance, Sir Charles Wood, the Secretary of State for India, who had been impatient with Lancashire's demands for reductions of Indian duties in the 1850s, admitted that there were grave dangers for the government and Britain if the impending American Civil War created serious social problems. Yet Wood's dislike and incomprehension of the cotton masters, whom he described as 'a hopeless set [who will] do nothing effectual for themselves', was patently obvious (Harnetty 1972: 14–16; Longmate 1978: 219). However, a subsequent campaign supporting the removal of the duties gathered momentum from 1874, fanned by the onset of trade depression and fears over the development of the Bombay cotton spinning industry. Opinion varies over just how far it was pressure from Lancashire that led eventually to the abandonment of duties in 1882. It is certainly true that electoral volatility in the 1870s and 1880s meant that the county remained a force to be reckoned with and, in 1878, the Conservatives feared the loss of as many as 14 Lancashire seats if there was no sign of flexibility on the Indian tariff issue (Harnetty 1972: 33). However, clearly the timing of the abolition was not dictated by Lancashire pressure, but by Indian finances. Certainly the cotton interests were able to exert some leverage, not least because prevailing economic and political thought legitimised their demands. But it is also important to remember that those bodies formulating tariff policy – the India Office and the Government of India – were split by internal power struggles leaving room for alliances with pressure groups such as the cottonocracy (Redford 1956: 24; Dewey 1978: 38).

If Lancashire's late nineteenth-century expansion saw her manufacturers exporting a growing proportion of cotton goods, the United States domestic market grew apace in the late nineteenth century. Much of this market expansion came from the combination of sustained and rapid population growth after 1850 and the transport and institutional changes associated with the expansion of the national market. The combination of high natural rates of population increase and an influx of 40 million immigrants between 1850 and 1914, turned the United States into the largest and most rapidly growing domestic market in the Western world (Atack and Passell 1994: 213 and 232). This market, whilst increasingly sophisticated on the eastern seaboard, continued to be satisfied with standardised products and remained heavily protected.

Against a background of significant domestic market growth, other forces began transforming the profile of the American cotton industry and eventually radically altered its competitive balance. The rapid expansion of cotton manufacturing in the South, on the basis of the formation of numerous small firms, reversed the trend towards local and indeed national oligopoly in cotton, unlike experience in so much of manufacturing in the United States at this time. Certainly there had been ante-bellum activity in the cotton industry in the Southern states, but its development had been a patchy and halting process and normally only occurred during raw cotton price downturns. Indeed, when cotton prices sagged, Southern firms advanced, but when cotton yields dropped and prices rose would-be millowners had trouble finding backers. However, as Table 6.5 shows, after 1880 extensive manufacturing development occurred in the Southern states. It was conventionally assumed that the beginnings of the industrialisation of the South were closely linked to the collapse of the plantation

Table 6.5. *Cotton spindle activity (regional): the rise of the South (ms)*

Year	Total US	South	% of total
1860	5.2	0.3	5.21
1870	7.1	0.3	4.12
1880	10.6	0.5	4.71
1890	14.4	1.4	9.64
1900	19.5	4.0	20.76
1910	28.3	9.8	34.80

Sources: Galenson 1985: 2; Lemert 1933: 38.

society based on slavery, which was signalled by the Civil War (Mitchell 1921: 91). However, continuities exist between the ante-bellum factory development in the Southern states and the post-bellum expansion of the Piedmont region, which suggest that other forces were also at work (Griffin 1964: 27–53). Of these, one of the most important was the labour effects of the economic stagnation which followed the collapse of slavery and which created a supply of cheap white labour, which could no longer be gainfully employed in agriculture (Wright 1986: 126–7). Technology also played a part, since the perfection of the ring spinning frame in the 1860s and 1870s and the development of the automatic loom in the late 1880s made it easier to employ the mainly unskilled ex-agricultural labour (Jeremy 1996: 234). Not surprisingly, therefore, mules were barely used at all in the South in the late nineteenth century (Galenson 1985: 41).

At first, in line with earlier developments, cotton manufacturing was entirely financed by local communities, especially in North Carolina, the home of much of the ante-bellum Southern cotton industry. However, trade credit from Northern commission houses and machine makers underwrote the sustained expansion of an area with a weak banking system and no machine making industry and helped to stimulate expansion more generally (Beatty 1987: 55). As Table 6.6 shows, by 1910 cotton manufacturing was widely dispersed in the South, though most heavily concentrated in North and South Carolina and in Georgia.

Even before the First World War, the rise of the South had implications for strategic response throughout the cotton industry, although the most noticeable and obviously damaging effects did not arise until in the 1920s. Automatic technology originated in the North, where both the labour market and past machine-making traditions meant that rings were a logical technological choice, from the 1860s onwards, first in northern

Table 6.6. *Distribution of capacity by Southern states, spindleage and loomage (in 000s)*

	Establishments		Spindles		Looms	
State	1880	1910	1880	1910	1880	1910
South Carolina	14	145	82	4,019	1.7	88.4
North Carolina	49	292	92	3,174	1.8	50.9
Georgia	40	139	199	1,939	4.5	35.1
Alabama	16	61	49	947	0.9	15.8
Tennessee	16	29	36	293	0.8	4.4
Virginia	8	14	44	329	1.3	8.7
Mississippi	8	19	19	177	0.6	3.6
Texas	2	16	3	112	0.1	2.3
All other	11	16	37	241	0.6	2.9
Total	164	731	561	11,231	12.3	212.1

Source: Copeland 1912: 35.

Table 6.7. *Spinning technology in the cotton industry in the United States, 1870–1909 (ms)*

	North		South	
Date	Mules	Rings	Mules	Rings
1870	2.7	2.8	0.03	0.3
1890	4.4	6.4	0.1	1.4
1900	4.5	8.4	0.2	4.1
1909	3.7	11.7	0.2	10.0

Source: Galenson 1985: 41.

Massachusetts and then more extensively. As in Lancashire so within and between the textile regions there were differences in the distribution of rings and mules. This was particularly noticeable if North and South are compared, as Table 6.7 shows. Similarly the rate of diffusion of automatic looms was faster in the Southern states than it was in New England (Feller 1966: 320–47; McGouldrick 1968: 39–40; Feller 1974). However, between the communities which made up these regions there were also sharp disparities in patterns of technological change. In the South, for example, mule spinning may have been unusual, but in some communities, especially in North and South Carolina, mules were purchased between 1899 and 1909 (Cotton Yarn Association 1929: 9). Within New England, on the other hand, the installation of rings for coarse counts was delayed in Fall River until the late 1870s. This was slower than in the cotton towns north of Boston, where automatic looms were also introduced more rapidly later in the century (Mass 1984: 98; Cohen 1990: 28–54; Copeland 1912: 157). There were significant variations in both the technological and product orientations of these two New England regions during industrialisation. In addition, it is clear that despite similarities in both origins and ownership, differing labour market conditions created varying patterns of labour relations in Fall River and the mills of northern Massachusetts. Much depended upon the extent to which throstles had previously been used. Extensive in their use of relatively cheap and plentiful power first water frames and then throstles, Lowell-style corporations economised on skill in the production of relatively coarse yarns for mass markets. In their turn, since they could be operated by women and children, labour relations tended to be less confrontational than where men were employed as they were in Fall River.

Such divergences, even within the same state, became self-reinforcing during the nineteenth century. The decline in the use of female agricultural labour in northern Massachusetts did not herald the substitution of skilled male labour. Instead the Yankee young women employed until the 1840s were steadily replaced by unskilled Irish, French Canadians and Poles (female and male) (Sandberg 1969). Even where practice converged after 1860 this highlights the differing historical experience of Fall River and the towns of northern Massachusetts. Part of the ethos of the northern Massachusetts sheeting producers in the 1820s and 1830s had been vertical integration. In Fall River this came only when the perfection of steam power gave the largest employers the incentive to integrate forward into printcloth production.

From the 1820s and until the 1870s, therefore, the cotton manufacturers of northern Massachusetts and Fall River were manufacturing a different product for different segments of the home market, using different categories of labour. This had profound implications for the diffusion of both the ring frame and the automatic loom. That rings diffused more readily in northern Massachusetts than Fall River before 1870 is entirely predictable since the technological origins of the ring lay in the throstle. More interesting, however, are the implications of its distinctive past for the late nineteenth- and early twentieth-century development of Fall River. Large employers like the Fall River Iron Works certainly abandoned mules for coarse counts. Yet along with neighbouring centres elsewhere in southern Massachusetts and Rhode Island, which shared a similar technological, organisational, social and product heritage, Fall

River retained mule spinning for finer counts. As a result, by the 1920s 70 per cent of all yarn over 40s was produced in this region (Cotton Yarn Association 1929: 11).

Common state corporate legislation meant that, with its interlocking corporations, Fall River displayed similar organisational characteristics to the cotton towns of northern Massachusetts by 1870. Yet if the ownership structure of Fall River firms meant they shared the potential for collective strategies with their northern counterparts they were, in terms of technology, labour relations and product, dissimilar. In northern Massachusetts, therefore, the use of throstle spindles had vastly exceeded mules in the early stages of industrialisation. By 1870, on the other hand, whereas 90 per cent of Fall River spindleage was on mules, in the towns of northern Massachusetts the average proportion of mule spindleage was only 46 per cent, with over half of spindleage being on either rings or throstles. This was a fairly closely reflection of national patterns. Indeed after the American Civil War Fall River was the only large cotton town in the United States where spinning was done almost exclusively on mules (Cohen 1990: 28–54, 157; Copeland 1912: 70).

The unusual concentration of mainly British, often militant, mule spinners in Fall River in turn created distinctive patterns of labour relations. Hence a wave of mule spinning strikes in the 1870s had far more serious consequences for Fall River producers than for firms in northern Massachusetts. In the Lowell district, rather than being prostrated, firms maintained production levels at around half capacity throughout the strikes by using rings. This proved instructive to Fall River employers. It meant that after the success of their collective strategy to defeat the mule spinners in 1875, they rapidly replaced mules at sub-40s counts with rings (Cohen 1990: 156–7).

Since the Southern states were the most rapidly growing segment of the cotton industry this contributed to the rapid shift to the new technology in the American cotton textiles overall. While using the same technology, the South enjoyed increasing labour cost advantages and by 1900 wages of adult cotton workers were 59 per cent lower than those in the North. In addition, more lax labour laws meant that Southern producers employed a higher proportion of cheap child labour than was the case in the North (Oates 1975: 118; Lea 1975b: 492). Southern employers were also in a stronger position to control their workforces and hold down wages than those in the North by the late nineteenth century. Whereas the effectiveness and prevalence of paternalism was on the decline in both New England and the mid-Atlantic states, Southern mills were inseparable from their mill villages. Such paternalism had its origins in the ante-bellum period but, against the background of impoverished Southern agriculture,

Table 6.8. *Product orientation of New England and Southern states (% of count 1889–1929)*

Year	under 20s	21–40	41+	41–60	61–80	80+
1889						
New Eng.	36.17	57.76	6.06	n/a	n/a	n/a
South	94.03	5.97	–	–	–	–
1929						
New Eng.	40.86	49.52	9.61	n/a	n/a	n/a
South	76.03	23.82	0.15	n/a	n/a	n/a

Source: Galenson 1985: 5.

millowners promoted their factories as an alternative to farm work. They used a combination of mill villages and family labour as devices to ease the transition from rural life to factory life, while creating a tractable workforce. Even with the combination of steam power and electricity which, by 1910, had freed manufacturers from unreliable water-powered sites, mill villages continued to be built in the South on the outskirts of towns. It is possible to exaggerate the extent to which these villages allowed millowners to dominate their operatives. They did not prevent labour unrest entirely, even in the 1880s and 1890s, when both the Knights of Labor and the National Union of Textile Workers came to the aid of Southern millworkers. Additionally, the rapid spread of small mills in the Piedmont region in this period meant that even when industrial action failed (as it always did) blacklisted millworkers often simply moved to another mill and another community. With labour turnover averaging 176 per cent per annum by 1907 this would seem to have been an option that was regularly used, giving a transiency level every bit as high as had been found in the North during industrialisation (Hall et al. 1986: 247–61). Even so, Southern millowners could restrain wages and alter working conditions in ways that were just not an option in the North.

The South's undermining of Northern cost advantages reinforced the need of bulk producers to cut costs and to modernise. More generally, however, Southern competition encouraged the movement by the bulk producers of New England into finer goods, as Table 6.8 shows, and for the first time brought them into direct competition with Philadelphia. Intense competition and deep uncertainty were, however, anathema to those running the Massachusetts corporations, where profitability depended upon standardised product and high throughput. Thus efforts to move up market and diversify were frequently problematic and bankruptcies increased as a result. At the troubled Boott Mills, for instance, after 1905, management consultants noted that a bewildering array of cloths were being produced. It was a trend which continued so that immediately prior to the First World War 12 different fabrics were being made by the mills and within this range a vast number of types of any one category. This strategy, whilst precipitated initially by the growing competitive advantage of Southern mills at the coarser end of the market, stemmed also from the greater efficiency of some other bulk producers. Boott Mills also came under pressure to move up market from their selling house Wellington, Sears who held a significant financial stake in the mills and who stood to make larger profits from finer cloths. Across New England the numbers of liquidations mounted in all the main textile centres. The only exception to this depressing trend was in such fine centres as New Bedford – for the majority of firms the move merely reduced potential scale economies (Gross 1993: 103–4; Wolfbein 1944).

Inevitably these strategic changes by the bulk producers had implications for Philadelphia, which went beyond product choice to include the organisation of both their labour relations and their commercial arrangements. In the middle of the nineteenth century Philadelphia's flexible specialisation had been based upon small-firm paternalism and the development of common interests and aspirations between entrepreneurs and a skilled workforce. By the 1880s, changes in patterns of immigration meant that the impact of this 'fraternal paternalism' was weakening. The shifting competitive environment, however, brought with it new pressures. Attempts to cut wages during the depression in the 1890s, in order to compete with the bulk producers, brought strikes and the eventual demise of the system. Strikes, mainly orchestrated by the Knights of Labor, became a growing problem and in response the Textile Manufacturers' Association, while maintaining its position as a lobbying group, formed the Philadelphia Manufacturers' Association to deal collectively with labour difficulties. Yet the extent and durability of collectivism in the Philadelphia labour market should not be exaggerated. This is because the structure of firms and characteristics of the skilled and individualistic workforce provided a distinct limitation confining owners' activity to periods of crisis, rather than being a consistent element of strategy among employers and employed (Scranton 1983: 256 and 354; Scranton 1989: 46 and 58–9).

The essence of competitive advantage for Philadelphia's proprietary capitalists was their product, rather than their price strategies. Yet in the face of threats from New England some manufacturers chose to forgo some quality and styling in order to compete on price, a contest in which flexible producers were doomed to failure. More successful was the decision to move into the production of goods such as lace, silk hosiery and other specialty lines which had previously been imported (Scranton 1989: 10; Knowlton 1948: 182–203). This move, however, depended upon protection and hence upon the city's newly found lobbying prowess *vis-à-vis* the Republican government (Scranton 1989: 226).

Changes in product strategy also had implications for commercial arrangements. In the past Philadelphia's manufacturers had to deliver seasonal flexibility in the face of rapid changes in demand in the New York fashion market. This meant that sales agents, with their emphasis on price, were less appropriate for Philadelphia than direct selling. Until the 1890s the majority (though not all) relied for their market information on personal contact through twice-yearly trips to New York and on the services of jobbers who purchased goods outright, while giving advice on likely trends and styles. In the 1890s the combination of the increasing pressure from the bulk producers and a major trade depression, which led to panic among jobbers, forced a change in selling practices in Philadelphia. Increasingly jobbers operated on a sample basis rather than placing large orders for stock. Dealing with them, as a result, became more complex and unsatisfactory. Direct dealing with retailers, however, involved a round season presence in New York and the extensive use of travellers, which was beyond the resources of Philadelphia's smaller firms. Certainly larger manufacturers increasingly used these means to by-pass jobbers while those using selling agents tried to find ways of abandoning them. For many smaller firms changes in distribution ultimately caused them to close, a trend which continued into the twentieth century (Scranton 1989: 69, 226–7 and 323–47).

As capacity increased, in the industry as a whole, exporting was an alternative strategy for firms in the bulk section of the industry in both the North and the South, especially in bad years. As a consequence, in this period cloth exports rose from 150m yards in 1882–4 to reach 467m yards in 1913 (Robson 1957: 358). United States cotton firms achieved some relatively short-term success in the northern Chinese province of Manchuria when, after 1885, New England producers of sheetings, drills and jeans successfully penetrated the Chinese market. Trade marks were widely used by all importers to Manchuria, and the Maine firm, Pepperell's, established a prominent position in jeans by 1906 (Clarke 1914: 245). However, in a low income market, price was of overwhelming importance. This meant that increasingly the mainly coarse and unbleached American exports to the province came from the Southern states, with their relatively low labour costs. Indeed, in this period some Southern mills were exceptionally export-oriented. For example, the Piedmont Manufacturing Company of Greenville, South Carolina, the

South's first really large-scale success, sold over half of its output for export. It was not alone, and by 1900 the South exported 10 per cent of its products as compared with a mere 3 per cent of production from New England (Galenson 1985: 36).

For a while the price competitiveness of American goods threatened the position of British exporters in this and more generally in the Chinese market. By 1905, as a result of their success in coarser fabrics, United States exporters held 36 per cent of the Chinese market as against Britain's 56 per cent, though British exporters retained advantage in finer shirtings and sheetings in southern China. However, the American gain proved to be short-lived and by 1914 the United States share of the Chinese market had fallen back to just 8 per cent, though the market still represented quite an important share of her exports. This was partly as a result of the renewed competitiveness of Britain in some categories of goods, especially in the jeans market. Of far greater significance, however, was the growing penetration of cheaper Japanese goods (Tyson 1968: 113). More generally, exports increased to Canada and Latin America, and in the years immediately before the First World War the Philippines became increasingly important (Cotton Yarn Association 1929: 19).

The increase in exports did not, however, mark a major strategic shift in the orientation and culture of the majority of American firms before the First World War. Consequently, they exported only 6.5 per cent of their cloth output between 1910 and 1913 representing only 4 per cent of the world market (Robson 1957: 4). One obvious reason why American firms were not more export-oriented was the sustained growth of their vast domestic market. Before the First World War, therefore, buoyant domestic markets absorbed most United States produced cloth, absolving the majority of manufacturers from the need to penetrate markets where competition was keener. However, there were a number of reasons, linked to the nineteenth-century culture of business and to the perceptions which it reflected, which explain why, when they tried to export, many firms encountered difficulties.

In the first place the domestic focus of the industry meant that there was not a sophisticated network of American export houses and overseas banks to serve the cotton industry in the late nineteenth century. However, the mainly European trading companies, in both the Far East and Latin America, adopted an increasingly cosmopolitan approach to commerce as competition intensified before the First World War. Quite simply they would trade in anything for which there was a market, irrespective of the country of origin (Chapman 1992: 107–24). Limited export success, by United States cotton textile producers, was therefore less the direct result of the absence of institutional support and more related to Americans' insensitivity to the specific tastes of particular markets. This led to mistakes which rendered any cost advantages on individual types of cloth irrelevant, since the wrong types of fabric were often supplied (Marrison 1975: 326–32). In addition, concentration on long production runs reduced flexibility in the face of local requirements. Copeland, writing in 1912, summed up the obstacles to successful international performance by United States cotton manufacturers as follows:

The American manufacturers . . . have not attempted to meet the demands of the local trade in the various countries. They have not sent out trained agents equipped with a knowledge of the foreign language to study the conditions and solicit orders, nor have they established branches in the commercial cities whereby they could carry on transactions with the native merchants. Every manufacturer of finished cotton goods knows that the tastes of the inhabitants of the different sections of the US, even, are not the same. . . . Yet it has usually been assumed that goods for which there was a demand here could be sold in Cuba, Venezuela, Madagascar or British India. . . . Moreover they have been unwilling to make up packages containing a variety of patterns, although such requests have been acceded to by German and English shippers, who have not tried to force the foreign buyer to accept a large quantity of a single design or quality. These are the real obstacles to the expansion of our foreign trade in cotton fabrics. (Copeland 1912: 228–9)

In any event before the First World War American goods could not compete in many Asian markets, in part because of a combination of slow and unscheduled deliveries, careless packing and the lack of resident agents. The position did not dramatically improve, in cotton textiles, when dissatisfaction with foreign agencies led the United States to establish the China and Japan Trading Company before 1914 (Sugiyama 1988: 285–6).

It is instructive that, before the First World War, it was only in the Philippines, which as Figure 6.2 shows accounted for 21 per cent of United States exports of cotton cloth, that a sustained and substantial growth of exports was achieved. This stemmed mainly from a combination of colonial expansion and tariff protection and as such was largely artificial. Acquired in 1897, at a time when both Europe and Japan were reinforcing their Imperial possessions in the Orient, these islands were retained for both their strategic and economic value. In the light of Japan's occupation of Formosa and Britain's annexation of Hong Kong, the islands were initially seen as a vital staging post for expanded trade with China and hence to the export potential of Southern mills (Williams 1929: 253). Indeed in 1897 *The Century* concluded that:

It is as a base for commercial operations that the islands seem to possess the greatest importance. They occupy a favoured location, not with reference to any one part of any particular country of the Orient, but to all parts. Together with the

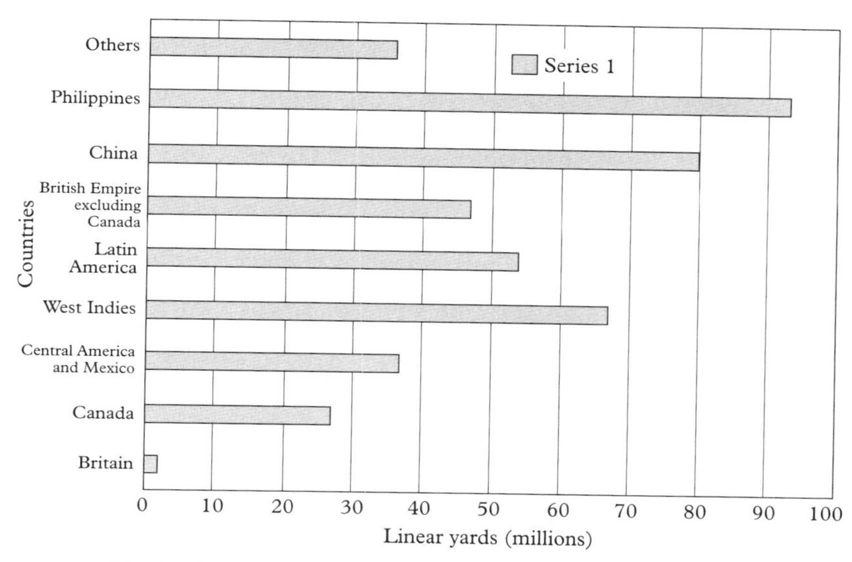

Fig. 6.2 Destinations of United States cotton cloth exports
Source: Cotton Yarn Association 1928:19

islands of the Japanese Empire, since the acquirement of Formosa, the Philippines are the pickets of the Pacific, standing guard at the entrance to trade with the millions of China, Korea, French Indo-China, the Malay Peninsula and the Islands of Indonesia to the South. (quoted in Williams 1929: 322)

The dramatic growth in cotton goods exports to these islands did not stem either from manufacturing advantages or from commercial expertise, but was closely related to the closed door tariff policy which the United States government imposed on the Philippines under the 1909 Tariff Act. This legislation, which excluded all foreign imports but allowed in United States goods duty free, had profound implications for trade patterns, so that by 1913 50 per cent of all Filipino imports came from the United States as compared with 13 per cent in 1908 (Williams 1929: 327). The overall poor performance of United States goods in export markets would seem, therefore, to have been a direct consequence of business cultures based upon serving home demand. Overseas markets were, on the other hand, for little more than dumping surpluses.

The declining personal political power of the Boston Associates was one of the slippages which, in the years after the Civil War, stimulated the development of more formalised employers' associations in New England. This was not the only factor, however, since the intensification of economic change and rapid postwar expansion in the cotton industry as a whole, the emergence of more effective trade unions, and an increasing trend towards factory regulation were also critical. This was a period of burgeoning domestic demand, when 7 million new spindles were added and when centres like New Bedford and Fall River came to dominate the markets for fine yarn and cloth and for print cloth respectively. But it was also a period of rapid change when expansion was punctuated by serious fluctuations, where from the 1880s industrial development in the South began to cause unease and where Massachusetts labour laws became increasingly stringent and trade unions better organised and more militant. At the level of individual communities interlocking bulk corporations retained a significant degree of power. However, across the region, in the face of growing competitive pressures, those running New England's corporations felt a sense of impotence and unease which led to the formation of first the New England Cotton Manufacturers Association in 1865 and in 1880 the Arkwright Club (Galambos 1966: 11–23).

These two organisations had differing objectives and, to a large degree, these were reflected in their business strategies. The New England Cotton Manufacturers Association was conceived as and remained a conduit for information about rapidly changing technology. The Arkwright Club, however, was a response to changes in the Massachusetts labour laws and was from the start more interventionist in its aims, representing mainly larger and older mills. It was set up:

> to promote consultation among all those having charge of the important trusts involved in the management of the cotton and woollen and allied industries, to cultivate good understanding and concerted action in all matters pertaining to the general interests of those industries, and to ensure mutual protection in all cases where they are in any way endangered. (Quoted Galambos 1966: 23)

Initially it fulfilled the role of a political lobbying organisation and thus filled the gap left by the Associates, though increasingly its aim along with other newly formed associations was to restrict competition. This became especially acute in the 1890s and in the years immediately before the First World War with the onset of a depression in New England, which was undoubtedly precipitated by the rise of the South and its growing dominance of the coarse goods market. This development, by disturbing the delicate competitive balance of previously complementary regions of Massachusetts and Philadelphia, had profound implications for the experience and strategies of firms in the North and saw the onset of vicious price cutting campaigns. At a time when the operation of anti-trust laws was fairly lax, the response by the Arkwright Club and other 'dinner-club' associations such as the Spinners' Association, was to attempt to introduce informal price and output controls, which were inevitably of limited impact. However, in the close-knit environment of Fall River, in 1900, a more radical experiment was tried in an effort to stabilise the sector. The city's mills co-operated in forming a selling agency to eliminate competition between mills. Yet in the face of persistent Southern competition even such co-ordinated activity was unsuccessful (Freyer 1992: 29; Galambos 1966: 33–7). Although, as in Britain, the relative failure of price fixing spawned some amalgamations in American textiles in the late 1890s, including American Thread, New England Cotton Yarn and United States Cotton Duck, the continued proliferation of tiny mills in the South limited their effect on the concentration of individual sectors (Lamoreaux 1985: 3). As a further complication it is interesting to note that whilst New Englanders were enthusiastic, if relatively unsuccessful pursuers of price fixing, pricing committees were always problematic in Philadelphia where flexible specialisation inhibited collusion and where sectoral associations remained heavily localised and weak (Scranton 1997: 330).

National comparisons

The forces for change in the British and American cotton industries, which were felt between the American Civil War and the First World War and played out within and between individual communities, left the two industries with sharply different profiles especially with respect to technology. Where the Americans used ring spinning frames and automatic looms, in their quest to achieve high labour productivity to compensate for high wages, the British favoured mules and plain looms because they allowed them flexibility. British technology was skill intensive and had evolved, by the late nineteenth century, to produce a wide range of yarns and cloths, sometimes using raw cotton that was variable in quality. American technology, on the other hand, was resource intensive, producing mainly standardised goods for a mass market (Broadberry 1997: 4). By 1913, therefore, whilst 81 per cent of British spindleage was mules, in the United States 87 per cent of spindleage was rings. The diffusion of the automatic loom was even slower in Britain with only a tiny number installed before the First World War (Robson 1957: 355). Similarly there were contrasts in the organisation of work and in labour relations between much of the American cotton industry and Britain. In Britain, for example, the organisation of work was craft based with accepted piece rates negotiated with trade unions and institutionalised in Wages Lists, whilst in the United States individual millowners set wages in accord with local conditions.

It is interesting that the peculiarities in terms of organisational structure and labour relations were not entirely borne out with respect to plant size. As Table 6.9 illustrates, throughout the nineteenth century the

Table 6.9. *The size of mills in the United States and Lancashire, 1850–1890 (average spindleage)*

	United States All Mills	Lancashire Spinning	Lancashire Combined
1850	3,290	11,818	18,621
1860	4,766	15,368[a]	19,634[a]
1870	7,426	18,342	31,494
1880	14,153	27,385[b]	25,955[b]
1890	15,691	38,618	30,169

Notes:
[a] Figure for 1861.
[b] Figure for 1878.
Sources: Copeland 1912: 6 and 11; Farnie 1979: 215 and 316.

average spindleage of American mills was quite modest, reflecting the diversity of scale across the industry as a whole. It is true that there were more large plants in America than in Britain and that giants, like Amoskeag with 650,000 spindles or Fall River Iron Works with 466,800, dwarfed anything on the other side of the Atlantic, especially when it is remembered that these were vertically integrated firms with substantial loomage. However, the standard size of a new spinning mill in Britain was 100,000 spindles by 1890 and matched the average for New England and vastly exceeded the American norm (Farnie 1979: 217; Copeland 1912: 142). Moreover the rise of the cotton industry in the Southern states did not replicate the scale of plant to be found in New England. In the cotton-growing states, although the majority of mills combined spinning and weaving, limited financial resources meant they were, initially at least, generally comparatively small-scale with an average spindleage of 15,363 by 1910 (Oates 1975: 100; Copeland 1912: 35).

There are a number of reasons why the dramas being played out at the community level reinforced national contrasts in the profiles of the two industries. These include the complex interrelationship between product and market orientation, with technological and organisational change and which, combined with dynamics of the competitive process, reinforced national differences in the orientation of the two industries.

Technology and labour arrangements are inseparable from product so it is not surprising that product choice continued to diverge. Consequently despite the progressive coarsening of British cloth during the nineteenth century, output remained infinitely finer than in the rest of

Table 6.10. *Production of cotton yarn in the United States, by count (%)*

Date	Up to 20s	21s–40s	Over 40s	Total
1899	58.0	36.8	5.2	1,467
1904	52.5	39.3	8.2	1,530
1909	49.8	42.5	7.7	2,037
1914	45.6	47.3	7.1	2,170

Source: Cotton Yarn Association, *Statistical Information Concerning Spinning in the United States* (Manchester 1928) p. 11.

the world and most especially in the United States. Fifty per cent of British spindles were engaged in sub-40s yarn production while in the United States, on the other hand, 93 per cent of yarn output was sub-40s in 1914, as Table 6.10 indicates. In addition, while Lancashire produced an ever increasing diversity of goods, 80 per cent of output, in the years before the First World War, was of staple products (Burgy 1932). As illustration of the low level of competitive advantage which the American industry had in fine goods, 90 per cent of the United States' tiny imports of cotton yarn came from Britain and were made up virtually exclusively of counts over 60s. Similarly, as an exporter of finer yarn and high quality cloth to European and Far Eastern markets, British performance remained strong throughout the late nineteenth and early twentieth centuries (Tyson 1968: 105–15). Clearly such significant variations in the product profile, themselves a result of the type of skill levels and the character of workforces, help to explain national variations in technological choice. This is especially so when it is remembered that they were reflected in continued sharp wage differentials, as Figure 6.3 shows, and United States wage costs remained among the highest in the world (Clark 1987: 150). However, the high level of protection and domestic orientation of the majority of firms made such comparisons and the international competitive failure of much American output purely academic.

There were also sharp disparities in structure, since whereas a large proportion of the American industry was vertically integrated, in Britain there was an increasing trend towards spatial and vertical specialisation in the years before the First World War. Thus, whilst in Britain the proportion of spindles and looms in integrated mills fell from 53 per cent and 83 per cent respectively in 1850 to 23 per cent and 35 per cent in 1914, with just 16 per cent of all firms integrating the two processes, the trend was reversed in the United States. With the exception of Philadelphia, where the ante-bellum process of specialisation and concentration on batch

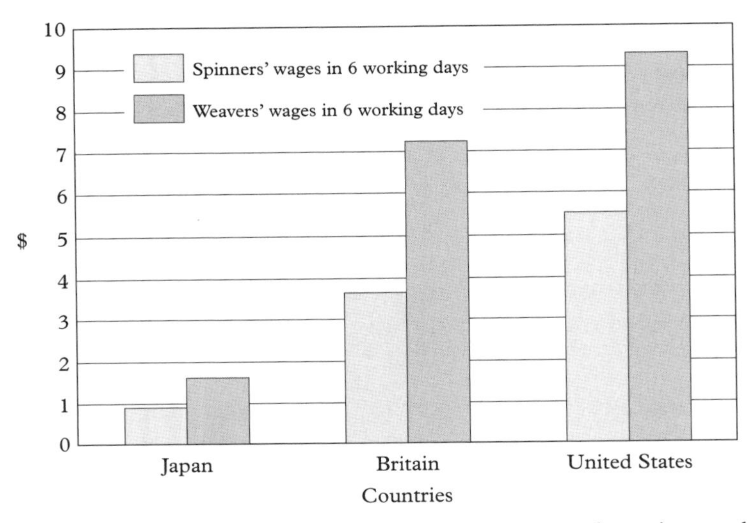

Fig. 6.3 Wage costs for spinning 20s ring warp and weaving on plain looms in Japan, England and the United States, 1912
Source: Clark 1914: 191–4

rather than bulk production was reinforced during the late nineteenth century, the integration of spinning and weaving became more and more common. Therefore in the United States, by 1914, 39 per cent of Northern firms and 56 per cent of firms in the rapidly developing South combined spinning and weaving.

Vertical integration can be a reflection of the inability of the producers of intermediate goods to meet the needs of manufacturers of finished goods or can arise when high transaction costs result from poor communications and flows of information (Langlois and Robertson 1989: 363). It is also most likely where markets are relatively uniform and where there are potential scale economies from long production runs. The popularity of vertically integrated spinning and weaving plants can in part be understood in the context of the United States' position as a newly developing country in the early part of the nineteenth century, while the domestic orientation of the industry brought with it significant scale economies. The continuing trend in the late nineteenth century, as the industry's growth centre moved South, is a reflection of similar influences, in a region which, whilst not entirely innocent of industrial development, lacked networks of skilled workers and effective local commercial arrangements which could have acted as intermediaries between producers of yarn and cloth. Moreover the domestic market orientation of the South meant there were potentially substantial economies of scale.

Clearly in the American case, therefore, there was an intimate link between technological choice and the level of integration. However, the idea that vertical specialisation precluded the choice of mass production technology in Britain is not sustainable. Internationally there are numerous examples where ring spinning and automatic looms were adopted in industries where spinning and weaving were separated (Saxonhouse and Wright 1984). Conversely levels of integration in the American cotton industry were not matched in any other country, not just in Britain. This suggests that it was the extraordinary circumstances in the United States which led to a particular configuration of technology and organisation rather than this being a relationship which was repeated internationally (Farnie 1979: 315; Chapman and Ashton 1913–14: 491–2).

While historical differences in the development of the British and American cotton industries help to explain their diverging technological profiles the crucial factor speeding up the process was the rise of cotton manufacturing in the Southern states. It was not just the case that the South was the most rapidly growing textile region with conditions favouring the adoption of automatic technology, but the impact which this had upon the competitive process in the North increased the rate of technological change there too. Although this pushed many New England producers up market, the persistent need to compete on price increased the demand for rings for all counts to compensate for higher labour costs. These were not the same pressures as those at work in Lancashire. Certainly cost competitiveness remained vital and was strongly enforced by Manchester's merchants and middlemen. But all the trends favoured and reinforced demand for the still versatile and profitable mule, especially in the dominant and burgeoning town of Oldham. Indeed, labour productivity gains continued to be made on this technology right up to the First World War (Broadberry 1997: 189; Marrison 1996a: 253–63).

Summary

Between 1860 and 1914 both the British and American cotton industries expanded dramatically. However, the internal and external pressures to which firms in the two countries responded were strikingly different. Whereas in Britain the period saw the dramatic growth of Empire and especially the Indian market against a background of growing foreign competition, in the United States the principal stimulus to expansion came from a vast and secure domestic market. Before 1860 strategic response in the two industries had diverged and there had emerged distinctive business and community cultures. A number of forces reinforced business culture in the British and American cotton industries. Consequently, although there were changes in product strategy, American firms remained predominantly production driven. Similarly, in Britain the increasingly specialised commercial arrangements and ancillary industries reflected the market orientation of strategies within and between regions. Equally the intensification of price competition and the emergence of collusive arrangements and holding companies stemmed from community ties.

The significance of locality in family firm strategy is assumed to decline as economies mature. It is certainly the case that district level organisations began to give way to industry-wide arrangements in the late nineteenth and early twentieth centuries and that growing urbanisation and suburbanisation reduced the effectiveness of personal contact. However, in both Britain and the United States, major changes at the level of communities, after 1860, had substantial implications for the competitive process within the industry and for the relationship of one town to another. In the first place technological strategies and firms' characteristics were moulded by the past capabilities of communities, while any changes for the industry could also result from significant initiatives in individual centres. Therefore, whereas in Britain the rise of Oldham was a major reason for the emergence of Lancashire's specialised structure, in the United States the rise of the South had lasting implications for the technological and organisational responses of firms in New England and Philadelphia. This approach, therefore, differs from institutional interpretations which explain British technological strategies in terms of the extent to which labour relations and structure deviated from a supposed American norm (Mass 1984: 248–54; Lazonick 1981a: 31–8; Lazonick 1986). In this analysis the varying profiles of the industries by 1914 have been shown to stem from *entirely different competitive processes* rather than from institutional rigidities which prevented British businessmen from behaving like their American counterparts. It certainly is not clear that Lancashire firms would have been much better off with United States-style strategies, for although there was a substantial labour productivity gap there is no evidence to suggest that this made the majority of American firms internationally competitive in this period (Clark 1987: 150; Broadberry 1997: 189).

The analysis of change at the community level also reveals some problems with explanations of national patterns of technological diffusion based upon institutional rigidities (Lazonick 1981c: 89–109; Lazonick 1990).This is because comparative analysis of the diffusion of ring spinning, in the British and American cotton industries, has been based upon comparisons of experience in Fall River and Oldham which, it has been revealed, cannot be taken as being representative of their respective industries. The discussion of Oldham and Fall River separately from their national contexts has, therefore, important consequences for the interpretation of technological strategies from the 1870s. Clearly the two towns shared many characteristics in terms of product, technology and the character of the workforce. Yet, whereas Oldham was the major mule town in an industry where most spinning was done on mules (Sandberg 1984: 388), Fall River's spinning technology was exceptional. This places the more rapid replacement of mules with rings, at sub-40s counts, in Fall River after the 1870s, in a rather different light. Quite simply, irrespective of the cost advantages of rings over mules at coarser counts, Fall River employers were following the lead of their northern Massachusetts counterparts, where long before 1870 first throstles and then the ring had been extensively used. They had, moreover, been able to observe at close quarters the superior experience of towns such as Lowell during a major strike. Conversely, quite apart from the continued profitability of mules, Oldham employers had fewer incentives to replace mules with rings in the 1870s and 1880s since they lacked the first-hand knowledge of the strategic advantages of such a move irrespective of the profitability of such a decision.

The analysis of change in the British and American cotton industries between the American Civil War and the First World War at the local level, has highlighted the complexity of the process of change and the shifting nature of competition and the structure of business in this period. The early twentieth century especially was a period of considerable expansion in both industries, yet in both lay the seeds of decay which, in the interwar period, would tear communities apart. For Lancashire's cotton towns, but especially for Oldham, the Edwardian era was truly an Indian summer which ended in 1914, whilst in the United States world war merely brought a stay of execution to cotton firms in New England especially, but also in Philadelphia. The next chapter will explore the way the profile of the two industries changed in the interwar period, the implications for communities and for the effectiveness of pressure groups in their fight to save their industries.

7 Prosperity and decay in war and peace, 1914–39

Despite the dramatic expansion of United States cotton manufacturing in the late nineteenth century, Lancashire remained the home of the world's largest cotton industry before the First World War. Yet, during the war and afterwards the increased capacity and continued labour productivity growth in the United States meant that by 1924, the United States had overtaken Britain as the largest producer of cotton cloth (see Table 7.1). During the 1920s and more especially the 1930s, on the other hand, both industries encountered the increasing competitive threat of Japan at home and abroad. The Japanese share of world cotton textile exports outstripped Britain by 1933, a lead which she sustained throughout the 1930s, as Figures 7.1 and 7.2 demonstrate.

By the outbreak of the First World War, despite common technological origins, the British and American cotton industries had developed along quite different trajectories. Distinctiveness in the experience of industrialisation, in government–industry relations, in commercial policy and in the characteristics of product and factor markets meant that the historical forces shaping business strategy were strikingly dissimilar. The sharpest contrast came in the product and market orientation of the two nations, with Britain having the world's most export-oriented cotton industry. On the other hand, efforts to penetrate the Far Eastern market had only marginally reduced the legendary reliance of the United States cotton industry on its domestic market. The divergent evolution of the two industries and the resultant contrasts in organisation and capabilities make the shared experience of difficulties and decay in the interwar period all the more remarkable – their explanation is one of the principal themes of this chapter.

In the period up to the First World War the experience of the two industries can be best understood with reference to the relationships within and between business communities. The question arises of how far the disruption of the First World War destabilised such relationships and set in train a string of events which irreversibly altered the profile of individual communities, and hence the competitive environment of the two

Table 7.1. *The British and United States cotton industries, 1919–37*

	United States				Britain			
Date	Spindleage (m) (%) rings	Loomage (000) (%) automatics	Cloth output (m sq yards)	Numbers employed (000)	Spindleage (m) (%) rings	Loomage (000) (%) automatics	Cloth output (m square yards)	Numbers employed (000)
1919	34.4	692	6,317	431	59.2	791	n/a	n/a
1924	35.8	700.3[a]	8,264[a]	472	59.5	792	5,589	792
1930	32.1[b]	699	7,693[c]	372	57.7	704	3,179	564
1937	27.0 (98.1)	573[d] (68.4)	8,785	400[e]	38.8 (27.8)	505[d] ([e]2.9)	3,640[d]	409

Notes:

[a] Figure for 1923.
[b] Figure for 1928.
[c] Figure for 1929.
[d] Figure for 1936.
[e] Figure for 1940.

Sources: Mitchell 1988: 332–81; Robson 1957: 339–59; Cotton Yarn Association 1929: 7; Atack and Passell 1994: 523).

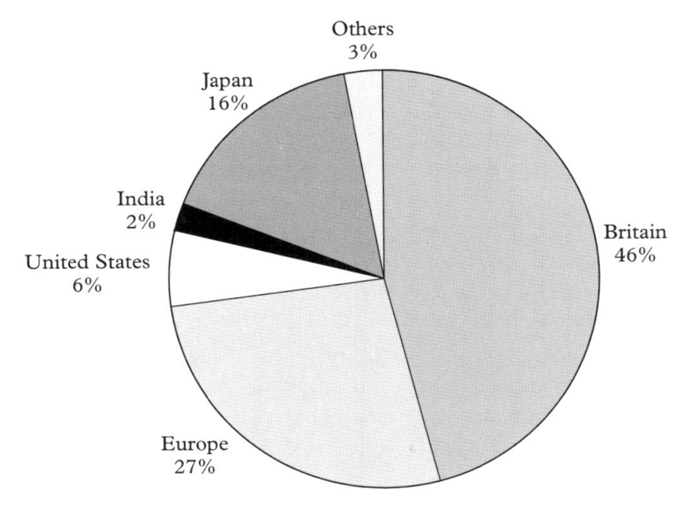

Fig. 7.1 World trade in cotton cloth, 1926–8
Source: Robson 1957: 4

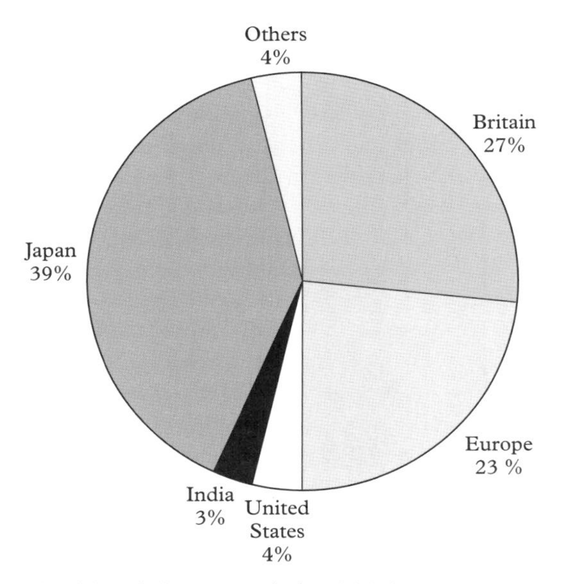

Fig. 7.2 World trade in cotton cloth, 1936–8
Source: Robson 1957: 4

industries. In this context, it is also important to establish how far, albeit in different ways, the First World War acted as a catalyst to strategies which, in their different ways, either helped to create over-capacity or did little to alleviate its worst symptoms. Previous networks were put to the test whilst new ones emerged as, nationally and internationally, collusion became the accepted way to handle market failure.

The impact of the First World War

Between 1914 and 1920 the British and American cotton industries were subject to a range of diverging pressures which contributed to their respective difficulties in the 1920s and 1930s. For the United States, wartime demand and the enthusiasm generated by the postwar boom stimulated a capacity increase in all the cotton manufacturing regions. This, in turn, brought an intensification of competitive pressures in the postwar years. In Britain, on the other hand, the problems stemmed less from the direct internal impact of the war as from its lasting repercussions for the international economy. This contributed to a decline in export markets from which the industry was never to recover and which shaped strategies throughout the interwar period.

The First World War irreversibly tilted the international balance of economic power away from Europe towards a bipolar world where the United States' international standing was vastly enhanced (Kennedy 1988: 249–330). The dramatic expansion of United States manufacturing capacity, in general, began after 1880. However, the First World War placed the United States in a unique position to begin in earnest to capitalise on trading and investment opportunities in the developing areas of the world. Consequently its business community displayed increasing optimism about long-term prospects in both South America and the Orient, as well as for war demand from Europe (Wilson 1971: 158). The United States was thus transformed into a major exporter, not just of foodstuffs and raw materials, but also of manufactured goods, especially the products of the Second Industrial Revolution. There was consequently considerable industrial expansion. Between 1914 and 1918 the manufacturing labour force grew from 8.2m in 1914 to 10.2m in 1918, whilst this was accompanied by substantial technological and business change (Fearon 1987: 7).

The cotton industry received a less dramatic stimulus than manufacturing industry generally from the First World War. Nevertheless, patterns of foreign and domestic demand were affected. This, in turn, stimulated an expansion of capacity and changes to production strategies in all of the cotton manufacturing regions. Piece goods exports rose

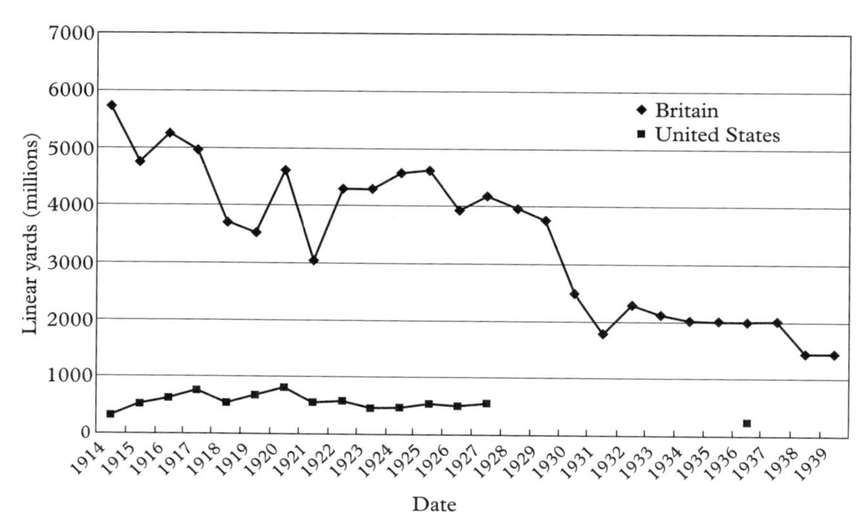

Fig. 7.3 British and United States cotton cloth exports, 1914–39
Source: Mitchell 1988; Robson 1957: 358; Cotton Yarn Association 1928: 18

during and immediately after the war and their geographic scope increased, but they remained a tiny fraction of Britain's exports as Figure 7.3 shows. During the war and postwar boom, which lasted until 1920, average United States cotton piece goods exports rose by 53.9 per cent and whilst a subsequent decline occurred in the 1920s some wartime export growth was sustained. Despite Japanese competition, which was severe in the Far East, high shipping costs and other restrictions disrupted supplies of cotton goods in the British Dominions and created new export opportunities for American cotton textile producers. As a result the United States gained an additional share of the Indian market during the war and firms believed that both the high quality and favourable price differential, *vis-à-vis* British goods, would enable them to maintain sales gains when hostilities ceased and conditions returned to normal.[1] In addition, exports of American cotton goods also expanded during the war and its aftermath to Canada, Mexico, and Cuba and Central America generally. The unusual conditions even allowed some penetration of European markets.[2] The First World War also increased the domestic market for cotton cloth, though relatively modestly because

[1] United States Department of Commerce, *The United States in India's Trade*, Washington 1939, p. 15.

[2] United States Tariff Commissioners, *The Japanese Cotton Industry and Trade*, Washington 1921, p. 148.

Table 7.2. *Size of mills in the United States, 1904–27 (spinning and weaving mills)*

	Av. looms per mill	Av. spindles per mill
Cotton growing states		
1904	543	18,181
1919	736	29,171
1927	724	29,319
New England states		
1904	1,453	54,989
1919	1,724	69,286
1927	1,910	80,006

Source: Lemert 1933: 121.

the United States did not enter the conflict until 1917. However, military demand for cloth for uniforms and for tyre fabrics for automobiles, combined with opportunities overseas, brought a surge of demand which created a sellers' market that brought temporary relief to a beleaguered New England cotton industry and to Philadelphia (Scranton 1989: 10).

Capacity rose as new and larger mills were built, as shown in Table 7.2. Yet the idea that there was a general expansion in the scale of firms is misleading in this period, for any growth in the average size of mills was far less noticeable in the South, where the bulk of new capacity was added, than in the North. Seventy-five per cent of the increase in operating spindleage, between 1914 and 1920, occurred in the Southern states, especially in North Carolina where numerous small and isolated mills were built at a time of low entry barriers and high profits (Minchin 1997: 7). The shift in active spindleage from North to South continued throughout the interwar period, as Figures 7.4 and 7.5 demonstrate, with the proliferation of small mills increasing the intensity of competition (Michl 1938: 146).

Dividend payments were largely sustained in the British cotton industry during the war. Nevertheless, in other respects, the wartime experience contrasted sharply with that in the United States. After a sustained period of expansion, from 1900 onwards, capacity growth stagnated and exports suffered a collapse from which they did not recover (Figure 7.3). By 1918 cotton piece exports were 64 per cent of their 1914 level with the principal losses coming in the Indian market, as Figure 7.6 shows. There cost, policy, competitive and demand changes combined to undermine the previous dominance of British cotton goods. With its exceptional degree of export orientation, the British cotton industry had always been exposed to

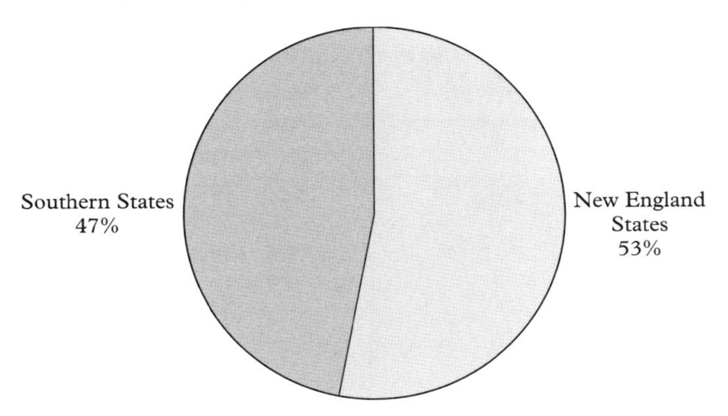

Fig. 7.4 Active spindleage in the United States cotton industry, 1921–2
Source: Michl 1938: 148

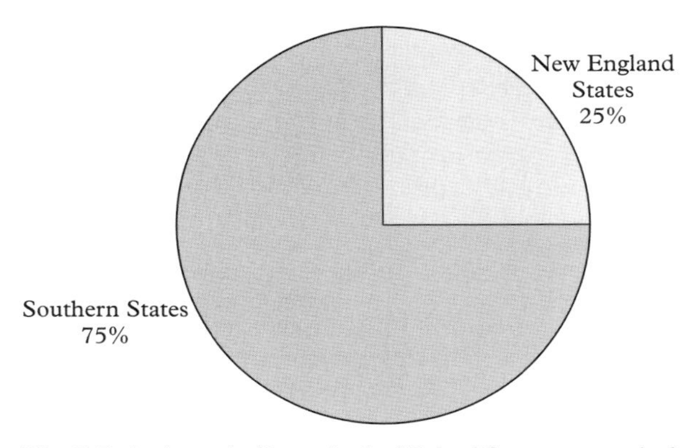

Fig. 7.5 Active spindleage in the United States cotton industry, July 1937
Source: Michl 1938: 146

the fluctuations of the international economy and was especially susceptible both to the disruption and disorder which the First World War created in the international economy and to the train of political events in the subcontinent, for which the war was a catalyst. More generally in the Far East and elsewhere, Lancashire became extremely vulnerable to Japanese competition (Tyson 1968: 111; Dupree 1990b: 102; Wurm 1993: 196).

The sustained rise in freight rates, combined with government controls on shipping, drastically restricted the supplies of American cotton used by Lancashire in production for the Indian market. Output of Lancashire's cotton mills dropped to 70 per cent of capacity and eventually to 50 per cent by March 1918. In terms of the war effort, even this level of produc-

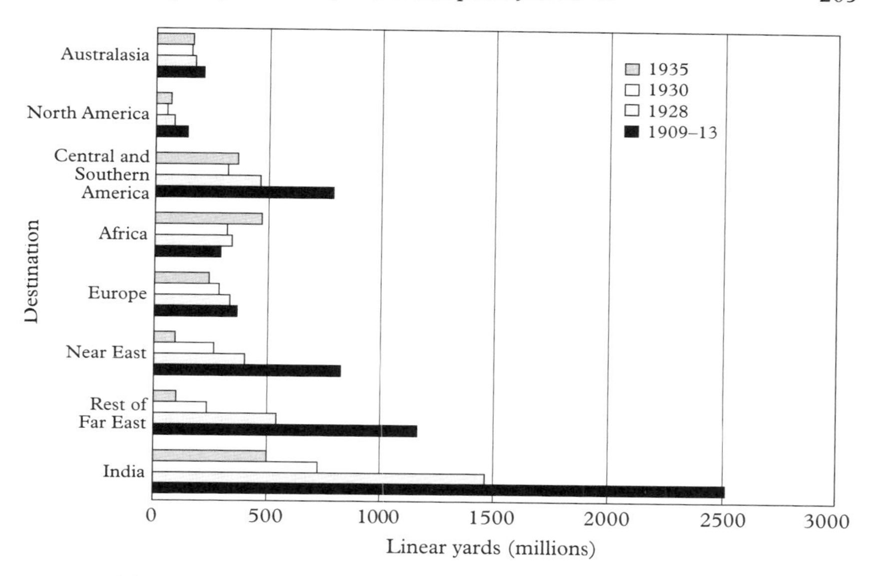

Fig. 7.6 Destinations of British cotton cloth exports, 1909–35
Source: Clay 1931: 48; Burnley and District Cotton Industry Study Group 1937: 18

tion may have been wasteful of resources and of increasingly scarce labour, but did create shortages of both yarn and cloth in Indian markets, fostering one of the stimuli which encouraged growth in the Bombay cotton spinning industry (Tomlinson 1979: 496; Singleton 1994: 617). In addition, the war had direct implications for Indian tariff policy and led to a fundamental shift in both the level and implications of tariffs. India entered the war with a revenue tariff of just 3.5 per cent on cotton cloth; by 1917 this had reached 7.5 per cent (Tomlinson 1977: 55). The combined stimulus of a tariff, which was creeping from raising revenue towards being protective, with the sharp decline in supplies of cotton goods from Lancashire, encouraged import substitution in India. As a result, in the course of the war, India's share of her own domestic market rose by around 20 per cent to 40 per cent (Tomlinson 1979: 504).

The wartime expansion of the Indian cotton industry was modest in comparison with the Japanese over the same period. Before 1914 Japan had successfully infiltrated the Chinese market, undermining earlier American gains there and squeezing the British. However, in common with the United States, the Japanese industry benefited from the market possibilities offered by the war. As the British Consul in Osaka affirmed, the First World War:

accorded to the [Japanese cotton industry] its great opportunity. . . . Not only did Japanese manufacturers find themselves [protected] from competition in their main market – China – but owing to the incapacity of England and other regular suppliers . . . they were able to build up a great trade in substitute goods with markets to which they had not previously found entry. (Quoted in Robertson 1990: 88)

Between 1913 and 1918, therefore, Japanese cotton cloth production grew by 55 per cent, while piece good exports quadrupled and also expanded in scope to include British India. Consequently Japanese piece goods imports to India rose, from just 0.44m linear yards in 1911–12 to over 238m linear yards in 1918–19, and Japan's share of India's imports rose from 1 per cent to 21 per cent (Tomlinson 1979: 499; Hardach 1987: 279). Whilst this represented only 7 per cent of the total Indian market and expansion was temporarily checked during the 1920s, it was a precursor of renewed Japanese export growth in the Far East during the 1930s (Tomlinson 1994: 347).

Given the disproportionate reliance of Lancashire on Far Eastern and especially the Indian market, the long-term implications of these changes were considerable and are captured in Figure 7.6. Indeed it has been calculated that the overall loss in trade volume, which was largest in the Indian market but also occurred in China, Latin America and the Near East between 1913 and 1928, was the equivalent of around a third of England's cotton weaving capacity (Robertson 1990: 91).

Postwar boom and slump: problems of over-capacity

The First World War had profound, if contrasting, implications for the economic environments faced by cotton manufacturers in both Britain and the United States. Set alongside these changes, the intense postwar boom, which lasted until the collapse in world trade in 1920–1, served to reinforce the differences in the two industries, whilst contributing to the difficulties which both faced in the 1920s. In Britain, after more than four years of war, the boom saw shortages of producer and consumer goods. These and other inflationary pressures led to dramatically spiralling prices and spinning margins in the cotton industry, as shown in Figure 7.7, while, as Figure 7.8 demonstrates, dividends rocketed. Whereas in the United States this encouraged mill building and re-equipment, especially in the South, in Britain the war and its aftermath continued to disrupt the building and equipping of new mills (Daniels and Jewkes 1928: 170). Consequently buoyant price conditions and high dividends encouraged speculation rather than modernisation.

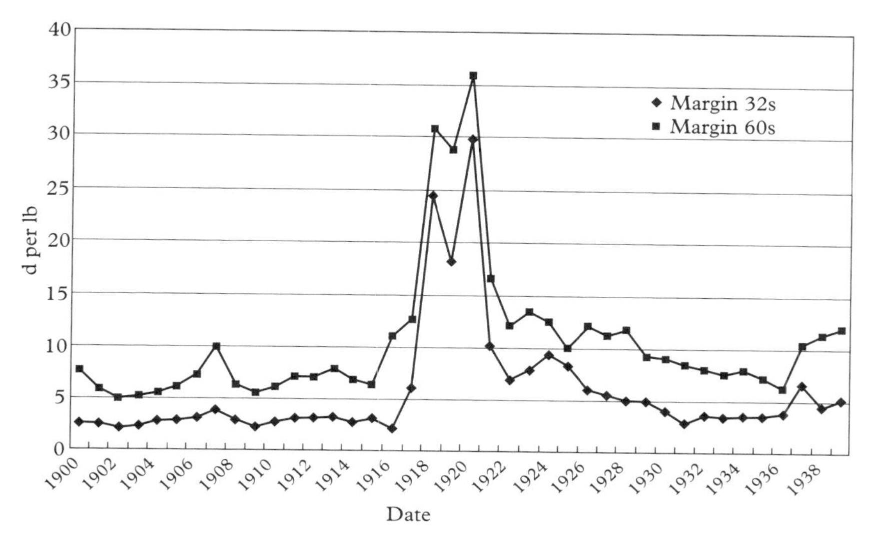

Fig. 7.7 Margins on 32s and 60s twist, 1900–39
Source: Robson 336–7

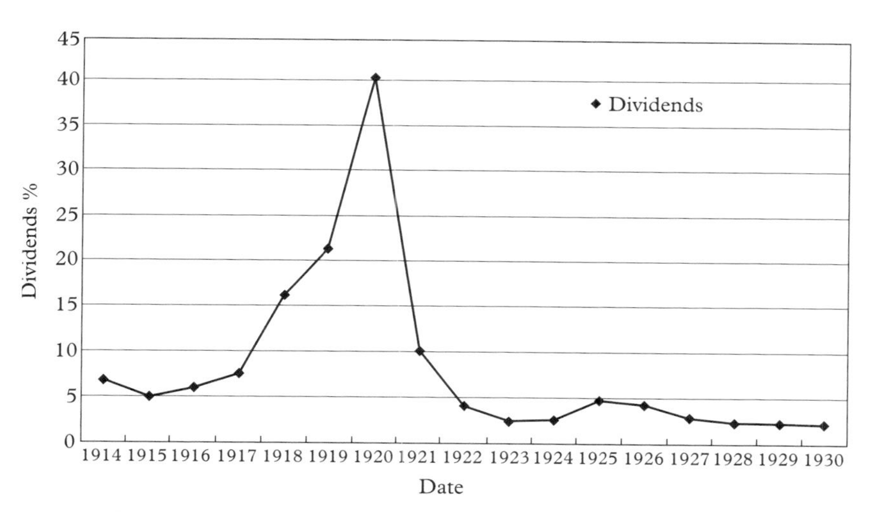

Fig. 7.8 Dividends in Lancashire spinning (public companies), 1914–30
Source: Robson: 338

Partly stimulated, no doubt, by the activities of the newly formed Oldham and District Share Exchange (set up at the height of speculation in October 1919, in competition with the official exchange) mill sales, especially in the American section, gathered pace. In the latter half of 1919 alone 150 mills changed hands, the majority being subsequently refloated at vastly inflated capitalisations. As in the prewar building boom, financial syndicates, who formed loosely grouped holding companies, were especially active in this period. The majority of members of these syndicates were local men, whose personal fortunes had been bolstered by share dealings before the war. London-based financial groups did play a part, however, as in the case of the Amalgamated Cotton Mills Trust. Formed in October 1918, this group purchased 15 mills, including the massive Horrocks Crewdson and Co, and acquired in total 17,500 looms, 786,000 mules, 548,000 rings and 117,000 doubling spindles. This diversified trust also included holdings in the Beecham Trust, Dunlop Rubber and the Tyre Investment Company (Toms 1997; *Textile Mercury* 29 November 1919, 13 December 1919, 3 January 1920; Clay 1931: 22).

The Amalgamated Cotton Mills Trust was established at the height of spiralling dividends and dismissed as pure speculation (Robson 1957: 157). Yet close analysis of its constituent parts and internal strategies suggests that it was a carefully constructed, closely managed grouping. Moreover, its reliance on a London financial syndicate masks an initiative which relied upon the complementarity of a number of closely connected firms. The Amalgamated Cotton Mills Trust Ltd was not, therefore, a random grouping of mismatched and failing businesses. Instead it produced a diversified array of fabrics ranging from shirtings, drills and sheetings for the Indian and Chinese market, through voiles, poplins and fancy goods for the home market to lace, sewing and hosiery thread, fine Egyptian yarn and tyre threads while also including a cotton waste manufacturer. This vertical grouping also embraced a shipper and vitally an innovative clothing firm, the Cellular Clothing Company Ltd (Amalgamated Cotton Mills Trust Ltd 1920). Such diversity provided a sound basis for access to a wide range of markets, but created potentially serious managerial problems. However, the constituent firms were already tied together by personal contact, ties of ownership and business ties. It is not clear how far Sir Frank Hollins' general penchant for mergers may have lain behind the amalgamation and Horrockses, Crewdon and Co Ltd's temporary inclusion. Certainly this nineteenth-century merger had created important connections between members of the giant Preston firm of Horrockses and Bolton, the home of the majority of the subsidiary firms. What is apparent, however, is that at the heart of the Amalgamated

Cotton Mills Trust Ltd was a critical core of Bolton firms, themselves tied together by the holding company John Haslam and Co Ltd. This holding company within a holding company controlled the seven key firms which gave the amalgamation its distinctive features as a vertical grouping and helped to provide direction. This group of firms had an internal rationale prior to the amalgamation which was further reinforced by a complex web of interlocking directorships extending across all subsidiaries of the Amalgamated Cotton Mills Trust Ltd. The six managing directors, who interestingly did not include Hollins, were represented on the boards of all subsidiaries whilst the majority of directors sat on the boards of at least four subsidiary companies.[3] However, the firm did not enjoy spectacular success in the 1920s and although it remained profitable, the group withheld dividends for most of the period (Clay 1931: 26a).

Yet, if the Amalgamated Cotton Mills Ltd was a carefully considered flotation it was the exception. Most such activity in this period was highly speculative. At the height of the boom, shares were trading at seven or eight times their original value and, in all, 23,832,000 spindles, 46 per cent of Lancashire's total, changed hands. This development proved to have lasting and damaging consequences for the character and adaptability of much of the industry throughout the interwar period (Daniels and Jewkes 1928: 173–4).

The geographic and sectoral distribution of recapitalised firms depended to a fair degree upon the ownership and investment patterns of firms that had evolved before the First World War. The prevalence of public, as opposed to private companies in the Oldham area, meant that the majority of recapitalised firms were in the town and its environs, whilst those areas of Lancashire where private companies continued to predominate, such as Bolton and the weaving towns of the north-east, saw far less activity. Accordingly 56 per cent of refloated companies lay in the coarse 'American' spinning section around Oldham, as compared with 19 per cent in the fine Egyptian section that had gravitated to Bolton, whilst only 14 per cent of Lancashire's loomage was affected (Daniels and Jewkes 1928: 175; Bowden and Higgins 1998: 327).

Postwar expansionary and inflationary pressures were less extreme in the United States than in Britain. Nevertheless high profitability and the expectation that advantages in export markets, brought about by chaos in Europe, would continue, encouraged an air of optimism and prosperity and led to further expansion of capacity. During the postwar boom the experience of the United States cotton industry seemed to replicate that of the highly successful industries of the Second Industrial Revolution.

[3] *Skinner's Cotton Trade Directory,* 1923.

Yet, whereas automobiles, machinery and consumer durables experienced high profitability, burgeoning dividends and share values and rising exports until the late 1920s, the Prosperity Decade largely passed the cotton industry by. Despite an impressive expansion of output underpinned by the sustained improvement in labour productivity growth, which had begun during the late nineteenth century and had been further encouraged by the war, the cotton industry performed poorly long before the Great Depression (Learned 1930: 501–12). In 1930, Claudius T. Murchison, President of the Cotton Textile Institute, wrote:

> King Cotton is sick. Though his illness was somewhat intensified by the stock market crash of 1929 and the ensuing events, it is in no sense due to that episode. He has not been a well monarch since 1923. From that time to the present . . . he has been steadily growing worse. The event is all the more alarming in that the illness [has] persisted for some years and in fact reached a highly aggravated state during a period when all of the other important personifications of American business were enjoying the best of health. (Murchison 1930: 1)

A chronic sickness infected all the textile regions of the North. At a time when, in manufacturing as a whole, the value of securities was spiralling upwards, those of cotton manufacturing companies fell by half. New England mill stocks were becoming worthless and the level of dividends declined by some 80 per cent during the 1920s. Indeed, by 1929 dividends had fallen to just one-fifth of their 1923 value. Organisational deficiencies and the stultifying effect of a moribund family firm culture, combined with union strength, have sometimes been assumed to lie at the heart of the North's problems. Firms were generally slower to innovate and introduce automatic technologies, especially Draper looms, than their Southern competitors. In a trend which began before the First World War many New England producers, and especially those in Fall River and New Bedford, had preferred to modify existing technology than to risk new investment. Sales of Draper looms to the North did rise considerably during the First World War and in several postwar years outstripped those in the South. Even so, by 1929 whilst 80 per cent of looms were automatic in the South, the level of automation was only 59 per cent in New England (Mass 1984: 168–9; Feller 1974: 571). Since Draper looms reduced but did not remove the cost advantage enjoyed by Southern manufacturers, there is no clear-cut evidence that by innovating New England manufacturers improved their prospects. When it is remembered that Fall River's bankrupted companies were using an above-average proportion of automatics, it is hard to sustain the idea that technical change would have dramatically improved the fortunes of the North. Formerly profitable and even relatively new mills went out of business throughout Massachusetts. For example, Bay State Corporation, which had been built after the First World War at a total cost of $4,000,000 and described as the 'lowest cost wide-sheeting producer', was eventually put up for sale for just $200,000 in 1929 (Feller 1974: 577; Smith 1944: 119; Murchison 1930: 22; Clay 1931: 52).

The apparently more dynamic South, where mills were exclusively equipped with rings and relied heavily on automatic looms, did not entirely escape the malaise. There, whilst business failure was rarer, prosperity was also surprisingly illusive. In the cotton growing states, employment was irregular and only half of Southern mills paid a regular dividend during much of the 1920s. In addition, mill property fell sharply in price and the value of stocks plummeted by $100m in the six years before the Wall Street Crash. Consequently an index of 25 leading Southern mill shares showed a decline of more than 50 per cent between 1923 and July 1930 (Clay 1931: 52). Even giants like the denim producers of Greensboro faced poor returns. Thus the company's President complained:

> Yes we managed to make some money up there in Greensboro. We have large mills, a tremendous unit, enormous production and consequent low overheads. In recent years, it has been revamped and re-equipped with new and up to date machinery, has been 'efficiency-ised' by experts and aside from its President, whom modesty eliminates from the running, we believe it to be well and ably managed. I have made its tax returns also, and I happen to know that in this same 6 year period I was talking about 1924–29 inclusive, it averaged earning of 3 and 4⁄10 per cent on its investment – less than ordinary saving bank interest. (Quoted in Murchison 1930: 33–4)

Similarly Dan River Mills, Danville, Virginia, another of the South's larger and innovative firms, experienced low returns, with net profits, between 1922 and 1931, averaging less than $900,000. In both 1924 and 1930, on the other hand, they recorded heavy losses, the first in their history. Throughout the period Dan River paid out dividends which were in excess of profits. These difficulties meant that after 1923 the firm was unable to pay workers their 'economy dividend' – an integral part of their system of industrial democracy – on a regular basis. Set alongside efforts to intensify work, this, in turn, made the firm vulnerable to labour unrest which exploded into a strike in 1930. Difficulties continued and in 1938 a loss of over $1m was recorded (Smith 1960: 191–2; Wright 1986: 147). These problems were felt even more acutely by the numerous small firms in the South where bankruptcy rates rose strikingly and where mills were sold for a fraction of their original worth (Clay 1931: 53).

Over-capacity and over-production lay at the heart of the troubles of the United States cotton industry in the 1920s. Their origins lay in the strategies pursued in the nineteenth century and were accentuated by the

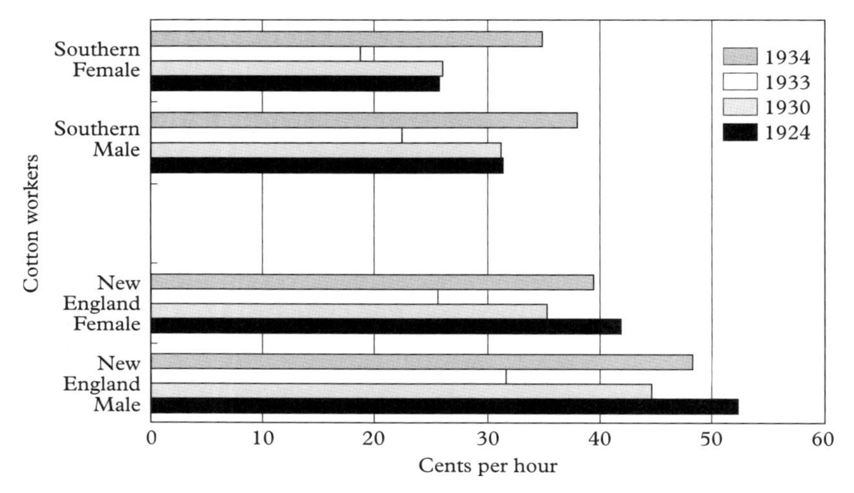

Fig. 7.9 Average United States cotton textile wage rates, 1924–34
Source: Michl 1938: 150

First World War in the four distinctive cotton regions. Indeed, it was only the stimulus of the First World War which provided a stay of execution for the bulk producers of Massachusetts. However, the war contributed to the chronic problems and rising stocks which bedevilled the entire industry and helped to erode profit margins after 1923.

Wartime demand had led to a partial reversal of the trend away from staples in the North, especially in New Bedford, and doubtless helps to explain the concurrent rise in investment in Draper looms. This city, which had developed a good prewar reputation in the finer end of the market, shifted production in favour of military demand for twills and towards tyre fabrics. As a result surplus postwar capacity emerged, when re-ordered mills were unable to sustain their position against the South. This was especially the case because, despite the recruitment of black labour in Northern mills during the war, wage differentials between the two regions remained substantial as Figure 7.9 demonstrates, with 1924 wages being on average 40 per cent higher in the North than in the South. In addition, the war had induced the introduction of night shifts, which persisted throughout the 1920s in the South, where labour laws were lax and where hours worked by individual workers were on average 13 per cent longer than in the North (Donald 1951: 37). Northern manufacturers, with some justification, saw this as a major source of over-production and falling prices and as the major basis of Southern competitive advantage (Wright 1986: 198–9, 208).

A minority of the larger and more successful New England firms were

Table 7.3. *Branches of Northern firms in Alabama, Georgia, North and South Carolina, 1931*

Number of firms	Northern firms	Branches
20		29
14	Massachusetts	23
1	Maine	2
5	Rhode Island	10
1	Maryland	2
2	New Hampshire	2
4	Pennsylvania	4
Total 47		72

Source: Lemert 1933: 156.

able to develop a successful and creative response to this environment. In the mid-1920s, for example, the Maine firm of Pepperells developed its marketing division and achieved a combination of the scale economies of long runs with the flexibility of a wide product range. It did this by rationalising production at its Biddeford factory to concentrate on towelling and cotton blankets. At the same time it consolidated, first with Massachusetts Cotton Mills of Lowell in 1926 to produce complementary goods such as draperies, work clothing and ginghams and in 1929 with Granite Mills of Fall River to begin rayon production for the fashion markets of Boston and New York. However, the firm's investment did not end with New England and eventually became secondary to the ownership of two further complementary mills in the South. As a result of these policies Pepperells achieved better than average performance in the late 1920s and 1930s (Knowlton 1948: 233–43).

Whilst the establishment of Southern branches became increasingly normal, as demonstrated in Table 7.3, the environment forced the majority of firms, in New England and the South, into a price war of increasingly damaging intensity and which the North was bound to lose. In the first place, in the North both tighter labour laws and trade unions inhibited attempts to cut wages and 'stretch out' work to cut costs, whilst the increasingly depressed climate discouraged further modernisation there.

The problems in Philadelphia from the mid-1920s onwards were more complex. Until 1925 Philadelphia had benefited from the Prosperity Decade. The depth of skill capabilities had allowed her flexible producers to achieve substantial growth in fashion hosiery and fabrics for automobile and furnishing upholstery. However, Southern producers soon encroached even on these markets. In addition, the growing need to hold stocks to accommodate the changing requirements of buyers increased the problems of the flexible producers (Scranton 1989: 325 and 461).

The decline of the North in the 1920s was precipitous. In New England, for example, in just six years between 1923 and 1929, waves of bankruptcies and liquidations meant that 5,400,000 spindles were scrapped and thousands became jobless. Mill closures occurred in all the New England states between 1923 and 1933. In Massachusetts, the number of mills declined from 245 to 137, in Rhode Island from 153 to 93 and in Connecticut from 69 to 35. In New Bedford about two-thirds of the town's corporations had closed, and in Manchester, New Hampshire, the liquidation of the giant Amoskeag works precipitated the loss of 10,000 jobs. Fall River too became a ghost town and in 1931 the city's position became so precarious that the Commonwealth of Massachusetts assumed control of its financial affairs (Michl 1938: 147–8; Scranton 1997: 339). In Philadelphia, although the decline was less sharp than in New England, 400 firms closed, with a permanent loss of 30,000 jobs between 1925 and 1939 and the vitality of an industrial district based upon flexibility and quality was lost (Murchison 1930: 22; Scranton 1989: 325; Scranton 1997: 340). As Figure 7.5 demonstrates, by 1937 only a quarter of United States spinning capacity remained in New England.

The British cotton industry also experienced serious difficulties in the 1920s. Falling demand with the collapse of overseas markets was accompanied by a rise in fixed costs and difficulties in achieving cost savings from wage reductions or productivity improvement. The high degree of vertical and spatial specialisation in Lancashire, which had emerged before 1914, meant that differing sectors and the towns which relied on them had varying experiences in the 1920s, before the onset of world depression swept the entire industry into turmoil and decline (Robson 1957: 7–8).

The First World War had had profound implications for Britain's position in her main Asian market which were not reversed when peace was restored. Instead political and economic conditions in British India became increasingly delicate in the 1920s. These trends, combined with the growing penetration of the Indian market by the Japanese, especially in the 1930s, meant that Lancashire's prime prewar market continued to shrink throughout the interwar period, as highlighted in Figure 7.6. This was not all, however, for British monetary policy and the commitment to restore and maintain the gold standard at prewar parity also damaged the cotton industry's fortunes in the 1920s.

In an era when industrialisation was spreading rapidly, the prewar size of the Lancashire cotton industry was unsustainable (Tomlinson 1994: 373). Yet the speedy loss of the industry's largest market was remarkable. By 1939 Lancashire's piece goods trade with India fell to just 6 per cent of the level it held on the eve of the First World War (Chatterji 1992: 3). This reflected the extent to which a chain of events, precipitated by the First World War, had lasting repercussions on the postwar economy and politics of India and on the size of the Indian market available to all exporters.

Nationalist pressures were one reason for the decline of Lancashire's market in India. The boycott of first British yarn and then cloth, inspired by Gandhi, gathered momentum in 1921. This movement reached a peak in 1930 when Marwari distributors and importers in Calcutta, which handled 65 per cent of postwar British imports, began cancelling orders in Manchester. Such boycotts led to a further contraction of Lancashire's trade with India and to outrage in Lancashire where it stimulated protests and lobbying of Cabinet ministers (Chatterji 1992: 347–51; Tomlinson 1977: 116).

Price competitiveness had always been important in the Indian market, but it became ever more critical in the 1920s. This was because shifts in the terms of trade, against primary producers, reduced Indian real incomes. The growth of the Bombay mill industry and Gandhi's emphasis on handloom weaving meant that a growing share of the Indian market was supplied domestically. Lancashire exporters were squeezed by Indian competition at the coarser end of the market in sheeting, dhooti and shirtings. On the other hand, falling incomes meant that the tariff undoubtedly had a marginal effect, especially after it was increased to 15 per cent in 1930 (Tomlinson 1977: 113–14; Dupree 1990b: 101–17). However, after 1928 and especially in the 1930s, driven by growing political pressures, in the Far East, Japanese competition became an increasingly potent threat in India and in many other of Lancashire's principal markets. The Manchuria incident precipitated a boycott of Japanese goods in China which in turn stimulated a drive to increase the scale and scope of Japanese exports (Wurm 1993: 217–19). By 1933 the volume of Japanese piece good exports had overtaken Lancashire to reach 2,087m square yards (Robertson 1990: 89).

Generally Japanese competitive advantage in cotton textiles in this period derived partly from lower labour costs as compared with Western producers. However, a business organisation which involved a combination of vertical holding companies to ensure a complementarity of shipping, financial and commercial services for industry, with one of the most effective collusive trade associations, contributed enormously to the international competitive advantage of the industry and to its ability to keep costs low.[4] In the 1920s these advantages allowed Japanese producers to

[4] United States Bureau of Foreign and Domestic Commerce, *Cotton Goods in Japan and their Competition in the Manchuria Market*, Special Agent's Series, No. 86, 1914, pp. 58–64.

undercut both British and Indian manufacturers in the Indian market and British exporters more generally. Further, a savage depreciation of the yen against the dollar in 1933, from $48.8 to $25.2, helped to make the price competitiveness of Japanese cotton goods in world markets almost unassailable (Rooth 1993: 181–2).

The general consequences for Lancashire exports of these trends are well known and are summarised in Figures 7.3 and 7.6. Cloth exports fell dramatically although yarn exports were less vulnerable though tiny in comparison to cloth. Nevertheless the fate of the spinners, who had only a limited reliance on yarn exports, was critically dependent upon the fortunes of the weavers, so that both sectors were terminally damaged. Moreover, the spinners were seriously weakened by the speculative excesses of the postwar boom, with the American section experiencing profound difficulties throughout the interwar period. In finishing, the bleaching sector suffered most from both the continued contraction of the Indian market and from the shift in domestic clothing demand towards printed and dyed fabrics. The printing sector, on the other hand, remained fairly robust during the 1920s and benefited from the import of bulk grey cloth between 1925 and 1930 (Robson 1957: 8). The onset of world depression in 1929 and the accompanying decline in primary product prices further reduced the markets for cotton goods and profits vanished in all sectors. Unemployment in Lancashire rose dramatically, never falling below 10 per cent between 1926 and 1938 and peaking at 38.5 per cent in 1931. A fifth of the unemployment in the 1930s was in the weaving belt with unemployment in Darwen and Blackburn standing at 42.7 per cent and 47.9 per cent respectively (Tomlinson 1994: 354 and 356; Singleton 1995: 218; Chatterji 1992: 149; Wurm 1993: 250). There was, consequently, a permanent shrinkage in the industry in the 1930s and the number of insured workers fell by a third between 1924 and 1938 (Board of Trade Report 1946: 7).

Although some decline in the level of spatial specialisation occurred in Lancashire during the interwar period, there was considerable variation in the level of employment across the county in the 1920s. As Figure 7.10 demonstrates, spinning generally struggled and never regained its 1921 level. The seemingly buoyant employment conditions in weaving are partly distorted by the favourable performance of Nelson and Colne. In spinning quite noticeable contrasts occurred between towns, depending upon their particular specialisms and how dependent they were upon the Indian market and upon how seriously they had been affected by the postwar speculation. These variations were especially noticeable in Oldham and Bolton, reflecting the differing market conditions faced respectively by the 'American' and 'Egyptian' sections of the industry. Consequently, Oldham firms struggled throughout the 1920s, with the

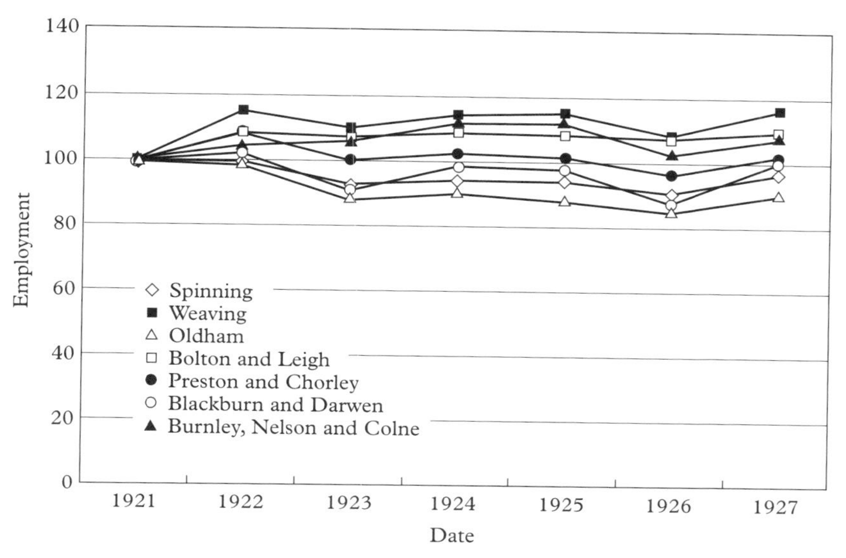

Fig. 7.10 Employment in Lancashire cotton towns, 1921–7
Source: Daniels & Jewkes 1928: 190

annual reports of the once-powerful Oldham Master Cotton Spinners Association (OMCSA) bearing testimony to a decade when any sign of prosperity was illusive. This began with the slump of 1921 which was described as 'the most serious depression ever experienced by the cotton trade'[5] and continued with barely any respite throughout the decade, so that a despairing annual report describes 1927 as 'one of the most trying and disheartening of all the years of depression since the boom of 1919–20, for those engaged in the American section of the cotton industry, whether as spinners or as manufacturers.'[6]

Dismal trading conditions were not the only problem in the 1920s however, for, as Figure 7.7 demonstrates, margins in the American section, whilst higher than before the First World War, were unlikely to compensate for the increased fixed costs faced by the heavily indebted mills which averaged at £1,710 per 1,000 spindles for refloated companies (Daniels and Jewkes 1928: 177). By contrast, in towns like Bolton and Leigh, where reflotation was limited and which were oriented towards the spinning of finer counts using mainly Egyptian cotton, employment levels were generally more stable and trading conditions more buoyant. In weaving, largely

[5] Oldham Master Cotton Spinners Association, *Annual Report*, 1921, p. 3.
[6] Oldham Master Cotton Spinners Association, *Annual Report*, 1927, p. 3.

untouched by fixed interest charges, the main determinant of experience was market orientation. Figure 7.10 confirms that Blackburn, with its concentration on dhooties for the Indian market, faired worst, whereas the more varied and higher quality orientation of Nelson and Colne and the fancy orientation of Preston's large employers created more favourable market conditions (Daniels and Jewkes 1928: 162–3; Clay 1931: 20; McIvor 1996: 185).

It is clear, therefore, that whilst the British and American cotton industries shared the common problem of over-capacity in the interwar period, its origins were quite distinct. Whereas Lancashire faced an unprecedented and unpredictable collapse in its principal overseas markets, the market for American cotton goods declined comparatively only marginally, although the growth of demand failed to live up to expectations. Instead the glut, after 1920, was a reflection of a cumulative growth in capacity so that the growth of output soon outstripped the growth of demand. In both cases, whilst the First World War precipitated the onset of difficulties, their precise direction was moulded by the historical forces which had shaped the industries. In Britain these were the symbiosis between the late nineteenth-century expansion of coarse production, the rise of the City and government economic and political strategies in India, which made the industry extremely vulnerable to changes in the international economy. In the United States, on the other hand, the competitive, technological and organisational structure of the industry, which was inseparable from its domestic orientation, interacted in the postwar world to create a glut.

To understand why output exceeded demand in both countries manufacturers' behaviour should also be set against fundamental changes in consumption patterns which affected firms in both countries. In the 15 years between the outbreak of the First World War and the Great Crash of 1929 women's fashion was transformed in the Western world. Wartime Utility clothing had seen some simplification of dress, but after the First World War skirts became shorter and less full and in 1925 came the revolution which shocked the establishment on both sides of the Atlantic: the coming of the short skirt. Although skirts lengthened again in the 1930s changes in women's lifestyle and attitudes meant the trend was never reversed (Laver 1969: 229–33). This fashion change inevitably reduced demand for cotton cloth in the United States and Europe at the very time when other forces generated a collapse in overseas markets. For British firms this inevitably limited the ability to shift from overseas to the home market. For the heavily domestically oriented firms of the United States the change caused panic, especially since a growing taste for silk dress material among the affluent meant that cotton cloth was increasingly used at the cheaper end of the market. This was not the only change in consumption patterns, however, for in the United States the demand for drills, ginghams and damasks collapsed, being replaced by demand for textiles for use in the production of tyres, automobiles and electrical goods (Hall et al. 1986: 265; Wright 1995: 47).

Strategic response: collusion, collective stability and government–industry relations

The internal and external forces affecting the economic environment faced by British and American cotton manufacturers in the interwar period elicited a range of responses. In the United States manufacturers continued to invest in new technology in the South (and even the North) in the 1920s. In the South 'stretch out' saw the use of double shift systems which increased levels of machinery utilisation and the squeezing of more work out of operatives. Productivity rose with rising implementation of production monitoring devices and the continued spread of automation and the use of electric motors, with output per worker rising in Southern mills by 76 per cent and real hourly earnings by 44 per cent in the interwar period (Wright 1995: 47). There erupted a sustained price war between North and South which became associated with wage cutting campaigns that soured labour relations (Hall et al. 1986: 265). As margins fell during the 1920s, both New England and Southern rapid-throughput mills tended to build stocks rather than run on short time, to avoid a rise in average costs. This was a strategy which ironically made their problems worse and led margins to fall even further (Scranton 1989: 379–85; Wright 1986: 208; Markham 1950: 79). The trend towards over-production was further encouraged by the separation of manufacturing from selling and the close financial relationship between commission houses and the mills they represented. This gave the commission houses a vested interest in encouraging the manufacturers to produce, then using their own excess stocks to drive prices down and maximise sales and hence their commission revenue. The mills for their part kept producing to cover overhead costs (Wood 1986: 37; Minchin 1997: 8).

If, in the United States, the growing intensity of competition between North and South was a prominent feature of this period, in Lancashire too the internal competitive environment changed, as the level of local specialisation began to diminish. The declining overseas demand for the goods of the 'American' section led companies, within reasonable technological limits, to shift product and market strategies and drove

> firms to seek new outlets in cloths that they did not formerly make. . . . The large firms of a district like Burnley, which has lost most of its bulk trade with China, or Blackburn which has suffered similarly in its trade with India, have turned to production for the less depressed home market and have branched out into new types of product. The results are first that the decline in number of looms is not materially greater in the districts which formerly specialised in the trade that has been lost; secondly, that the depression in the weaving industry has spread to all sections and districts. (Clay 1931: 21)

Attempts to shift product inevitably had technical limitations and intense competition through price cutting was a common response, whilst the rate of technological change remained slow, with rings representing only 27.8 per cent of total British spindleage by 1937 while, in the same year, only 2.9 per cent of all looms were automatics (Robson 1957: 339).

During the 1920s there was a growing awareness, on both sides of the Atlantic, that over-capacity was part of a long-term trend, rather than a reflection of temporary changes. Strategies varied, but intensified price competition was a common feature, whilst efforts to reduce labour costs by improving productivity met with mixed success. These pressures in turn encouraged the business communities in both Britain and the United States to take collective action, which intensified government–industry relations, influenced commercial policy and stimulated amalgamations. However, differences in the origins of the problems and in the historical development of institutions and of the industries, meant that whilst there were striking similarities in the strategies adopted, the detail and emphasis of responses, whether at the level of the firm or the industry, or by government, at times diverged. This was particularly noticeable in the responses to the effects of damaging price competition. In Britain, therefore, while price stabilisation remained a priority, in the 1930s efforts were also, admittedly somewhat haltingly, directed towards accommodating a permanent market shrinkage. In the United States, on the other hand, the very intensity of price cutting strategies in the South meant that throughout, rightly or wrongly, more priority was given to trying to limit output of all firms, rather than to reducing the level of productive capacity. What is clear is that in both countries the very depth of the difficulties faced in the cotton industry made defensive measures more common than innovative strategies. In addition, on both sides of the Atlantic, voluntary restraints on price and output proved problematic and it required statutory powers to achieve any fundamental changes.

In both the United States and Britain competition has been described as atomistic in the late nineteenth century and interwar period. In the United

States the rise of the South prevented the emergence of the oligopolistic structure which developed in many American industries (Markham 1950: 75–6). In Britain, on the other hand, despite some changes in the financial structure of firms and the late nineteenth-century wave of amalgamations, competition within sectors – apart from finishing, where an extremely effective, powerful and profitable cartel developed – was intense. Nevertheless, collective attempts to resolve the respective problems of the cotton industry, by no means entirely successful, began in the 1920s and were accompanied by changes in the negotiating structure of the industry to achieve a semblance of unity.

Unlike the position in the United States, interwar British governments tacitly and, by the 1930s, explicitly supported co-operative action and attempts at collective stabilisation were more openly collusive, albeit often short-lived and problematic. In Lancashire, certainly in spinning, this trend was inseparable from the difficulties which beset that proportion of the industry which had undergone financial reconstruction during the postwar boom. This was because less than half the value of shares were paid up so that the majority of firms were burdened with fixed interest loans from the banks. When the boom collapsed, in 1921 a network of debt remained which seriously hampered any efforts to modernise and rationalise the industry in the 1920s, whilst making a combination of short time working and price maintenance an attractive, if unstable, way to ensure that prices covered costs (Bamberg 1988: 84; Utley 1931: 47; Bowden and Higgins 1998: 327–8). Short time working, whether organised or informal, hitherto the favoured solution to short-term fluctuations, became, from the early 1920s, a long-term response to difficulties. At the same time efforts to secure price maintenance in spinning, weaving and finishing were orchestrated respectively by the Federation of Master Cotton Spinners Association (FMCSA), the Cotton Spinners and Manufacturers Association (CSMA) and variously by the Federation of Calico Printers (FCP) and other finishing associations (McIvor 1996: 192–3; Clay 1931: 27).

The level of success of collusive agreements depends upon a combination of the proportion of capacity involved, the extent of division within a sector, the level of concentration, the extent to which it was possible to police an agreement and upon the state of trade. In the Lancashire cotton industry, a further determinant of success or failure was the extent to which schemes could accommodate the high levels of specialisation. Conversely the opportunity and incentive to maximise individual, as opposed to collective, profits will be greatest where there are numerous firms, where profits are falling and where agreements fail to reflect differing cost structures. Accordingly, easily the most durable and successful collusive arrangement was in printing which, during the interwar period, developed an unrivalled culture of co-operation. Dominated and strongly supported by the Calico Printers Association, the FCP embraced 97 per cent of the industry, enabling its members to behave as quasi-monopolists. Price maintenance in calico printing began in 1916 and a postwar arrangement dated from 1918, when a complex agreement accommodated the wide range of specialisms in the trade. Unlike the majority of Lancashire's collusive agreements this proved to be relatively robust and had sufficient flexibility to become institutionalised until after the Second World War, despite a break during the 1930s. Yet the ability of printers, as service providers, to engage in non-price competition, ultimately did undermine the agreement (Cook and Cohen 1958: 184).

The organisation strove hard to maintain control of capacity and to constrain potentially damaging competition. Thus, as in 1919, the Federation was prepared to purchase printworks to 'prevent the works getting into the hands of customers' (presumably shippers).[7] They were sometimes, as in 1921, susceptible to pressure from their customers to reduce their prices, but they did this as a group rather than through competitive price cutting, showing a collective awareness of a growing threat of grey cloth being exported to be printed. Nor were they averse to adjusting prices upwards if conditions allowed.[8] It was a measure of their success that firms within the industry and, most particularly the Calico Printers Association, remained profitable throughout the 1920s, a phenomenon which undoubtedly contributed to the durability of the evolving arrangement. Only the extreme pressures of depression brought the arrangement to an end in 1932 (Clay 1931: 29; Cook and Cohen 1958: 184).

In contrast to the endurance of price maintenance in printing, arrangements elsewhere for organised short time and even more so for price maintenance, proved problematic and at best sporadic. In both spinning and weaving less than 80 per cent and 65 per cent of capacity respectively were organised during the 1920s and 1930s, whilst it is a commonplace that local variations in product, market, in support for employers' associations and in attitude made it difficult to gain consensus on any sectoral arrangements. This meant that whereas FCP was, after 1922, the sole organisation for the printing sector, FMCSA and CSMA embraced numerous and disparate local associations of spinners and manufacturers (McIvor 1996: 191; Bowden and Higgins 1998: 330–2). To secure either an organised restriction of working hours or a price maintenance scheme,

[7] Greater Manchester Record Office (GMRO), Federation of Calico Printers, Minutes, 10 January 1919.

[8] GMRO, Federation of Calico Printers, Minutes, 25 October 1921; 14 March 1924.

80 per cent of each association was required to vote in favour – a rare outcome in such diverse and varied sectors, where even individual towns lacked a consensus. In Blackburn in 1925, for instance, although there was a recognition that intense competition benefited no one and that collusion had brought prosperity to the finishers, there was little consensus over organised short time proposals.[9] Nevertheless on average 15 per cent of all operatives were on short time work in the interwar period, though difficulties of securing agreements for different sectors meant that much of it was on an informal rather than an organised basis, and thus unpredictable and potentially destabilising (Bowden and Higgins 1998: 332–3).

The achievement of sectoral price maintenance agreements in spinning and weaving was even more difficult than organised short time, until the late 1930s. The legendary individualism of Lancashire's spinners and manufacturers is doubtless important, whilst the refusal by Sir Frank Platt to allow the Lancashire Cotton Corporation, of which he was Chairman, to join the FMCSA clearly weakened this group's bargaining power (Dupree 1987: 253). However, explaining the limits of price collusion, orchestrated by industry-wide organisations, is more complex. The difficulty with attempts at price association, such as the failed Cotton Yarn Association of 1927, is that they were an attempt to achieve price stability across a sector wherein firms faced both differing markets and had differing cost structures. In spinning, the division of the producers into those using predominantly American cotton and those using mainly Egyptian cotton is well known. The heavily indebted American section was encouraged to collude to ensure that prices covered costs, but ironically falling markets for coarse yarns, throughout the 1920s, encouraged price cutting. In the Egyptian section, on the other hand, reasonable profits made the Bolton spinners more inclined to support price agreements (Bowden and Higgins 1998: 339). This might have been avoided had there been a will to introduce sectional price agreements, but the Oldham spinners opposed attempts to differentiate between sections, perhaps fearing the loss of bargaining power which their numerical strength brought them in the FMCSA. It was only in the mid-1930s, after the advantages of localised price agreements, such as the Royton ring spinning arrangement, became obvious, that the Oldham spinners began to favour sectional arrangements. These made way for legally binding price agreements critically linked to scrapping of capacity under the Cotton Industry Reorganisation Act of 1939.[10]

[9] Lancashire Record Office (LRO), Blackburn and District Cotton Employers' Association Minutes, 31 August 1925.

[10] Oldham Master Cotton Spinners Association, *Annual Reports* 1935–7.

In weaving during the 1920s the response to price maintenance varied, but was at best lukewarm with the framing of any collective agreement vastly complicated by varying cost structures. The stumbling block to discussions in 1923 appears to have been the difficulty of producing standardised costings between towns.[11] Ultimately, however, attempts at price fixing amongst spinners and weavers were undermined by the 1,200 or so export shippers who demanded specific cloths at specific prices and competed intensely with each other as well as encouraging internal competition in the industry. A 1937 report from the Burnley and District Cotton Industry Study Group condemned the exporters' position arguing that:

> Internal competition between merchant and merchant and manufacturer and manufacturer often leads to unremunerative prices without any expansion of demand. On many occasions cloths are sold far more cheaply than is necessary and the confidence in the cloth is destroyed by the very fact of these price reductions. Furthermore, this same competition leads to an infinite variety of cloth constructions where such variety is not only unnecessary but is definitely harmful.[12]

Whereas the calico printers had sufficient collusive power to impose their prices on the merchants the manufacturers did not. Indeed discussions on the possibility of exporters by-passing the shippers revealed the relative power of the merchants who, it was alleged, would boycott any manufacturers undertaking their own shipping in any market.[13] Only a minority of large firms moved into marketing during this period and whilst these firms generally enjoyed above-average profits this was by no means universal, whilst the Calico Printers Association's move into marketing proved problematic (Chapman 1996: 91).

Nevertheless, the origins of employers' associations lay in industrial relations with FMCSA and CSMA being cornerstones in the collective bargaining process. Accordingly from 1928, in an effort to cut costs, especially in weaving, employers pursued co-ordinated wage cutting strategies and attempted to raise productivity through the eight looms system. With industrial relations soured by long-term short time both experiments failed and led to a wave of strikes between 1929 and 1932 (Fowler 1988: 115–19).

The difficulties of co-ordinating innovation in a vertically specialised industry encouraged some organisational change in collective representation and, at the initiative of the Manchester Chamber of Commerce, the Joint Committee of Cotton Trade Organisations (JCCTO) was founded

[11] LRO, Colne and District Coloured Goods Manufacturers Association, Minutes, 23 October 1923.

[12] Burnley and District Cotton Industry Study Group, *Report on Marketing* (Manchester: Sherratt and Hughes), 1937, p. 27.

[13] LRO, North Lancashire Textile Employers, Minutes, 8 December 1930.

in 1925. Initially it embraced merchants, manufacturers and converters and in 1928 widened to include trade unions. Its principal objective was to achieve stability, greater efficiency and industry-wide reorganisation. Thus the JCCTO established the Cotton Trade Statistics Bureau to gather information that might facilitate stabilisation. In addition, the Shirley Institute, the industry's scientific facility, was set up in 1919 and initiated work efficiency studies in the 1930s. It also engaged in research extending across fibres, dyestuffs and textile machinery and received financial support from levies on the different sectors of the industry (Singleton 1991: 69; Board of Trade 1946: 129–31).

The JCCTO had backed the doomed Cotton Yarn Association, the failure of which marked a new phase in its strategy, when it began actively to promote amalgamations as the most effective way of stabilising the industry, removing over-capacity, stimulating innovation and improving competitiveness. However, the overwhelming reason for the policy shift was the precarious financial state of the American section of the spinning industry. Given the close intertwining of local interests, this crisis threatened the stability of the banking system, a situation which increasingly alarmed Montagu Norman, Governor of the Bank of England. In 1929 he coerced the debtor mills into the Lancashire Cotton Corporation (LCC), an amalgamation designed to acquire 10 million spindles underwritten by the Bankers' Industrial Development Company. This was followed in the same year by the establishment of the Combined Egyptian Mills and the Quilt Manufacturers' Association (Robson 1957: 214–15; Bamberg 1988: 87–92).

In theory, by facilitating the scrapping of redundant and obsolete capacity and the production of complementary goods by the remaining units, these amalgamations should have facilitated industrial rationalisation. However, although by 1934 LCC had scrapped 3 million spindles, over-capacity remained in the fine section of the industry and the Corporation itself performed poorly, having inherited many mills on the verge of bankruptcy (Kirby 1974: 147–51). Co-ordinated, if limited attempts to promote amalgamations in Lancashire, therefore, stemmed in large part from the financial repercussions of the speculative postwar boom and did not contribute significantly to the rationalistion. The same financial imperative for amalgamation did not exist in the weaving sector and the 1930 proposals of Sir Horace Wilson, chief industrial adviser to the government, were treated with great scepticism in Lancashire's weaving districts.

Further unsuccessful attempts at voluntary price agreements, the initiative of LCC, made it essential for the industry to find alternative ways of reducing capacity. Accordingly in 1934 the spinning industry approved a scheme to scrap 10 million spindles and obtained statutory powers to deal with redundancy. There was, however, growing urgency for promoting a lasting and orderly contraction of the industry as a whole. The difficulty of achieving the necessary price stability on a voluntary basis led to industry-wide pressure for government intervention, though difficulties in securing agreement to any scheme across the industry remained a protracted and painful process. Eventually in 1939 parliament passed the Cotton Industry (Reorganisation) Act, which fixed internal minimum prices and quotas establishing the Cotton Board as the means of control for orchestrating change in the industry. It was a matter of profound frustration that many of the clauses of this Act were immediately laid aside to meet the demands of war (Robson 1957: 216–17; Board of Trade 1946: 11).

Business strategies were not all defensive in this period, however, and some firms, including the William Birtwistle group, successfully shifted from overseas to home market and used branding and direct selling to achieve it. This grouping of five spinning and weaving firms, in the Preston and Blackburn region, was controlled by the Birtwistle family through interlocking directorships, but retained independent trading identities. In the interwar period the group moved into direct selling for the home market, in the face of the collapse of its traditional Indian market. Between 1921 and 1937 they developed a chain of 38 retail stores, first in Lancashire and then country-wide, under the name John Hawkins, along with a large mail order business. In the 1930s they finalised plans for the production of a hard-wearing cotton dress fabric which was retailed under the brand name of Miss Muffet.[14]

In the United States regionally based trade associations developed in New England in the late nineteenth century, reinforced in Massachusetts by the collective power of the interlocking corporations (Gross 1993: 86). Even before the mid-1920s these associations were united in their support for tariff policy although diverging regional interests made agreement on production levels implausible. However, in 1926 the cumulative pressure of falling profit margins and rising levels of bankruptcy led to the establishment of the Cotton Textile Institute (CTI) as a national stabilising organisation not unlike the JCCTO in Britain. It had the two-fold objective of stabilising supply and demand in the industry, while at the same time promoting improved efficiency. By the collection of price, output and market data the CTI aimed to reduce over-production by giving firms sufficient information to stabilise their market share. At the same time it sought to stimulate demand for cotton cloth by investigating

[14] William Birtwistle Group of Mills, *Centenary 1851–1951*, Preston 1951.

new uses for cotton and included its use in civil engineering (pioneered in North Carolina in 1926). Further, by promoting education and research and improvements in cost accounting it intended to improve overall industrial efficiency (Galambos 1966: 55–85).[15]

Before 1933, in sharp contrast to the position in Britain, all efforts at industry-wide control of output in the United States must be seen in the context of anti-trust. This was because of fears that any stringent controls would precipitate legal action and meant that the CTI eschewed any action which might be interpreted as being outside the law. In any event with only one-third of the industry covered by the CTI and with many members lukewarm in their support, any truly collusive action by the CTI would have been doomed. Very limited levels of integration of marketing in textiles meant that there was a dichotomy of interest between the commercial and industrial sectors of the industry, which was very similar to that found in Britain. However, in the United States the real fault line was regional, rather than sectoral, and stemmed also from the competitive structure of most of the industry. Enthusiasm both for membership and for the philosophy of control was greatest amongst the older and larger firms in New England, whilst as in the period before the First World War achieving any form of unity in Philadelphia was problematic. New Englanders had most to gain from the policy, had evolved a culture of co-operation which stretched back over 100 years and faced bankruptcy from its failure. In the South, on the other hand, there was greater support for competition and only a limited willingness to restrict output. This divide was especially highlighted by the difficulties faced by the CTI in implementing the so-called 55–50 strategy, designed to reduce over-production by limiting night-work. The idea was that mills working days only should have a self-imposed limit of 55 hours whilst those with night shifts should work for 50 hours. The failure of Southern producers to comply with the letter, let alone the spirit of this policy, signalled the end of attempts to secure relief for the industry internally, and the beginning of political manoeuvrings for reform by the CTI. Thus the intensely competitive structure of the industry worked against collusion and the only truly effective price fixing arrangement was made between those large firms, including Dan River Mills, which produced mainly branded goods and were able to peg prices during the 1920s. This arrangement was, however, quite separate from the CTI and broke down with the Crash of 1929 (Galambos 1966: 139–72, 123–4).

Roosevelt's National Industrial Recovery Act (NIRA) of 1933 altered the rules of the game faced by industry and, in the cause of overcoming

[15] *Manchester Guardian Commercial*, 4 October 1935, Supp. p. 8.

the worst impact of the Depression, it loosened the girdle of anti-trust. Accordingly, for a brief interlude, cartels became legal, stringent restrictions on the hours of work were introduced, as were a national minimum wage and a recognition of the right for workers to organise. However, the NIRA did not provide any long-term relief for the North since it was only effective for a couple of years until the Supreme Court declared it unconstitutional. Worse, Southern employers never conceded the right for workers to organise even after the Wagner Labor Relations Act of 1935 (Barkin 1957: 399). In 1935 spindleage hours rose again and by 1937 35 per cent of Southern firms worked three shifts. Although the Fair Labor Standards Act of 1938 imposed a national minimum wage on Southern textiles, the regional restructuring of the industry had been confirmed (Wright 1986: 213–16).

Whilst there were amalgamations in this period, there were no organised attempts to promote mergers in the United States that were equivalent to those in Britain. However, the wider issue of integration was a central theme in the numerous investigations into the ills of the industry in the 1930s. These mainly Harvard-based studies saw vertical integration as a universal panacea for an industry which, it was believed, had suffered from a failure to emulate the more dynamic and successful capital intensive sectors of American industry. Interestingly the Wharton investigator, Davis, and his collaborators, who were more in tune with the requirements of Philadelphia's flexible producers, were more sceptical about the gains from integration, especially at the quality end of the market (Scranton 1989: 459; Davis 1938). In the event, as in Britain, in America's early 1930s mergers tended to be horizontal rather than vertical and to be defensive rather than creative. Thus in 1930 and 1931 56 per cent of all mill mergers were horizontal, although from 1937 there was a growing trend towards vertical integration in the United States cotton industry (Markham 1950: 79).

As in Britain, even in the 1930s, a few firms were able to respond creatively and even appear to thrive in these difficult conditions. Of these perhaps the most notable example is Burlington Mills, Burlington, North Carolina, founded by Spencer Love in 1923. Although initially engaged in cotton weaving, this firm, at the suggestion of its New York selling agency, experimented with weaving cotton bedspread fabrics with a rayon filling and moved into silk weaving for women's dress material. Low labour costs enabled them to undercut competitors in Pennsylvania and New England. This proved to be the precursor of a highly successful move into the production of unfinished rayon dress material during the 1930s which the firm sold direct to converters in the women's garment industry, by-passing the selling agencies. Diversification did not end there, however, for in 1938 Love moved his firm into women's silk hosiery. Burlington continued to grow during the Depression, acquiring a number of failed mills, and by 1940 it was a giant employing 12,000 operatives in 32 mills (Wright 1995: 48–64; Schusteff 1992: 354).

Whilst enterprises such as Spring Industries Inc of South Carolina thrived and others such as Pepperel in New England and the Southern firm of Cannon Mills pursued non-price competition through branding and direct selling, such a level of growth, innovation and creativity was rare in this period (Ring 1992: 378; Scranton 1997: 337). The majority of cotton firms, intent on defensive measures, confronted divided interests and often limited representation meaning that despite institutional developments, collective efforts to achieve industry-wide stability were broadly unsuccessful in both the United States and Britain. Between 1930 and 1932 the entire United States cotton industry operated at a net loss of over $200m, whilst in the same period profits also disappeared in virtually all sectors of the British industry. It was a reflection of the extraordinary impact of the Depression, but it indicated the extreme pressures faced by defensive organisations, which owed their very existence to crisis and economic difficulties.

The events of the interwar period intensified government–industry relations, especially over commercial policy, in ways which would benefit the industry or at the very least prevent any further deterioration. These attempts to shape the external as well as the internal environment, facing the two cotton industries, were certainly marked by nineteenth-century experience. However, the volatile conditions of the interwar period led to some significant changes in stance and highlighted growing divisions within Lancashire over free trade, whereas in America cotton manufacturers remained devoutly protectionist.

The prewar significance of the Indian market to the British cotton industry inevitably meant that from the First World War onwards the Indian tariff and Gandhi's boycott of Lancashire goods assumed significant and, indeed, disproportionate importance in Lancashire. Raised at a time when Lancashire's political influence was untarnished, if by no means overwhelming, this conflict highlights the complexity of commercial policy formulation. The London government's agreement to increase the Indian tariff coincided with a £100m loan from the Indian government to Britain for the war effort. Offered without any consultation with the Indian people, this loan created serious budgetary problems for India and thus became dependent upon tariff increases to raise revenue. Such increases were inevitably unpopular with the Lancashire cotton lobby. However, the financial needs of the war effort and the political imperative to sustain the impression of Imperial unity meant they were introduced and maintained after the war (Constantine 1995: 262; Tomlinson 1977: 57–8).

During the 1920s and especially the 1930s, the Manchester Chamber of Commerce remained Lancashire's mouthpiece and made enormous efforts to forge new relationships with the government, both as an adviser and as representative of the industry. Raymond Streat, its Secretary, proved a tireless ambassador, building close personal relationships with key political figures, especially the Earl of Derby – dubbed the 'King of Lancashire' for his championing of the industry. Articulate, urbane and with finely tuned political antennae, Streat appeared the ideal negotiator, seemingly equally at home in Manchester or with London politicians (Dupree 1987, vol. I). Yet the difficulties he and his colleagues encountered on Indian tariffs highlights the complexities of lobbying on commercial policy, whilst demonstrating the growing limitations of Lancashire's bargaining power with government. A number of factors made progress tortuous and these ranged from the political complexity of all decisions involving India in this period, to the limited political power of Lancashire's MPs and Lancashire concerns. In addition, an in-built and mutual distrust which existed between all branches of manufacturing in Lancashire and the merchant-dominated Manchester Chamber of Commerce, created at times a climate of confusion regarding whose views the Chamber were championing.

The main obstacle to progress was the delicacy of the Indian political position after the First World War. Fiscal autonomy became a potent symbol of the growing Independence movement in India between 1918 and 1921, and when the surfacing of Nationalist tensions coincided with increasing budgetary difficulties in the subcontinent the government in London was left with little alternative but to sanction the bolstering of the wartime tariff. The increase of duties from 7 per cent to 11 per cent in 1921, despite opposition from Lancashire was, therefore, an attempt to pacify the Nationalists, whilst simultaneously raising revenue (Chatterji 1992: 202–4). Indian import tariffs had not peaked in 1921, however, and in 1930 they were raised to 15 per cent reaching 25 per cent a year later. Given the disquiet which this caused and the energy used to gain relief from it, it is ironic that the impact of the Indian tariff on Lancashire was more psychological than actual (Tomlinson 1994: 348).

From 1930 the Chamber of Commerce became increasingly involved in trying to achieve preferential treatment for Lancashire's goods in India. Whilst the commitment of the Chamber of Commerce to free trade had wavered during the First World War and its opposition to safeguarding was milder than might have been expected during the 1920s, it was not until 1930 that its directors made their first unequivocal protectionist statement in 50 years (Dupree 1987, vol. I: 90; Marrison 1996a: 265–6). In addition, the introduction of British tariffs and the move towards Imperial Preference, signalled by the Ottawa Agreement of 1932, led to a new international trade environment which in turn created a novel role for the Chamber of Commerce. It marked the beginning of a series of meetings between British cotton trade representatives and their counterparts abroad, to prepare the way for intergovernmental negotiations on trade (Dupree 1990b: 103–4). This move was not universally popular in Lancashire and, when plans for an industry mission to India were first discussed at the end of 1931, the Blackburn Chamber of Commerce expressed disquiet. Whether this stemmed from its historical suspicion of the Manchester Chamber of Commerce, which would dominate such a mission, or reflected the by no means implausible belief that, in promoting an industrial mission, the Government avoided responsibility for the success or more likely failure of such talks, is unclear.[16] Either way it serves to highlight the sensitivity and the difficulty of achieving any progress on commercial policy in this period.

Broadly, any support which the government showed for Lancashire throughout the 1920s and 1930s had to be weighed against the budgetary and political consequences for India. This became especially noticeable in the 1930s, as the National Government strove to achieve constitutional reform for India at a time when the Lancashire cotton industry was in a state of collapse. In 1933, the Manchester Chamber of Commerce and FMCSA prepared a joint statement opposing the idea of fiscal autonomy to be given as evidence before the Joint Select Committee on Indian Constitutional Reform. This unprecedented co-operation was a measure of the depth of concern over Indian tariffs that was felt throughout Lancashire.

Ultimately the MCC/FMCSA evidence was changed and Lancashire's views on Indian tariffs were couched in such moderate terms that their thrust was lost. This became the centre of a major, if brief, political controversy initiated by Winston Churchill, who invoked the Privileges Committee of the House of Commons against Lord Derby and Sir Samuel Hoare. He accused them both of using undue influence on members of the Manchester Chamber of Commerce to persuade them to change their evidence. Although the case was thrown out and Churchill has been cast as a mischief maker opposed to Indian Reform, the true origins of the changes remain somewhat obscure and the consequences for Lancashire and its relations with the government unclear. Streat, who

[16] LRO, Blackburn and District Cotton Employers' Association, Minutes, 17 December 1931.

was intimately involved in the case, was contemptuous of Churchill's intentions, emphasising that it was the delicate position reached in the India Mission talks in November 1933 which led to the change. He was also critical of both his colleague Sir Thomas Barlow who he felt had panicked and of those in the industry who condemned the emasculation of Lancashire's evidence, believing them to be politically naïve. Streat was doubtless correct that the majority of manufacturers lacked his experience and understanding of political negotiation. Yet the Privileges Committee was composed entirely of members nominated by Party Whips of all three parties who supported the government's policy in India and was clearly not objective (Churchill 1959: 595). Equally, whilst Streat was keen to emphasise the importance of the India Mission for Lancashire, taking it as a sign of the high esteem with which the industry was held by the government, it is probable that his position at the centre of the talks led him to overestimate the importance attached to the industry he represented. It is not clear, therefore, whether the true motive for the changes was indeed to salvage the India Mission and secure something for Lancashire or rather that a breakdown of the talks, precipitated by the evidence, would have had serious and wide political implications for relations between London and the subcontinent.

At the very least this episode serves to emphasise the extent to which Lancashire interests were a relatively minor priority for a government facing the likelihood of Indian Independence and the consequences which this would have, especially for the City of London. Certainly the Lees–Mody Pact of November 1933 brought agreement to the principle of amending Indian tariffs on imported cotton goods which was followed in 1936 by a reduction of the tariff on Lancashire goods to 20 per cent (Robson 1957: 265; Dupree 1990b: 110). However, this shift mainly reflected continuing Japanese import penetration of the Indian market and was set alongside a 75 per cent tariff against foreign, especially Japanese, goods. The best that can be said is that without the pressure which the cotton industry's representatives brought to bear, it is likely that market conditions would have been even worse (Dupree 1990b: 106–8).

In such a difficult environment, Lancashire's case cannot have been helped by the lack of mutual understanding and sympathy which existed between the Manchester Chamber of Commerce and industrialists. There is growing evidence that the historical support for free trade more closely reflected the attitudes of the directors of the Chamber than its industrial members, even though there was no overwhelming clamour for protection before the First World War (Marrison 1996b: 90–113, 226). Divisions arose on issues of policy, however, since there were clearly marked social and cultural differences which made it hard for the two groups to understand each other. In his diary Streat made no secret of his contempt for the industrialists he was representing and whilst some (though not all, Oldham and Blackburn being important exceptions) employers' association minutes frequently reveal considerable parochialism, such an attitude cannot have helped to create an impression of unity.

Clearly the barriers facing Lancashire manufacturers were considerable, extending to negotiations with Japan. In the 1930s, Japanese competition became of far greater significance for Lancashire's markets than the Indian tariff and 'the reaction to [it] . . . bordered on hysteria'.[17] There were attempts to persuade the Japanese to introduce voluntary quotas. The complicated negotiations needed to achieve restraint in Britain's overseas markets and especially in India, failed in 1934. This stemmed, not least, from suspicions in India that any Anglo-Japanese agreement would merely divide up the Indian market. The breakdown of efforts to achieve voluntary restraints was a prelude to endeavours to establish an international cartel in world cotton markets and to an Anglo-Japanese conference in 1934. Market sharing was seen by the British government, who initiated the negotiations, as a means of encouraging rationalisation of the Lancashire cotton industry whilst enticing Japan back into the international arena following the Manchuria incident. As it happened, the negotiations at the Anglo-Japanese Conference were doomed. They offered little to the Japanese who had most to gain by expansion and little from the stability favoured by Lancashire (Wurm 1993: 256–87). The collapse of negotiations heralded the introduction of Empire quotas on Japanese goods, a move which, in the short term, was helpful to Lancashire. As a result Japanese piece good exports to the Empire fell from 157.7m yards in 1933 to 35.5m yards in 1935 with Lancashire's rising from 173.9m yards to 277.7m yards in the same period. Yet, whilst Britain's cotton interests could claim a strategic success, the sanctions simply led the Japanese to intensify their efforts in other markets, especially in the Middle East, where Japanese piece good exports rose from 129m yards in 1931 to 505m yards, predominantly at Lancashire's expense (Wurm 1993: 287; Shimizu 1986: 49 and 61).

In the light of such limited progress and the seemingly inexorable loss of traditional export markets the question arises of why, in view of rising tariffs in India, Lancashire's larger firms did not move from pursuing export strategies to undertaking FDI. After all this had been the rational response of firms, including the Scottish thread manufacturer J. and

[17] LRO, Blackburn and District Cotton Employers' Association, Minutes, 17 December 1931.

P. Coats and English Sewing Cotton, to rising tariffs in, for example, the American market before the First World War (Wilkins 1989: 364–5). Moreover, a number of Britain's international trading companies had built cotton factories in British India by this period.[18] There is no conclusive evidence that Lancashire firms considered and rejected this option, but there are a number of possible reasons why it was not favoured. In the first place, with the exception of the Lancashire Cotton Corporation, many of the larger vertically integrated firms, such as Rylands, Ashton Brothers, Horrockses or the vertical grouping Birtwistles, which might have had the resources and managerial capabilities to expand overseas, were far less dependent upon the Indian market than the myriad small firms making up the bulk of the Lancashire industry. These large firms produced fairly high quality goods and their branded fabrics enjoyed a special standing in the domestic market so that the attraction of FDI, particularly given the political instability of India in this period, was limited. For the mass of small firms in towns like Blackburn and Burnley investing overseas was just not an option.

The postwar boom's collapse in 1920 immediately brought a united call from the cotton industry in the United States for improved protection, even though imports were minimal at this time. This was the standard response to difficulty from an industry whose history had been inseparable from the development of the tariff and which, despite some reductions in nominal tariffs in 1899 and 1904, remained one of the United States' most heavily protected industries. The accumulated knowledge and experience of the increasingly labyrinthine United States tariff system, which this history brought, undoubtedly made it easier for representatives of the cotton industry to secure protection (Schattschneider 1935: 165). As a result duties on higher value cotton products were increased significantly under the Fordney McCumber Tariff of 1922, to the benefit especially of Philadelphia producers. Manufacturers were generally satisfied with the rates achieved in the 1920s, even though they gained little from the Smoot Hawley Tariff Revision of 1930 (United States Tariff Commission 1929; Galambos 1966: 61).

The calls for protection in 1921 were clearly a reflex response of an industry suffering the beginnings of internal crisis. However, they were renewed with vigour in the 1930s when cotton manufacturers were exposed to a rise in imports. At the very time that the United States cotton industry was struggling with the intensely painful process of regional restructuring, it faced, as Britain in India and elsewhere, a surge

[18] I am grateful to Geoffrey Jones for providing me with information from his forthcoming book *Merchants to Multinationals: British Trading Companies in the nineteenth and twentieth centuries* (Oxford: Oxford University Press 2000).

of imports from Japan whose exporters were searching for markets following the Manchuria incident. Between 1932 and 1935 cotton piece goods imports from Japan, mainly low priced bleached goods used for underwear and handkerchiefs, rose from 789,000 square yards to 19,121,000 square yards to make up 60 per cent of total United States cloth imports, although this was less than 0.3 per cent of total domestic consumption of cotton manufactures (Michl 1938: 179). A combination of rising anti-Japanese feeling and a sense of righteous indignation at the first low labour cost competition in their sacred domestic market since 1816, led to an outraged and aggrieved response among already beleaguered New England manufacturers.

In an impassioned speech in New York, in 1934, the Governor of Massachusetts complained, 'Any individual who has followed the course of the invasion of America by the Empire of Japan who still harbours the delusion that reciprocal trade agreements will result in regulation to provide protection for American workers is certainly a fit subject for a psychopathic institution' (quoted in Tupper and McReynolds 1937: 414–15).

Nor did their pleas fall on deaf ears, for Roosevelt agreed to the tariff being raised by 46 per cent, on selected items (i.e. those which made up the bulk of imports from Japan). This move was a precursor to a voluntary quota on Japanese cotton piece goods exports to the United States, negotiated informally by the CTI and representatives of a Japanese export association in 1936, and vastly outweighed the support which Lancashire received from the British government (Bidwell 1939: 15).

International competitiveness

The painful adjustment and limited strategic response of the British cotton industry, in the face of irreversible changes in the interwar world economy, has stimulated considerable debate. Emphasis has especially been laid upon the forces which inhibited rationalisation and modernisation. Equally it is clear that despite the collapse of New England, the United States emerged from the interwar period as the world's largest producer of cotton textiles, dwarfing a much depleted Lancashire in terms of both output and capacity (Robson 1957: 358). This points to the more dynamic response of a technologically and organisationally advanced industry which was not constrained by past traditions. It also implies that with a profile more in line with that in the United States, the Lancashire cotton industry would have responded better to the pressures of the interwar period. Conversely it has been argued that it was the intertwined institutional rigidities in business structure and in labour relations which made

Lancashire's response to the collapse of her overseas markets so inadequate (Lazonick 1986).

In comparison with the United States automation came slowly to the British cotton industry and higher rates of innovation would have definitely been an advantage, though one which would not have restored Lancashire goods to competitiveness. Moreover, to conclude that the principal reason for a limited technological response lay in institutional rigidities is to underestimate the impact of the economic environment both inside and outside Lancashire in the interwar period. There is, for example, little evidence that technological inertia, in this period, stemmed predominantly either from union opposition or from institutionalised collective bargaining. In the first place in the 'American' section especially around Oldham, the nineteenth-century hotbed of labour radicalism, the collapse of markets drastically undermined union power as membership of the spinning union dwindled from 9,538 in 1920 to 5,131 in 1937. Consequently, whilst there was no attempt to amend the work practices of mule spinners, it was easy to replace mules with rings. Equally, in weaving a worsening of labour relations and an upsurge of strike activity between 1929 and 1932 should not be interpreted simply in terms of opposition to new technology and work practices. Activism was most prevalent in the finer sections of the trade where better economic conditions had bolstered union power, the upheaval reflected a souring of labour relations, due to long-term short time, rather than overt opposition to new technology (Fowler 1988: 113–19). In spinning, on the other hand, a more crucial influence on investment decisions in the 'American' section were the financial constraints on reconstructed firms, which meant that, irrespective of the views of operatives, new investment was a luxury few could afford. Moreover, throughout the industry, including areas and sectors where firms were not burdened with heavy debts, there were few incentives to invest (Kirby 1974). For instance a leading member of the Burnley Master Cotton Spinners and Manufacturers Association observed that: 'Even if the operatives put no obstacle in the way of automatics individual employers were not prepared to spend money attaching [them] and run further risk, as they were not sure to be able to sell their products'.[19]

This is not to argue that Lancashire's craft-based work practices were not better suited to the conditions of the nineteenth century than to the twentieth or that achieving change through the system of collective bargaining was anything other than slow and ponderous. Rather it is to

[19] LRO, Burnley Master Cotton Spinners and Manufacturers Association, Minutes, 27 November 1930.

suggest that the role of shopfloor relations in inhibiting technological change in the interwar period should not be exaggerated, especially in comparison with the United States, where there were long-term variations in the development of labour relations (Kirk 1994). Diverging rates of re-equipment and productivity growth between the United States and Britain reflect far more the differences in the origin and magnitude of market difficulties confronting the two industries. Moreover, the opportunity for relocation of cotton manufacturing to greenfield sites in the United States cotton growing states, inevitably increased the rate of technological change whilst low levels of labour organisation and lax labour laws facilitated the introduction of other productivity enhancing measures such as double shifts.

It is also not clear that, despite differing origins in interwar problems, taken as a whole, strategies in the United States were much more creative than in Britain. Policies on both sides of the Atlantic were marked as much by reaction as by creativity and by defensiveness rather than innovation. Moreover the survival of the United States cotton industry owed a great deal to the ability to achieve regional restructuring, against a background of protection, than to any intrinsic superiority of performance. It is certainly true that there was technological inertia in the Lancashire cotton industry which had damaging long-term consequences. However, it has become equally clear that in many respects, in the interwar period, export opportunities were dwindling rather than being lost. The question remains, therefore, of whether an organisational and technological profile more in line with the United States would have limited the market losses and eased the adjustment process in Lancashire, as has been suggested (Lazonick 1990: 138–9; Lazonick and West 1995: 245). For this to be so, the distinctive structure and productivity advantages of United States manufacturers would need to have been translated into international competitive advantage.

The international competitive advantage of economies has been measured by their share of world manufactured exports. Gauged in these terms, United States industry generally was exceptionally successful in the late nineteenth and early twentieth centuries, with its share rising from 6 per cent to 22 per cent between 1870 and 1929 (Lazonick 1991: 14). Yet if the high profitability of the 1920s largely passed the United States cotton industry by, so too did the dramatic export growth which was so much a characteristic of experience in the capital-intensive industries.

The volume of United States cotton piece good exports did grow impressively between 1914 and 1921. However, this should not be confused with an increasing share of world markets or with a lasting competitiveness of American cotton goods, as occurred in other products.

Table 7.4. *United States revealed comparative advantage, 1913–37*

Sector	1913	1929	1937
Textiles	0.2	0.2	0.2
Automobiles	1.5	2.9	2.5
Industrial equipment	1.7	1.6	1.6

Source: Calculated on the basis of statistics from Tyszynski 1951: 277–81.

Despite dramatic growth in terms of output and labour productivity, the United States cotton industry accounted for only 4 per cent of world exports of cotton textiles prior to 1914, rising to a mere 6.3 per cent by 1929 and falling back again in the Great Depression, as Figure 7.2 demonstrates. Thus, as Table 7.4 illustrates, in striking contrast with such industries as automobiles or industrial machinery, the United States cotton industry did not display a revealed comparative advantage at any time between 1913 and 1937.

Clearly the productivity and cost advantages, which came from American technology and production methods, were not translated into penetration of foreign markets in cotton textiles on the scale that might have been expected. It has been implied that the Southern producers were trapped by a 'tariff induced export blockage' in the 1930s (Scranton 1989: 383). However, whilst the depressed world markets, economic nationalism and spiralling levels of protection of the early 1930s were not conducive to export growth, they were not the origin of the low level of export penetration by United States cotton manufacturers. In the first place they were constraints faced by all cotton textile producers, but seem to have had a greater impact on some countries than others. It is especially striking from Figures 7.1 and 7.2 that the cotton industries of Continental Europe successfully retained their share throughout the interwar period. In addition, there is evidence that, except during the First World War, American cotton firms experienced difficulties penetrating and maintaining their position in many foreign markets. Moreover, before 1939 export success, which was often fairly short-lived, was restricted to a relatively narrow range of products and to markets where competitive forces were not intense, as highlighted in Figure 7.11. The Manchuria market was lost to the Japanese by 1914, whilst more generally in the Far East American success was limited to the Philippines which consumed between 14 per cent and 20 per cent of United States exports in the 1920s. This was not, however, a reflection of the competitive advantage of United States goods, but stemmed from a closed door policy

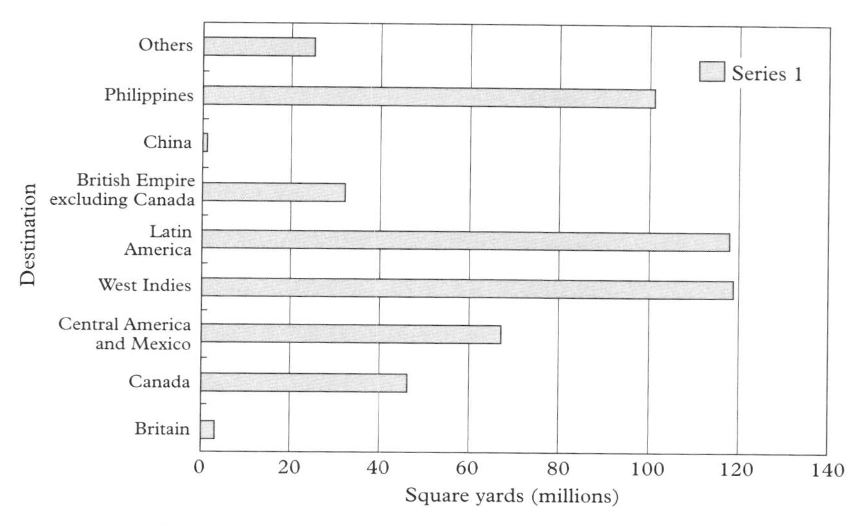

Fig. 7.11 Destinations of United States cotton cloth exports, 1926
Source: Cotton Yarn Association 1928: 19

against the rest of the world. Similarly they enjoyed some import penetration in those Central and Latin American Republics where the American government was exerting informal influence and had negotiated bilateral trade arrangements (Wilson 1971: 159–60).

In the developed world, on the other hand, it is significant that United States exporters were only really successful in culturally similar societies like Canada. In Europe cultural barriers to trade were by no means insurmountable. However, Europe comprised a collection of highly sophisticated and diverse markets where there were, in any event, long established craft-based textile industries. The relatively coarse, standardised cotton fabrics produced by Southern manufacturers for the United States home market and the Philippines could not hope to compete in these discerning markets, other than in wartime. This limitation was not lost on contemporaries searching for a solution to the difficulties of the industry. Thus Kennedy wrily admitted that: 'Attempts [to expand exports] are beset with difficulties, first because of the fact that only a relatively few classifications of American cotton goods have a normal market abroad. In other words our export markets are and always have been limited to certain few types of goods' (Kennedy 1936: 157). Indeed, although the war had provided a window of opportunity for United States cotton firms, they failed to capitalise on it in the long term. More generally, between 1922 and 1934 exports of cotton piece goods, by the United States, fell from 587m square yards to 223m square yards, undoubtedly contributing to over-capacity

Table 7.5. *Comparative index of Japanese and United States cotton yarn and goods, 1914–20 (Japanese price as % United States)*

	Yarns		Cloth	
	Coarse (20s)	Medium (40s)	Coarse	Medium
1914	69	84	74	122
1915	74	81	77	132
1916	66	69	76	122
1917	75	86	79	119
1918	69	74	69	98
1919	105	108	93	159
1920	85	94	81	119

Source: US Tariff Commission 1921: 128.

and helping to erode profit margins at home (Michl 1938: 176). Much of this erosion was again due to Japanese competition, especially in the early 1930s following the Manchuria incident. In the Philippines alone the United States' share of imports fell from 67 per cent in 1933 to 40 per cent in 1934, whereas Japan's share rose accordingly from 23 per cent to 52 per cent (Michl 1938: 177).

The extreme domestic orientation of merchants in the American cotton industry was declining even before the First World War when some United States trading companies had begun to appear, reducing reliance on foreign agents. They clearly lacked experience, but market penetration and subsequent loss of markets after 1918 include limited price competitiveness and attitudes to some foreign markets which ranged from arrogance to incomprehension. Even before 1914 many American goods were not price competitive in Asian markets (Sugiyama 1988: 286), whilst by 1920 the Japanese enjoyed price competitiveness over the United States, as Table 7.5 shows, in coarse and medium yarns and coarse cloths which stemmed from a combination of longer Japanese hours, lower wages and lower freight costs. The position was even gloomier in the 1930s, when one commentator concluded that:

> As a matter of fact, instead of there being any genuine prospect of increasing our exports of cotton goods abroad, we are rather in the process of losing our existing markets. Attempts to hold up wage and price levels has destroyed a large part of our export trade. Competition from Japanese goods has been particularly severe in the Philippine and Latin American markets. In the Philippines, our former best export market, with our goods entered free of duty and Japanese goods paying full duties, Japanese prices are 15–60 per cent lower than for comparable American textiles. (Kennedy 1936: 158)

These factors, combined with highly effective vertical collusion, as well as the use of inferior cotton and heavy size, made the United States extremely vulnerable to Japanese competition in the interwar period.

Limited export success and loss of markets gained during the First World War were also the result of insensitivity to the specific tastes of particular markets, whilst long production runs reduced flexibility in the face of local requirements. In the interwar period United States commercial firms found the Indian market especially problematic, and not just because of the peculiar political and economic influences, which meant that its market for foreign goods dwindled in the interwar period. A report from the Bureau of Commerce suggested that perhaps the most important obstacle to the success of United States trading companies in India, in this period, was their newness. Their perception was that it was difficult to compete with the reputation that long establishment had brought British export houses. This supposed superiority stemmed from networks of contacts dating back over 100 years plus British power and influence traceable to the seventeenth century and the establishment of the East India Company. Whilst this report doubtless exaggerated the prowess of British firms, the observation certainly has some validity (United States Department of Commerce 1939: 9). Inexperience and an insularity born of domestic scale meant a limited appreciation of the foreign and a bafflement with India. American trading companies found Indian culture quite impenetrable and complained:

> In India it is extremely difficult, if not impossible, to obtain satisfactory credit references or bank reports concerning many importers. This not because the importers are weak in capital resources, or of doubtful reputation, but because there is no satisfactory machinery for the collection and dissemination of worthwhile credit reports. There are banks in India able to furnish information regarding some importers; but their task is made extremely difficult by the complicated arrangements under which many importers sometimes operate – as for instance when business members of a large family share, under Hindu or Mohammedan law, certain of their rights and obligations with other members of the family who may not be in business at all. Thus one of 6 Hindu brothers may do an import business with very little liquid capital, but he may possess family property rights which enable him to secure any necessary financial accommodations. On the other hand, should he default on an obligation as an importer, he could not be sued upon his expectation of realizing his equity in the family fortune.[20]

The problems of an unfamiliar market were not the only reasons why United States cotton textile export performance was lacklustre. A misplaced confidence in the expected slowness of the recovery of war-torn

[20] United States Department of Commerce, *The United States in India's Trade* (Washington 1939), p. 71.

Europe meant that United States exporters displayed considerable arrogance in Indian and other markets. All American exports to the Indian market dwindled in the interwar period, of cotton goods specifically it was suggested that: 'With regard to cloths, close attention to market requirements is essential. In the past, the Bureau's office in Calcutta has reported that in many cases American fabrics appear to be bought by the Indian dealer rather than sold.'[21]

The explanation of the relatively poor interwar export performance of the United States cotton industry can be traced to the historical forces shaping the American cotton industry in the nineteenth century. This had created a symbiosis between technology, organisation and product which placed limits on the markets it could serve abroad and upon the number of firms likely to export. Southern firms began exporting quite early but mainly to low labour cost markets or where there was direct competition with Japan (see Figure 7.11). These were markets in which, despite the United States' high growth rates of labour productivity, potential long-term competitiveness was limited. Table 7.5 has shown the extent of Japanese price advantages over their American competitors, which stemmed from low labour costs, organisation and long working hours. In 1924 the introduction of the Toyoda automatic loom was to have profound effects for Japanese productivity, raising it from between 3 and 19 times and contributing hugely to the growing dominance of Japanese cotton goods in world markets (Mass and Lazonick 1990: 41).

Empirical evidence on the United States' industrial trade patterns, in the 1960s, suggests that there is a strong relationship between total factor productivity growth and exports (Weiser and Jay 1972: 462). On this basis the poor export showing of the United States cotton industry before 1939 implies that high labour productivity growth, from the late nineteenth century, was the result of relative capital growth, rather than improved efficiency. More research is needed to confirm this hypothesis. However, the exceptional vulnerability of the United States cotton industry to low labour cost competition, when American technology diffused so readily from the late nineteenth century onwards, does confirm the idea that efficiency gains must have been limited. In the 1920s sharp rises in wage costs, in both the Northern and Southern sectors of the industry, further exacerbated the problem (Wright 1986: 148).

Just as the extreme domestic orientation of the American cotton industry helps to explain why manufacturers found it difficult to penetrate foreign markets, the apparently limited efficiency changes in the industry can partly be explained by the experience of industrialisation, at the heart

[21] United States Bureau of Commerce, 1939, p. 26.

of which, with the exception of Philadelphia, was economisation of skill. In northern Massachusetts, for example, the emphasis had been on skill reduction in the production of standardised cloths. In Fall River in the 1870s, on the other hand, damaging strikes, initiated by the militant mule spinners unions, hastened the replacement of mules with skill-saving rings (Cohen 1990: 156–7). This trend inevitably continued when the industry began its dramatic rise in the South in the 1880s and accounts for the sharp increases in labour productivity that resulted from the substitution of machinery for skill. This is not the same thing as improving the efficiency with which all resources were used. Moreover, since it was a development which occurred against the background of the tariff, the problem of international price competitiveness was not of overwhelming importance.

The objective of national self-sufficiency in the United States and the attendant domestic orientation of the industry both reinforced and was reinforced by the evolution of organisational capabilities and product strategies in cotton manufacturing. These trends also contributed in important ways to the development of cloths and techniques which were distinctively American.

In some industries, tariffs have fostered innovation as a precursor for export penetration (Lazonick and West 1995: 247). This was patently not the case with cotton textiles. The coincidence of the development of the cotton industry with the evolution of the tariff influenced the culture of the industry as a whole. This meant that in general, throughout the late nineteenth century and interwar period, cotton goods enjoyed higher levels of protection than other industries. Thus, although by 1930 the average nominal tariff on cotton goods was 46 per cent, it was only 35 per cent on metals and 31 per cent on chemicals (Keesing and Wolf 1980: 10).

The 'infant industry' argument for tariffs cannot, therefore, be sustained for cotton goods. Instead, protection ensured an extraordinarily high domestic orientation. This helps to explain why United States cotton goods faced such a narrow range of potential markets abroad. In addition, and critical to the industry's vulnerability to low labour cost competition, Wright was able to conclude that 'the American industry had grown up behind a tariff wall since the Civil War, and had long since priced itself out of foreign markets' (Wright 1986: 148). His conclusion supports the idea that labour productivity gains were not converted into the overall efficiency improvements necessary for a good performance in world markets.

This analysis has raised serious doubts concerning the international competitiveness of the United States cotton industry in the interwar period. The considerable labour productivity advances, of American cotton producers after 1880, were not translated into a share of world exports commensurate with the growth and modernisation of the industry through to the 1920s. It is not enough to say that American cotton manufacturers faced such a large domestic market that they had no need to export. All the evidence suggests that when competitive pressures forced them to sell their products abroad, they found it an often chastening experience.

This finding has important consequences for understanding American competitive performance in the interwar period and for interpreting British economic decline. Lazonick has argued that in the twentieth century the basis of international competitive advantage shifted from British-style proprietary capitalism to corporate capitalism along American lines (Lazonick 1991: 45–9). There are strong grounds for accepting this conclusion with regards to such industries as motor vehicles or consumer durables. However, the model fits less well with cotton, where labour productivity improvements stemming from rapid throughput technology, in vertically integrated corporations in America, did not guarantee penetration into foreign markets. In the industries of America's Second Industrial Revolution the productivity gains which derived from technological and organisational strategies were intimately linked to the development of internal marketing facilities by firms. This, combined with the growing tendency towards FDI after 1914, helped to overcome the commercial disadvantages which American firms faced abroad. In cotton, on the other hand, such integration of commercial activity with manufacturing was delayed until the development of the giant textile and clothing conglomerates in the 1950s (Markham 1950: 82). Yet even with such initiatives American cotton firms performed poorly in high income markets (Tomlinson 1994: 523–6). This suggests that in textiles generally the gains from full-scale integration may be less than in other industries. At the same time, it illustrates the long-term consequences for design and cloth type of an industry whose development depended heavily upon a relatively undiscerning rural market. It is surely significant that the only fashion cloth in which United States cotton producers have enjoyed international competitive advantage, in the twentieth century, has been denim. Perfected as a fashion good in the United States in the 1920s (Murchison 1930: 111–12), this cloth was to be the most potent symbol of a Frontier cloth culture which developed in the nineteenth century. As a model to halt what Singleton has seen as the inevitable decline of the British cotton industry in the face of third world development, the United States was singularly inappropriate (Singleton 1990: 44–5).

Summary

Over-capacity dogged cotton manufacturers in Britain and the United States, throughout the interwar period. It sapped their profits, created an air of despondency and above all encouraged collusion as a defensive response. Collusive arrangements were tortuous and unstable and regional and sectoral fault lines, which frequently reflected difference in attitude and expectations as well as in product and market orientation, meant collective agreements were frequently extremely bad-tempered if they could be forged at all. The very difficulty of stabilising two mature industries in a period of deep uncertainty left industrialists on both sides of the Atlantic with little alternative but to turn to their governments to legitimise their efforts. That in both cases this was forthcoming in the 1930s is a measure of the extent to which politicians, even in anti-trust America, feared the dire social and economic consequences of market failure. There is no question that such anti-competitive policies were rarely associated with innovation and modernisation. Yet it is hard to see how these objectives could have been achieved had a more intensely competitive environment prevailed. If nothing else, prolonged depression and uncertainty were psychologically draining, whilst new investment was dependent upon an expectation of a return, which was lacking on both sides of the Atlantic for much of the interwar period.

Changing competitive pressure and attempts at collusion served to blur some of the regional and sectoral divisions which so characterised both industries. Yet if product, financial and organisational structures began to alter it is hard to detect any fundamental shifts in the underlying business culture either in the differing regions of the United States or in Lancashire's cotton towns and vertically specialised sectors. However, expectations of the future were transformed, especially in those regions and sectors most seriously affected by decline. In New England the realisation that the future of textiles lay in the South was a revelation which took nearly two decades to sink in. After a decade of 'profitless prosperity' and declining demand for heavily ornamented fabrics Philadelphia made what was effectively its last flexible shift in textiles into hosiery, upholstery and curtains but still saw its employment fall by half by 1939 (Scranton 1997: 338).

In Lancashire an atmosphere of despair became embedded in attitudes in this period as it slowly registered with industrialists that they were not facing a short-term downturn, but a prolonged contraction. Whilst it is hard to sustain the argument that vertical and spatial specialisation constrained technological change, a lack of appreciation of the concerns and attitudes within different sectors and over comparatively small geographic distances, characterised all intra-industry relations. These were reinforced by the survival of local and sectoral employers' associations until the 1960s, even though wage negotiations were conducted via national organisations. Most striking are the well-known differences in perception, attitudes and social standing of the merchants who dominated the Manchester Chamber of Commerce and industrialists and brought to life in Raymond Streat's diaries. What is particularly noticeable in the 1920s and 1930s is how spectacularly parochial were the concerns of especially the north-eastern weaving towns of Nelson and Colne. There, employers' association minutes were more likely to be concerned with the quality of the rail service to Manchester than with the problems of foreign competition. This was not, it has to be said, a feature shared by their neighbours in Blackburn or by the well-organised spinners in Oldham, where wide-ranging discussions on the problems of foreign competition, the silver question and Indian tariffs were frequent. Yet it serves to illustrate how far removed from strategic thinking, relating to the future of the industry, were the majority of manufacturers and how localised their concerns remained.

The chapter also serves to demonstrate ways in which Lancashire was beginning to break down as a classic industrial district dependent for its success upon a combination of self-reinforcing indigenous skill, subsidiary industries and innovation based upon local knowledge (Sunley 1992: 306). Long-term short time began to erode the skill base and possibilities for collaboration between employers and unions, whilst depressing prospects reduced workers' enthusiasm for entering cotton mills. Equally poor returns on investments sharply reduced Lancashire's demand for new machinery and helped to erode the profit margins of the county's principal machine makers (Farnie 1990: 169–70). It is interesting and instructive that one of the most notable community-based initiatives in the period did not relate to technology or the fostering of skill, but to the establishment of mechanisms within individual communities and across Lancashire to monitor creditworthiness. Accordingly during the 1920s both the Federation of Calico Printers and Colne's manufacturers discussed the possibility of establishing 'a credit and business morality bureau based upon information supplied by members'[22] whilst by 1927 the Manchester Cotton Spinners and General Lancashire Commercial List had been established and provided detailed information on the standing of all firms. Although banks regularly kept security lists to assist

[22] Colne and District Coloured Goods Manufacturers Association, Minutes, 16 May 1923.

them in their overdraft and lending policy, it was unusual for the initiative to come from within the industry. For a county where business secrecy was embedded, this departure from confidentiality was a reflection of the depth of anxiety and the attendant fear of bankruptcy. The information contained in the list was not treated lightly, with subscribers instructed to keep the volume 'under lock and key'.[23]

If the interwar period made manufacturers increasingly nervous of the future it did not precipitate any fundamental change in the organisation of the industry or in the relationship between manufacturers with finishers, merchants and packers. The collusive arrangements of the finishers can have done little to improve the long-term competitiveness of the industry, especially in the Far East, whilst the overseas merchants and packers retained a stranglehold on the industry which, whilst a frequent source of complaint, remained unchallenged. Changes did, however, occur in the home trade with challenges from expanding retailers such as Marks and Spencer (Chapman 1990: 179–82). In the export trade, however, around 1,200 shippers maintained their position as the commercial antennae of the industry and contributed to the failure of attempts to create stability in manufacturing.

In the United States the interwar period marked the decisive shift of the nucleus of the cotton industry from New England and the mid-Atlantic states to the cotton growing states of the South. The First World War had bolstered the position of New England's bulk producers, but gave them only a passing respite, while in Philadelphia changing tastes and increasingly disadvantageous selling arrangements put the capabilities of the industrial district under extreme pressure. Responses to the changed world varied from despondency and defeat, through a range of defensive and largely unsuccessful arrangements, to innovation and the establishment of Southern branches. The difficulties of Northern producers in meeting the challenge of the South bore an uncanny resemblance to the problems Lancashire firms faced in meeting the threat of Indian and Japanese competition, at a time when dismal or non-existent profits deterred investment.

The rise of the South and the demise of the North as the heart of cotton manufacturing in the United States is complicated by regional differences in the culture of business. It was not just the case that Northern producers could not compete with the South because of outmoded technology and nineteenth-century business attitudes. New England complaints about low labour costs and weak labour laws in the South reflect

[23] Manchester Central Library, *Manchester Cotton Spinners and General Lancashire Commercial List, 1927*. I am grateful to Douglas Farnie for alerting me to the existence of this list.

the localism of development in a country which is, after all, a continent. The culture of business in the South was dramatically different from that in the North, but it was only rarely reflected in the dynamic and innovative strategies of large firms. Instead the distinctiveness of the Southern cotton industry, in this period, lay in the power of the company village and its symbiotic relationship to usually small mills formed in the boom years during and after the First World War. Generally Southern millowners were able to continue to pay low wages until the New Deal, at least, because state laws allowed it and trade union organisation was inhibited by tightly controlled mill villages. Yet the idea of labour docility, as the crucial component of Southern competitiveness, can be taken too far, as previously quiescent labour relations were disrupted by strikes in the late 1920s and 1930s most especially the general textile strike of 1934 which was masterminded by the American Federation of Labor, Textile Workers Union. In addition, the growing importance of Northern finance and the spread of more modern management techniques began to undermine the power of Southern mill village paternalism (Carlton 1982; Hall et al. 1986: 242–86).

A consequence of the distinctive organisation of the cotton industries of Britain and the United States and their differing development, is to be found in the conduct of government–industry relations in the interwar period. It is striking that whereas in the United States it was the industrialists who, through the CTI, pressed the government on commercial policy, in Britain the power base lay with the Manchester Chamber of Commerce. It is not that a substantial mercantile community had failed to emerge in New York, which linked cotton manufacturers to the domestic market. Rather the vertical integration of manufacturing meant that New York did not fulfil the role of co-ordinator of an increasingly vertically and spatially specialised industry serving diverse foreign markets. On the other hand, the cumulative growth of commercial wealth in Manchester, in the nineteenth century, accorded the members of its long-established Chamber of Commerce considerable power and influence both locally and nationally. It is particularly noticeable that whereas the cotton interests in the United States were relatively successful in achieving their objectives, in Britain the process was often extremely protracted. Lancashire did not lose from the tortuous negotiation process in India or from the failure of the cartel negotiations with Japan, but success was often long in coming and complicated to achieve.

The explanation for the difficulties the British cotton lobby faced can easily be found in the shock waves which shattered the very foundations of the international economy, from 1914 onwards, and in the lack of political as well as economic unity in Lancashire. The collapse of overseas markets undermined the Chamber of Commerce's faith in trade liberalism and ultimately the political influence of cotton interests. However, the sometimes limited success of cotton's representatives, in moulding commercial policy in their favour, was not just a reflection of the relative decline of the industry, for difficulties began in the First World War. Instead it is clear that the aims of commercial policy cannot be separated from wider economic, international and diplomatic issues. In the late nineteenth century and in the years before the First World War there was a coincidence of interest between Lancashire, British commercial and financial policies and the City of London. In the interwar period this broke down and was further complicated by increasing tension in India and more widely in the Far East. These trends meant that despite endeavouring to bring relief to their industry or at least prevent further deterioration, Lancashire's representatives were increasingly faced with policy decisions that at best brought them little comfort and at worst seemed to run counter to their interests. Indeed the Ottawa Agreement and subsequent adjustments to the Indian tariff were but a hollow victory for Lancashire and one which was to haunt them after 1945, when Commonwealth imports, allowed into Britain duty free under its terms, became a growing problem. In the United States, by contrast, although competing interests in big business and finance became increasingly internationalist after the war, it was not until the 1930s that they found political expression (Wilson 1971: 1–16; Ferguson 1989: 8–9). In the 1920s, however, United States commercial policy was in the hands of the Republicans, the party which had, 'for two generations advertised protective tariffs as the sovereign remedy for all the ills that industry is heir to' and which favoured the protection of labour-intensive industries (Schattschneider 1935: 86). Even with the political changes of the 1930s, the requests by the cotton interests for protection against Japanese competition were treated sympathetically, not least because they were in accord with United States policy in the Pacific.

8 The turbulent years, 1939–80: the politics of decline

Two decades of difficulty for the British and American cotton industries were followed by the outbreak of the Second World War, which did nothing to balk the trend of Lancashire's collapse or the shift of the United States cotton industry from North to South. The Lancashire cotton industry became far more automated in the 1960s, with the scrapping of redundant machinery, yet this did little to halt the inexorable decline of the industry. Accordingly, in the next 20 years Lancashire's demise was virtually complete, as Table 8.1 shows, with almost the last vestiges of a dying industry vanishing in the 1981 recession. In the United States, between 1950 and 1970, 300,000 textile jobs were lost in New England alone, whilst an increasingly capital-intensive industry, which was based upon multi-fibres, continued to develop in the South. In the 1970s and early 1980s, however, unemployment in the Southern states began to rise at an alarming rate and numerous businesses closed or were taken over (Gaventa and Smith 1991: 182). Nevertheless the cotton and related industries survived, albeit on a diminished scale and, by 1983, the United States had the distinction of being home to the world's most 'productive' textile industry.

The shifting role of business communities has been inseparable from the evolution of cotton manufacturing from the eighteenth century. Similarly, in the second half of the twentieth century the decay of communities based upon cotton and the demise of industrial districts, deprived of their dynamism, is a reflection of the collapse of the industry. Yet it remains to be seen to what extent a 'culture of decline' infected businesses and what similarities and contrasts can be detected in the way in which communities in Lancashire and in the American South tried to alter their fate. This highlights the importance of placing the issue of industrial decline in the context of wider social, political and economic conditions. Clearly supply-side deficiencies are important – it is hard to consider industrial performance without focusing on technology, entrepreneurship and the management and organisation of business. Yet these need to be set in the context of the expectations of success of any decision,

Table 8.1. *The British and United States cotton industries, 1941–80*

Date	Britain				United States			
	Spindleage (m) operating (% rings)	Loomage (000) operating (% automatic)	Cloth output (m linear yards)	Numbers employed (000)	Spindleage (m) operating	Loomage (000) operating (% shuttleless)	Cloth output (m linear yards)	Numbers employed (000)
1941	16.49 (n/a)	293 (n/a)	2,150	297	n/a	n/a	10,432	412[1]
1945	14.44 (n/a)	216 (n/a)	1,569	209	n/a	n/a	8,720	415
1950	34.5 (30)	358 (n/a)	2,207	316	23.0	369[2]	11,200	277
1960	13.7 (24)	155 (26)	1,380	148	20.0	326	9,328	254
1970	3.3 (94)	68	780	96	19.6	302[3] (7.6)	6,246	222
1980	1.5 (n/a)	26	399	50	17.3	n/a	4,456	78[4]

Notes:

[1] Figure for 1942.
[2] Figure for 1955.
[3] Figure for 1976.
[4] Figure for 1982.

Sources: Cotton Board, *Quarterly Statistics*; Singleton 1991: 142; International Federation of Cotton and Allied Trades, *International Cotton Industry Statistics Supplement*; Mitchell 1988: 370–1; *Cotton: Monthly Review of World Statistics.*

which will be critically influenced by market conditions, by the views of close associates, usually from within the business community, and by prevailing government policy.

The impact of the Second World War

The Second World War altered trading patterns and had a number of lasting implications for the cotton industry worldwide and for the industries of Britain and the United States in particular. Moreover, differing sources of raw materials and timing of entry into the war meant that its impact varied (Robson 1957: 12–13; Cotton Board Trade Letter, March 1949: 4). As a result the Second World War proved to be a stimulus to the American cotton industry, especially in the Southern states. By 1945 only 20 per cent of the nation's cotton spindles remained in the North (Minchin 1997: 7). In Britain the war was a serious constraint and dislocation to British production and markets was much more profound and prolonged than had occurred between 1914 and 1918. Whereas in the First World War Lancashire's mills remained running, in 1940 a government concentration scheme was introduced which closed down a significant proportion of capacity and well over half of spindleage and loomage lay idle by the end of the war. Equally in spinning and weaving, employment fell by 38 per cent and 39 per cent respectively (Singleton 1994: 602; Cotton Board Trade Letter, March 1949: 5). The motivation was simple: with the industry entirely dependent on imported raw cotton, the British government needed to save scarce and hazardous shipping for vital supplies of food and armaments. Moreover, the measure was also inspired by the desire to release labour for war work in the supposedly safe north-west of England (Miles 1968: 25). As a result, between 1940 and 1945 British raw cotton consumption fell by 48 per cent, with output of cotton cloth falling by a similar amount. Exports fell even further and in 1945 were just 43 per cent of the 1940 level. This led inevitably to import substitution in such regions as Latin America and to the penetration of British markets by foreign competitors (Mitchell 1988: 355 and 357).

Wartime gaps in overseas markets left by British and Japanese producers were increasingly met by an expansion of Indian and United States production, both of which had the advantage of being raw cotton producers. From being a tiny interwar exporter the United States emerged, for the first and only time in its history, as the world's dominant exporter of cotton cloth. In response to opportunities at home and abroad United States cotton cloth output rose accordingly from 8,420m square yards in 1939 to 11,108 m square yards in 1942 even though it fell back by about 20 per cent over the next three years (Vitkovitch 1955: 258).

Despite the introduction of price controls (Simpson 1966: 58), very limited wartime restrictions on output distinguish the experience of the United States cotton industry from that in Lancashire. Even when the United States entered the war in 1941 and the armed forces and war industries swallowed 100,000 cotton workers or 20 per cent of the total workforce in the next four years, this was a far smaller loss of employment than had occurred in Lancashire. In addition there was some substitution of black for white labour in this period. At Dan River Mills the proportion of blacks had risen to 15 per cent by 1946 beginning a shift which was to continue, albeit very slowly, in the postwar period (Smith 1960: 509). In any event any shortfall in cotton textile output was more than compensated for by the wartime expansion of man-made fibre production. The versatility of man-made fibres, especially for industrial uses, and the peculiar advantages which the United States enjoyed in the production of synthetics meant that output of both cellulosics and synthetics expanded dramatically. It was a trend which was not matched in Britain. In the United States, therefore, whilst cellulosic production rose from 380m lbs in 1939 to 854m lbs in 1946, in Britain the increase over the same period was a mere 4 per cent (Robson 1958: 27). This helps to explain the transformation of the largest manufacturing firms in the United States into multi-fibre users.

There do not seem to have been significant productivity gains in the United States cotton industry during the Second World War, the three-shift system already being in place. Some Southern producers, such as Dan River, had difficulties meeting stringent government standards. In general, though, production-oriented strategies of both New England and Southern producers were ideal for both allied and domestic government demand for standardised products such as sheeting and cambrays, as well as drills and twills for uniforms and many firms thrived (Smith 1960: 434–62; Knowlton 1948: 265).

Wartime import substitution in both the Far East and Latin America meant that export volume and hence the buoyancy of overseas trade was lower in the postwar world than it had been in the 1930s. As a result although world cotton piece good production rose from an estimated 37.5m square yards in 1936–7 to 40.9m square yards in 1955 the volume of exports had fallen by 27.7 per cent over the same period and only in high income markets were there possibilities for export growth. Nevertheless the immediate postwar period featured an extraordinary sellers' market as the cotton industry of Japan was temporarily incapacitated while the dramatic expansions of the cotton industries of Hong Kong and Pakistan lay ahead. It offered considerable opportunities to manufacturers in Britain and the United States and they collectively contributed 64 per cent of world cotton piece goods exports in 1946 (Robson 1957: 359;Vitkovitch 1955: 264).

The ability of cotton manufacturers in the United States and Britain to respond to the opportunities of the postwar sellers' market was undoubtedly influenced by their contrasting wartime experiences. Therefore, although clearly justified in terms of the war economy, the concentration scheme seriously inhibited Lancashire's recovery after 1945. Following two decades of decline, which had discouraged new investment, a relatively high proportion of British capacity was obsolete whilst the machinery which had lain idle had deteriorated. In addition, it became harder to recruit good, new workers to the cotton industry, generating serious fears of a labour shortage. This stemmed partly from the interwar image of an industry which habitually worked short time and partly from the competing attractions of Lancashire's defence-related industries, many of which continued to grow after 1945 (Miles 1968: 33). There were, by contrast, few similar constraints on the United States cotton industry which led to sharp differences in immediate postwar experience.

Table 8.1 demonstrates that although output declined in the latter part of the Second World War postwar recovery was impressive taking output 27 per cent above the 1937 level. However, while the late 1940s marked a temporary halt to the decline of the cotton industry, output levels did not regain their prewar volume. In terms of export experience both cotton industries benefited from the postwar sellers' market. Yet what is more striking is that, as Figure 8.1 shows, although both countries were unable to sustain this position and, as British cotton piece goods exports continued to decline never regaining their prewar level, both were exporting similar volumes as world markets shrank.

Still United States cotton manufacturers would assuredly lose world market share as the industries of Continental Europe and Japan recovered and as Asian production generally began to grow. British exporters also lost market share, since they had been undermined either by import substitution or foreign competition during and after the war. In comparison with the interwar period easily the most striking change, highlighted in Figure 8.2, was in the position of India, which soon ceased importing British cotton goods altogether, becoming instead a major exporter to Britain. Only to British West Africa, Rhodesia and New Zealand was there any increase in the volume of piece goods exports before 1950, an increase which reversed by 1955. Britain's accession to GATT in 1947 was partly to blaim for losses in Commonwealth markets in the early 1950s, since these countries could no longer allow British goods preferential tariff rates whereas Britain was also subject to revived Japanese competition. Moreover in the 1950s and 1960s both India and Pakistan

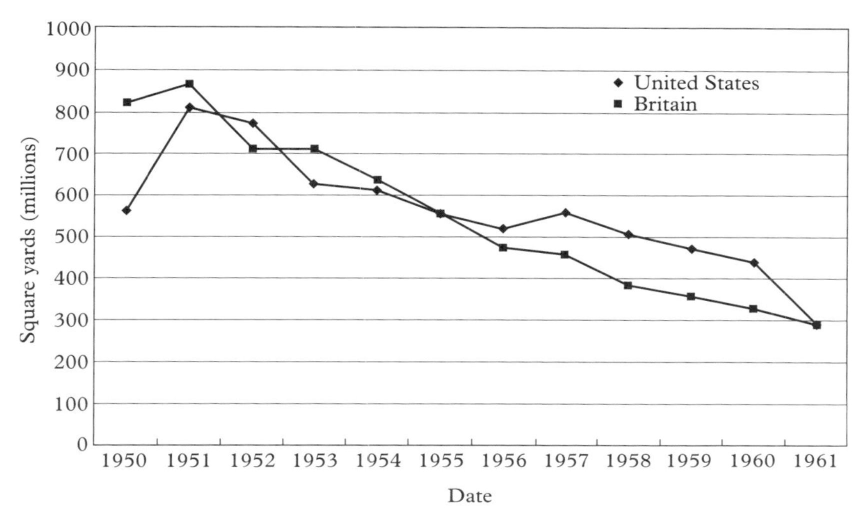

Fig. 8.1 Volume of British and United States cotton cloth exports, 1950–61
Source: Robson 1957: 358; *Cotton Board Quarterly Bulletin*

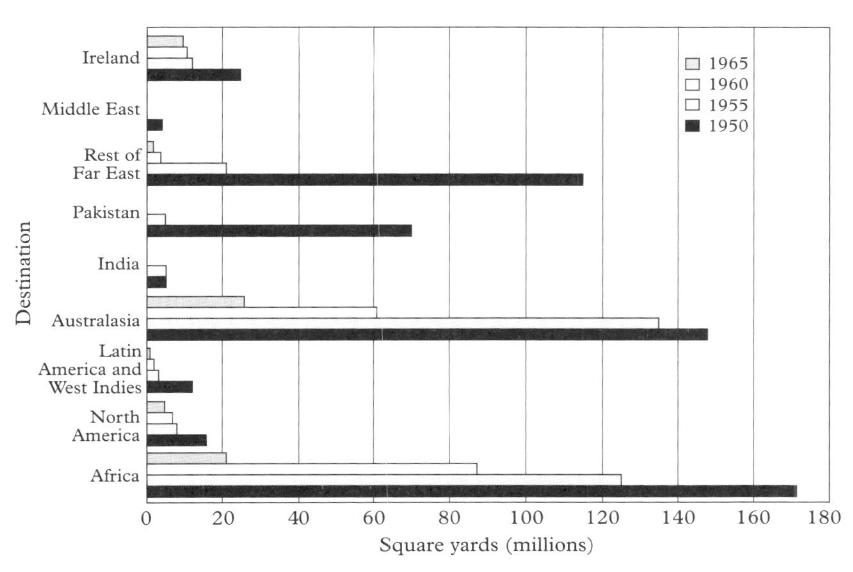

Fig. 8.2 Destination of British cotton cloth exports, 1950–65
Source: Singleton 1991: 118

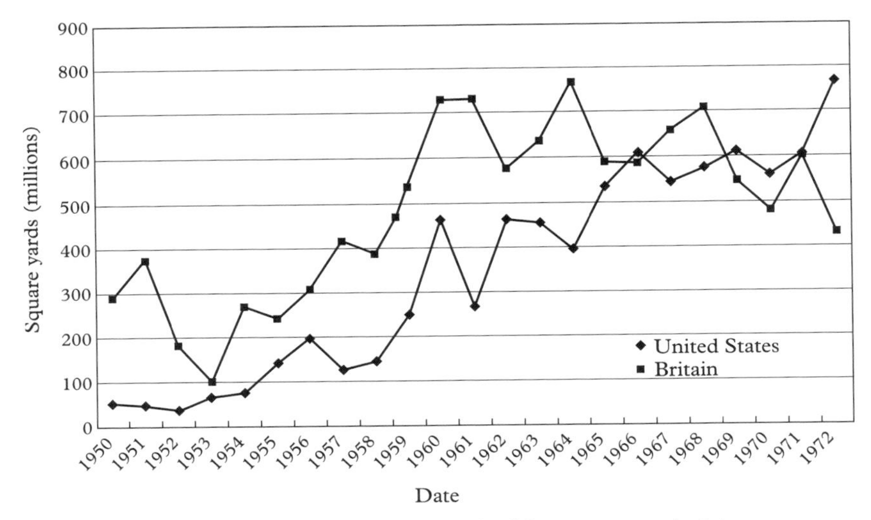

Fig. 8.3 Volume of British and United States cotton cloth imports, 1950–72
Source: Cotton Board: *Quarterly Statistics*; *Cotton: Monthly Review of World Statistics*

enjoyed relatively high rates of tariff protection (Dupree 1990a: 110; OECD 1965: 66).

The damaging impact of declining cotton piece good exports in the 1950s was inevitably far greater for Lancashire than for the United States and was more likely to deter investment and modernisation thus contributing to collapse. This was not merely because the fall in volume was greater but because despite some postwar reduction in the export orientation of the British cotton industry, it remained heavily dependent on overseas markets with over a quarter of cotton cloth destined for export between 1950 and 1966. By contrast, the United States cotton industry retained an exceptional domestic orientation after 1945 and on average a far smaller proportion of output was exported by United States producers than by British (see Table 8.5), although Figure 8.4 does demonstrate some shifts in direction. Yet for an industry with such a vast domestic market the consequence of any decline in exports would have had only a marginal effect on strategy and morale and future prospects.[1] The collapse of the postwar sellers' market in 1952 witnessed a rise in imports of cotton piece goods in both the United States and Britain as Figure 8.3 demonstrates, while Figures 8.5 and 8.6 indicate that imports to Britain came

[1] Cotton Board, *Quarterly Statistics.*

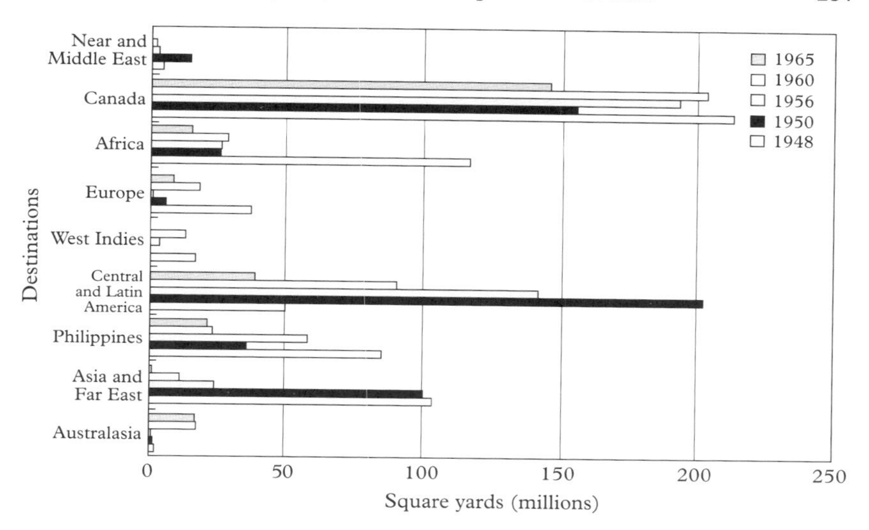

Fig. 8.4 Destination of United States cotton cloth exports, 1946–65
Source: Cotton Board: *Quarterly Statistics*; *Cotton: Monthly Review of World Statistics*

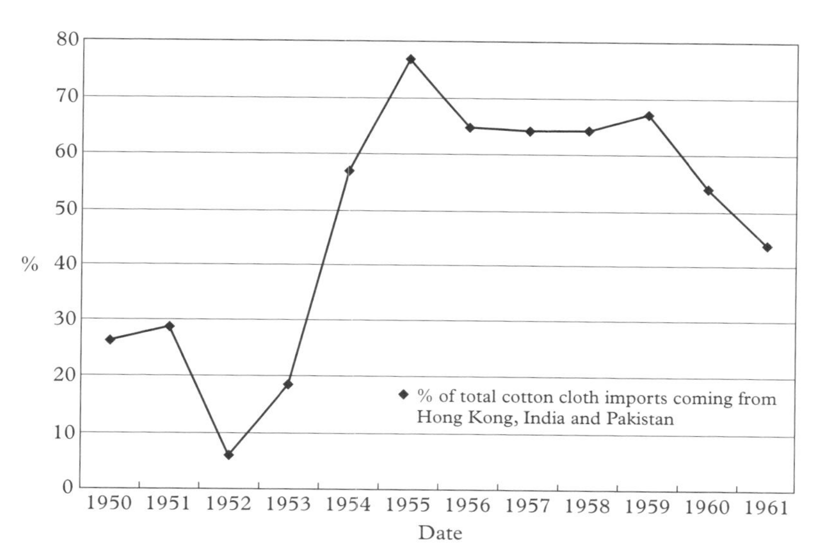

Fig. 8.5 Proportion of total British cotton cloth imports coming from Hong Kong, India and Pakistan, 1950–61
Source: Cotton Board: *Quarterly Statistics*

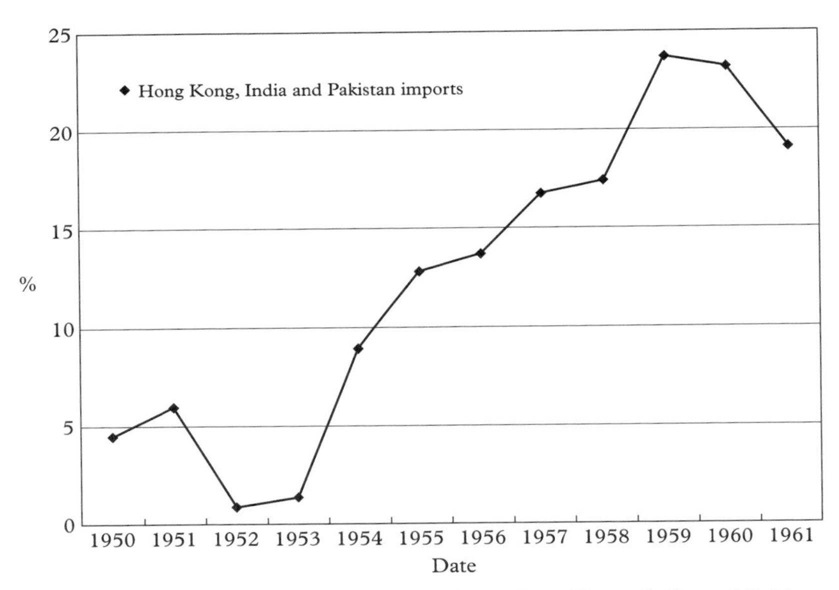

Fig. 8.6 Imports of cotton cloth from Hong Kong, India and Pakistan as a proportion of British domestic consumption, 1950–61
Source: Cotton Board: *Quarterly Statistics*

predominantly from the Commonwealth and made up a rising proportion of domestic consumption. Similarly in the United States imports came largely from the low labour cost economies of the Far East.

Response to such changing market conditions and efforts to maintain competitiveness varied in Britain and the United States embracing investment in new technology to improve productivity, development of new products, experimentation with new work practices, diversification, organisational change and collusion. More than anything, however, the period from 1950 to 1980 was marked by growing political lobbying as industrialists tried to persuade governments of the need to protect them from the chilling wind of import penetration. Cotton industry jobs were dwindling in both Britain and America from the early 1950s. In Britain between 1951 and 1960 105,000 jobs were lost in the cotton industry with employment in spinning and weaving each falling by around 40 per cent. In the United States, on the other hand, a total of 138,000 cotton industry jobs vanished between 1945 and 1960. In reality import penetration was only part of the explanation for the job losses but it was a sufficiently emotive issue to become central to campaigns by cotton interests on both sides of the Atlantic.

Strategic response in the postwar world

In Britain, continued flows of duty free imports deterred substantial investment between 1950 and 1959 since they contributed to declining profits and dismal expectations of future returns. Certainly the banks were prepared to lend and backed Cyril Lord's flamboyant empire building in the 1950s, but overall the industry seems to have stood still and at best invested defensively rather than creatively (Singleton 1991: 141–54). The technological profile of the industry only really began to change in favour of greater automation after the Cotton Industry Act of 1959 hastened the scrapping of surplus capacity. Faith in mule spinning initially remained firm, though a limited shift to rings occurred as a short-term strategy to handle the joint impact of high taxes on fine yarns, as a result of Purchase Tax, and the shortage of mule labour. Ironically the much condemned Yarn Spinners Agreement of 1947 may have encouraged innovation through increasing certainty by providing minimum margins (Higgins 1993a: 211–34). It is interesting to note that, in terms of R&D, the record of expenditure, at 0.4 per cent of annual turnover by large British firms, actually bettered that in the United States where firms expended only 0.1 per cent of net sales on research. This suggests that most of the criticism of the neglect of research by textile industrialists stems not from international comparisons, but from comparisons with far more technology-intensive sectors (Singleton 1991: 142; Huffmire 1973: 33–4).

Productivity could also be improved by changes in work practices and in a preamble to their report on the Musgrave experiment of 1946 the Cotton Board quoted the Platt Report which observed:

> Work load assessments are not made in British mills, the number of units supervised having [been] in the past ascertained empirically and combined with wage rates in the drawing up of 'wage lists' which under modern conditions do not permit the most economical utilisation of labour ... the scientific assessment of an operative's load would appear to be an aspect of modernisation to which the attention of the appropriate parties might be directed with a determination to arrive at a solution. . . . Revision of wage rates and workers' duties should be based on scientific rather than empirical methods, and should aim at increasing both the productivity and the wages of labour. (Cotton Board 1948: 1)

The Musgrave experiment was the Cotton Board's attempt to introduce work study in negotiation with unions and managers at the Musgrave Spinning Company's No. 7 Mill, in Bolton. The mill employed industrial consultants, Production Engineering Ltd, who drew up a redeployment plan and on the basis of the trial it was shown that it was possible to reduce numbers employed by 20 per cent and increase output per hour by 15 per cent and for the remaining workers to achieve a 30 per cent improvement in earnings. This proved so popular with management and the workforce that it was retained after the end of the experiment (Cotton Board 1948: 7). Other work study schemes were initiated by the Shirley Institute and in 1949 the Cotton Board opened a work study school in Manchester. However, although both initiatives found favour with the government, wider implementation was fraught with difficulty, varied regionally and was especially unpopular in coarse spinning areas such as Oldham, whilst their progress seems to have been inhibited by the Evershed and Aronson Wages Lists. These difficulties undoubtedly reduced the ability of the cotton industry to contribute to the export drive of the 1940s whilst leading to further loss of competitive advantage in the 1950s. Yet, if the postwar period from the 1940s until 1980 is taken as a whole, labour relations were amazingly quiescent in Lancashire and changes such as the introduction of shift working were accepted with little opposition. Declining relative wages in cotton and good alternative employment opportunities meant that if workers were dissatisfied, they went elsewhere. Even more so than in the interwar period, cotton unionism was in retreat and membership falling, so that bargaining power was terminally eroded (Singleton 1991: 65–88, 168–90).

For the most part collusive arrangements and price maintenance did little to stabilise the declining Lancashire cotton industry after the Second World War and changes in the law, relating to Monopolies and Restrictive Practices, meant that by the 1960s they were outlawed. The Yarn Spinners Association was established in 1947 to avoid the problem of 'weak selling'. However, the maintenance of an agreement in a declining sector was a thankless task made hopeless by growing interest from the Monopolies Commission. In 1958 the Restrictive Practices Court upheld a ruling that the yarn agreement inflated prices and led to a loss of export markets, despite the defence that by creating greater certainty, price maintenance in spinning was benign and supportive. As in the interwar period, under pressure from both finishers and merchants and with significant internal divisions of their own, weavers found it hardest to secure and maintain any price agreements and postwar efforts were aborted in the 1950s (Singleton 1991: 199–204). In calico printing, however, a price fixing scheme was introduced in 1949 as soon as government controls were removed, in an attempt to maintain stability. There was outrage among calico printers over the 1954 Monopolies Commission report, seen by the sector as savage in its attack on price maintenance, contradictory of the principles of the Cotton Industry Enabling Act of 1939 and likely to damage the industry as a whole. The culture of collusion in printing, which had evolved in the interwar period, proved very resilient and it was not until 1961 that fears of renewed attention from the Restrictive Practices Court led the FCP to abandon recommended minimum prices. Even then covert collusion continued and an 'Information Service' was set up in the same year, membership of which was to be a possible condition of membership of the Federation. Members would report prices and all reports were to be 'in code' and, whilst there was some uneasiness about powers of inspection, there can be little doubt that the purpose of this arrangement was to constrain competition.[2]

By the 1960s the remnants of the Lancashire cotton industry were absorbed by the man-made fibres industry in a wave of mergers which created a high level of vertical integration and the world's most concentrated textile industry. By 1966 the four dominant firms of Courtaulds, English Sewing Cotton, Viyella International and Carrington Dewhurst controlled Lancashire's cotton interests and within them were strong vertical groupings as mergers included both backward and forward integration, while both Viyella International and Carrington Dewhurst were financed by ICI (Singleton 1991: 221–30). Yet the outcome of the mergers was a dismal failure in terms of overall competitiveness and the survival of a textile base in Lancashire. The management style of firms does not seem a conclusive reason for success or failure since some, such as Courtaulds, mixed features of multi-divisionality with a holding company structure whilst the Viyella group was a multi-divisional company lacking strategic direction. In many respects it was firms outside these conglomerates, such as Shiloh and Smith and Nephew, which performed best during the 1960s and 1970s and were able to maintain both profitability and individuality through serving specific niches (Singleton 1997: 129–31; Millington 1995: 25–7; Foreman-Peck 1995).

There is little evidence in this period that scale alone could provide the basis of competitive advantage in textiles in the developed world and there is much to suggest that flexibility, within innovative networks, has led to greater resilience and better performance. By the 1960s Lancashire no longer represented a dynamic industrial district based on textiles. Forty years of difficulties and uncertainty had eroded the link between evolving skill and competitive advantage, whilst the strength of localism had degenerated into a fatalistic parochialism. Yet it is hard to escape the feeling that government policy in this period meant that Lancashire's industrialists were operating in an environment which undermined the very strengths which could have proved their salvation and encouraged a corrosive defeatism.

[2] GMRO, FCP, Minutes, 23 June 1961 and 26 January 1962.

Clearly it was inconceivable that Lancashire could have regained even prewar shares of world cotton piece exports: for the developing world was importing less, whilst British producers, with outmoded technology, had lost cost competitiveness in many traditional markets. Yet there emerged a vicious cycle which helped to choke off the very innovation and investment which could have allowed a smaller and more modern industry to thrive in high income markets. It is striking that neither Britain nor the United States was particularly successful in fashion markets overseas after 1945. The United States was unable to maintain a substantial foothold in any high income market except Canada, whereas Britain made no impact at all in Europe, as Figures 8.2 and 8.4 show. For Britain, lacking the United States' large, high income domestic market and facing rising import penetration from low labour cost producers, this was especially unfortunate. As cotton textile production increased in the developing world, from the 1950s onwards, and the proportion of total world output exported declined, these were the only markets in which established cotton industries could hope to maintain an advantage.

Britain's poor success in high income markets with high quality and high value added fabrics stemmed from a number of causes. If the history of the United States cotton industry made it difficult for firms to penetrate high income overseas markets, the development of Lancashire as an industrial district should have rendered its structure and capabilities ideal for expansion into markets where quality and flexibility were the keys to success. In this segment of world markets an admittedly much-reduced Lancashire cotton industry should have been able to compete effectively and move up market, a course of action which was successfully pursued in Continental Europe. Such a strategy would have moderated Lancashire's decline. Yet it only occurred to a modest degree and with very limited success.

During the postwar period, a number of factors including wartime Utility schemes, inexperience in Continental European markets, supply-side weaknesses, structural changes and government policy inhibited any efforts to move in this direction. At the same time the legacy of Empire reinforced commercial links with Commonwealth markets on the one hand, whilst distancing Britain from the emergent, discerning markets of the EEC after 1957, on the other. This in turn slowed down any move up market and isolated the British industry from the influence of Continental textile designs, which were to become so important in the postwar world.

In the Second World War the government concentration scheme controlled the wartime capacity of the cotton industry, whilst from 1941–52 the Utility scheme regulated the type of goods produced and the design of clothing and furniture. Used in conjunction with rationing and price controls, Utility was intended to provide a supply of durable, serviceable clothing and by December 1942 the scheme was in place. It included specifications for cloth types and clothing design, controls on prices and profits, nominated designated manufacturers, provided guarantees for quality and gave tax advantages to producers of Utility goods which were to be exempt from Purchase Tax (Sladen 1995: 11, 36–7).

There is general agreement that Utility was essential to the British war economy and that it successfully achieved its objectives and may also have had some positive long-term benefits for both the cotton and clothing industries in terms of standardisation, quality-control and productivity (Wadsworth 1948; Worswick 1947; Sladen 1995: 101). However, in terms of establishing a lasting foothold in, for example, European markets, the Utility programme, and more especially its retention until the 1950s, almost certainly proved a hindrance. Success in high quality markets depends on a combination of the flexibility and productivity of a skilled workforce with the design and quality of its products. Permanent loss of skilled workers during and after the Second World War made it more difficult for Lancashire firms to compete and contributed to the disintegration of the self-sustaining skill base of the industrial district, which numerous recruitment drives and education schemes could not reverse. Moreover the persistence of Utility and austerity measures into the 1950s choked any enthusiasm for new fabric designs and stifled any moves up market (Sladen 1995: 101). Equally, the continued exemption of Utility fabrics from Purchase Tax, until 1956, constrained home demand for finer cloths and led to a shift out of fine production into long runs of coarser cloth. This in turn restricted the ability to build export markets on domestic capabilities (Higgins 1993a: 353; Dupree 1990a: 118–19). This was especially ironic, since by 1958 fine poplin shirtings were one of relatively few fabrics in which Britain enjoyed both price and quality advantages in the increasingly competitive and potentially lucrative German market (Cotton Board 1958: 49–50). This was not all, however, for United States tariffs, adjusted in the interwar period to offer increased protection for the finer end of the market, continued to work against Britain in the 1950s. In 1956, during talks at the American Embassy, Raymond Streat complained:

> I reminded them that US tariffs on cotton goods had been since the days of the Fordney-McCumber Tariff Act in the 1920s excessively high and much higher than ours. The concessions under the US reciprocal trade act had, in our opinion, never cut deep enough to remedy this basic inequality. We had never wanted, hoped or expected to export cotton goods to the US on a scale which could possibly have injured the US cotton industry. We would have been richly content at

> any time since the end of the Second World War to have something between half and one percent of the American home market, or from 60 to 120m yards, whereas the best we had got in any one year was just about 10m. Their tariff structure was irrational bearing more heavily on the more expensive goods, and the customs appraisal methods in the past had greatly impeded trade. (Dupree 1987, vol. II: 860)

Yet even without these constraints, the question remains of whether Lancashire's skill base was really such a good foundation for a move up market. Vertical and spatial specialisation had certainly brought flexibility in meeting the needs of diverse markets, but Lancashire's forte was not design and the best efforts of the Cotton Board 'Colour and Design Centre' had only limited effect. In 1958 German consumers dismissed Lancashire design as tasteless and lacklustre, and given the frustration felt by fashion designers over British textile producers, one feels a certain sympathy for them (Jarvis 1997: 92–9). Nor, interestingly, were there many signs of textile design flair in the 1960s for British manufacturing firms. London may have become the fashion hub of the world but rather than moving up market, British manufacturers continued to try and compete in low quality textiles. By this time the combination of a major skills shortage and the creation of large conglomerates reinforced a trend to standardised products for the mass market. Equally, the demands of the major retailers, especially Marks and Spencer, for low price standardised garments may well have sapped initiative and inhibited change (Schoeser 1996: 207–9; Singleton 1996: 322). Against the backdrop of two decades of high levels of duty free Commonwealth imports Lancashire was doomed to slide into obscurity.

The position of the United States differed from Britain since, despite the background of a continued shift of the cotton industry and indeed textiles as a whole to the Southern states (as Figure 8.7 shows) and of a declining industry, investment levels were relatively high. Relying heavily on retained profits often amassed during the prosperous war years, larger textile firms, in particular, engaged in fairly energetic levels of investment in modernisation and diversification programmes. Accordingly expenditure on new plant and machinery rose from an average of $460m per annum in the 1950s to $760m in the 1960s across the textile industry as a whole, though this, as much as anything, reflects a shift into manufacturing using synthetics and man-made fibres across the industry, rather than the experience of cotton alone. The emphasis continued to be on saving labour, economising on skill and new technology and methods and the proportion of obsolete capacity fell from 29 per cent in 1962 to 17 per cent by late 1968. Against such growing capital intensity, integration and diversification also rose, as firms turned to synthetics and into sectors

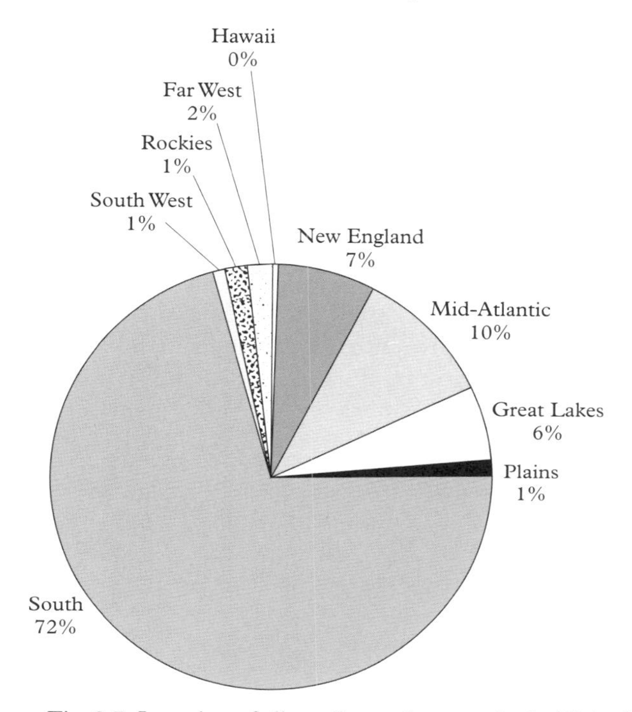

Fig. 8.7 Location of all textile employment in the United States, 1978
Source: Toyne et al. 1984: 5–12c

such as tufted carpets and hosiery. However, only a few large firms moved into finished goods production, the majority lacking the necessary design and marketing expertise. Merger activity, which had begun before the Second World War, gathered momentum and in North Carolina alone there were 542 mergers in textiles with 90 mills, 1.6m spindles and 23,000 looms changing hands. This trend continued and between 1948 and 1954 there were 117 textile-related mergers in the United States as a whole. Despite increasing government interest in the monopoly implications of textile-related mergers, a massive 748 consolidations and acquisitions occurred between 1955 and 1964 (Wood 1986: 173–4; Simpson 1966: 57). As part of this process there emerged a number of large dominant firms including Burlington Industries Inc., J. P. Stevens and Lowensteins, the experience of which provide insights into the process of change occurring in this period.

During the Second World War Spencer Love, founder of Burlington Mills, had been director of the Bureau of Textiles, Leather and Clothing of the War Production Board, a position which helped to ensure that his firm had a guaranteed source of profit from government contracts. This, combined with the opportunities for growth, which a stock market listing brought, allowed Love to expand Burlington Mills in ways which would significantly widen the markets the firm could serve. Between 1945 and 1962 the firm achieved a high level of diversification into a massive array of fabrics and hosiery. Although Love disposed of his converting operations during the 1950s, he retained his selling agency and increasingly moved into branded goods such as Cameo hosiery and Lees carpets, which were sold direct to retailers or through mail order catalogues. By 1954 Burlington was the world's largest textile company and was organised under a multi-divisional structure, changing its name to Burlington Industries Inc. the following year. By 1961 it ranked 50th in *Fortune*'s listing of the 500 largest United States industrial companies, employing 62,000 workers in 122 plants and with assets valued at $614m in both the United States and overseas. A period of slower expansion occurred during the 1960s, followed by some rationalisation in the 1970s, so that by 1979 the corporation consisted of 98 plants in the United States with 22 plants in nine overseas countries, but remaining America's largest textile giant standing at 129th in the *Fortune* 500 (Wood 1986: 169–70; Wright 1995: 77).[3]

No other textile firm matched Burlington Industries' growth in terms of sales, assets, employees or product range. In 1961 the family dominated J. P. Stevens, which was the second largest United States textile firm employed 34,000 workers in 42 cotton, woollen, worsted and synthetic cloth manufacturing plants mainly in North and South Carolina with some in New England. This New York selling agency had expanded into Southern cotton manufacturing in 1946, also on the strength of profits from wartime government contracts. It absorbed 11 textile firms, capitalising on the financial ties which it enjoyed with manufacturing firms and enabling it to have full control over the lines which it sold. At the same time it secured a merger with another branch of the family business, which owned ten New England woollen and worsted mills. Backward integration also characterised the growth of M. Lowenstein and Sons, New York converters which, in 1946 and 1947, took a controlling interest in grey cloth mills in Alabama, North and South Carolina initially to secure a supply of goods for their finishing operations (Simpson 1966: 58).[4]

These three prominent examples of business growth reflected general trends in textiles and in the cotton industry in particular and had repercussions for the profile of the industry. Some of the giants of the interwar

[3] *Moody's Industrial Manual*, 1961, 1974, 1979; *Fortune*, May 1980.
[4] *Moody's Industrial Manual*, 1961.

period continued to flourish, including Pepperell Manufacturing Company and Cannon Mills (Markham 1950: 87). However, the new giants which emerged, whilst profitable and dynamic in the interwar period, owed their expansion to accumulated wartime profits which allowed them to alter the structure of American textile production and distribution. One result of the wave of merger activity from 1946 onwards was that the power of the selling agent diminished significantly, and as early as 1946 75 per cent of sales were direct. In addition, the emergence of the conglomerates significantly blurred the divisions between different categories of textiles and, as product ranges became more diverse, there was an increase in the use of the multi-divisional form of organisation. However, although the cost efficient giants like Burlingtons were able to undercut competitors in their scramble for customers, textiles did not become an oligopolistic market. By 1963 Burlington's market share was still only 5 per cent of sales, since the Southern textile industry continued to include numerous small producers and the level of concentration was lower than in Britain. In general, if there was a spread of conglomeration, mills remained very small employing as few as 300 workers and mills were no larger in the 1950s than they had been in the 1920s (Huffmire 1973: 33; Simpson 1966: 57–8; Singleton 1997: 133–4; Minchin 1997: 7–9).

Still there was a growing concentration of ownership in the Southern textile industry, and by the 1950s 42 interests controlled 20 per cent of production. This shift in ownership patterns, combined with the social changes stemming from the Second World War, contributed to the further shift of the industry south. Yet companies began selling off mill housing signalling the demise of the company village. This was a time when improved living standards, the product of rising wartime wages, altered consumption patterns of millworkers enabling them to buy cars, consumer durables and aspire to home ownership (Minchin 1997: 21). However, although the decline of the mill village coincided with rising levels of strike activity, unionisation remained very limited and strike action, such as that in 1951, largely unsuccessful. Consumerism rendered workers unwilling to engage in long strikes and, for the still overwhelmingly white workforce, the Ku Klux Klan was able to turn unions into a race issue. Additionally giants like Burlington and J. P. Stevens abandoned traditional low wage policies and used higher wages (by the standards of the South) and modern employee relations programmes as weapons against unions and avoiding unionisation in the 1940s and 1950s. With continued weak unions, wages remained lower in the South than the North in the 1950s and hastened the further decline of textile production in New England and the mid-Atlantic states as plants continued to close or move their operations south (Minchin 1997: 69–167).

The textile giants were certainly cost efficient, but it is not clear how far they altered the international profile of the United States cotton industry or its ability to compete in high income markets. In the interwar period, the production-driven United States cotton industry had lacked the capabilities and more especially the flexibility to enjoy lasting success in diverse overseas markets. The mass production of a standardised product by unskilled labour, which had evolved in the nineteenth century to serve frontier markets, had been reinforced by the shift of the industry south. Until the 1920s luxury fabrics and fine yarns were almost always imported and often from Britain. In the postwar world firms in closer contact with their markets were able to improve the quality and design of their products and become far more market conscious. Yet market sensitivity remained domestic and it is fair to say that the trend towards homogeneity in both clothing and furnishing fabrics, which stretched from the 1930s to the 1960s, benefited the giant producers whose branding strategies gave them opportunities for non-price competition. Exporting on any scale to a diverse range of economies, with varying tastes and preferences and sharply segmented markets, was another matter. It complicated production and eroded cost advantages in goods other than towellings and sheetings or mass produced clothing like denim jeans which became fashion goods during the 1960s. Even then the textile manufacturers were dependent upon apparel makers such as Levi Straus and Blue Bell to set the trend. It was not until 1980, ironically immediately prior to the dramatic collapse of the Southern textile industry, that United States denim producers, such as Cone Mills, Greensboro, were able to by-pass the apparel makers and sell direct in Europe while others created a fashion for United States co-ordinated bed linen and towels. More generally American firms, despite or perhaps because of their scale and capital intensity, lacked the flexibility and even the technology for success in diverse markets (Toyne et al. 1984: 8.4; Scranton 1997: 340).[5] Indeed, whilst United States textile firms retained a productivity advantage in 1980, the rate of innovation, especially the introduction of the shuttleless loom, was slower than in the European Union which had gained the technological initiative (Toyne et al. 1983: 5–19c; Singleton 1997: 150).

Nevertheless, in comparison with Britain until the 1970s and more especially in the 1980s, cotton manufacturing in the United States declined but investment remained buoyant and innovation continued. It may simply have been the case that United States businessmen were culturally more enthusiastic about innovation and investment than their

[5] *Fortune*, 5 May 1980.

British counterparts; after all the productivity gap in textiles dated from the nineteenth century. Yet the expectations of return on investment are a critical determinant of the decision to invest and these are affected by the level of certainty in a particular sector. The prospect of rising import penetration from low labour cost producers was a scourge facing both industries, yet its impact on expectations depended upon the extent to which it was possible to persuade the government that cotton interests deserved protecting.

Campaigns for protection

In Britain in the 1950s and 1960s the reluctance of successive governments to protect the cotton industry, in the face of Far Eastern and especially Commonwealth competition, has been well documented (Dupree 1990a; Singleton 1990: 129–49) and needs only brief reiteration here. In striking contrast to experience elsewhere in the developed world and especially in the United States, British governments, at best, gave low priority to the protection of the cotton industry whether against low labour cost imports or to allow for industrial regeneration. Instead of enhanced protection they favoured the scrapping of obsolete and surplus capacity and the re-equipment of the remaining core of the industry (Miles 1968: 46–54). At worst their commercial policies worked directly against Lancashire and were formulated without consultation with the Cotton Board who represented the industry (Dupree 1990a: 119–20).

Lack of government consultation with the Cotton Board on a key policy issue was particularly noticeable with regard to the Anglo-Japanese Trade Agreement of 1954. In an effort to correct the imbalance in trade between Japan and the sterling area in 1952, the British government agreed to a range of measures which heightened Japanese competition in both Commonwealth and British markets. These included encouragement to Commonwealth countries to accept Japanese imports, measures to allow the removal of import quotas on Japanese goods, whilst Japan was also given limited access to the British domestic market. Since cotton textiles were an important part of this trade, the agreement undermined Lancashire in both home and overseas markets and most especially in those overseas markets upon which the industry was especially dependent. The agreement was greeted by a mixture of outrage and disbelief in the industry and in the House of Commons. It was a humiliation for the Cotton Board which highlighted its limited bargaining power and undermined its standing in the industry and hence its ability to act as an effective mouthpiece for the diverse interests represented. This was especially unfortunate since growing Commonwealth imports soon overshadowed

Table 8.2. *Tariffs on cotton textiles in industrialised economies in 1966 (%)*

	EEC	United Kingdom	United States	Japan
Cotton yarn	8	7.5	5–29	5–7.5
Woven fabrics	14–19	17.5	7.75–33	10–25
Ribbons	16–21	17.5–20	5–42.5	10–25
Tulle, lace and embroidery	14–22	25	19–60	15–30

Source: GATT 1966: 80.

worries of renewed Japanese competition (Dupree 1990a: 119–20). Consequently, at the very time when the industry needed a powerful pressure group, the ability of the Board to fulfil this role was clearly fading.

As far as the manufacturing interests of Lancashire were concerned, the most galling aspect of government policy was its inflexibility regarding duty free Commonwealth imports, a legacy of the Ottawa Agreements of 1932. The origins of these agreements lay in the sterling area, based upon Imperial Preference that was constructed after the abandonment of the gold standard and free trade in 1931. While British goods were to enter the Empire at preferential rates, the Ottawa Agreements laid down that all goods qualifying for Empire preference entered Britain duty free. In the 1930s the assumption had been that Empire imports would comprise predominantly raw materials; in the postwar period they included Commonwealth cotton goods. That these arrangements were not modified until 1972 placed Lancashire at a significant disadvantage in comparison with other developed economies. This is because whilst, as Table 8.2 shows, British tariffs on foreign produced goods were very much in line with those of both Europe and the United States, UK producers were alone in facing duty free imports from Hong Kong, India and Pakistan which were after all the most rapidly growing sources of cotton textile exports.

Lancashire's campaign for protection against Commonwealth imports lasted from the 1950s until the 1970s and saw many attempts to secure modification of the free entry policy. This mainly involved pressure for quotas on imports, but there was also support for tariffs. The frustration of spinners and manufacturers was summed up at a FMCSA meeting in February 1955 when they resolved that:

> this meeting affirms its grave concern at the immediate and potentially increasing threat to employment, stability and confidence in the cotton industry from the imports of cotton cloth and yarn. . . . It expresses its profound dissatisfaction at the Government's unwillingness to take action to safeguard the vital interests of

the workpeople and employers in the Lancashire cotton industry and urges strong representations to be made directly to the government.[6]

The campaign was orchestrated in a number of ways and by more than one body. From 1950 until 1969 the Cotton Board, which had the often difficult task of representing all sections of the industry, was the official link between the cotton interests and the Board of Trade. The Cotton Board concentrated on efforts to secure quotas of Commonwealth imports on the basis of voluntary agreements. They rarely enjoyed the confidence of the entire industry and from the start were seen as too compliant by the more extreme employers, such as Cyril Lord. In 1962 dissatisfaction with the Cotton Board's conduct of the campaign for protection led to the foundation of the Textile Action Group (TAG). This group of militant activists was formed at a meeting between a group of Oldham employers and some East Lancashire manufacturers in the boardroom of an Oldham mill. This body aimed to stimulate legislative change on imports, to encourage the marking of cloths to show their country of origin and encourage retailers to 'buy British'. They planned to do this by direct action from local groups and letter writing campaigns, rather than simply relying on the Cotton Board. Within a few weeks branches were formed in Halifax, Keighley, Silsden, Todmorden, Barnoldswick, Nelson, Burnley, Preston, Wigan, Ashton, Stockport and West Horton (Lazer 1975: 274).[7] Whilst raising the visibility of the campaign (sometimes in unwelcome ways) TAG did not achieve any more spectacular success than the Cotton Board.

In the 1950s local employers put pressure on backbench Conservative MPs, often in vulnerable marginal seats, by local employers' associations, whilst links between the United Textile Factory Workers Association and the Labour Party kept the issue alive during Labour's period of opposition (Lazer 1975: 57). In addition, leading textile industrialists argued strongly for protection at every available opportunity. Therefore in 1965, Courtaulds' outspoken chairman, Sir Frank Kearton, argued for regenerative tariffs in a powerful speech to stockholders:

It is clear that given the right investment, the textile industry can contribute more to economic growth than most other industries. But such investment depends on confident long term planning. This in turn means that Lancashire must have some assurance, in the next few vital years, that the UK will not continue to be the world's dumping ground for cotton type textiles. All other countries regard their domestic textile industries as vitally important to general economic well being. I have never been able to understand why some quarters seem so hostile to

[6] *Textile Weekly*, 18 February 1955. [7] *Manchester Guardian*, 9 May 1962.

Lancashire's traditional industry, and are so ready to contemplate its decline. Common sense surely would urge that it is re-established and revitalised. (Quoted in Knight 1974: 54)

Kearton's view was also transmitted to the Permanent Secretary to the Board of Trade and echoed by the newly established Textile Council in 1969 in *Conditions for Progress*, in which it was suggested that: 'government should make an early and firm announcement of tariff and quota policy beyond 1970' (quoted in Lazer 1975: 106).

Efforts to secure relief from Commonwealth imports were fraught with difficulty and during the 1950s and 1960s all the evidence suggests that both Conservative and Labour governments were unwilling to yield to the Cotton Board's demands for a reversal, or at least a modification, of this policy. In 1952, for instance, in his address to the Cotton Board Conference in Harrogate, the President of the Board of Trade, Peter Thorneycroft, dubbed by the blunt and vocal Cyril Lord as the 'hangman of Lancashire', dismissed the pleas of the industry for support and protection against Commonwealth imports. He concluded that:

My final word to you is this. The Government has no feather-bed to offer you and very little shelter in the harsh winds of competition which are blowing through the world today. We will try to give you what help we can. We will try to mould the trading patterns to suit you. We will try to limit the burdens put upon you. But, in the last resort no government can help you. Your future depends on the same qualities of skill, courage, enterprise and high endeavour which have carried you so nobly and so far.[8]

Nor was there any evidence of a softening of this view, which was reiterated at the Cotton Board conference in 1955. In addition Thorneycrof pointed out that Commonwealth imports still made up only 10 per cent of domestic consumption so that erosion of export markets and the maintenance of external competitiveness were a more serious problem for the industry. More significantly he made it clear that the interests of the national economy were better served by greater trade liberalisation than by the protection of the cotton industry (Cotton Board 1956: 4). Earlier that year the Cotton Board had even gone so far as to send a deputation to meet Winston Churchill, but again to no avail. In a statement in the House of Commons on 3 May 1955 he stated that: 'We would be reluctant to take action against imports from India, particularly action which would discriminate against India compared with other parts of the Commonwealth. Special considerations of Colonial policy arise in the case of Hong Kong' (Cotton Board 1956: 4). What Churchill feared was that any concessions for Lancashire, especially with respect to India,

[8] *Cotton Board Trade Letter*, November 1952.

might risk Indian tariff preferences on other British goods (Dupree 1987, vol. II: xxiv).

With such minimal government enthusiasm, efforts by the Cotton Board to negotiate voluntary quotas with the cotton masters of Hong Kong, India and Pakistan in the 1950s were doomed and it was not until 1958 when Macmillan threw his weight behind the negotiations that agreement was reached. Even then the quota for Hong Kong was much higher than anticipated (Lazer 1975: 243; Dupree 1990a: 110–28; Singleton 1991: 136; Cotton Board 1956). Once the Long Term Arrangement (LTA) was negotiated under the auspices of GATT in 1961 to allow for an orderly expansion of exports of cotton goods from the developing to the developed world, the British government was tardy in its use of it, much to the chagrin of Lancashire (Tomlinson 1994: 352; Singleton 1991: 135–7; Knight 1974: 110; Textile Council 1969: 128; GATT 1966: 83).[9] Against this background the system of global quotas covering yarn, cloth and made-up goods, introduced in 1966, came too late to be of any significant benefit to Lancashire and did not stem the flow of imports (Singleton 1991: 139; Miles 1976: 197). It was not until 1972, in preparation for joining the European Community, that tariff arrangements were finally altered.

The campaign for government support began in the United States in the 1950s, when the cotton interests complained that their industry was being crippled by the impact of government support schemes for raw cotton, which placed them at a disadvantage in cotton purchases in comparison with foreign competitors. In addition they were threatened by imports of cotton goods first from Japan and later from Hong Kong and India (Aggarwal and Haggard 1983: 259–60; Robson 1957: 262–3). Additionally, especially with regards to the industrial reconstruction of Japan and the tariff concessions granted in 1955, they believed that American foreign policy objectives worked against their increasingly obsolete industry and threatened 2.4 million jobs (Hunsberger 1961: 258 and 310; Brandis Buford 1982: 8–10). These factors created discontent which was vigorously and effectively articulated by the American Cotton Manufacturers Institute (ACMI), which represented 80 per cent of the industry (Aggarwal and Haggard 1983: 10; Bauer, de Sola Pool and Dexter 1964: 10).

In the United States, in contrast to the relative impotence of the British cotton interests in general and the Cotton Board in particular, the cotton textile lobby became extremely powerful after the Second World War. It did not succeed in reversing the public commitment of governments to

[9] Federation of Master Cotton Spinners Associations, *Annual Report 1965*, p. 97.

Table 8.3. *Effective rates of protection for textiles in the United States and Britain in 1962*

	United States	Britain
Thread and yarn	31.8	27.9
Textile fabrics	50.6	42.3

Source: Belassa 1965: 57.

world trade liberalisation, but it was successful in gaining a number of major concessions in terms of non-tariff protection. In addition, despite the commitment of the United States government to tariff reductions, which saw a series of tariff cuts to cotton goods in 1955, 1962 and 1971, the American cotton industry with *ad valorem* tariffs of 16 per cent and 23.8 per cent on yarns and fabrics respectively was, in 1974, amongst the most highly protected in the developed world. Certainly these rates were significantly higher than the 8.6 per cent and 14.3 per cent duties imposed by the European Community (Keesing and Wolf 1980: 44). Taking the whole of the period from 1950 to 1971 the contrast with Britain is even starker. In the first place the effective rate of protection remained higher in the United States than in Britain, as Table 8.3 shows. In addition, of course, the United States industry was protected against the imports of such Commonwealth countries as India, Pakistan and Hong Kong. Moreover, although the cotton interests in the United States were not able to reverse government promotion to freer trade, they were able to obtain some moderation in tariff reductions. In the Kennedy Round, for example, 56 per cent of textile and textile products experienced no reductions or reductions of less than 50 per cent (Evans 1971: 284).

The United States cotton industry was, therefore, shielded from international competition by higher and more comprehensive tariffs after the Second World War than were British firms. In addition, American cotton manufacturers received more extensive non-tariff protection than could be secured by the Cotton Board and were generally a more potent political force. Thus they achieved far more wide-ranging government responses to their difficulties than was the case in Britain. In the 1950s, for example, Japanese import penetration, directly encouraged by tariff reductions introduced in 1955, was portrayed as the major threat to the health of the cotton industry. The ACMI exerted sufficient pressure on its government to achieve an intergovernmental agreement in 1957 which placed a binding quota on Japanese imports of cotton goods with no guaranteed growth (Brandis Buford 1982: 11). This proved acceptable to the ACMI who concluded:

It is our considered opinion that the plan, if adequately enforced, is basically sound and workable and that it should dissolve promptly the cloud of doubt and uncertainty which has disrupted US cotton textile markets for almost two years. . . . It is logical that the Japanese exporters will also benefit from more orderly marketing conditions in this country. (Brandis Buford 1982: 11)

This was just the start of a series of relatively successful campaigns to secure government support for the industry. These included the establishment of a Congressional subcommittee on the Domestic Textile Industry in 1958 which was to 'conduct a full and complete study of all factors affecting commerce and production in the textile industry of the United States' (Brandis Buford 1982: 11). The so-called Pastore Committee concluded that, aside from achieving productivity gains, textiles had not experienced the dramatic postwar rise in prosperity achieved in other sectors. In addition, it suggested that so great was the decline in cotton textiles that both Congress and the administration should review all policies contributing to that decline. Finally, it secured confirmation from the Office of Civil and Defense Mobilisation that the cotton industry was 'an essential industry and an essential part of the nation's mobilisation base' (Brandis Buford 1982: 11). Consequently the Pastore Committee justified the need to maintain high levels of textile capacity and employment on the somewhat dubious grounds of national security. On this basis it recommended the introduction of import quotas and the termination of the two-price raw cotton system (Brandis Buford 1982: 11).

The idea of unilateral action by the United States on textile quotas was not feasible and there was little response from the Eisenhower administration to the Committee's demands. These recommendations were encapsulated in John F. Kennedy's Seven Point Plan of 1961 which was a crucial part of his electoral campaign. This scheme established a government-sponsored research programme to facilitate change in the industry, altered depreciation allowances on textile machinery to encourage scrapping and provided assistance from the Small Business Administration. It also established a government support scheme to offset the two-price raw cotton system. It was, however, especially imaginative with respect to the impact of import penetration. Kennedy agreed to initiate an international conference to establish a multilateral arrangement for an orderly growth of world cotton textile exports. The idea was to reduce the disruption of markets in industrialised countries which economic growth in the developing world caused. At the same time, the seventh point of the plan used the alleged national security standing of the industry as a basis for special case pleading under Trade Agreements, leaving open the possibility of unilateral protective measures (Aggarwal and Haggard 1983: 279).

Implemented in 1961, the Seven Point Plan was infinitely more supportive of the domestic industry than the 1959 Cotton Industry Act had

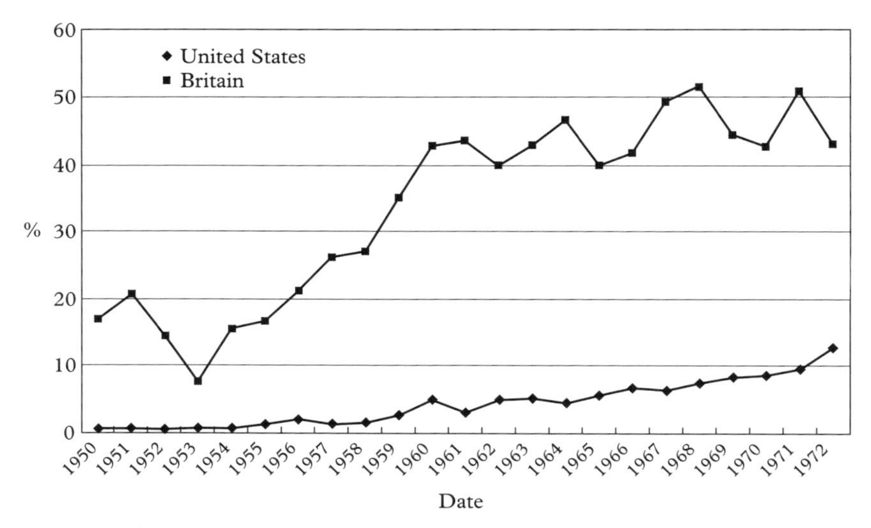

Fig. 8.8 Import penetration of cotton cloth in Britain and the United States, 1950–72
Source: Cotton Board: *Quarterly Statistics*

been in Britain. It was designed to encourage the transformation of the industry in a relatively secure external environment. Easily the most significant consequence for the cotton industry was the hastily convened international conference of representatives of developed and developing economies in Geneva. This resulted in the Short Term Arrangement followed swiftly, in 1962, by the Long Term Arrangement (LTA) which allowed for a controlled growth of imports of 5 per cent per annum. However, where imports from one participating country threatened to disrupt the domestic market of another, restraint could be called for (Brandis Buford 1982: 20–6; Simpson 1966).

The LTA, which was successively renewed until 1973, fell short of the ACMI's demands for non-tariff protection for all textiles. It did, however, mark a major and welcome step forward in the industry's quest for special treatment. Successive United States administrations had the opportunity to protect their national cotton industry behind the respectability of an international agreement. Kennedy had, therefore, found an international solution to a potentially embarrassing domestic economic and political problem (Aggarwal and Haggard 1983: 377). For the cynical, it is instructive that with far lower levels of import penetration than occurred in Britain, as was shown in Figure 8.8, the United States invoked the LTA far more frequently. Indeed between 1962 and 1965 the United States took restrictive action against the cotton goods of Argentina, Brazil, Colombia,

Table 8.4. *Nominal tariff rates on textiles and apparel, 1973–87*

	Thread and yarn	Fabrics	Apparel
USA			
1973	14.5	19.0	27.0
1987	9.0	11.5	22.5
European Community			
1973	8.0	14.5	16.5
1987	7.0	10.5	13.5
Japan			
1973	9.0	12.0	18.0
1987	7.0	9.5	14.0

Source: Singleton 1997: 179.

Mexico, Pakistan, the Republic of China, Hong Kong, India, Israel, Jamaica, Korea, Spain, Portugal, the Philippines, Poland, Yugoslavia, Turkey, Japan, Greece and the United Arab Republic, covering a range of 49 categories of goods. By 1972 the United States had constraints on imports from 30 suppliers (GATT 1966: 83; Simpson 1966: 29; Anson and Simpson 1988: 109).

An important consequence of the LTA was that developing countries began to shift production towards synthetics which were not covered by the agreement. This signalled the start of a new series of campaigns in the United States in the late 1960s and early 1970s which, following the pattern of the cotton campaigns, culminated in a new international trade treaty, the Multifibres Arrangement (MFA) which was concluded late in 1973. As with LTA the initiative and much of the political pressure for MFA came from the United States and followed renewed domestic pressure for protection against imports of synthetics first from Japan in 1969–71 and subsequently from East Asia (Destler, Fukui and Sato 1979; Brandis Buford 1982: 44; Keesing and Wolf 1980: 39). Quite apart from quota arrangements under MFA the United States retained higher tariff protection than any other developed economy through to the 1980s, as shown in Table 8.4.

The politics of protection

The explanation of precisely why cotton textile interests in Britain proved less successful in influencing governments than was the case in the United States is a complex issue. It involves the interaction of historical, cultural and politico-economic domestic forces with changes in both the international balance of power and in foreign economic policy on either side of the Atlantic.

One possible explanation of the greater success of United States campaigns for cotton protection, as compared with those in Britain, is the legacy of nineteenth-century experience. It could simply be that with a history so closely linked to the development of the tariff (Ratner 1972) the American cotton interests had much more experience in lobbying for protection than their British counterparts, with their free trade traditions.

Certainly there were historical precedents for differences in bargaining power to be found in the interwar period. In the 1920s and 1930s British governments were prepared to make only marginal concessions to Lancashire, when their interests were damaged as a result of changing policy with regard to India. In the United States, on the other hand, Roosevelt, who needed the Southern Democrats' support, was quick to concede to the demands of the cotton interests for enhanced protection against Japan, even though they came in 1936, just two years after the passage of the Reciprocal Trade Act, a first step towards trade liberalisation by the United States (Bauer, de Sola Pool and Dexter 1964: 25–6). This pattern continued in the postwar period, especially after 1955, when in the United States the coalition of cotton and textile interests emerged as a major political force that had to be neutralised every time successive governments, from Kennedy to Reagan, wanted to make any progress on its central objective of multilateral trade liberalisation. Yet to conclude that the superior bargaining power of United States cotton manufacturers was the result of greater and longer experience than was the case in Britain, is to oversimplify the issues.

In studying the effectiveness of pressure groups in achieving import protection, economists have identified a number of significant influences. Of these, the most important determinants of success have been the relatively small number of firms in the industry (Olson 1971), combined with a high degree of geographic concentration and a rapid growth of import penetration. Against this background, it has also been predicted that pressure groups would be most likely to gain protection for an industry which is both highly labour intensive and which accounts for a high level of employment, whilst producing a commodity which makes up only a small proportion of consumers' budgets. Moreover protection was most likely to be successful when only a small share of output was exported and where there were relatively low levels of foreign direct investment by firms in the industry (Anderson and Baldwin 1981: 14).

Some contrasting economic forces provide a partial explanation of why pressure groups in the United States were more successful in securing pro-

Table 8.5. *Proportion of British and United States piece good output exported, 1950–72*

Date	Britain	United States
1950	36.9	5.0
1951	37.4	7.0
1952	39.9	7.0
1953	36.7	5.6
1954	30.5	5.7
1955	31.2	4.9
1956	29.4	5.0
1957	28.0	5.9
1958	26.9	5.4
1959	26.0	5.1
1960	25.3	4.7
1961	23.3	5.2
1962	21.4	4.5
1963	20.9	4.2
1964	19.3	4.4
1965	18.8	3.3
1966	16.9	3.8
1967	16.9	6.6
1968	19.0	7.7
1969	17.7	8.8
1970	17.8	8.9
1971	19.7	9.9
1972	15.5	13.5

Sources: Robson 1957: 358; Cotton Board, *Quarterly Statistics*; *Cotton Monthly Review of World Statistics*, 1965–72.

tection than was the case in Britain. In the first place, the United States cotton industry was historically far less export-oriented than was the case in Britain, a trend which continued in the postwar period, as Table 8.5 shows. Moreover, in the 1950s, as Figure 8.8 demonstrates, although both were experiencing similar rates of growth of import penetration, in the United States cotton piece good imports started from a far lower base, so that the shock factor is likely to have been greater than in Britain.

These historical trends in market orientation, in turn, influenced attitudes towards foreign competition in the United States. As a consequence, even though import penetration was a fraction of the level in Britain, cotton manufacturers were simply noisier in their complaints than their British counterparts. High nineteenth-century tariff barriers meant that United States cotton manufacturers had built up their industries under the assumption that the vast domestic market was their preserve. Cotton manufacturers remained firmly protectionist and, in 1961, one former textile executive pointed out in a letter to the *New York Times*:

> We would welcome imports which were improvements on our own; our objection is to import of imitations of our own products coming in only because they are lower in price because they are made under cheaper foreign wages and standards. . . . We are looking for no temporary adjustment. Therefore we want permanent protection, whether by tariff or quota or both, that will maintain our American standards today, tomorrow and forever. (Quoted in Hunsberger 1961)

Any infiltration or threat of incursion into the domestic market was, therefore, treated with alarm and outrage, for cotton manufacturers in the United States did not believe that foreign producers had an inalienable right to penetrate their markets. A casual glance through the business news pages of *Textile World* in the 1950s and early 1960s confirms the view that American textile men were always outraged by foreign incursions into their market, even though they were not averse to dumping in the neighbouring Canadian market.[10] Similarly in 1961, for example, on the eve of the Geneva meeting on the proposed Long Term Arrangement on cotton textiles, the ACMI called for 'recognition that growth of the American textile market is not created for overseas manufacturers and that they have no vested right to any part of it' (Brandis Buford 1982: 24).

Raymond Streat has observed that British manufacturers were far more gentlemanly than their American cousins in their cries for protection. This cultural difference may well have stemmed, in part at least, from contrasting historical influences on the market orientation of the industry (Cotton Board Trade Letter, 1949: 3). However, apparent British restraint should not be exaggerated for, as the campaign for protection gathered momentum, so it became more raucous especially when orchestrated by Cyril Lord during the 1950s and by TAG in the 1960s (Dupree 1987, vol. II: 885).

If differences in the market orientation of the two industries were significant in influencing the cultures and styles of campaigning, the impact of other economic forces on bargaining power was nothing like as conclusive. The relative labour intensity of the cotton industry in high income economies made the industries of both the United States and Britain ideal candidates for successful campaigns for protection. However, since the American industry was more capital-intensive than the British this clearly does not explain differences in bargaining power. Secondly, lacking a national low labour cost alternative, such as the Southern states of the United States, it is true that British firms were more inclined to

[10] *Textile World*, July 1957, p. 23.

undertake foreign direct investment than their United States counterparts. Yet, there is little evidence that this was sufficient, in the period in question, to explain differences in bargaining power (Clairmonte and Cavanagh 1981: 139; Knight 1974: 55).

High levels of economic and geographic concentration increase the effectiveness of pressure groups. In Britain the cotton industry continued, albeit to a somewhat reduced degree, to be concentrated in Lancashire while in the United States the proportion of cotton textile manufacturing located in the Southern states grew apace. It has been suggested, however, that any collective action in Lancashire was hampered by the lasting influence of vertical and spatial specialisation, which made it difficult for the industry to speak with one voice (Wurm 1993: 198). This argument must be taken seriously since the Manchester Chamber of Commerce reverted to a staunch support for trade liberalism and the calico printers proved arch enemies of import controls from 1951 onwards. For instance, at the time of the Anglo-American Cotton Textile Mission to Japan the Federation of Calico Printers observed: 'Until the Lancashire manufacturers are able and willing to make cloth in sufficient quantity and of suitable qualities at a saleable price, the unrestricted importation of foreign cloth for finishing in the UK is essential for the maintenance of the maximum export trade in finished goods' (Minutes, FCP, 10 May 1951).

Nor did they seriously modify this view, but remained vocal in their opposition to the restriction of imports right through to the 1960s. Inevitably past spatial specialisation within Lancashire contributed to political divisions which reduced bargaining power. Thus Liberal MPs maintained their historical support for free trade, especially in towns less affected by the coarse imports from the Commonwealth. In the 1958–9 session of the Bolton and District Textile Works Managers Association, for example, A. F. Holt, the Liberal MP for Bolton West, spoke in favour of free trade to a not unenthusiastic audience, whose livelihood lay at the finer end of the cotton industry.[11] The persistence of an exceptionally strong sense of local identity that survived even as product distinctions blurred, remained a problem in Lancashire. Again in 1958 the Rochdale and District Cotton Crisis Action Committee complained of the lack of co-ordination of the various towns on the question of Commonwealth imports.[12] Higher levels of vertical integration in the United States inevitably avoided the same level of internal squabbling and increased bargaining power accordingly, whilst it will emerge, in the context of

[11] Bolton and District Textile Works Managers Association, 1958–9, *Annual Report*. I am grateful to Steve Toms for drawing my attention to this speech.

[12] LRO, Burnley Master Cotton Spinners and Manufacturers Association, Minutes, 3 December 1958.

American politics, that any localism proved a strength rather than a weakness.

Yet, if differing organisational structures affected the bargaining power of interest groups in Britain, nothing so simple as variations in economic and geographic concentration explain the contrasting bargaining power of cotton industry pressure groups on either side of the Atlantic. This is because, even though levels of integration were lower in Britain than in the United States, concentration ratios in textiles were 44.2 and 34.5 respectively making British levels marginally higher. More significantly in both cases, these were low relative to such sectors as automobiles and therefore reflected a comparatively limited level of national bargaining power (Nelson 1963: 37; Hannah 1983: 144).[13]

Clearly, simple economic analysis cannot explain why the cotton interests were so much more effective in influencing government policy in the United States than in Britain. Nor are cultural variations, which shaped attitudes to import penetration, the whole story. A full appreciation of the success or failure of interest groups to mould government policy, is dependent upon both the structure of the political system, and wider policy objectives both of which are in turn shaped by historical forces (Davis and North 1971).

In the United States the political system is decentralised, with power divided between the president and Congress. Under this arrangement the majority party in Congress may differ from the head of state. Its origins can be traced back to the early post-Revolutionary period. Suspicious of concentrations of influence, America's founding fathers sought to divide power within the government and within society, an objective entrenched in the Constitution. As a consequence the identity and legislative power of individual states were preserved, with control divided between federal and state governments. In turn, within the federal government, executive power was to rest with the president whilst legislative power was to lie with Congress, as the guardians of state interests. Members of Congress, mindful of a desire for re-election, have been able to put local interests ahead of national ones. This has meant they have tended to weigh up the likely local consequences of any policy initiative and vote accordingly, rather than necessarily along party lines. The Seventeenth Amendment of 1913, which required that senators should be elected rather than being the placemen of the state legislatures, inevitably reduced the power of interest groups in United States politics, as is witnessed by voting patterns on the Smoot Hawley Tariff of 1930 (Davis and North 1971: 67; Callahan,

[13] It should be noted that the United States concentration ratio is a four-firm ratio for 1954 and the United Kingdom is a five-firm ratio for 1957.

McDonald and O'Brien 1994: 683–90). However, the power of the president continued to be moderated by Congress with its wide representation, whilst the threat of the presidential veto in turn has moderated the influence of Congress (Davis and North 1971: 62; Lees 1969: 36, 189).

There is also a complex committee structure in Congress which facilitates the legislative process and further reinforces the power of interest groups. In the United States, Congressional Committees are established by the legislature not the president, so that Congress controls the membership. This committee structure means that Congress has had the opportunity of filling committees with sympathetic members and has frequently exercised this privilege (Rowley et al. 1995: 97–8; Lees 1969: 135). Inevitably those members of Congress who served on committees exerted most influence on the path of legislation (Baldwin 1985: 50). It is interesting, therefore, to note that John Pastore, who chaired the Subcommittee on Domestic Textiles, was a senator from Rhode Island, whilst the first members were the senators representing South Carolina and New Hampshire (Brandis Buford 1982: 16).

In terms of the formulation of foreign commercial policy, the United States Constitution divided executive and legislative power between president and Congress. Consequently, although presidential influence over commercial policy stemmed from responsibility for conducting foreign relations, under Article I, Section 8, Congress had the right to regulate foreign commerce and to raise duties and taxes (Feller and Wilson 1976: 106–7; Rowley et al. 1995: 124). This clear division of responsibility continued until the 1930s. The president directed foreign affairs whilst taxation, including the raising of tariffs, remained the responsibility of Congress. With tariffs viewed essentially as an issue of domestic, as opposed to foreign, economic policy in a relatively isolationist economy, there was relatively little conflict of interest.

By authorising the president, for a three-year period, to make tariff cutting agreements with other countries, Roosevelt's 1934 Reciprocal Trade Act altered this balance. It passed the power to adjust tariffs from Congress to the executive (Bauer, de Sola Pool and Dexter 1964: 26). This has meant that the president and the State Department have been able to take the initiative in formulating foreign economic policies, in line with broader strategic foreign policy objectives such as the economic reconstruction of Europe and Japan. However, by retaining the right to veto a further three-year extension of this power, Congress has continued to monitor the process, giving due consideration to such issues as the implications of policy for domestic industry and employment (Baldwin 1985: 34–5). Therefore, any postwar United States president wishing to make any progress on trade liberalisation, has required the support of

Table 8.6. *Southern voting patterns on major United States trade legislation, 1922–62*

Textile district	Employment	Textile vote by representative			
		1922	1930	1955	1962
Georgia (4th District)	22,830	L	L	P	L
Georgia (7th District)	24,000	L	L	P	L
N. Carolina (9th District)	61,700	L	L	P	P
N. Carolina (10th District)	41,800	L	L	P	P
N. Carolina (11th District)	39,170	L	L	P	P
S. Carolina (3rd District)	36,300	L	L	P	L
S. Carolina (4th District)	51,000	L	L	P	L

Source: Bauer, de Sola Pool and Dexter 1964: 360.

Congress at the very time when the power of the Southern bloc vote became a major source of political compromise (Pastor 1980: 53; Moe 1991: 106–29). In addition, the continued power of Congress has meant that campaigning commitments by potential presidents could not simply be empty promises to win votes; for were undertakings not ratified, Congressional support could be withdrawn from major initiatives.

In such an environment the cotton industry interest groups in the United States have been able to exert considerable influence over the political process. Moreover, the mergers during the 1940s and 1950s and the formation of such giant combines as the Burlington Mills Corporation, M. Lowenstein and Sons Inc., J. P. Stevens and Textron, brought a growing unity of economic interest between North and South which shared the damaging effect of import penetration in the 1950s and 1960s (Markham 1950: 83–5; Simpson 1966: 57–9). It proved to be a powerful mix because the managers of the Northern-owned Southern mills were their one-time owners, who retained prominent positions in close-knit local elites and hence remained in regular and personal contact with Congressmen. So close were the ties between the two groups that, in the Second World War, the relationship between Southern millowners and Democratic Congressmen has been likened to incest. Such close ties meant that, mindful of their prospects for re-election, Southern Democrats were, between the mid-1950s and mid-1970s, increasingly prepared to abandon their historical and partisan allegiance to liberalism and vote in line with local interests. This meant that the ACMI's letter writing campaigns, as Table 8.6 indicates, significantly influenced voting patterns on the renewal of the Reciprocal Trade Act in the mid-1950s, a pattern which was reinforced during the 1960s (Bauer, de Sola Pool and Dexter 1964: 359–62; Galbraith 1981: 149; Baldwin 1985: 15–29).

From the mid-1950s the political strength of United States cotton interests to influence voting patterns was further enhanced by the formation of successful alliances with both the clothing and man-made fibres sections of the industry, all also increasingly located in the Southern states. By the early 1960s, on the other hand, the ACMI was also able to compel the National Cotton Council, an association of previously free trade cotton growers, and the Textile Workers of America to join them. The result was a combination of sectors and interests which became a formidable political force representing the united interests of the declining North with the politically potent South (Aggarwal and Haggard 1983: 257 and 274–7; Robson 1957: 45; Zeiler 1992: 76).

The threat of the Southern bloc vote was, therefore, a critical feature of American trade negotiations in the 1950s and 1960s. Moreover, presidents needed the South to get elected in the first place and the prospect of the Southern bloc vote against major initiatives, of both strategic and electoral importance, was enough to ensure that the cotton interests secured major concessions (Brandis Buford 1982: 15–35; Destler et al. 1979; Keesing and Wolf 1980: 39).

Kennedy's desire for tariff reductions, which culminated in the Trade Expansion Act of 1962, stemmed from a wish to neutralise the impact of the EEC common external tariff on United States business and agricultural interests. To achieve this wider objective he had to carry the representatives of the cotton industry groups with him, a group of 128 Congressmen who, throughout the 1950s, had voted as a group against freer trade (Baldwin 1985: 15–35; Pastor 1980: 63). This could only be achieved by fulfilling promises made in his electoral campaign. In August 1960, as Democratic nominee, he had published a letter to Governor F. Hollings of South Carolina in which he acknowledged the need for an industry-wide remedy if rising unemployment was to be avoided in both the textile and apparel industries (Brandis Buford 1982: 17). This became the foundation of his 1961 Seven Point Plan for textiles which guaranteed the vital support of the ACMI for the Trade Expansion Act in 1962 (Pastor 1980: 109). The Hollings resolution freed normally protectionist Congressmen to vote for liberalisation. As a further reward, the cotton industry was faced with below-average tariff reductions of 25 per cent and 27 per cent respectively on cotton cloth and cotton yarn, as compared with the norm of 36 per cent and a maximum of 50 per cent (Brandis Buford 1982: 33). The need to ratify electoral promises made to the textile coalition by prospective presidents remained a feature of 1960s and 1970s politics whether presidents were Democrat or Republican. Thus in 1968, in an effort to secure the Republican nomination, Nixon promised to stem rising flows of textile imports. It was a promise which tied him into lengthy, frustrating and costly negotiations with the Japanese over imports of synthetics between 1969 and 1971, at the very time he was trying to improve US–Japanese relations (Destler et al. 1979: 69–71).

From being a marginal, often divided pressure group with a facility for lobbying Congress over protection, the United States cotton industry therefore emerged as a significant political force capable of threatening major pieces of trade liberalising legislation, unless concessions were granted. This position simply was not replicated in Britain as a result of a combination of differences in both the political system, structural arrangements in the industry and the wider macroeconomic objectives of governments during the 1950s and 1960s.

The British parliamentary system is far more centralised than in the United States, with power resting firmly with the prime minister, who is also leader of the government. In addition, the prime minister will also be the leader of the majority party in the House of Commons, where voting on all major policy issues will be along party lines. In Britain, therefore, executive and legislative power are united with the executive dominating the legislative process (Krasner 1978: 57–61). Policy is, therefore, made by the prime minister and the cabinet and ratified by a parliament in which the government will be the majority party. Unlike Congressional Committees where membership may be the placemen of Congress the composition of British Select Committees is determined by the executive without favour to local interest groups.

The system of government in Britain has limited the power of pressure groups to block major initiatives. In the twentieth century the combination of centralised political power in a parliamentary system, with the vagaries of the timing of British elections, has meant that the impact of local, sectional interests has often been relatively limited. With the important exceptions of the City of London, with its close-knit networks of contact with the Treasury (Cain and Hopkins 1993: 265–7) or the defence related industries with aspirations in accordance with government foreign policy, local or industrial interest groups have had a relatively marginal influence on economic policy formulation.

The cotton industry groups' impact on policy was greatest around general elections and concessions were granted if there was anxiety about the outcome of an election, especially when there were signs of backbench revolt during economic downturns. Prior to the 1955 election it appears that it was the industry rather than the government that made cotton an issue, yet with a small majority and with East Lancashire having twice as many marginal seats as the national average, the Conservative government had to take the industry seriously. In the event, if anything, this election weakened the case of cotton with the government, since Labour made few gains in cotton seats and Thorneycroft was later able to take the view that there was no mandate for protection (Lazer 1975: 170–90). The impact of cotton issues was, however, stronger in 1957–8 when there were nine marginal Lancashire constituencies and the cotton interests gained some concessions from the Conservative government. From 1957, therefore, there are signs that the Conservatives, at Macmillan's instigation, began secretly to put their weight behind the inter-industry talks on Commonwealth imports, on the grounds that it would reduce the human costs of the planned run-down of the cotton industry. This supportive position continued with the 1959 Cotton Industry Act which provided a government assisted scheme of scrapping as a prelude to modernisation (Miles 1968: 46–54). Again in 1962, in the depths of a major slump in the industry and a Conservative opinion poll collapse, fears for the future of their seats led five Conservative MPs to vote with the opposition in the cotton industry debate. Edwin Taylor, the MP for Bolton East, was perfectly explicit when he announced: 'My majority is so small that I must be in danger. If the government do not do what I believe they must do then I shall not hesitate to vote against them' (quoted in Lazer 1975: 284). It is an illustration of the impact of a centralised electoral system, however, that although Labour promised much for cotton during its electoral campaign, support within the party was at grassroots level rather than in the cabinet of the new government. As a result, little by way of additional protection was delivered and after 1964 there were no major debates on cotton for 18 years (Lazer 1975: 326).

The merger wave of the 1940s and 1950s significantly increased the political effectiveness of American cotton interests. In Britain the equivalent merger wave, which restructured the industry along vertical rather than horizontal lines and led to a significant rise in concentration, was delayed until the 1960s. The wave of amalgamations began in 1963 as a struggle for control of Lancashire's dwindling capacity between the major man-made fibres producers Courtaulds and ICI. Within three years, what remained of the cotton industry was in the hands of four combines, Courtaulds, Viyella International, English Sewing Cotton and Carrington Dewhurst. Often portrayed as a last-ditch attempt to stem the decline of the Lancashire cotton industry by radical restructuring (Lazonick 1986: 37; Singleton 1991: 209–28), the amalgamations, which made the British cotton industry the most heavily concentrated in the world (Anson and Simpson 1988), were also designed to increase bargaining power with government. Indeed Sir Arthur Knight, Deputy Chairman of Courtaulds, admitted that this lay behind his company's acquisition of Fine Spinners and Doublers and the Lancashire Cotton Corporation, which he believed were essential if there was to be 'any prospect of influencing government attitudes over imports' (Knight 1974: 49).

That the industry, in reality, exerted so little leverage and that tariff protection against the Commonwealth was not achieved until 1972 is a measure of the textile interests' limited bargaining power with government, especially as compared with the United States. This was partly because the tight ties of ownership between the remnants of the Lancashire cotton industry and the combines did not lead to further geographic concentration, in the way that had happened in the Southern states of the United States. Moreover, neither Courtaulds nor Viyella International had their origins in Lancashire and had geographically scattered industrial interests within Britain (Coleman 1969: 24–36; Singleton 1991: 221). However, since Lancashire still remained a significant home to the remains of the industry and hence a potential political power base this cannot be the whole story. More important in terms of explaining differences in bargaining power was the cross-sectoral alliance between the United States manmade fibre producers and clothing industries and the cotton industry to form a powerful coalition of dynamic and declining industries. In Britain the man-made fibres producers became prominent owners of Lancashire so that this formidable display of collective unity between the strong and the weak was missing. In addition, it is worth noting also that the cultural environment found in the Southern states of the United States was quite unlike the relations which existed in Lancashire between MPs and millowners where there was a considerable cultural divide between the majority in parliament and industrialists.

In a centralised political system bargaining power is also dependent upon the ability of a group to capture public imagination and this, outside Lancashire, the cotton industry singularly failed to do. The decline of cotton in Lancashire was not associated, in the 1950s and 1960s, with vast social problems. Certainly some towns, especially Oldham, Burnley and Bolton, experienced depopulation, as Figure 8.9 shows. This shrinkage came of out-migration and declining birth rates in an ageing population. But it hardly warranted national action, especially since unemployment did not rise sharply because other industries, most particularly defence-related, expanded (Department of Economic Affairs 1965: 40). Cotton problems lacked the enthusiastic support of the TUC and received little encouragement from the serious press. The National Chambers of Trade did pass a resolution backing cotton's demand for import controls and there was some backing from the Federation of British Industry (FBI) but, in representing a wide range of export industries whose interests could be damaged by protection for Lancashire, this was never wholehearted. Not

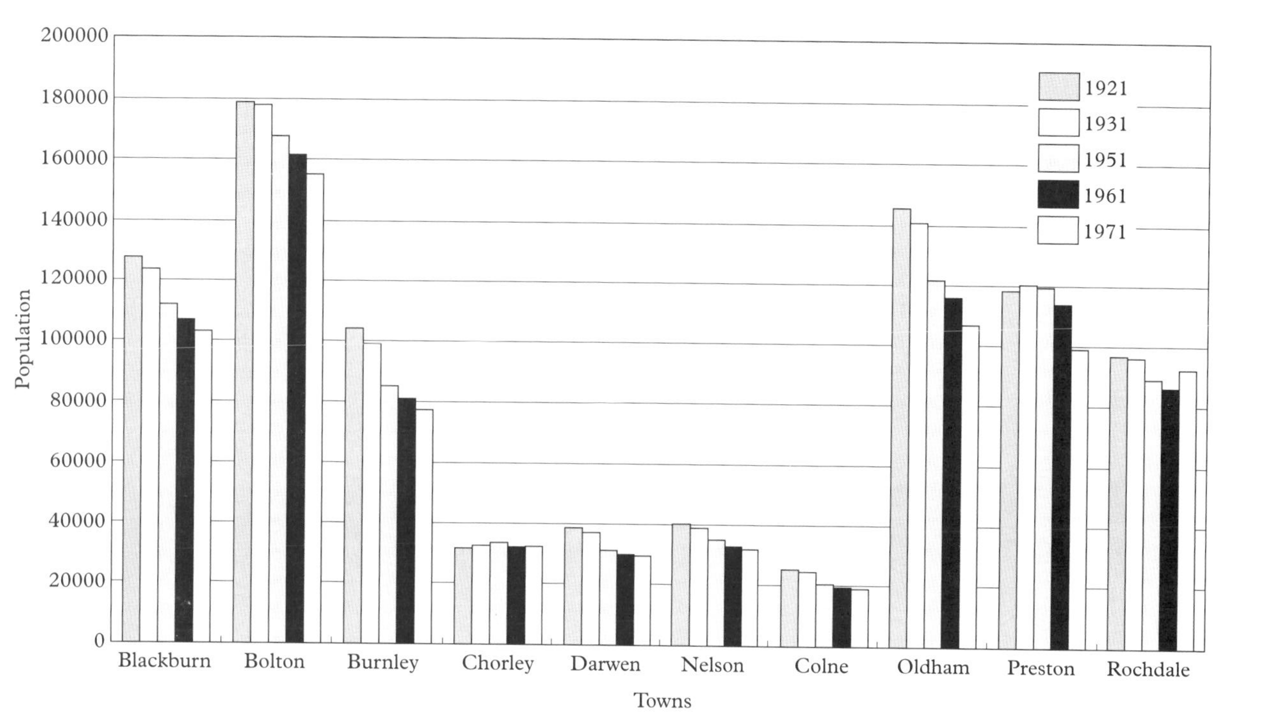

Fig. 8.9 Population change in the main Lancashire cotton towns, 1921–71
Source: Census Reports 1921–71

even the whole of Lancashire supported protection, since north of the Ribble cotton had never been economically significant. For those looking to enhance the economic potential of the county as a whole, cotton was not only largely irrelevant, but also no longer held any prospect of prosperity. The Lancashire and Merseyside Industrial Development Association and the North West Regional Board for Industry were impervious to requests to urge restrictions of grey cloth imports on government. This was quite simply because they did not believe it would benefit Lancashire as a whole and would quite probably damage the expanding defence and electronic sector and they were undoubtedly correct (Lazer 1975: 196).

It is clear that differences in the development of the political systems of the United States and Britain meant that the relative power of interest groups, to bend government policy in their favour, varied. It is not, however, sufficient to conclude that the limited success of Lancashire's protectionist campaigns was entirely the result of a more centralised political system than prevailed in the United States or of a more successful propaganda campaign. In any event industries such as defence did receive preferential treatment by British governments in this period. It is clear therefore that differences in the wider economic and political objectives of the two governments had discrete implications for the two industries in this period.

The United States' commitment to world trade liberalisation gave governments greater flexibility in responding to the demands for concessions by the cotton interests than did Britain's commitment to the Commonwealth. More than anything it was the centrality of the Commonwealth to British macroeconomic policy in the 1950s and 1960s which explains why both Tory and Labour governments were reluctant to increase the protection of the cotton industry. In the 1950s, therefore, Churchill feared that any concessions to Lancashire, especially with respect to India, might risk Indian tariff preferences on other British goods whilst there was a strong humanitarian case for promoting industrial development in Hong Kong. Perhaps surprisingly the Labour Party, so critical of government policy when in opposition, was only slightly more amenable to the reversal of the policy on duty free imports than the Tories though they introduced a blanket surcharge of 10–15 per cent on all imports in 1964–6.[14] However, with a commitment to alleviating world poverty it would have been politically damaging and deeply contradictory to have introduced a tariff specifically against Commonwealth imports (Lapping 1970: 76).

Perhaps the most important policy impediment to enhanced protection for Lancashire against imports from Hong Kong, Pakistan and India

[14] Federation of Master Cotton Spinners Associations, *Annual Report*, 1966, p. 21.

was the vital role which Commonwealth sterling balances played in British macroeconomic policy regarding the sterling area in this period (Dupree 1987, vol. II: xxiv; Bell 1956). During the Second World War Britain had relied on credits, mainly from Empire banks, to purchase imports and these were held as sterling balances in London amounting to £3,567m by 1945. By the end of 1957 trade patterns within the sterling area meant they had risen to £3,912m, a third of which were held by colonial banks including of course those based in Hong Kong (Conan 1961: 55). Any introduction of import restrictions on Commonwealth cotton goods would have provoked a withdrawal of these sterling balances and a major sterling crisis, thus fundamentally undermining British economic policy. It was a constraint for which there was no equivalent in the United States and it effectively meant that the United States' position as the champion of trade liberalism was a far smaller obstacle to protection of the cotton industry than was Britain's commitment to the Commonwealth. It was, therefore, no accident that the introduction of duties on imported Commonwealth cotton goods was delayed until 1972 when the sterling area ended (Cain and Hopkins 1993: 285).

Finally all campaigns for protection should be placed in the context of wider considerations of international economic policy and diplomacy. In the world which emerged after 1945 it is impossible to ignore that the shift in the international balance of power from Europe, and especially from Britain, to the United States was complete and that this had consequences for domestic policy formulation in the two countries. The considerable international political and economic power of the United States gave presidents the option of shifting domestic economic problems into the international arena, as Kennedy had done in 1961 and Nixon in 1973. The UK's diminished international prestige after 1945 meant that such actions simply were not options for British administrations.

Summary

The scale of the United States cotton industry, by 1980, sits somewhat uneasily against notions of product cycle decline of staple industries in mature economies. The operation of the product cycle predicts the decline of the cotton industry in the developed world and its expansion in the developing economies of the Far East and Southern Europe in the twentieth century. It can also explain why, in recent years, developed economies have faced rising levels of import penetration from the developing world. Rapid international diffusion of relatively simple technologies meant that in industries which were labour- rather than technology-intensive, such as textiles, revealed comparative advantage passed from early industrialisers to later developers, from relatively high to relatively low labour cost economies. Spindleage and loomage in the developed world was on average 14 per cent and 19 per cent lower in 1963 than it had been in 1958. In Hong Kong, on the other hand, spindleage grew by 68 per cent and loomage by 130 per cent although India and Pakistan achieved much more modest increases. Similarly by 1963 21.8 per cent of textile imports to Western Europe, North America and Japan came from Asia and overwhelmingly from Hong Kong (OECD 1965: 91).

Against this background, the collapse of the Lancashire cotton industry, which reached such massive proportions through the artificial growth of the Indian market in the nineteenth century, is entirely predictable (Singleton 1991, 1996). Yet it is especially instructive to note that, just as in the interwar period so after the Second World War, although the scale of output of the United States cotton industry dwarfed all others in the developed and the developing world, her industry did not display a revealed comparative advantage any more than Britain's did (Singleton 1997: 18). Increasingly, United States commentators have been convinced that the industry survived because of the protection it had received, rather than because of its international competitiveness (Toyne et al. 1983: 8–21). In Britain, by contrast, cotton manufacturers had little bargaining power with governments and after the Second World War many elements of policy were diametrically opposed to the interests of their industry. It is certainly fair to say that in the policy climate of the period, tariffs, especially against Hong Kong, represented a forlorn hope on the part of Lancashire cotton manufacturers. Yet, after two decades of squeezed profits in the interwar and the wartime concentration periods, duty free imports at best inhibited innovation. Lancashire industrialists can be criticised for the defensiveness of their response and an absence of the creativity found, say, in Continental European textile industries. However, the environment in which they operated discouraged innovation whilst the commercial organisation of the industry both as regards the past role of the shipping houses and the postwar role of the big retailers (quite different from the Continental position) discouraged the evolution of strategies based on adding value.

Singleton is undoubtedly correct to conclude that international shifts in comparative advantage made protection a waste of resources after 1945 (Singleton 1990: 129–49). Yet, despite an international liberalisation of world trade, at the prompting of the United States following the Second World War, textile protection has remained a fact of life and nowhere more prominently than in America. This was patently not so in Britain, where the political power of Lancashire, in reality never that significant, eroded further after the Second World War as the industry declined. British governments, therefore, remained relatively unmoved when the objective of Commonwealth development led to competition in both foreign and domestic markets. The cotton industry in the United States did not reverse their government's commitment to internationalism, any more than British interests undermined British commitment to Commonwealth trade and development. However, in contrast to the position in Lancashire, American cotton manufacturers were able to secure government concessions for the industry and be confident of government support when their domestic markets were threatened. Moreover, the international standing of the United States meant that her government was in a position to influence the direction of international agreements for textiles in ways which favoured American cotton interests. In addition, cotton manufacturers could be confident that such agreements would be interpreted in the most favourable possible way.

In a number of ways, this analysis of campaigns for protection, of the British and United States cotton industries since 1945, confirms the importance of comparing the political and institutional environment surrounding business. In the first place it has shown how critical was the influence of national differences in the development of political institutions in shaping the bargaining power of interest groups. In the second, implicit in the discussion has been the long-term historical implications of institutional development for both cotton industries. Thus, whereas Lancashire's dramatic expansion had been inseparable from Empire, and especially India, the rise of the cotton industry in the United States was just as closely associated with the tariff. These trends had profound implications for the two industries in the changed world after 1945. It left Lancashire with the legacy of the Ottawa Agreements, at a time when British governments were anxious to promote Commonwealth development. In the United States, on the other hand, past associations with protection continued to work in the cotton industry's favour despite changing national policies. Finally, differences in the institutional environment were among a range of factors which affected the structure of the two industries and their ability to survive after 1945.

The relative weakness of protection of cotton textiles was hardly the only explanation for the demise of cotton manufacturing in Lancashire in the late twentieth century. Equally, there was no economic case for protection. However, the relative success of cotton manufacturers in the United States, in campaigns for protection, in the 1950s and 1960s, as compared with their Lancashire counterparts, undoubtedly had a bearing on their respective industrial profiles. Clearly obsolete machinery, in comparison to the United States, goes some way towards explaining why the Lancashire cotton industry declined so rapidly. However, if set alongside two decades of interwar decay and depressing market trends, during and after the Second World War, the resistance of British governments to pleas for protection represented the final straw (Dupree 1990a: 123–5). There was simply, as Singleton has shown, little incentive to invest in productivity enhancing technology in a deeply uncertain and depressing market environment (Singleton 1991: 141–67). Indeed it has been argued that European cotton industries displayed similar structural and technical weaknesses as Britain in the 1950s, but were protected and imposed import restrictions which breached GATT and allowed for successful modernisation (Bardan 1973: 8–35). In the United States, on the other hand, not only had wartime and postwar trends been more favourable to the cotton industry than was the case in Britain, but the growing awareness of their political power, especially after 1960, and relatively high tariff and non-tariff barriers encouraged investment by cotton manufacturers.

Before 1945 the relatively high level of protection afforded to American industry generally helped to give it its distinctive characteristics of high productivity, capital intensity and standardisation (Nelson and Winter 1982: 139). In the postwar period the enjoyment of relatively high levels of protection reinforced these trends. Even as United States tastes became increasingly sophisticated, the size of the domestic market allowed continued product homogeneity. Larger and highly rationalised mills therefore produced a limited array of fabrics (Toyne et al. 1983: 8–21). After 1961 the combination of still relatively high tariffs and the active use of the LTA by successive administrations encouraged a wave of productivity enhancing investment which reinforced existing trends in the industry (Isard 1973: 402–15). Conversely in the 1960s, the United States Department of Commerce argued that it was vital that the disruptive effects of unexpected imports be avoided because the psychological effect of being unable to predict market changes would reduce levels of investment (Bardan 1973: 28).

Yet the long-term consequences of the protection of the American cotton and textile industries may be less encouraging. In the first place productivity enhancement has led to a rise in unemployment during the 1970s and 1980s. Moreover, the reinforcement of trends towards standardisation has meant that, with the doubling of imports between 1973 and 1985, many United States firms have looked for overseas markets and found it difficult to move over from production-oriented methods to those geared towards meeting market diversity. As a consequence between 1981 and 1984 alone there have been 231 plant closures and numerous Southern textile centres have become ghost towns (Gaventa and Smith 1991: 183–5).

Interestingly the analysis of the implications of differing political institutions must also bring into question the notion that Lancashire's decline was principally the result of institutional rigidities. Certainly differing historical experience does help to explain why Lancashire's postwar decline came earlier and was more precipitous than occurred in the United States. However, it was not simply the case that varying economic forces had created two industries with contrasting organisational and technological structures and consequently differing capacities for change, as Lazonick has suggested (Lazonick 1986). There were significant long- and short-term differences in the investment environment faced in the United States and Britain. In addition, long-term political and cultural influences were every bit as important, to the formulation of business strategy, as the legacy of past forms of capitalism. Combined with twentieth-century changes in the balance of international power, these influences meant that United States cotton manufacturers had greater power to mould commercial policy in their favour than was the case for Lancashire's cotton interests.

9 Conclusion

Contrasts and continuities: the long-term trends

Between 1750 and 1950 cotton cloth achieved a worldwide popularity unrivalled by any other fibre for use in clothing, furnishing and industrial fabrics. It was versatile, washable and became attractive for high and low income markets. The East India Company had imported painted calicoes into Britain in the early eighteenth century and helped to make cotton cloths fashionable. It was, however, a combination of technological change and commercial developments which made cotton goods cheap and widely used in working-class dress. Relatively rudimentary technologies were developed in Britain's traditional textile areas, especially those where fustians had been produced, and these dramatically increased labour productivity and made new products available, whilst a combination of changes in motive power and business organisation increased total factor productivity, lowering costs and the price of goods. Factory-based cotton spinning spread from 1770 onwards in Britain. However, this also initially led to an expansion in the traditional craft-based sectors such as handloom weaving and machine-making, again in existing textile areas, reinforcing their skill base. The East Midlands, North Wales and southern Scotland saw vigorous activity in the eighteenth century, but it was in Lancashire and adjacent areas of Cheshire where, by 1800, most cotton spinning mills were found. There too the foundations were laid for the nineteenth-century emergence of a sophisticated industrial district.

Eighteenth-century cotton spinning technology was simple and diffused easily to Britain's European trading partners, but most especially to the United States, where a common language and historical ties eased its transplant across the Atlantic. For Americans industrialisation held the prospect of economic prosperity to underpin the political independence achieved in 1776. This encouraged state-induced industrial espionage. Despite the efforts of British industrialists and the government to secure the fruits of ingenuity for British benefit, Americans fairly easily gained information about technology, smuggled parts of machines or their plans and enticed skilled workers from leading firms to emigrate. It was harder for them to ensure that these technologies took root and thus the early spread of cotton manufacturing, in the United States, was slow and tortuous until the 1812 war with Britain provided a window of opportunity. The spread of factory-based cotton manufacturing in the United States gathered pace after 1820 and, despite shared technological origins, the principal characteristics of the two cotton industries soon diverged. By the 1830s businessmen in New England had adapted British technologies and devised methods of organising work in ways which were distinctly American. In the other cotton manufacturing regions of Pennsylvania and the Southern states, technological and organisational styles had also evolved which were both distinguishable from each other and British traditions. Later on in the century the development of automatic machinery by American machine makers broke the umbilical cord of technological dependence of America on Britain for ever.

It was the divergence of American methods of cotton manufacturing, from those in Britain, which first attracted the attention of contemporaries in the 1840s. They harboured what was then almost certainly a morbid and unfounded fear of foreign competition. More recently historians have been eager to find an explanation of the relative and absolute decline of Britain's major nineteenth-century export industry and have often viewed it through American spectacles and found it wanting. Yet whilst the general quest for productivity enhancing devices, to compensate for factor market deficiencies and especially for shortages of skill, did play a critical role in moulding strategic choice in the American cotton industry, the explanation of national differences in business behaviour is more complicated. Recognising the influence of differences in institutional, social, political and cultural forces is vital.

The legal environment, as it impinged on company formation, on combination, on labour relations, or on tariffs, by laying down the formal 'rules of the game' provided a crucial backdrop to business behaviour. Consequently just as an institutionalised suspicion of joint stock companies in Britain, embedded in the 1720 Bubble Act, helped to reinforce the position of the versatile partnership in British business, in many New England states the legal framework favoured the corporation. Equally, it is conceivable that the repeal of the Combination Laws in 1825, in Britain, contributed to and reinforced craft control of cotton manufacturing in ways missing in the United States during industrialisation. Yet laws have been shown to be socially and politically determined, changeable in the face of altered economic circumstances and open to variations of interpretation. Examining the impact of the institutional environment on decisions in the British and American cotton industries has demonstrated this complexity. There was, for example, a close relationship between company law and the type of family firm to evolve during industrialisation. Yet it is also clear that within the confines of an institutional arrangement, lay room for interpretation which was clearly dependent upon economic and social forces and hence on the needs of both families and firms.

That family firms differed in the British and American cotton industries stemmed partly from variations in laws, but also because they were operating against contrasting economic and social backdrops. Whilst there are some parallels between the exploitation of isolated water sites by the early cotton masters in eighteenth-century Britain and greenfield site development in the United States, the similarities should not be overdrawn. Early factory colonisation in Britain may have been costly but could be financed by individual family partnerships or with the flexibility which came from networks of partnerships. The scale of underdevelopment, problems of communications, the absence of banks or any other financial infrastructure, to be found even in the United States' coastal areas meant that large-scale factory investment was quite beyond the resources of individual family corporations, still less partnerships, and required a type of collective activity that was simply not necessary in Britain. This contrast alone helps to distinguish the policies and, indeed, the culture of British and American family firms. The idea of collective support for community development, a comparative rarity in Britain, was a vital element of the American psyche. It influenced business attitudes and the behaviour of family firms in important ways that are especially noticeable in Massachusetts, but which can be detected in varying forms wherever greenfield site development was undertaken. Attitudes to the family in the United States were also unlike those in Britain with attachment to the building of a dynasty less noticeable. Yet this contrast can be overdrawn, especially in New England where it was the desire to protect existing wealth and prestige which helped to drive the strategies of the Boston Associates after the Embargo War.

Labour market differences between Britain and the United States have been widely discussed by those basing their comparative analysis on relative factor prices. Whilst there can be no denying that the relationship between the price of capital and labour is crucial to technological choice, this does not address perhaps the greatest contrast between labour behaviour between a country of recent settlement and a small, relatively densely populated island – the level of transiency. Throughout the cotton manufacturing areas of the United States there is evidence that high labour turnover was accepted, by workers and employers alike, as an integral part of American life. In Britain, by contrast, movement was over relatively short distances and, whilst factory colonisers at times complained about the 'migratory spirit' of the workforce and set about devising ways of retaining labour, the order of magnitude was far less and in general rarely gave rise to comment. Indeed the difficulty of getting any reliable labour turnover figures, other than for a few unrepresentative factory colonies, suggests that millowners in Lancashire were not especially worried by it. Yet, in trying to make sensible comparisons about labour strategies, in the two cotton industries, turnover is an important consideration for it held implications for the ability of labour to organise and for technological choice. The high level of transiency in the United States, in comparison with Britain, undoubtedly contributed to the relatively low level of trade union organisation and the comparative ineffectiveness of strike action. At the same time it helped to mould technological choice, since in Britain the reinforcement of skills, within a geographically small industrial district, encouraged the use of skill-intensive technology. By contrast, in the United States high transiency rates with, after 1840, a rising proportion of immigrants in the cotton industry, encouraged the use of skill-saving technologies. Only in those cotton manufacturing areas of the United States which attracted skilled migrants, such as Philadelphia and Fall River, were skill-intensive technologies favoured.

The prominence given to the giant firms of northern Massachusetts, from the 1830s onwards, and the tendency towards scale in American business generally during the Second Industrial Revolution, has led to the assumption that Britain's increasingly specialised cotton firms were dwarfed by those across the Atlantic. Yet close examination of experience during the second half of the nineteenth century, the interwar period or indeed the period after 1945 shows that the prominence of giants, first in New England and later in the Southern states, obscured the overall picture, certainly with respect to plant size. While individual firms were often enormous in the United States, historically the barriers to entry into cotton manufacturing remained relatively low and the average size of mills smaller than in Lancashire. Moreover, until the 1950s competitive pressures ensured that levels of concentration remained low in both industries. Thereafter, it is true that the position changed and successive waves of mergers on both sides of the Atlantic led to an increase in the level of market power enjoyed by large firms. Somewhat surprisingly, however, it was in Britain that the takeover of the remnants of the cotton industry by man-made fibres producers led to higher levels of concentration than in the United States. There the persistence of still small, Southern cotton mills reduced the market power of the multi-fibre giants.

One of the most widely discussed contrasts between the British and American cotton industries has been the level of vertical integration and to understand its significance it is important to place it in context. With regards to the industries of the Second Industrial Revolution, vertical integration has been associated with the achievement of cost efficiency, using rapid throughput technology and rising market penetration from internalising marketing. Yet, if there are clear efficiency gains for capital- and technology-intensive industries these are less obvious in cotton manufacturing. Additionally, when the experience of the British and American cotton industries is compared it is clear that, during industrialisation, the dissimilarities were less stark since the trend to vertical specialisation in Britain only became noticeable after 1850. More strikingly, the high level of vertical integration in the United States cotton industry was unusual internationally until after the Second World War and not just in comparison with Britain. In part this may have been a reflection of the problems of business in a country of recent settlement, where vertical integration could be a response to limited infrastructure. In addition, the extreme and unusual home market orientation of the United States cotton industry, which persists even today, undoubtedly contributed to the structure of firms. The equally unusual export orientation of Lancashire firms had well-known implications for business strategy and contributed to vertical specialisation but, more importantly, to spatial specialisation. Lancashire's specific regions produced a range of categories of goods and individual towns had specific technological and product orientations. This in turn was related to the development of specialist services and was inseparable from the evolution of distinctive machine-making techniques in specific towns over long periods of time. In addition, a crucial aspect of Lancashire's development was the nineteenth-century proliferation of specialist yarn dealers, finishers, converters and overseas shippers in Manchester which meant that the majority of Lancashire manufacturers had no perception of the markets they served.

Lancashire's spatially specialised towns, with their intense horizontal competition, could not be more different from the collective and integrated approach to be found in the prominent northern Massachusetts towns such as Lowell, where interlocking corporations produced largely complementary cloths. However, it is important to remember that whilst there may have been far fewer specialist agents and converters in New York than in Manchester, very few United States firms integrated either converting or marketing until after the Second World War. In theory the close financial ties between agents and manufacturers could have enhanced the market awareness of producers, yet most of the evidence suggests that selling agents exploited manufacturers and often pursued policies which worked against them. In addition, the extreme domestic orientation of United States producers meant the development of specialist overseas trading companies was delayed until the late nineteenth century. Whilst this did not prevent firms from exporting, since foreign agents were happy to handle their goods, it undoubtedly contributed to an insularity which characterised American cotton manufacturers.

Separated from direct contact with their markets, many of Lancashire's cotton manufacturers also displayed insularity and a concern with the local which bordered on parochialism. The persistence of local employers' associations, which communicated with sectoral ones, reinforced this attitude through to the 1960s. Yet, in contrast with the position in the United States the Lancashire mercantile community was truly international both in its membership and orientation. The numerous immigrant merchants who settled in Manchester gave the community a cosmopolitan air and provided access, through a complex web of contacts and partnerships, to myriad overseas markets.

Insularity among United States cotton manufacturers clearly stems, in part, from the availability of the world's largest domestic market during the second half of the nineteenth century, whereas the Lancashire cotton industry, with its legendary export orientation, would have been only a fraction of its size without overseas markets. Confidence in access to the domestic market in America was, however, enhanced by entrenched protectionism which can be traced from its origins in 1816 right through to the aftermath of the Second World War. This led American producers to be hostile to even tiny foreign imports and to make investment decisions on the basis that the home market was theirs by right. With growth dependent upon access to overseas markets, the tradition of free trade became equally firmly entrenched among Lancashire's merchants, and whilst the stranglehold of *laissez faire* in Lancashire may have been exaggerated, only the dire conditions of the 1930s depression really shook that faith.

Faith in access to a secure domestic market by United States cotton manufacturers was also a reflection of an ability to mould government policy in ways which were never shared by Lancashire's cotton manufacturers, even at the height of their political and economic power in the nineteenth century. Differences in the relationship between localities and the government had important implications for state–industry relations in the two countries. The American Constitution maintained the strength of localities, giving their representatives the capability to make local business views bite with the federal government. In Britain, on the other hand, the industrial interests lacked any parliamentary representation prior to 1832. Certainly this and the local government reforms of the 1830s brought the potential of national political leverage and growing civic identity. However, any bargaining power over issues of government policy (even the anti-Corn Law campaign) was diluted by internal divisions, by the greater political leverage of the City-based elites and by a political system which was heavily centralised, where executive and legislative power was and is united.

These contrasts had lasting implications for the power of interest groups and in no area more noticeably than in trade policy. Setting aside differences in attitude, stemming from the foreign commercial policy, the United States Constitution divided executive and legislative power between president and Congress. Consequently, although presidential influence over commercial policy stemmed from responsibility for conducting foreign relations, under Article I, Section 8, Congress had the right to regulate foreign commerce and to raise duties and taxes. Since Congress, rather than the president, determined tariffs this meant that local interest groups had a direct input into the tariff-making process, in sharp contrast to the position in Britain. The potential for political influence by cotton manufacturers was obviously greater in the United States than in Britain. Nevertheless, until 1945 the political power of the cotton industry should not be overplayed since political divisions, between the geographically separate textile regions, made consensus every bit as difficult to achieve as it was in politically fragmented Lancashire. Moreover for Lancashire's cotton interests a major complicating factor in the nineteenth century and interwar period was India. The complexity and sensitivity of the political and economic situation there meant that the success or failure of campaigns to achieve tariff reductions depended crucially upon the state of Indian finances and the degree of internal pressure for independence. Similarly after 1945 Lancashire's attempts to achieve relief from duty free Commonwealth imports conflicted with monetary, economic and humanitarian objectives of governments.

Differences in the market orientation of the two industries undoubtedly had consequences for the type of goods produced, with the greater uniformity of a domestic market leading to a tendency towards standardised products in the United States not shared in Britain. However, in many ways the more striking contrast lay in the coarseness of yarns and cloths, with the average count of yarn being markedly and consistently lower in the United States than in Britain, throughout the nineteenth century, even when growing reliance on the Indian market reduced the average count of yarn exported from Lancashire.

Against these canvases the British and American cotton industries grew apace, especially after 1860, and by the interwar period United States output had outstripped Lancashire, to make it the world's most productive cotton industry, a position it retained. By the First World War the well-known divergences in the overall profile of the two industries were clear, with far higher levels of automation in the United States' vertically integrated corporations than among Lancashire's specialised, proprietary capitalists. Labour relations had also shifted further apart, with collective bargaining in Lancashire increasingly based upon unwieldy negotiating procedures between amalgamated employers' associations and amalgamated unions, a process which served to reinforce the power of labour over the organisation of work and to institutionalise piece rate lists. Yet, in the United States, negotiation was local and especially at the level of the firm, and control was firmly centralised in the hands of employers. The biggest disparity lay in levels of labour productivity, with the emergence of a consistent productivity gap in favour of the United States. Yet since neither industry was proof against problems of over-capacity and depression in the interwar period, albeit for different reasons, it is hard to sustain the notion that the United States cotton industry was necessarily organised in a superior way. Moreover given that the lack of uniformity in business behaviour stemmed from strikingly varying conditions, which emerged over a long historical period, the idea of making generalisations about the quality of entrepreneurial decisions becomes suddenly very complicated and inconclusive. This is not to suggest that entrepreneurship or individual decisions on innovation are unimportant. Rather, it is to argue that conclusions about business attitudes and business strategy cannot and should not be made simply on the basis of long-term national generalisations. Neither can it be assumed that shifting circumstances and changes in the competitive environment did not affect behaviour in ways which could tilt the orientation of an entire industry.

Change, variety and networks

Long-term, national differences in the evolution of the British and American cotton industries mask striking local variations within each industry, which are vital to understanding both the evolution of the competitive process and of the development of contrasting national profiles. Consequently, although it is perfectly appropriate to generalise about deep-seated national characteristics, it is vital to explore the relationships which developed within local communities, the connections among local communities and the impact of often major changes upon those linkages.

The tendency, when analysing the American cotton industry, to focus upon the giant vertically integrated corporations of New England stems partly from their prominence but also from the large share of total output they produced during the nineteenth century. Yet focus on the bulk producers, founded by the Boston Associates, obscures both the diversity of the United States cotton industry in the nineteenth century and the extent to which there had emerged, in the ante-bellum period, four locally distinctive and largely non-competing cotton regions which drew their characteristics as much from their local communities as from national trends. American cotton firms in the ante-bellum period were embedded in the communities of which they were part, and local social and economic characterisitics demonstrably shaped the strategies they pursued. They were also inseparable from networks which evolved within the communities, providing information and helping to reduce uncertainty. At the same time businessmen also joined wider externally operating networks which facilitated communication with state and federal governments.

The development of the bulk producing corporations in northern Massachusetts owed much to the wealth and aspirations of the Boston Associates, reflecting a co-operative form of family firm strategy based upon the business corporation. Fostered by the Commonwealth of Massachusetts as a vehicle for development, the business corporation became entrenched in the life of the state long before the rise of cotton manufacturing. For the Associates it provided the obvious vehicle for their ambitious project to create an alternative income flow from commerce, whilst extended kinship links underpinned by interlocking directorships created a distinctive and powerful form of collective family capitalism. The *raison d'être* of these firms was the security of their founders, a consideration which permeated everything from product and financial strategies to the management of labour, matters inseparable from technology. As a consequence the interlocking northern Massachusetts corporations produced bulk sheetings initially primarily for frontier markets and employed Yankee female labour. Community development was overtly paternalistic and the enterprises closely controlled dormitory accommodation. In addition, the economic rise of the Boston Associates is hard to separate from their political power which allowed them, from 1816 until the American Civil War, to sway governments on tariff policy in ways that benefited their interests.

Yet if the northern Massachusetts corporations came to dominate the American cotton industry, in terms of their sheer volume of output, they were not representative of the industry as a whole in the ante-bellum period. Even within Massachusetts, there evolved differences in the profile and strategy of firms whilst in Pennsylvania and, especially, Philadelphia, a vertical network of specialised firms emerged, depending upon a craft workforce for their success. With such networks of specialist businesses united by ties of ethnicity, firms within each sector competed with one another more on the basis of quality than on price and produced a variety of goods for the fashion markets of the eastern seaboard. In a social environment quite distinct from the greenfield sites of northern Massachusetts, employers were also paternalists but their paternalism was aimed at mainly male skilled operatives. Based on the blurring of aspirations between employers and employed it operated in an environment where low barriers to entry enabled workers to aspire to be bosses. As with the paternalism of the bulk producers, it was only partly successful, but served to reinforce competitive strategies based upon the skill of the workforce.

Slow factory development in the cotton-growing states should not obscure the early stirrings of industry in societies dominated by slavery and agriculture. Often as a counter to a downturn in the raw cotton market, community-based factory development also occurred particularly in the North and South Carolinas. Production was mainly locally oriented and cloth of the coarsest construction, while paternalism was designed to accommodate the social underpinnings of plantation society.

These local variations moulded strategy in the nineteenth and twentieth centuries but their characteristics were in no sense set in tablets of stone. Indeed, sometimes dramatic external shocks led to localised changes which, by altering the pattern of competition, shaped the technological and product profile of the entire industry in important ways. Until the American Civil War firms in the cotton textile regions of the United States produced goods for different segments of the domestic market. The Civil War had remarkably little detectable immediate impact on business strategy, other than to move Philadelphia producers into wool. However, its aftermath and the decay of subsistence family-farm agriculture in the South helped to precipitate a change which brought bulk and batch producers into competition and ultimately undermined the Northern states as the home of the cotton industry.

The rise of Southern manufacturing led bulk producers to move up market and to proliferate cloth types, while in Philadelphia there was a growing trend to novelties and specialties. Markets became increasingly crowded and, whilst the First World War brought a stay of execution for the North, the interwar period was marked by chronic over-capacity which encouraged growing, if irrational, cries for greater protection. Efforts, complicated by diverging regional interests, also surfaced, aiming to achieve some version of collective stabilisation. The changed competitive environment also served to confirm the dominant position of automatic technology in the American cotton industry, for it became universal in the rapidly growing South. In the North, by contrast, the majority of firms either moved south, innovated or went bankrupt with a few blundering on for years. In the postwar period cotton became a truly Southern industry, which was increasingly dominated, though not entirely overwhelmed, by the giant capital-intensive conglomerate, multi-fibre producers most of which had enjoyed high wartime profits.

The emergence of Lancashire as an advanced and sophisticated industrial district derived from a combination of market forces and diverse community-based strategies by family firms. There the role of community was every bit as important to the formulation of family firm policies as it was in the United States. Mainly informal ties, between interconnected families, were strengthened by more formalised business meetings in such organisations as Chambers of Commerce and the Manchester Royal Exchange. Ties of credit and attempts to affect attitudes in communities through paternalistic bonds between employer and employed meant that the boundaries of family firms were local. Networks of trust arose from more than just kinship ties or even the ties of religion, being underpinned by the shared outlook and attitudes of the local community. Just as in the United States, so in Lancashire, significant variations appeared in the economic basis and the social and political profile of individual communities during the nineteenth century. These were noticeable in the years before the 1830s and were reinforced by changes later in the century. There were consequently sharp differences which surfaced in the evolution of such key cotton towns as Oldham, Bolton, Rochdale, Preston and Blackburn, which were linked to variations in their traditional economic base, in landholding patterns and in social orientation. These mirrored contrasts in the origins of enterprise, in the size and structure of firms and hence in family firm behaviour. Most noticeable were the contrasts between dynastic Bolton and the small-scale entrepreneurship of Oldham in the Industrial Revolution. Played out in social and political variations in experience, such distinctions also remained inseparable from the divergent technological traditions of the two towns. Since the early emergence of cotton manufacturing owed much to the existence of traditional machine-making skills, as well as to skilled operatives, Bolton and Oldham developed distinctive technological capabilities which the expansion of export markets served to reinforce. Manchester, the commercial hub of the Lancashire cotton industry, also exhibited locally particular characteristics. In the eighteenth century and early nineteenth century its social, political and economic life was dominated by a Nonconformist 'charmed circle' of mainly Unitarian merchants who, for a while, were the driving force behind the Manchester Chamber of Commerce. These Nonconformist merchants formed the respectable, moderate and moneyed face of the Anti-Corn Law League. In Lancashire as a whole an elite of dynastic families emerged which, by the 1860s, were able to pursue distinctive strategies which were dependent upon accumulated wealth and long-standing goodwill. Yet even within this group there were sharp differences in social, religious and political status.

The British picture then was rather more complex than the mainly regional divisions found in the United States. As the nineteenth century progressed export growth, to a wide range of destinations, served to reinforce the trend towards spatial and vertical specialisation and hence to the economic and social diversity of the country. However, just as in the United States shocks and radical external changes generated a chain of events that altered the competitive structure of the industry and consequently the behaviour of family firms. The initial catalyst for change was the American Civil War, less for the poverty and despair which it caused than for the innovation which it encouraged at the community level. This was especially noticeable where shortages of American raw cotton and the need to use sub-standard Indian cotton stimulated a resourceful and innovative response by firms. In Oldham this confirmed the use of adapted mules for coarser counts while creating wealth especially among machine makers which could subsequently be used to finance the development of large joint stock mills. At the same time the Civil War proved to be a stimulus to the weaving towns of north-east Lancashire and hence contributed to both spatial and vertical specialisation. The financial repercussions, in the so-called American section of the industry, continued to be felt after the turn of the century and after the First World War when syndicates developed based upon the wealth amassed through Oldham's mill building companies.

Oldham's growth into Lancashire's largest concentration of spinning mills was heavily dependent upon the combination of the opportunities of the Indian market and the peculiarities of the town's financial arrangements, whilst its technological tradition ensured that its expansion relied on mules. This growth occurred in what has been described as the 'Indian summer' of the cotton industry, in the years before the First World War. Its repercussions, by reinforcing the wealth of the syndicates, continued to reverberate in the dismal decades of the interwar period. In the feverish speculation of the postwar boom these mainly locally based groups prominently promoted that wave of reflotations and financial reconstructions of cotton spinning mill companies which proved so soon to be financially crippling to the American section of the industry. Consequently, if the international turmoil, set in train by the First World War, was a major reason for the collapse of many Lancashire markets, the heavy indebtedness of especially Oldham companies also made creative response immensely difficult. Close market ties between Oldham and those towns such as Blackburn and Burnley (which had owed their rise to a combination of the Indian market and Oldham yarn) meant these centres were also devastated. Conversely the mainly privately owned firms, in the Bolton-based Egyptian section, fared far better in the interwar period, as did the related weaving towns of Nelson and Colne. Dragged down neither by high levels of debt in over-capitalised firms nor by the same level of market loss suffered in the American section, these towns experienced a measure of prosperity at least until the 1930s.

Competitiveness and decline

The prime purpose of this book has been to explore the causes and consequences of differences in the development of business behaviour in the cotton industries of Britain and the United States, rather than to compare their international competitiveness. This is because the sharply contrasting orientation of the two industries meant that firms were only rarely competing directly, certainly before the Second World War. What this study has revealed, however, is that by the interwar period both industries were experiencing serious difficulties and neither was especially internationally competitive. Yet, whereas the Lancashire cotton industry suffered terminal decline after the Second World War, this was not matched in the United States. The scale of cotton manufacturing's survival, at least to the 1970s in the United States, was partly due to the scale of the domestic market and to manufacturers' continued ability to influence government policy. Of course American cotton entrepreneurs expressed public outrage to gain policy modifications and the trade press reveals an industry in almost constant anguish. However, the peculiar social and political configurations of post-Second World War America worked in textiles' favour in important ways.

After 1945, in the United States, Southern cotton manufacturers benefited from the emergence of a powerful Southern bloc vote, which vastly enhanced the ability of the textile industry, as a whole, to influence government policy. Even though the merger wave had altered and depersonalised ownership patterns during the 1940s and 1950s, close ties between mill-managers (their one-time owners) and politicians at the community and state level ensured that senators were aware of cotton manufacturers' desires for protection of their beloved domestic market. Nor could they doubt the consequences for their political careers if they failed to deliver. Similarly at the national level successive presidents depended upon the South for election and, in office, faced the defeat of cherished policies if they did not take the Southern bloc vote seriously. Confidence that their voice would be heard must surely have encouraged companies' high levels of investment witnessed in the 1960s and 1970s.

In Lancashire, on the other hand, analysis confirms the widely held view that the economic and social diversity that was inseparable from vertical and spatial specialisation made it difficult for the industry to speak with one voice, especially when under pressure, as in the interwar period or after the Second World War. Even had the waters not been muddied by the successive difficulties of the Indian and Commonwealth questions, governments could be forgiven for confusion over what Lancashire wanted by way of support and relief. There was nothing so clear-cut as a simple campaign for protection conducted by an industry in difficulties. This was especially noticeable in the 1950s and 1960s when sectoral divisions regarding the desirability of duty free Commonwealth imports were one of the forces which helped to make Lancashire a fairly impotent pressure group. This interestingly contrasts with the position in the United States, where the regional divisions which had reduced bargaining power before the Second World War were largely removed. Moreover, no equivalent of the Southern bloc vote aided the British cotton industry. Lancashire was politically divided even in the cotton communities, and certainly between the areas south of the Ribble and those rural areas to the north which were only fleetingly touched by cotton. This meant that even without differences in the two political systems, in comparison with the United States, Lancashire had none of the political muscle enjoyed by Southern manufacturers.

This is not all, however, for despite a series of debates in the House of Commons in the 1950s and 1960s 'the cotton question' never really assumed national importance. Before 1980 the decline of the Lancashire cotton industry caused waves within textile circles and certainly altered the physical environment of those communities for which it had once been a life-blood. The demolition of mill chimneys and the proliferation of museums and industrial heritage centres have changed the character of many veteran cotton communities. Yet in the 1950s and 1960s, although some towns became depopulated, the demise of the cotton industry did not cause massive unemployment and hence social problems. This further reduced any potential for constructing a strong case for intervention on its behalf. Again the position of Lancashire's communities and their interplay with national politics contrasts with the American South where fears for social and racial tension were real and powerful in the same period. These forces meant that whilst the case for protection of cotton manufacturing was no stronger in the United States than in Britain after the Second World War the American industry suffered far less precipitous decline before 1980. Even though the 1980s were a dire decade for textiles in the United States, one is left with the impression of an industry which could still rely on some level of sympathy from its government.

This study does not demonstrate or aim to demonstrate the superiority of Lancashire firms over United States firms. Rather it undertakes to make sense of the peculiarities and similarities which can be detected in the two industries focusing on bilateral rather than multilateral comparisons. Yet, since so much of the discussion of decline in the British economy in general and the cotton industry in particular has been viewed from an American starting point, this restriction seems justified. In placing the evolution of the British and United States cotton industries in their national and local contexts and examining their courses against a long-term historical backdrop, it has been possible to explore the changing forces which led to the similarities and peculiarities of business behaviour in each country and to differences in the culture of business. By demonstrating the complexity of the forces at work it highlights the hazards of viewing British business, and especially the cotton industry, from an American perspective in ways which have implications for the study of business more generally. Much more research is needed if we are to understand why and how firms develop in distinctive ways and the forces shaping their capabilities. Internationally comparative studies help us appreciate the relationship between distinctive economic, social, political and cultural forces and business and hence allow the analysis of diversity rather than simply presuming convergence.

References

Abercrombie, N. and Hill, S. 1976, 'Paternalism and Patronage', *British Journal of Sociology*, 27: 413–29.

Adams, Donald R. Jr. 1970, 'Some Evidence on English and American Wage Rates, 1790–1830', *Journal of Economic History*, 30: 499–520.

Afleck, Diane Fagan 1987, *Just New from the Mills: Printed Cottons in America*, North Andover, Mass.: Museum of American Textile History.

Aggarwal, Vinod K. and Haggard, Stephen 1983, 'The Politics of Protection in the US Textile and Apparel Industries', in Zysman, John and Tyson, Laura (eds.) *American Industry in International Competition*, Ithaca: Cornell University Press.

Aldcroft, D. H. 1964, 'The Entrepreneur and the British Economy, 1870–1914', *Economic History Review*, 17: 113–34.

Allaire, Yvan and Firsirotu, Michaela E. 1984, 'Theories of Organisational Culture', *Organisational Studies*, 5, London.

Alvesson, Mats J. and Lindkvist, P. 1993, 'Transaction Costs, Clans and Corporate Culture', *Journal of Management Studies*, 30: 427–52.

Amalgamated Cotton Mills Trust Ltd 1920, *Concerning Cotton: A Brief Account of the Aims and Achievements of the Amalgamated Cotton Mills Trust Limited and its Component Companies*, Manchester: Amalgamated Cotton Mills Trust Ltd.

Anderson, B. L. 1966, 'Aspects of Capital and Credit in Lancashire during the Eighteenth Century' (unpublished MA thesis, University of Liverpool).

1972, 'The Attorney and the Early Capital Market in Lancashire during the Eighteenth Century', in Crouzet, F (ed.) *Capital Formation in the Industrial Revolution*, London: Methuen.

Anderson, Gary M. and Tollison, Robert D. 1985, 'Ideology, Interest Groups and the Repeal of the Corn Laws', *Journal of Institutional and Theoretical Economics*, 141: 197–212.

Anderson, Kym and Baldwin, Robert E. 1981, 'The Political Market for Protection in Industrial Countries: Empirical Evidence', *World Bank Staff Working Paper*, 492.

Anderson, M. 1971, *Family Structure in Nineteenth-Century Lancashire*, Cambridge: Cambridge University Press.

Anon., 1897, 'The New Cotton Combination: The English Sewing Cotton Company Ltd', *The Drapers Record*, 611–17.

Anon., 1980, 'Corporate Culture: The Hard to Change Values that Spell Success or Failure', *Business Week*, 27 October.

Anson, Robin and Simpson, Paul 1988, *World Textile Trade and Production Trends*, London: Economist Intelligence Unit Special Report.

Ashmore, Owen 1969, *The Industrial Archaeology of Lancashire*, Plymouth: Latimer Trend and Co.

Ashton, T. S. 1953, 'The Bill of Exchange and Private Banks in Lancashire 1790–1830', in Ashton, T. S. and Sayers, R. S (eds.) *Papers in Monetary History*, Oxford: Oxford University Press.

Aspin, C. 1964, *James Hargreaves and the Spinning Jenny*, Helmshore: Helmshore Local History Society.

Atack, J. 1979, 'Fact in Fiction? Relative Costs of Steam and Water Power: A Simulation Approach', *Explorations in Economic History*, 16: 409–37.

Atack, J. and Passell, P. 1992, *A New Economic View of American History*, New York: W. W. Norton.

1994, *A New Economic View of American History from Colonial Times to 1940*, New York: W. W. Norton & Co.

Augur, Philip John 1979, 'The Cotton Famine, 1861–5: A Study of the Principal Towns during the American Civil War' (unpublished Ph.D thesis, University of Cambridge).

Baack, B. D. and Ray, E. J. 1974, 'Tariff Policy and Income Redistribution: The Case of the US in 1830–60', *Explorations in Economic History*, 11: 103–22.

Bailyn, B. 1950, *The New England Merchants in the Seventeenth Century*, Cambridge, Mass.: Harvard University Press.

Baldwin, Robert E. 1985, *The Political Economy of US Import Policy*, Cambridge, Mass.: MIT Press.

Bamberg, J. H. 1988, 'The Rationalization of the British Cotton Industry in the Inter War Period', *Textile History*, 19: 83–102.

Bardan, B. 1973, 'The Cotton Textile Agreement, 1962–72', *Journal of World Trade Law*, 7: 8–35.

Barkin, Solomon 1957, 'Labour Relations in the United States Textile Industry', *International Labour Review*, 75: 391–411.

Bauer, R., de Sola Pool, I. and Dexter, L. 1964, *American Business and Public Policy*, Chicago: Aldine.

Beatty, Bess 1987, 'Lowells of the South: Northern Influences on the Nineteenth Century North Carolina Textile Industry', *Journal of Southern History*, 53: 37–62.

Belassa, B. A. 1965, 'Tariff Protection in Industrial Countries: An Evaluation', *Journal of Political Economy*, 22.

Bell, P. W. 1956, *The Sterling Area in the Post-War World: Internal Mechanism and Cohesion*, Oxford: Oxford University Press.

Bender, Thomas 1975, *Toward an Urban View: Ideas and Institutions in Nineteenth Century America*, Lexington: University of Kentucky Press.

Bendix, R. 1956, *Work and Authority in Industry*, New York: Wiley.

Ben-Porath, Yoram 1980, 'The F-Connection: Families, Friends and Firms and the Organization of Exchange', *Population and Development Review*, 6: 1–30.

Bidwell, Percy W. 1939, *The Invisible Tariff: A Study of the Control of Imports into the United States*, New York: Council on Foreign Relations.

Biggart, Nicole Woolsey and Hamilton, Gary H. 1992, 'On the Limits of a Firm

Based Theory to Explain Business Networks: The Western Bias of Neo-classical Economics', in Nitin, Nohria and Eccles, Robert C (eds.) *Networks and Organizations: Structure, Form and Action*, Boston: Harvard Business School Press.

Bils, Mark 1984, 'Tariff Protection and Production in the Early US Cotton Textile Industry', *Journal of Economic History*, 44: 1033–46.

Blank, Stephen 1978, 'Britain: The Politics of Foreign Economic Policy, the Domestic Economy and the Problem of Pluralist Stagnation', in Katzenstein, Peter (ed.) *Between Power and Plenty: Foreign Economic Policies of Advanced Industrial States*, Madison: University of Wisconsin Press.

Board of Trade 1946, *Working Party Reports: Cotton*, London.

Bolton and District Textile Works Managers Association, 1958–9 Minutes.

Bowden, Sue and Higgins, David 1998, 'Short-Time Working and Price Maintenance: Collusive Tendencies in the Cotton Spinning Industry, 1919–1939', *Economic History Review*, 51: 319–43.

Boyson, R. 1970, *The Ashworth Cotton Enterprise*, Oxford: Oxford University Press.

Brandis Buford, R. 1982, *The Making of Textile Trade Policy, 1935–81*, Washington: American Cotton Manufacturers Institute.

Breen, T. T. 1986, 'An Empire of Goods: The Anglicization of Colonial America, 1690–1776', *Journal of British Studies*, 25: 467–99.

Bremner, Robert H. 1970, *Children and Youth in America*, Cambridge, Mass.: Harvard University Press, Vol. I.

Broadberry, S. N. 1997, *The Productivity Race: British Manufactures in International Perspective, 1850–1990*, Cambridge: Cambridge University Press.

Brody, David 1989, 'Time and Work during Early American Industrialism', *Labour History*, 15: 5–46.

Brogan, Hugh 1985, *The Penguin History of the United States of America*, London: Penguin.

Brown, John C. 1992, 'Market Organization, Protection and Vertical Integration: German Cotton Textiles before 1914', *Journal of Economic History*, 52: 339–51.

Brown, L. 1958, *The Board of Trade and the Free Trade Movement, 1830–42*, Oxford: Clarendon Press.

Buck, N. 1925, *The Development and Organisation of Anglo-American Trade, 1800–1850*, New Haven: Yale University Press.

Burgy, Herbert 1932, *The New England Cotton Textile Industry: A Study in Industrial Geography*, Baltimore: Johns Hopkins University Press.

Burnley and District Cotton Industry Study Group 1937, *Report on Marketing*, Manchester: Sherratt and Hughes.

Butt, 1971, *Robert Owen: Prince of Cotton Spinners*, Newton Abbot: David and Charles.

Bythell, D. 1968, *The Handloom Weavers*, Cambridge: Cambridge University Press.

Cain, P. J. and Hopkins, A. G. 1993, *British Imperialism: Innovation and Expansion, 1688–1914*, London: Longman.

Calico Printers Association 1899, *Company Prospectus*.
Callahan, Collen M., McDonald, Judith A. and O'Brien, Anthony Patrick 1994, 'Who Voted for Smoot-Hawley?', *Journal of Economic History*, 54: 683–90.
Carlton, David L. 1982, *Mill and Town in South Carolina, 1880–1920*, Baton Rouge: Louisiana State University Press.
Carosso, Vincent P. and Sylla, R. 1991, 'US Banks in International Finance', in Cameron, Rondo and Boirykin, V. I. (eds.) *International Banking, 1870–1914*, New York: Oxford University Press.
Casson, M. C. 1982, *The Entrepreneur*, London: Mark Robertson.
1991, *The Economics of Business Culture: Game Theory, Transaction Costs and Economic Performance*, Oxford: Oxford University Press.
1993, 'Entrepreneurship and Business Culture', in Brown, Jonathan and Rose, Mary B. (eds.) *Entrepreneurship, Networks and Modern Business*, Manchester: Manchester University Press, 30–54.
Casson, M. C. and Rose, Mary B. 1997, 'Institutions and the Evolution of Modern Business', *Business History*, 39: 1–8.
Catling, H. 1970, *The Spinning Mule*, Newton Abbot: David and Charles.
Chandler, A.D. Jr. 1977, *The Visible Hand: The Managerial Revolution in America*, Cambridge, Mass.: Harvard University Press.
1990, *Scale and Scope: The Dynamics of Industrial Capitalism*, Cambridge, Mass.: Harvard University Press.
Chandler A. D. Jr. and Tedlow, R. 1985, *The Coming of Managerial Capitalism: A Casebook on the History of American Economic Institutions*, Homewood: Richard D. Irwin.
Chapman, S. D. 1967, *The Early Factory Masters*, Newton Abbot: David and Charles.
1970, 'Fixed Capital Formation in the British Cotton Industry, 1770–1815', *Economic History Review*, 23: 235–66.
1981, 'The Arkwright Mills', *Industrial Archaelogy Review*, 6: 5–27.
1987, *The Cotton Industry and the Industrial Revolution*, Houndmills: Macmillan.
1992, *Merchant Enterprise in Britain: From the Industrial Revolution to World War II*, Cambridge: Cambridge University Press.
1996, 'The Commercial Sector', in Rose, Mary B. (ed.) *The Lancashire Cotton Industry: A History since 1700*, Preston: Lancashire County Books.
Chapman, S. D. and Butt, J. 1988, 'The Cotton Industry', in Feinstein, C. H. and Pollard, S. (eds.) *Studies in Capital Formation in the United Kingdom, 1750–1920*, Oxford: Clarendon Press.
Chapman, S. J. 1899, 'The Regulation of Wages by Lists in the Spinning Industry', *Economic Journal*, 9: 592–9.
1900, 'Some Policies of the Cotton Spinners' Trade Unions', *Economic Journal*, 10.
Chapman, S. J. and Ashton, T. S. 1913–14, 'The Size of Businesses Mainly in the Textile Industries', *Journal of the Royal Statistical Society*, 78: 469–549.
Chatterji, B. 1992, *Trade, Tariffs and Empire: Lancashire and British Policy in India, 1919–1939*, Oxford: Oxford University Press.
Child, J. 1964, 'Quaker Employers and Industrial Relations', *Sociological Review*, 12: 393–415.

Church, Roy 1993, 'The Family Firm in Industrial Capitalism: International Perspectives on Hypotheses and History', *Business History*, 35: 17–43.
Churchill, Randolph S. 1959, *Lord Derby: King of Lancashire*, London: Heinemann.
Clairmonte, Frederick and Cavanagh, John 1981, *The World in their Web: Dynamics of Textile Multinationals*, London: Zed Press.
Clark, G. 1987, 'Why isn't the Whole World Developed? Lessons from the Cotton Mills', *Journal of Economic History*, 47: 141–73.
Clark, Victor S. 1929, *History of Manufactures in the United States Vol. I*, New York: Carnegie Institute.
Clarke, W. A. Graham 1914, *Cotton Goods in Japan and their Competition in the Manchuria Market*, Special Agents Series No. 86, Washington.
Clay, Henry 1931, *Report on the Position of the English Cotton Industry*, Manchester: Securities Management Trust.
Coase, R. H. 1937, 'The Nature of the Firm', *Economica*, 4: 386–485.
Cochran T.C. 1971a, 'The Entrepreneur in Economic Change', in Kilby, P. (ed.) *Entrepreneurship and Economic Development*, New York: Free Press.
1971b, *Frontiers of Change*, New York: Oxford University Press.
1985, *Challenges to American Values: Society, Business and Religion*, New York: Oxford University Press.
Cohen, I. 1990, *American Management and British Labor: A Comparative Study of the Cotton Spinning Industry*, New York: Greenwood Press.
Cohen, Stanley 1962, 'Northeastern Business and Radical Reconstruction: A Re-Examination', in Andreano, R (ed.) *The Economic Impact of the Civil War*, Cambridge, Mass.: Harvard University Press.
Coleman, D. C. 1969, *Courtaulds: An Economic and Social History, Vol. II*, Oxford: Oxford University Press.
Coleman, Peter J. 1963, *The Transformation of Rhode Island, 1790–1860*, Providence: Brown University Press.
Collier, F. 1964, *The Family Economy of the Working Classes in the Cotton Industry*, Manchester: Manchester University Press.
Collins, Bruce 1990, 'American Enterprise and the British Comparison', in Collins, B. and Robbins, K. (eds.) *British Culture and Economic Decline*, London: Weidenfeld and Nicolson.
Commons, J. R. 1934, *Institutional Economics*, New York: Macmillan.
Conan, A. R. 1961, *The Rationale of the Sterling Area*, London: Macmillan.
Constantine, Stephen 1995, 'Britain and the Empire', in Constantine, Stephen, Kirby, Maurice W. and Rose, Mary B. (eds.) *The First World War in British History*, London: Edward Arnold.
Cook, Lesley P. and Cohen, Ruth 1958, *The Effects of Mergers*, London: George Allen and Unwin Ltd.
Copeland, Melvin T. 1909–10, 'Technological Development in the Cotton Industry since 1860', *Quarterly Journal of Economics*, 24: 109–59.
1912, *The Cotton Manufacturing Industry of the United States*, Cambridge, Mass.: Harvard University Press.
Cotton Board, Trade Letters 1949–54.
1948, *Musgrave Experiment*, Manchester.
1949–61, *Quarterly Statistical Review*, Manchester.

1956, *The Cotton Industry and the Consequences of Unlimited Imports*, Manchester.
1958, *Western Germany: The Market for Britain's Cottons*, Manchester.
Cotton Spinning Productivity Team 1950, *Report of a Visit to the USA in 1949 of Productivity Team Representing the Cotton Industry*, London.
Cotton Textile Institute 1929, *Special Report on Extending the Uses of Cotton*, New York.
1938, *Cotton Facts and Figures: Statistical and Economic Material Relating to the Cotton Textile Industry*, New York.
Cotton Weaving Productivity Team 1950, *Report of a Visit to the USA in 1949 of a Productivity Team Representing the Cotton Weaving Industry*, London.
Cotton Yarn Association 1928, *Statistical Information Concerning Cotton Spinning in the United States of America*, Manchester.
1929, *Statistical Information Concerning Cotton Spinning in the United States of America*, Manchester.
Cottrell, P. L. 1980, *Industrial Finance, 1830–1914*, London: Methuen.
Craig, F. W. S. 1977, *British Parliamentary Election Results, 1832–85*, London: Macmillan.
Crick, W. F. and Wadsworth, J. E. 1936, *A Hundred Years of Joint Stock Banking*, London: Hodder and Stoughton.
Crouzet, F. 1972, *Capital Formation in the Industrial Revolution*, London: Methuen.
1982, *The Victorian Economy*, London: Methuen.
Curzen, G. Jose de la Torre, Donges, Juergen B., Macbean, Alasdair I., Waelbroeck, Jean and Wolf, Martin 1981, *MFA Forever? Future of the Arrangement for Trade in Textiles*, London: Trade Policy Research Centre.
Cyert, R. M. and March, J. G. 1963, *A Behavioural Theory of the Firm*, New York: Prentice-Hall.
Dalzell, Robert F. 1987, *Enterprising Elite: The Boston Associates and the World They Made*, Cambridge, Mass.: Harvard University Press.
Daniels, G. W. 1920, *The Early English Cotton Industry*, Manchester: Manchester University Press.
1933, 'Samuel Crompton's Census of the Cotton Industry in 1811', *Economic Journal, Economic History Supplement II*.
Daniels, G. W. and Jewkes, J. 1928, 'The Post War Depression in the Lancashire Cotton Industry', *Journal of the Royal Statistical Society*, 91: 159–92.
David, Paul 1970, 'Learning by Doing and Tariff Protection: A Reconsideration of the Case of the Ante-Bellum United States Cotton Textile Industry', *Journal of Economic History*, 30: 521–601.
Davis, H. S. et al. 1938, *Vertical Integration on the Textile Industries*, University of Pennsylvania and Washington DC: The Textile Foundation Inc.
Davis, Lance E. 1957, 'Sources of Industrial Finance: The American Textile Industry: A Case Study', *Journal of Economic History*, 9: 189–203.
Davis, Lance E. and North, Douglass C. 1971, *Institutional Change and American Economic Growth*, Cambridge: Cambridge University Press.
Davis, R. 1979, *The Industrial Revolution and British Overseas Trade*, Cambridge: Cambridge University Press.

Deane, P. and Cole, W. A. 1962, *British Economic Growth, 1688–1959*, Cambridge: Cambridge University Press.

Dehn, R. M. R. 1913, *The German Cotton Industry*, Manchester: Manchester University Press.

Department of Economic Affairs 1965, *The North West, 1954–64*, London: HMSO.

Destler, I. M., Fukui, H. and Sato, H. 1979, *The Textile Wrangle*, Ithaca: Cornell University Press.

Dewey, C. 1978, 'The End of the Imperialism of Free Trade: The Eclipse of the Lancashire Lobby and the Concession of Fiscal Autonomy to India', in Dewey, C. and Hopkins, A. G (eds.) *The Imperial Impact: Studies in the Economic History of Africa and India*, London: Athlone Press.

Dickson, R. J. 1966, *Ulster Emigration to Colonial America, 1718–1775*, London: Routledge & Kegan Paul.

Donald, Gordon Jr. 1951, 'The Depression in Cotton Textiles, 1924–40' (unpublished Ph.D thesis, University of Chicago).

Dublin, Thomas 1975, 'Women, Work and Protest in the Early Lowell Mills: The Oppressing Hand of Avarice would Enslave Us', *Labour History*, 16: 99–116.

1979, *Women at Work: The Transformation of Work and Community in Lowell, Massachusetts, 1826–1860*, New York: Columbia University Press.

Dulles, Foster Rhea 1993, *Labour in America: A History*, Alington Heights, Ill.: Harlan Davidson, 5th edition.

Dupree, M. 1990a, 'Struggling with Destiny: The Cotton Industry, Overseas Trade Policy and the Cotton Board', *Business History*, 32: 106–28.

1990b, 'Fighting Against Fate: The Cotton Industry and the Government in the 1930s', *Textile History*, 21: 101–17.

1996, 'Foreign Competition and the Interwar Period', in Rose, Mary B. (ed.) *The Lancashire Cotton Industry: A History since 1700*, Preston: Lancashire County Books.

Dupree, M. (ed.) 1987, *Lancashire and Whitehall: The Diary of Sir Raymond Streat*, 2 vols. Manchester: Manchester University Press.

Dutton, H. I. and King, J. E. 1981, *Ten Per Cent and No Surrender: The Preston Strike 1853–54*, Cambridge: Cambridge University Press.

1982, 'The Limits of Paternalism', *Social History*, 7: 59–73.

Early, Frances H. 1980, 'A Reappraisal of the New England Labour Reform Movement of the 1840s: the Lowell Female Labor Reform Association and the New England Working Men's Association', *Histoire Sociale*, 13.

Edwards, M. M. 1969, *The Growth of the British Cotton Trade, 1780–1815*, Manchester: Manchester University Press.

Eiselen, Malcolm Rogers 1932, repr. 1974, *The Rise of Pennsylvania Protectionism*, Philadelphia: Porcupine Press Inc.

Elbaum, B and Lazonick, W. 1986, *The Decline of the British Economy*, Oxford: Oxford University Press.

Eldridge, J. E. T. and Crombie, A. D. 1974, *A Sociology of Organisations*, London: Allen & Unwin.

Ellison, Mary 1972, *Support for Secession: Lancashire and the American Civil War*, Chicago: University of Chicago Press.

Engels, F. (ed.) 1958, *The Condition of the Working Classes in England*, Oxford: Oxford University Press.
Evans, John W. 1971, *The Kennedy Round in American Trade Policy: The Twilight of GATT?*, Cambridge, Mass.: Harvard University Press.
Farber, Bernard 1972, *Guardians of Virtue: Salem Families in 1800*, New York: Basic Books.
Farnie, D. A. 1975, 'The Cotton Famine in Great Britain', in Ratcliffe, B.M (ed.) *Great Britain and Her World, 1750–1914*, Manchester: Manchester University Press.
1979, *The English Cotton Industry and the World Market, 1815–1896*, Oxford: Oxford University Press.
1990, 'The Textile Machine-Making Industry and the World Market 1870–1960', *Business History*, 32: 150–70.
1993, *John Rylands of Manchester*, Manchester: John Rylands University Library.
Fearon, P. 1987, *War, Prosperity and Depression: The US Economy, 1917–1945*, Oxford: Philip Allan.
Federation of Master Cotton Spinners Associations Ltd 1951–67, *Annual Reports*, Manchester.
Feller, I. 1966, 'The Draper Loom in New England Textiles, 1894–1914: A Study of Diffusion of an Innovation', *Journal of Economic History*, 26: 326–47.
1974, 'The Diffusion and Location of Technological Change in the American Cotton Textile Industry', *Technology and Culture*, 15: 569–93.
Feller, Peter Buck and Wilson, Ann Carlisle 1976, 'United States Tariff and Trade Law: Constitutional Sources and Constraints', *Law and Policy in International Business*, 8: 105–23.
Ferguson, Thomas 1989, 'Industrial Conflict and the Coming of the New Deal: The Triumph of Multinational Liberalism in America', in Fraser, Steve and Gerstle, Gary (eds.) *The Rise and Fall of the New Deal Order, 1930–1980*. Princeton: Princeton University Press.
Fitton, R. S. 1989, *The Arkwrights: Spinners of Fortune*, Manchester: Manchester University Press.
Fitzgerald, R. 1987, *British Labor Management and Industrial Welfare, 1846–1939*, London: Croom Helm.
Fong, H. D. 1932, *Triumph of the Factory System*, Tientsin, China: Chihli Press.
Foreman-Peck 1995, *Smith and Nephew in the Health Care Industry*, Cheltenham: Edward Elgar.
Forrester, R. B. 1921, *The Cotton Industry in France*, Manchester: Manchester University Press.
Fowler, Alan 1987, *The Barefoot Aristocrats*, Littleborough: George Kelsall.
1988, 'Lancashire Cotton Trade Unionism in the Interwar Years', in Jowitt, J. A. and McIvor, A. J (eds.) *Employers and Labour in the English Textile Industries, 1850–1939*, London: Routledge & Kegan Paul.
Fox, A. 1985, *History and Heritage*, London: Allen & Unwin.
Fox-Genovese, Elizabeth and Fox-Genovese, Eugene 1983, *Fruits of Merchant Capital, Slavery and Bourgeois Property in the Rise and Expansion of Capitalism*, New York: Galaxy Books.

Freifeld, Mary 1986, 'Technological Change and the Self-Acting Mule: A Study of Skill and Sexual Division of Labour', *Social History*, 11: 319–43.

French, M. 1994, 'Co-ordinating Manufacturing and Marketing: The Role of the Selling Agent in United States Textiles', *Textile History*, 25: 227–42.

Freyer, Tony 1992, *Regulating Big Business: Antitrust in Great Britain and America 1880–1990*, Cambridge: Cambridge University Press.

Fruin, W. Mark (ed.) 1998, *Networks, Markets, and the Pacific Rim: Studies in Strategy*, Oxford: Oxford University Press.

Gadian, D. S. 1978, 'Class Consciousness in Oldham and other North West Industrial Towns', *Historical Journal*, 21: 161–72.

Galambos, Louis 1966, *Competition and Co-operation: The Emergence of a National Trade Association*, Baltimore: Johns Hopkins University Press.

Galbraith, John K. 1981, *A Life in Our Times*, London: Penguin.

Galenson, Alice 1985, *The Migration of the Cotton Textile Industry from New England to the South, 1880–1930*, New York: Garland.

Garrard, J. 1983, *Leadership and Power in Victorian Industrial Towns, 1830–1880*, Manchester: Manchester University Press.

Garside, W. R. and Gospel, H. F. 1986, 'Employers and Managers: Their Organizational Structure and Changing Industrial Strategies', in Wrigley, C. J. (ed.) *A History of British Industrial Relations, Vol. I, 1870–1914*, Brighton: Harvester.

Gatrell, V. A. C. 1977, 'Labour Power and the Size of Firms in Lancashire Cotton in the Second Quarter of the Nineteenth Century', *Economic History Review*, 30.

1982, 'Incorporation and the Pursuit of Liberal Hegemony in Manchester, 1790–1839', in Frazer, D. (ed.) *Municipal Reform and the Industrial City*, Leicester: Leicester University Press.

GATT 1966, *A Study on Cotton Textiles*, Geneva.

1984, *Textiles and Clothing in the World Economy*, Geneva.

Gaventa, John and Smith, Barbara Ellen 1991, 'The Deindustrialisation of the Textile South: A Case Study', in Leiter, Jeffrey, Schulman, Michael D. and Zingraff, Rhonda (eds.) *Hanging by a Thread*, Ithaca: Cornell University Press.

Gerlach, Michael L. and Lincoln, James R. 1992, 'The Organization of Business Networks in the United States and Japan', in Nohria, Nitin and Eccles, Robert C. (eds.) *Networks and Organisations: Structure, Form and Action*, Boston: Harvard Business School Press.

Gerschenkron, A. 1953, 'Social Attitudes, Entrepreneurship and Economic Development', *Explorations in Entrepreneurial History*, 6: 1–19.

1966, *Economic Backwardness in Historical Perspective*, Cambridge, Mass.: Harvard University Press.

Gibb, George S. 1950, *The Saco-Lowell Shops: Textile Machinery Building in New England, 1813–1949*, Cambridge, Mass.: Harvard University Press.

Gitelman, H. M. 1967, 'The Waltham System and the Coming of the Irish', *Labor History*, 52: 227–53.

Godley, Andrew 1995, 'The Development of the UK Clothing Industry, 1850–1950: Output and Productivity Growth', *Business History*, 37: 46–63.

1996, 'Singer in Britain: The Diffusion of Sewing Machine Technology and its Impact on the Clothing Industry in the United Kingdom, 1860–1905', *Textile History*, 27.

Godley, Andrew and Westall, O. M. (eds.) 1996, *Business History and Business Culture*, Manchester: Manchester University Press.

Goldin, Claudia and Sokoloff, Kenneth 1982, 'Women, Children and Industrialization in the Early Republic: Evidence from the Manufacturing Censuses', *Journal of Economic History*, 42: 741–74.

Grampp, W. 1987, 'How Britain turned to Free Trade?', *Business History Review*, 61: 86–112.

Granovetter, Mark 1985, 'Economic Action and Social Structure: The Problem of Embeddedness', *American Journal of Sociology*, 91: 481–501.

1996, 'Coase Revisited: Business Groups in the Modern Economy', *Industrial and Corporate Change*, 4: 93–130.

Granovetter, Mark and Swedberg, R. (eds.) 1992, *The Sociology of Economic Life*, Boulder, Co.; Westview Press.

Grant, Wynn 1993, *Business and Politics in Britain*, 2nd edn, Houndmills: Macmillan.

1995, *Pressure Groups, Politics and Democracy in Britain*, London: Harvester Wheatsheaf.

Gray, Robert 1996, *The Factory Question and Industrial England, 1830–1860*, Cambridge: Cambridge University Press.

Gregory, Frances W. 1975, *Nathan Appleton: Merchant and Entrepreneur, 1779–1861*, Charlottesville: University Press of Virginia.

Griffin, Richard W. 1964, 'Reconstruction of the North Carolina Textile Industry, 1865–1885', *North Carolina Historical Review*, 4: 34–55.

Griffin, Richard W. and Standard, Diffee W. 1957, 'The Cotton Textile Industry in Ante-bellum North Carolina Part II: An Era of Boom and Consolidation, 1830–1860', *The North Carolina Historical Review*, 34: 131–64.

Gross, Laurence F. 1993, *The Course of Industrial Decline: The Boott Cotton Mills of Lowell, Massachusetts, 1835–1955*, Baltimore: Johns Hopkins University Press.

Guagnini, A. 1991, 'The Fashioning of Higher Technical Education in Britain: The Case of Manchester', in Gospel, H. (ed.) *Industrial Training and Technological Innovation: A Comparative Historical Study*, London: Routledge & Kegan Paul.

1993, 'Worlds Apart: Academic Instruction and Professional Qualifications in the Training of Mechanical Engineers in England, 1850–1914', in Fox, R. and Guagnini, A. (eds.) *Education Technology and Industrial Performance in Europe, 1850–1939*, Cambridge: Cambridge University Press.

Habakkuk, H. J. 1962, *American and British Technology in the Nineteenth Century*, Cambridge: Cambridge University Press.

Hall, Jacquelyn Dowd et al. 1986, 'Cotton Mill People: Work, Community and Protest in the Textile South', *American Historical Review*, 91: 245–86.

Hall, Peter Dobkin 1977, 'Family Structure and Economic Organization: Massachusetts' Merchants, 1700–1850', in Hareven, Tamara K. (ed.) *Family and Kin in Urban Communities, 1700–1930*, New York: Franklin Watts.

1984, *The Organization of American Culture, 1700–1900: Private Institutions, Elites and the Origins of American Nationality*, New York: New York University Press.

Hamilton, Gary G. and Feenstra, Robert C. 1995, 'Varieties of Hierarchies and Markets: An Introduction', *Industrial and Corporate Change*, 4: 51–91.

Hampden-Turner, C. and Trompenaars, F. 1993, *The Seven Cultures of Capitalism*, Doubleday.

Handlin, O. and Handlin, M. 1945, 'Origins of the American Business Corporation', *Journal of Economic History*, 5: 1–23.

1947, *Commonwealth: A Study of the Role of Government in the American Economy: Massachusetts, 1774–1861*, New York: New York University Press.

Hanham, H. J. 1959, *Elections and Party Management: Politics in the Time of Disraeli and Gladstone*, Cambridge: Cambridge University Press.

Hannah, L. 1983, *The Rise of the Corporate Economy*, London: Methuen.

Hardach, G. 1987, *The First World War, 1914–18*, Harmondsworth: Penguin.

Harley, C. Knick 1992, 'International Competitiveness of the Antebellum American Cotton Textile Industry', *Journal of Economic History*, 52: 559–83.

Harnetty, P. 1972, *Imperialism and Free Trade: Lancashire and India in the Mid Nineteenth Century*, Manchester: Manchester University Press.

Hawke, G. 1975, 'The United States' Tariff and Industrial Production in the Late Nineteenth Century', *Economic History Review*, 38: 84–99.

Helm, Elijah 1900–1, 'The Middleman in Commerce', *Transactions of the Manchester Statistical Society* (no vol. no.): 55–65.

Higgins, D. M. 1993a, 'Re-Equipment as a Strategy for Survival in the Lancashire Spinning Industry, c1945–c1960', *Textile History*, 24: 211–34.

1993b, 'Rings, Mules and Structural Constraints: The Lancashire Textile Industry, c1945–c1965', *Economic History Review*, 46: 342–62.

Hills, R. L. 1970, *Power in the Industrial Revolution*, Manchester: Manchester University Press.

Hobsbawm, E. 1968, *Industry and Empire*, London: Penguin.

Hodgson, Geoffrey M. 1988, *Economics and Institutions*, Cambridge: Polity Press.

Hoffman, W. 1958, *The Growth of Industrial Economies*, Manchester: Manchester University Press.

Hofstede, G. 1984, *Culture's Consequences: International Differences in Work Related Values*, London: Sage.

1994, *Cultures and Organizations*, London: HarperCollins

Hollis, P. 1974, *Pressure from Without in Early Victorian Politics*, London: Edward Arnold.

Honeyman, K. 1982, *Origins of Enterprise: Business Leadership in the Industrial Revolution*, Manchester: Manchester University Press.

Hood, Adrienne W. 1999, 'Industrial Opportunism: From Handweaving to Mill Production, 1700–1830', in Benes, Peter (ed.), *Textiles in Early New England: Design, Production and Consumption*, Boston: Boston University Press.

Hoppit, J. 1986, *Risk and Failure in English Business, 1700–1800*, Cambridge: Cambridge University Press.

Horwitz, Morton J. 1977, *The Transformation of American Law, 1780–1860*, Cambridge, Mass.: Harvard University Press.

Howe, A. C. 1984, *The Cotton Masters, 1830–1860*, Oxford: Clarendon Press.
1996, 'The Business Community', in Rose, Mary B. (ed.) *The Lancashire Cotton Industry: A History since 1700*, Preston: Lancashire County Books.
1997, *Free Trade and Liberal England, 1846–1946*, Oxford: Oxford University Press.
Huberman, Michael 1987, 'The Economic Origins of Paternalism: Lancashire Cotton Spinning in the First Half of the Nineteenth Century', *Social History*, 12: 187–92.
1996, *Escape from the Market: Negotiating work in Lancashire*, Cambridge: Cambridge University Press.
Hudson, P. 1986, *The Genesis of Industrial Capital: A Study of the West Riding Wool Textile Industry, c1750–1850*, Cambridge: Cambridge University Press.
Huffmire, D. W. 1973, 'Strategies of the United States Textile Industry in the Post World War II Period', *Journal of Business Policy*, 3: 31–7.
Hunsberger, H. S. 1961, *Japan in United States' Foreign Economic Policy*, Washington: US Government Printing Office.
Hunt, B. C. 1936, *The Development of the Business Corporation in Britain, 1800–1867*, Cambridge, Mass.: Harvard University Press.
Isard, Peter 1973, 'Employment Impacts of Textile Imports and Investment: Vintage Capital Model', *American Economic Review*, 30: 402–15.
Jarvis, Anthea M. 1997, 'British Cotton Couture: British Fashion and the Cotton Board, 1941–1959', *Costume*, 31: 92–9.
Jeffreys, J. B. 1977, *Trends in Business Organization in Great Britain since 1856*, New York: Arno Press.
Jeremy, David J. 1973a, 'British Textile Technology Transmission to the United States: The Philadelphia Region Experience', *Business History Review*, 47.
1973b, 'Innovation in American Textile Technology during the early Nineteenth Century', *Technology and Culture*, 14: 40–76.
1977, 'Damming the Flood: British Government Efforts to Check the Outflow of Technicians and Machinery, 1780–1843', *Business History Review*, 51: 1–34.
1981, *Transatlantic Industrial Revolution: The Diffusion of Textile Technologies between Britain and America, 1790–1830*, Oxford: Basil Blackwell.
1990, *Technology and Power in the Early American Cotton Industry: James Montgomery, the Second edition of his 'Cotton Manufacture' (1840) and the Justitia Controversy about Relative Power Costs*, Philadelphia: American Philosophical Society.
1993, 'Survival Strategies in Lancashire Textiles: Bleachers' Association Ltd to Whitecroft plc, 1900–1980s', *Textile History*, 24: 163–209.
1996, 'Lancashire and the International Diffusion of Technology', in Rose, Mary B. (ed.) *The Lancashire Cotton Industry: A History*, Preston: Lancashire County Books.
Jeremy, David, J. and Stapleton, Darwin H. 1991, 'Transfers between Culturally Related Nations: The Movement of Textile and Railroad Technologies between Britain and the United States, 1780–1840', in Jeremy, David J. *International Technology Transfer: Europe, Japan and the USA, 1700–1914*, Aldershot: Edward Elgar.
Jones, G. T. 1933, *Increasing Returns: A Study of the Relation between the Size and*

Efficiency of Industries with Special Reference to the History of Selected British and American Industries, 1850–1910, Cambridge: Cambridge University Press.

Jones, Geoffrey 1993, *British Multinational Banking, 1830–1990*, Oxford: Oxford University Press.

Jones, Geoffrey and Rose, Mary B. 1993, 'Family Capitalism', *Business History*, 35: 1–16.

Jones, S. R. H. 1994, 'The Origins of the Factory System in Great Britain: Technology, Transaction Costs or Exploitation?', in Kirby, M.W. and Rose, Mary B. (eds.) *Business Enterprise in Modern Britain*, London: Routledge & Kegan Paul.

Joyce, P. 1980, *Work, Society and Politics, The Culture of the Factory in Later Victorian England*, Brighton: Harvester Press.

1984, 'Labour, Capital and Compromise: A Response to Richard Price', *Social History*, 9: 67–76.

Kawakatsu, Heita 1998, 'The Lancashire Cotton Industry and its Rivals', in Bruland, Kristine and O'Brien, Patrick (eds.) *From Family Firms to Corporate Capitalism: Essays in Business and Industrial History in Honour of Peter Mathias*, Oxford: Clarendon Press.

Keesing, Donald B. and Wolf, Martin 1980, *Textile Quotas against Developing Countries*, London: Trade Policy Research Centre.

Kennedy, Paul 1988, *The Rise and Fall of Great Powers: Economic Change and Military Conflict from 1500–2000*, London: Fontana Press.

Kennedy, Stephen Jay 1936, *Profits and Losses in Textiles Cotton Textile Financing*, New York: Harper and Brothers Publishers.

Kenny, Stephen 1982, 'Sub-regional Specialization in the Lancashire Cotton Industry, 1884 -1914: A Study of Organizational and Locational Change', *Journal of Historical Geography*, 8: 41–63.

Kindleberger, C. P. 1964, *Economic Growth in France and Britain, 1851–1950*, Cambridge, Mass.: Harvard University Press.

Kinnealy, Christine 1998, 'Peel, Rotten Potatoes and Providence: The Repeal of the Corn Laws and the Irish Potato Famine', in Marrison, Andrew (ed.) *Free Trade and its Reception*, London: Routledge & Kegan Paul, 50–81.

Kirby, M. W. 1974, 'The Lancashire Cotton Industry in the Interwar Years: A Study of Organizational Change', *Business History*, 16: 145–59.

Kirk, Neville 1994a, *Labour and Society in Britain and the USA: Vol. I, Capitalism, Custom and Protest*, Cambridge: Cambridge University Press.

1994b, *Labour and Society in Britain and the USA: Vol. II, Challenge and Accommodation 1850–1939*, Cambridge: Cambridge University Press.

Knight, Arthur 1974, *Private Enterprise and Public Intervention: The Courtaulds Experience*, London: Allen & Unwin.

Knowlton, Evelyn 1948, *Pepperell's Progress: A History of a Cotton Textile Company 1844–1945*, Cambridge, Mass.: Harvard University Press.

Krasner, Stephen 1978, 'US Commercial Policy and Monetary Policy: Unraveling the Paradox of External Strength and Internal Weakness', in Katzenstein, Peter (ed.) *Between Power and Plenty: Foreign Economic Policies of Advanced Industrial States*, Madison: University of Wisconsin Press.

Kriedte, P., Medick, H. and Schlumbohm, J. 1982, *Industrialisation before Industrialisation*, Cambridge: Cambridge University Press.

Lamoreaux, Naomi R. 1985, *The Great Merger Movement 1895–1904*, Cambridge: Cambridge University Press.
1994, *Insider Lending: Banks, Personal Connections and Economic Development in Industrial New England*, Cambridge: Cambridge University Press.
Lander, Ernest McPherson Jr. 1969, *The Textile Industry in the Antebellum South*, Baton Rouge: Louisiana University Press.
Landes, David 1969, *Unbound Prometheus*, Cambridge: Cambridge University Press.
Lane, Joan 1977, 'Apprenticeship in Warwickshire, 1700–1834' (unpublished Ph.D thesis, University of Birmingham).
Langlois, Richard N. and Robertson, Paul L. 1989, 'Explaining Vertical Integration: Lessons from the American Automobile Industry', *Journal of Economic History*, 49: 361–75.
1995, *Firms, Markets and Economic Change: A Dynamic Theory of Business Institutions*, London: Routledge.
Lapping, Brian 1970, *The Labour Government 1964–1970*, London: Penguin.
Lary, Hal B. 1968, *Imports of Manufactures from Less Developed Countries*, New York: Columbia University Press.
Laver, James 1969, *Costume and Fashion: A Concise History*, London: Thames & Hudson.
Law, Brian 1996, *Fieldens of Todmorden: A Nineteenth Century Business Dynasty*, Littleborough: George Kelsall.
Lazer, H. 1975, 'Politics, Public Policy Formation and the Lancashire Textile Industry, 1954–1970' (unpublished Ph.D thesis).
Lazonick, W. 1979, 'Industrial Relations and Technical Change: The Case of the Self Acting Mule', *Cambridge Journal of Economics*, 3: 231–63.
1981a, 'Production Relations, Labour Productivity and Choice of Technique: British and United States' Cotton Spinning', *Journal of Economic History*, 41: 491–516.
1981b, 'Competition, Specialization and Industrial Decline', *Journal of Economic History*, 41: 31–8.
1981c, 'Factor Costs and the Diffusion of Ring Spinning in Britain prior to World War I', *Quarterly Journal of Economics*, 96: 89–109.
1983, 'Industrial Organization and Technological Change: The Decline of the British Cotton Industry', *Business History Review*, 57: 195–236.
1984, 'Rings and Mules in Britain: A Reply', *Quarterly Journal of Economics*, 99: 393–8.
1986, 'The Cotton Industry', in Elbaum, B. and Lazonick, W. (eds.) *The Decline of the British Economy*, Oxford: Oxford University Press.
1990, *Competitive Advantage on the Shopfloor*, Cambridge, Mass.: Harvard University Press.
1991, *Business Organization and the Myth of the Market Economy*, Cambridge: Cambridge University Press.
Lazonick, W. and West, J. 1995, 'Organizational Integration and Competitive Advantage: Explaining Strategy and Performance in American Industry', *Industrial and Corporate Change*, 4.
Lea, Arden J. 1975a, 'Cotton Textiles and the Federal Labor Act of 1915', *Labour History*, 16: 285–94.

1975b, 'Cotton Textiles and the Federal Labour Act of 1816', *Labour History*, 16: 485–94.

Learned, E. P. 1930, 'Mergers in the Cotton Industry', *Harvard Business Review*, 13: 501–12.

Lee, C. H. 1980, 'The Cotton Industry', in Church, R. (ed.) *The Dynamics of Victorian Business: Problems and Perspectives*, London: George Allen and Unwin.

Lee, R. D. and Schofield, R. S. 1981, 'British Population in the Eighteenth Century', in Floud, R. and McCloskey, D. N. (eds.) *The Economic History of Britain since 1700*, Vol. I, Cambridge: Cambridge University Press.

Lees, J. D. 1969, *The Political System of the United States*, London: Faber and Faber.

Lemert, Ben F. 1933, *The Cotton Textile Industry of the Southern Appalachian Piedmont*, Chapel Hill: University of North Carolina Press.

Lemire, B. 1979, *Fashion's Favourite: The Cotton Trade and the Consumer in Britain, 1660–1800*, Oxford: Oxford University Press.

1992, *Fashion's Favourite: The Cotton Trade and the Consumer in Britain, 1660–1800*, Oxford: Oxford University Press.

Leunig, Timothy 1996, 'The Myth of the Corporate Economy: Factor Costs, Industrial Structure and Technological Choice in the Lancashire and New England Cotton Industries, 1900–1913' (unpublished Ph.D thesis, University of Oxford).

Levitt, Sarah 1996, 'Clothing', in Rose, Mary B. (ed.) *The Lancashire Cotton Industry: A History since 1700*, Preston: Lancashire County Books.

Licht, Walter 1995, *Industrialising America: The Nineteenth Century*, Baltimore: Johns Hopkins University Press.

Lindstrom, Diane 1978, *Economic Development in the Philadelphia Region, 1810–1850*, New York: Columbia University Press.

Lipset, Seymour Martin 1967, *The First New Nation: The United States in Historical and Comparative Perspective*, New York: Anchor Books.

Littler, C. 1982, *The Development of the Labor Process in Capitalist Societies*, London: Croom Helm.

Lloyd-Jones, Roger 1998, 'The Manchester Business Community, the Trade Cycle and Commercial Policy', in Marrison, Andrew (ed.) *Free Trade and its Reception*, London: Routledge & Kegan Paul.

Lloyd-Jones, Roger and le Roux, A. A. 1980, 'The Size of Firms in the Cotton Industry, 1815–1841', *Economic History Review*, 33: 72–82.

Lloyd-Jones, Roger and Lewis, M. 1987, *Manchester and the Age of the Factory: The Business Structure of Cottonopolis in the Industrial Revolution*, London: Croom Helm.

Logan, Frenise A. 1965, 'India's Loss of the British Cotton Market after 1865', *Journal of Southern History*, 31: 40–50.

Longmate, Norman 1978, *The Hungry Mills*, London: Temple Smith.

Lyons, J. S. 1985, 'Vertical Integration of the British Cotton Industry, 1825–1850', *Journal of Economic History*, 45: 419–26.

Macrosty, Henry William 1907, *The Trust Movement in British Industry: A Study of Business Organisation*, London: Longman's and Co.

McCord, Norman 1958, *The Anti-Corn Law League, 1838–46*, London: George Allen and Unwin.

McCraw, Thomas (ed.) 1997, *Creating Modern Capitalism*, Cambridge, Mass.: Harvard University Press.
McGouldrick, Paul 1968, *New England Textiles in the Nineteenth Century: Profits and Investment*, Cambridge, Mass.: Harvard University Press.
McIvor, Arthur J. 1996, *Organised Capital: Employers Associations and Industrial Relations in Northern England, 1880–1939*, Cambridge: Cambridge University Press.
Marglin, S. 1974, 'What Do Bosses Do?', *Review of Radical Political Economy*, 6: 60–112.
Mariotti, Sergio and Cainarca, Gian Carlo 1986, 'The Evolution of Transaction Governance in the Textile-Clothing Industry', *Journal of Economic Behaviour and Organization*, 7: 351–74.
Markham, J. W. 1950, 'Integration in the Textile Industry', *Harvard Business Review*, January: 74–88.
Marrison, A. J. 1975, 'Great Britain and Her Rivals in the Latin American Cotton Piece Goods Market, 1880–1914', in Ratcliffe, B. M. (ed.) *Great Britain and Her World, 1750–1914*, Manchester: Manchester University Press.
1996a, 'Indian Summer, 1870–1914', in Rose, Mary B. (ed.) *The Lancashire Cotton Industry: A History since 1700*, Preston: Lancashire County Books.
1996b, *British Business and Protection, 1903–1932*, Oxford: Clarendon Press.
Marshall, A. 1890, *Principles of Economics*, London: Macmillan.
Marshall, J. D. 1968, 'Colonization as a Factor in the Planting of Towns in North West England', in Dyos, H. J. (ed.) *The Study of Urban History*, London: St Martin, 216–20.
Mass, W. 1984, 'Technological Change and Industrial Relations: The Diffusion of Automatic Weaving in the United States and Britain' (unpublished Ph.D thesis, Boston College).
Mass, W. and Lazonick, W. 1990, 'The British Cotton Industry and International Competitive Advantage: The State of the Debates', *Business History*, 32: 9–65.
Mather, F. C. 1974, 'The General Strike of 1842', in Quinault, R. E. and Stevenson, J. (eds.) *Popular Protest and Public Order*, London: Allen & Unwin.
Mathias, P. 1979, *The Transformation of England*, London: Methuen.
Meakin, B. 1905, *Model Factories and Villages: Ideal Conditions of Labour and Housing*, London: Garland.
Mendells, F. F. 1972, 'Proto-industrialization: The First Phase of the Industrialization Process', *Journal of Economic History*, 32: 241–61.
Merrick Dodd, E. 1954, *The American Business Corporation until 1860*, Cambridge, Mass.: Harvard University Press.
Michl, H. E. 1938, *The Textile Industries: An Economic Analysis*, Washington DC: Textile Foundation.
Miles, Caroline 1968, *Lancashire Textiles: A Case Study of Industrial Change*, Cambridge: Cambridge University Press.
1976, 'Protection of the British Textile Industry', in Corden, W. M. and Fels, G. (eds.) *Public Assistance to Industry: Protection and Subsidies in Britain and Germany*, London: Macmillan.
Millington, J. 1995, 'Shiloh's Survival Recipe', *Textile Monthly*, June: 25–7.
Milward, Alan S. 1984, *The Economic Effects of the Two World Wars on Britain*, Houndmills: Macmillan, 2nd edn.

Minchin, Timothy J. 1997, *What Do We Need a Union for?*, Chapel Hill: University of North Carolina Press.
Mitchell, B. R. 1988, *British Historical Statistics*, Cambridge: Cambridge University Press.
Mitchell, Broadus 1921, *The Rise of Cotton Mills in the South*, Baltimore: Johns Hopkins University Press.
Mizruchi, Mark 1982, *The American Corporate Network 1904–1974*, Beverly Hills, CA: Sage.
Moe, Terry M. 1991, 'Politics and the Theory of Organisation', *Journal of Law, Economics and Organization*, 7: 106–29.
Montgomery, Florence 1970, *Printed Textiles: English and American Cottons and Linens, 1700–1850*, New York: Thames and Hudson.
Montgomery, James 1836, *The Theory and Practice of Cotton Spinning or the Carding and Spinning Master's Assistant*, Glasgow: John Niven.
1840, *A Practical Detail of the Cotton Manufacture of the United States of America and the State of Cotton Manufacture of that Country Compared with that of Britain*, Glasgow: J. Niven Jr.
Moody's Industrial Manual, New York.
Moore, R. J. 1964, 'Imperialism and the Free-Trade Policy in India, 1853–4', *Economic History Review*, 17.
Murchison, Claudius T. 1930, *King Cotton is Sick*, Chapel Hill: University of North Carolina Press.
Musson, A. E. 1976, 'Industrial Motive Power in the United Kingdom, 1800–70', *Economic History Review*, 2nd Series, 29: 415–39.
Nelson, Ralph L. 1963, *Concentration in the Manufacturing Industries of the United States: A Mid Century Report*, New Haven: Yale University Press.
Nelson, Richard R. and Winter, Sidney G. 1982, *An Evolutionary Theory of Economic Change*, Cambridge, Mass.: Harvard University Press.
North, Douglass C. 1990, *Institutions, Institutional Change and Economic Performance*, Cambridge: Cambridge University Press.
Oates, Mary J. 1975, *The Role of the Cotton Textile Industry in the Economic Development of the American South East, 1900–1940*, New York: Arno Press.
O'Brien, P., Griffiths, T. and Hunt, P. 1991, 'Political Components of the Industrial Revolution: Parliament and the English Cotton Textile Industry, 1660–1774', *Economic History Review*, 2nd Series, 44: 395–423.
O'Connor, Thomas H. 1968, *Lords of the Loom: The Cotton Whigs and the Coming of the Civil War*, New York: Charles Scribner's Sons.
OECD 1965, *Modern Cotton Industry: A Capital Intensive Industry*, Paris: OECD.
Olson, M. 1971, *The Logic of Collective Action: Public Goods and the Theory of Groups*, Cambridge, Mass.: Harvard University Press.
Ouchi, William G. 1980, 'Markets, Bureaucracies and Clans', *Administrative Science Quarterly*, 25.
Parliamentary Papers 1836, *Poor Law Commissioners.*
Pastor, Robert A. 1980, *Congress and the Politics of US Foreign Economic Policy, 1929–1976*, Berkeley: University of California Press.
Peacock, A. E. 1984, 'The Successful Prosecution of the Factory Acts, 1833–55', *Economic History Review*, 37: 197–210.
Pearson, R. 1991, 'Collective Diversification: Manchester Cotton Merchants and

the Insurance Business in the Early Nineteenth Century', *Business History Review*, 65: 379–414.

Penrose, Edith T. 1959, *The Theory of the Growth of the Firm*, Oxford: Basil Blackwell.

Pincus, J. J. 1977, *Pressure Groups and Politics in Antebellum America*, New York: Columbia University Press.

Pollak, Robert A. 1985, 'A Transactions Cost Approach to Families and Households', *Journal of Economic Literature*, 23: 581–608.

Pollard, S. 1963, 'Factory Discipline in the Industrial Revolution', *Economic History Review*, 24: 513–29.

1965, *The Genesis of Modern Management*, London: Penguin.

1978, 'Labor in Great Britain', in Mathias, P. and Postan, M. M. (eds.) *The Cambridge Economic History of Europe*, Vol. VI, Part 1, Cambridge: Cambridge University Press.

1981, *Peaceful Conquest*, Oxford: Oxford University Press.

1983, *The Development of the British Economy, 1914–1980*, London: Edward Arnold.

1991, 'Regional Markets and National Development', in Berg, M. (ed.) *Markets and Manufacture in Early Industrial Europe*, London: Routledge & Kegan Paul.

Potter, David 1954, *People of Plenty: Economic Abundance and the American Character*, Chicago: University of Chicago Press.

Pressnell, L. S. 1956, *Country Banking in the Industrial Revolution*, Oxford: Clarendon Press.

Prude, Jonathan 1983, *The Coming of Industrial Order: Town and Factory Life in Rural Massachusetts, 1810–1860*, New York: Cambridge University Press.

Ratner, S. 1972, *The Tariff in American History*, New York and London: Van Nostrand.

Redford, A. 1926, *Labour Migration in England, 1800–50*, Manchester: Manchester University Press.

1934, 1956, *Manchester Merchants and Foreign Trade*, 2 vols., Manchester: Manchester University Press.

Report on Select Committee on Duties Payable on Printed Cotton Goods 1818, 279, Vol. III: 301.

Rezneck, S. 1932, 'The Rise and Early Development of Industrial Consciousness in the United States, 1760–1830', *Journal of Economic and Business History*, 4: 784–811.

Ring, Trudy 1992, Hast, A. (ed.) *International Directory of Company Histories*, Vol. V, London: St James' Press.

Roberts, D. 1979, *Paternalism in Early Victorian England*, London: Croom Helm.

Robertson, Alex J. 1990, 'Lancashire and the Rise of Japan, 1910–1937', *Business History*, 32: 87–105.

Robson, R. 1957, *The Cotton Industry in Britain*, London: Macmillan.

1958, *The Man-Made Fibres Industry*, London: Macmillan.

Rodgers, H. B. 1960, 'The Lancashire Cotton Industry in 1840', *Transactions of the Institute of British Geographers*, 28: 135–54.

Rooth, Tim 1993, *British Protectionism and the International Economy: Overseas Commercial Policy in the 1930s*, Cambridge: Cambridge University Press.

Rose, Mary B. 1979, 'Diversification of Investment by the Greg Family, 1800–1914', *Business History*, 21: 79–96.

1986, *The Gregs of Quarry Bank Mill: The Rise and Decline of a Family Firm, 1750–1914*, Cambridge: Cambridge University Press.

1989, 'Social Policy and Business: Parish Apprenticeship and the Early Factory System, 1750–1834', *Business History*, 31: 5–32.

1994, 'The Family Firm in British Business, 1780–1914', in Kirby, Maurice W. and Rose, Mary B. (eds.) *Business Enterprise in Modern Britain*, London: Routledge & Kegan Paul.

1996, 'Family Firm Community and Business Culture: A Comparative Perspective on the British and American Cotton Industries', in Godley, Andrew and Westall, Oliver (eds.) *Business and Culture*, Manchester: Manchester University Press.

Rosenberg, N. 1963, 'Technological Change in the Machine Tool Industry, 1840–1910', *Journal of Economic History*, 23: 414–43.

1967, 'Anglo American Wage Differences in the 1820s', *Journal of Economic History*, 27: 221–9.

1969, *The American System of Manufactures: Report of Commission on the Machinery of the United States*, Edinburgh: Edinburgh University Press.

1972, *Technology and American Economic Growth*, New York: Harper and Row.

1982, *Inside the Black Box*, Cambridge: Cambridge University Press.

Rostas, L. 1948, *Comparative Productivity in British and American Industry*, Cambridge: Cambridge University Press.

Rostow, W. W. 1968, *The Stages of Economic Growth*, Cambridge: Cambridge University Press.

1975, *How it all Began: Origins of the Modern Economy*, London: Methuen.

Rowley, Charles K., Thorbecke, Willem and Wagner, Richard E. 1995, *Trade Protection in the United States*, Aldershot: Elgar.

Roy, William G. 1997, *Socializing Capital: The Rise of the Large Industrial Corporation in America*, Princeton: Princeton University Press.

Rubinstein, W. D. 1981, 'New Men of Wealth and the Purchase of Land in Nineteenth Century England', *Past and Present*, 92: 125–47.

1993, *Capitalism, Culture and Decline in Britain, 1750–1990*, London: Routledge & Kegan Paul.

Russell, Alice 1987, 'Local Elites and the Working Class Response in the North West, 1879–1895: Paternalism and Deference Reconsidered', *Northern History*, 23: 153–73.

Sabel, C. and Zeitlin, J. 1985, 'Historical Alternatives to Mass Production: Politics, Markets and Technology in Nineteenth Century Industrialization', *Past and Present*, 108: 133–76.

1997, *World of Possibilities: Flexibility and Mass Production in Western Industrialization*, Cambridge: Cambridge University Press.

Sandberg, Lars G. 1969, 'American Rings and English Mules: The Role of Economic Rationality', *Quarterly Journal of Economics*, 73: 25–43.

Sandberg, L. H. 1968, 'Movements in the Quality of British Cotton Textiles, 1815–1913', *Journal of Economic History*, 29: 1–27.

1974, *Lancashire in Decline*, Columbus: Ohio State University Press.

1984, 'The Remembrance of Things Past: Rings and Mules Revisited', *Quarterly Journal of Economics*, 99: 387–98.

1987, 'Stubborn Mules and Vertical Integration: The Disappearing Constraint?', *Economic History Review*, 32: 87–94.

Saul, S. B. 1970, *Technological Change: The United States and Britain in the Nineteenth Century*, London: Methuen.

Savage, M. 1987, *The Dynamics of Working Class Politics*, Cambridge: Cambridge University Press.

Saxonhouse, G. and Wright, G. 1984, 'Rings and Mules around the World: A Comparative Study in Technological Choice', in Saxonhouse, G. and Wright, G. (eds.) *Research in Economic History*, London: JAI Press.

1984, 'New Evidence on the Stubborn English Mule and the Cotton Industry, 1878–1920', *Economic History Review*, 37: 507–19.

1987, 'Stubborn Mules and Vertical Integration: The Disappearing Constraint', *Economic History Review*, 40: 87–94.

Schattschneider, E. E. 1935, *Politics, Pressure and the Tariff: A Study in Free Private Enterprise in Pressure Politics, as shown in 1929–30 Revision of the Tariff*, New York: Prentice Hall.

Schoeser, Mary 1996, 'Shewey & Full of Work: Design', in Rose, Mary B. (ed.) *The Lancashire Cotton Industry: A History since 1700*, Preston: Lancashire County Books.

Schonhardt-Bailey, Cheryl, 1998, 'Interests, Ideology and Politics: Agricultural Trade Policy in Nineteenth Century Britain and Germany', in Marrison, Andrew (ed.) *Free Trade and its Reception*, London: Routledge & Kegan Paul.

Schumpeter, J. A. 1934, *The Theory of Economic Development*, Cambridge, Mass.: Harvard University Press.

Schusteff, S. 1992, 'Burlington Industries Inc.', in Hast, A. (ed.) *International Directory of Company Histories*, Vol. V, London: St James' Press.

Scranton, P. 1983, *Proprietary Capitalism: The Textile Manufacture at Philadelphia 1800–1885*, Cambridge: Cambridge University Press.

1984, 'Varieties of Paternalism: Industrial Structures and the Social Relations of Production in American Textiles', *American Quarterly*, 36: 135–57.

1986, 'Learning Manufacture: Shop Floor Schooling and the Family Firm', *Technology and Culture*, 27: 40–62.

1989, *Figured Tapestry: Production Markets and Power in Philadelphia Textiles, 1885–1941*, Cambridge: Cambridge University Press.

1997, '"Have a heart for the manufacturers!' Production, Distribution and the Decline of American Textile Manufacturing', in Sabel, Charles F. and Zeitlin, Jonathan (eds.) *World of Possibilities: Flexibility and Mass Production in Western Industrialization*, Cambridge: Cambridge University Press.

Seavoy, Ronald E. 1982, *The Origins of the American Business Corporation, 1784–1855: Broadening the Concept of Public Service During Industrialization*, New York: Greenwood Press.

Second Annual Report of the Poor Law Commissioners, 29, Pt. 1, 1836.

Seed, J. 1982, 'Unitarianism, Political Economy and the Anatomies of Liberal Culture in Manchester', *Social History*, 7: 1–25.

1986, 'Theologies of Power: Unitarianism and Social Relations of Religious

Discourse', in Morris, R. J. (ed.) *Class, Power and Social Structure in British Nineteenth Century Towns*, Leicester: Leicester University Press.

Shammas, Carole 1990, *The Pre-industrial Consumer in England and America*, Oxford: Oxford University Press.

Shelton, Cynthia 1986, *The Mills of Manayunk: Industrialization and Social Conflict in the Philadelphia Region, 1787–1837*, Baltimore: Johns Hopkins University Press.

Shimizu, H. 1986, *Anglo-Japanese Trade Rivalry in the Middle East in the Interwar Period*, Ithaca: Cornell University Press.

Siegenthaler, Hansjorg 1967, 'What Price Style? The Fabric Advisory Function of the Dry Goods Commission Merchant, 1850–1880', *Business History Review*, 41.

Silver, Arthur Wistar 1966, *Manchester Men and Indian Cotton, 1847–1872*, Manchester: Manchester University Press.

Silvia, P. T. 1975, 'The Position of Workers in a Textile Community: Fall River in the Early 1880s', *Labor History*, 16: 230–48.

Simpson, William Hays 1966, *Some Aspects of America's Textile Industry*, Columbia S.C.: The R. L. Bryan Co.

Singleton, J. 1990, 'Showing the White Flag: The Lancashire Cotton Industry, 1945–65', *Business History*, 32: 129–49.

1991, *Lancashire on the Scrapheap: The Cotton Industry, 1945–1970*, Oxford: Oxford University Press.

1994, 'The Cotton Industry and the British War Effort', *Economic History Review*, 47: 601–18.

1995, 'Debating the Nationalisation of the Cotton Industry, 1918–50', in Millward, R. M. and Singleton, J. (eds.) *The Political Economy of Nationalisation in Britain, 1920–1950*, Cambridge: Cambridge University Press.

1996, 'The Decline of the British Cotton Industry since 1940', in Rose, Mary B. (ed.) *The Lancashire Cotton Industry: A History since 1700*, Preston: Lancashire County Books.

1997, *The World Textile Industry*, London: Routledge & Kegan Paul.

Siracusa, Carl 1979, *A Mechanical People: Perceptions of the Industrial Order in Massachusetts, 1815–1880*, Middletown, Conn.: Wesleyan University Press.

Skinner's Cotton Trade Directory, 1923, Manchester.

Sladen, Christopher 1995, *The Conscription of Fashion: Utility Cloth, Clothing and Footwear, 1941–52*, Aldershot: Scolar Press.

Smith, Robert S. 1960, *Mill on the Dan: A History of Dan River Mills, 1882–1950*, Durham N.C.: Duke University Press.

Smith, T. R. 1944, *The Textile Industry of Fall River, Massachusetts*, New York: King's Crown Press.

Spence, C. C. 1965, *The Sinews of American Capitalism*, London: Macmillan.

Stigler, G. 1951, 'The Division of Labour is Limited by the Extent of the Market', *Journal of Political Economy*, 59.

Sturges, Kenneth 1915, *American Chambers of Commerce*, New York: Moffat Yard and Company.

Sugiyama, S. 1988, 'Textile Marketing in East Asia, 1860–1914', *Textile History*, 19: 279–98.

Sunley, Peter 1992, 'Marshallian Industrial Districts: The Case of the Lancashire Cotton Industry in the Inter-War Years', *Transactions of the Institute of British Geographers*, 17: 306–20.

Swain, John T. 1986, *Industry before the Industrial Revolution: North East Lancashire, 1500–1640*, Manchester: Manchester Chetham Society.

Sykes, R. A. 1980, 'Some Aspects of Working Class Consciousness in Oldham, 1830–1842', *Historical Journal*, 23: 167–79.

Taggart, W. 1923, *Cotton Mill Management: A Practical Guide for Managers, Carders and Overlookers*, London: Macmillan.

Taussig, F. W. 1931 and 1966, *The Tariff History of the United States*, New York: G. P. Putnam's Sons.

Taylor, Peter F. 1991, 'Popular Politics and Labour-Capital Relations in Bolton, 1825–1850' (unpublished Ph.D thesis, University of Lancaster).

Temin, Peter 1966a, 'Steam and Water in the Early Nineteenth Century', *Journal of Economic History*, 26: 187–205.

1966b, 'Labour Scarcity and the Problem of Industrial Efficiency in the 1850s', *Journal of Economic History*, 26: 277–95.

1988, 'Product Quality and Vertical Integration in the Early English Cotton Textile Industry', *Journal of Economic History*, 48: 891–907.

1997, 'Is it Kosher to Talk about Culture', *Journal of Economic History*, 57: 267–87.

Terrill, Tom E. 1973, *The Tariff, Politics and American Foreign Policy, 1874–1906*, Westport: Greenwood Press.

Textile Council 1969, *Cotton and Allied Trades: A Report on Present Performance and Future Prospects*, Manchester.

Textile Weekly.

Textile World.

Thomas, W. A. 1973, *The Provincial Stock Exchanges*, London: Frank Cass.

Thompson, E. P. 1967, 'Time, Work Discipline and Industrial Capital', *Past and Present*, 38: 56–97.

Thornblade, James B. 1971, 'Textile Imports from the Less Developed Countries: A Challenge to the American Market', *Economic Development and Cultural Change*, 19: 277–86.

Timmins, G. 1993, *The Last Shift*, Manchester: Manchester University Press.

1996, 'Technological Change', in Rose, Mary B. (ed.) *The Lancashire Cotton Industry: A History since 1700*, Preston: Lancashire County Books.

1998, *Made in Lancashire*, Manchester: Manchester University Press.

Tiratsu, N. and Tomlinson, J. 1993, *Industrial Efficiency and State Intervention: Labour 1939–1951*, London: Routledge & Kegan Paul.

Tomlinson, J. D. 1977, 'Anglo Indian Economic Relations, 1913–28 with Special Reference to the Cotton Trade' (unpublished Ph.D thesis, London School of Economics).

1979, 'The First World War and British Piece Goods Exports to India', *Economic History Review*, 32.

1994, *Government and Enterprise since 1900*, Oxford: Oxford University Press.

Toms, J. S. 1993, 'The Profitability of the First Lancashire Merger: The Case of Horrocks, Crewdson and Co Ltd, 1887–1905', *Textile History*, 24: 129–46.

1994, 'Financial Constraints on Economic Growth: Profits, Capital

Accumulation and the Development of the Lancashire Cotton Spinning Industry, 1885–1914', *Accounting Business and Financial History*, 4: 363–83.
1996, 'The Finance and Growth of the Lancashire Cotton Industry, 1870–1914 (unpublished Ph.D thesis, University of Nottingham).
1997, 'Windows of Opportunity in the Textile Industry: The Business Strategies of Lancashire Entrepreneurs, 1880–1914', *Business History*, 40: 1–25.
Toyne, B. et al. 1983, *The United States Textile Mill Products Industry: International Challenges and Strategy for the Future*, Columbia: University of South Carolina Press.
1984, *The Global Textile Industry*, London: Allen & Unwin.
Tryon, R. M. 1917, *Household Manufactures in the United States, 1640–1860*, Chicago: University of Chicago Press.
Tucker, Barbara M. 1979, 'The Family and Industrial Discipline in Antebellum New England', *Labour History*, 21.
1984, *Samuel Slater and the Origins of the American Textile Industry*, Ithaca: Cornell University Press.
Tupper, Eleanor and McReynolds, George E. 1937, *Japan in American Public Opinion*, New York: Macmillan.
Turner, H. A. 1962, *Trade Union Growth, Structure and Policy: A Comparative Study of the Cotton Unions*, London: Allen & Unwin.
Tyson, R. E. 1968, 'The Cotton Industry', in Aldcroft, D. H. (ed.) *The Development of British Industry and Foreign Competition, 1875–1914*, London: George Allen & Unwin.
Unwin, George 1904, *Industrial Organization in the Sixteenth and Seventeenth Centuries*, Oxford: Clarendon Press.
US Bureau of the Census 1960, *Historical Statistics of the United States from Colonial Times to 1957*, Washington DC: Government Printing Office.
US Bureau of Foreign and Domestic Commerce 1914, *Cotton Goods in Japan and their Competition in the Manchuria Market*, Special Agents' Series, No. 86 by Clarke, W. A. Graham, Washington.
US Department of Commerce 1939, *The United States in India's Trade*, Washington.
US Tariff Commission 1921, *The Japanese Cotton Industry and Trade*, Washington.
1929, *Textile Imports and Exports 1891–1927*, Washington.
Utley, Freda, 1931, *Lancashire and the Far East*, London: George Allen & Unwin.
Utton, M. 1974, 'On Measuring the Effects of Industrial Mergers', *Scottish Journal of Political Economy*, 31.
Vitkovitch, B. 1955, 'The UK Cotton Industry, 1937–54', *Journal of Industrial Economics*, 3: 241–65.
Wadsworth, A. P. and Mann, J. de Lacy 1931, *The Cotton Trade and Industrial Lancashire 1600–1780*, Manchester: Manchester University Press.
Wadsworth, H. 1948, 'Utility Cloth and Clothing Scheme', *Review of Economic Studies*, 16.
Wallace, Anthony 1978, *Rockdale: The Growth of an Industrial Village in the Early Industrial Revolution*, New York: Norton.
Wallwork, K. L. 1968, 'The Calico Printing Industry of Lancastria in the 1840s', *Transactions of the Institute of British Geographers*, 45: 143–56.

Walton, John K. 1987, *Lancashire: A Social History, 1558–1939*, Manchester: Manchester University Press.
1989, 'Protoindustrialization and the First Industrial Revolution: The Case of Lancashire', in Hudson, P. (ed.) *Regions and Industries*, Cambridge: Cambridge University Press.
Ward, D. C. 1987, 'Industrial Workers in the Mid Nineteenth Century South: Family and Labour in the Graniteville (SC) Textile Mill, 1845–1880', *Labour History*, 13: 328–48.
Ward, J. T. 1965–6, 'The Factory Movement in England, 1830–1855', *Transactions of the Lancashire and Cheshire Antiquarian Society*, 75–6: 186–210.
Wardley, P. 1991, 'The Anatomy of Big Business: Aspects of Corporate Development in the Twentieth Century', *Business History*, 33.
Ware, Caroline F. 1931, *Early New England Cotton Manufacture: A Study of Industrial Beginnings*, Boston: Houghton Miffin Co.
Weber, M. 1978, *Economy and Society*, trans. and ed. Roth, G. and Wittich, C. Berkeley: California University Press.
Weiser, L. and Jay, K. 1972, 'Determinants of the Commodity Structure of US Trade: Comment', *American Economic Review*, 62: 459–64.
Wells, L. T. 1968, 'Product Life Cycle for International Trade', *Journal of Marketing*, 3.
White, G. S. 1836, *Memoir of Samuel Slater: The Father of American Manufactures Connected with a History of the Rise and Progress of the Cotton Manufacture in England and America*, Philadephia, reprinted 1967 by Augustus M. Kelly Publishers, New York.
Wiener, M. J. 1981, *English Culture and the Decline of Industrial Spirit, 1850–1980*, Cambridge: Cambridge University Press.
Wilkins, M. 1989, *The History of Foreign Investment in the United States to 1914*, Cambridge, Mass.: Harvard University Press.
William Birtwistle Group of Mills 1951, *Centenary 1851–1951*, Preston (From W's).
Williams, Benjamin H. 1929, *Economic Foreign Policy of the United States*, New York: McGraw-Hill.
Williamson, O. E. 1980a, 'Emergence of the Visible Hand: Implications for Industrial Organization', in Chandler, Alfred D. Jr. and Daems, H (eds.) *Managerial Hierarchies*, Cambridge, Mass.: Harvard University Press.
1980b, 'The Organization of Work', *Journal of Economic Behaviour and Organization*, 1: 5–38.
1981, 'The Modern Corporation: Origins, Evolution, Attributes', *Journal of Economic Literature*, 19: 1537–68.
1985, *The Economic Institutions of Capitalism*, New York: Free Press.
1991, 'Comparative Ownership and Control: The Analysis of Discrete Structural Alternatives', *Administrative Science Quarterly*, 36: 269–96.
Wilson, Joan Hoff 1971, *American Business and Foreign Policy, 1920–33*, Lexington, Kentucky: University Press of Kentucky.
Wilson, John F. 1995, *British Business History, 1720–1994*, Manchester: Manchester University Press.
Winstanley, M. J. 1996, 'The Factory Workforce', in Rose, Mary B. (ed.) *The Lancashire Cotton Industry: A History since 1700*, Preston: Lancashire County Books.

Wolfbein, Seymour L. 1944, *The Decline of a Cotton Textile City: A Study of New Bedford*, New York: Columbia University Press.

Wood, Philip J. 1986, *Southern Capitalism: The Political Economy of North Carolina, 1880–1980*, Durham, N.C.: Duke University Press.

Woolfolk, George Ruble 1958, *The Cotton Regency: The Northern Merchants and Reconstruction, 1865–1880*, New York: Bookman Associates.

Worswick, G. 1947, 'Concentration – Success or Failure?', in Oxford University Institute of Economic Statistics, *Studies in War Economics*, Oxford: Blackwell.

Wortzel, Heidi Vernon 1982, 'Changing Patterns of Management in Lowell Mills', in Okochi, Akio and Yonekawa, Shin-ichi (eds.) *The Textile Industry and its Business Climate*, Tokyo: Tokyo University Press.

Wright, Annette C. 1995, 'Spencer Love and Burlington Mills, 1923–1962', *Business History Review*, 69: 42–79.

Wright, Gavin, 1979, 'Cheap Labour and Southern Textiles before 1880', *Journal of Economic History*, 39: 655–80.

1986, *Old South, New South: Revolutions in the Southern Economy since the Civil War*, New York: Basic Books.

Wurm, Clemens 1993, *Business, Politics and International Relations: Steel, Cotton and International Cartels in British Politics, 1924–39*, trans. Patrick Salmon, Cambridge: Cambridge University Press.

Young, Arthur 1771, *A Six Months Tour through the North of England*, Vol. III, London.

Zeiler, Thomas W. 1992, *American Trade and Power in the 1960s*, New York: Columbia University Press.

Zevin, R. B. 1971, 'The Growth of Cotton Textile Production after 1815', in Fogel, Robert W. and Engerman, Stanley L. (eds.) *The Reinterpretation of American Economic History*, New York: Harper and Row.

Zonderman, David A. 1992, *Aspirations and Anxieties: New England Workers and the Mechanised Factory System, 1815–1850*, Oxford: Oxford University Press.

Zysman, John 1994, 'How Institutions Create Historically Rooted Trajectories of Growth', *Industrial and Corporate Change*, 3: 243–83.

Index

Cambridge Studies in Modern Economic History

1 *Central and Eastern Europe 1944–1993: detour from the periphery to the periphery*
Ivan Berend
ISBN 0 521 55066 1

2 *Spanish agriculture: the long siesta 1765–1965*
James Simpson
ISBN 0 521 49630 6

3 *Democratic socialism and economy policy: the Attlee years 1945–1951*
Jim Tomlinson
ISBN 0 521 55095 5

4 *Productivity and performance in the paper industry: labour, capital and technology, 1860–1914*
Gary Bryan Magee
ISBN 0 521 58197 4

5 *An economic history of the silk industry, 1830–1930*
Giovanni Federico
ISBN 0 521 58198 2

6 *The Balkan economies c. 1800–1914*
Michael Palairet
ISBN 0 521 58051 X

7 *Grain markets in Europe, 1500–1800: integration and deregulation*
Karl Gunnar Persson
ISBN 0 521 65096 8

8 *Firms, networks and business values: the British and American cotton industries since 1750*
Mary B. Rose
ISBN 0 521 78255 4